GCE AS Level

City of Westminster College
219097
D0198481

AS Level for Edexcel

Health & Social Care

Series editor:
Neil Moonie

WITHDRAWN

www.heinemann.co.uk
✓ Free online support
✓ Useful weblinks
✓ 24 hour online ordering

01865 888058

Heinemann
Inspiring generations

City of Westminster College
Learning Services / Queens Park Centre

Heinemann is an imprint of Pearson Education Limited,
a company incorporated in England and Wales, having
its registered office at Edinburgh Gate, Harlow, Essex, CM20 2JE.
Registered company number: 872828

Heinemann is a registered trademark of
Pearson Education Limited

Text © Neil Moonie, Beryl Stretch, Anne Bates, Dee Spencer-Perkins, Jo Irvine 2005

First published 2005

10 09 08
10 9 8 7 6 5 4

British Library Cataloguing in Publication Data is available
from the British Library on request.

ISBN 978 0 435453 70 1

Copyright notice
All rights reserved. No part of this publication may be reproduced in any form or by any means (including photocopying or storing it in any medium by electronic means and whether or not transiently or incidentally to some other use of this publication) without the written permission of the copyright owner, except in accordance with the provisions of the Copyright, Designs and Patents Act 1988 or under the terms of a licence issued by the Copyright Licensing Agency, 90 Tottenham Court Road, London W1T 4LP. Applications for the copyright owner's written permission should be addressed to the publisher.

Edited by Neil Moonie
Designed by Lorraine Inglis
Typeset by TechType, Abingdon, Oxon

Original illustrations © Harcourt Education Limited, 2005

Illustrated by TechType, Abingdon, Oxon

Cover design by Wooden Ark Studio

Printed in China (SWTC/04)

Cover photo: © Getty Images

Picture research by Ginny Stroud-Lewis

Acknowledgements
Every effort has been made to contact copyright holders of material reproduced in this book. Any omissions will be rectified in subsequent printings if notice is given to the publishers.

Photo acknowledgements
Alamy Images – pages 46, 52, 140; Alamy Images/Malcolm Case-Green – page 151; Alamy Images/David Hoffman Photo Library – pages 125, 179; Alamy Images/Photofusion Picture Library – pages 11, 21, 119, 180, 221; Alamy Images/The Photolibrary Wales – page 180; Collections – page 180; Mary Evans Picture Library – page 259; Getty Images – pages 9, 204; Getty Images/Hulton Archive – page 120; Getty Images/Stone – pages 24, 26; Harcourt Education – page 220; Harcourt Education/Gareth Boden – page 109; Harcourt Education/Haddon Davies – page 9; Harcourt Education/Jules Selmes – pages 8, 152, 223; Harcourt Education/Ginny Stroud-Lewis – page 27; Harcourt Education/Tudor Photography – pages 33, 180; Harcourt Index/Corbis – pages 2, 9; Richard Smith – pages 89, 118, 133, 136, 206, 212, 236, 243, 298, 305.

Websites
Please note that the examples of websites suggested in this book were up to date at the time of writing. It is essential for tutors to preview each site before using it to ensure the URL is still accurate and the content is appropriate. We suggest that tutors bookmark useful sites and consider enabling students to access them through the school or college intranet.

Contents

Introduction to the 2005 edition iv

Unit 1 Human Growth and Development

1.1 Life stages and aspects of human growth and development 2

1.2 Factors affecting growth and development 20

1.3 Promoting health and well-being 46

Unit 2 Communication and Values

2.1 Communication 58

2.2 Care value base 80

2.3 Transmission of values 96

Unit 3 Positive Care Environments

3.1 Values and individual rights 108

3.2 Barriers to access 119

3.3 Creating a positive environment 128

3.4 How society promotes service users' rights 140

Unit 4 Social Aspects and Lifestyle Choices

4.1 Lifestyle choices and life course events 158

4.2 Social factors affecting health and well-being 173

4.3 Care professional/service user relationship 190

Unit 5 Activities for Health and Well-being

5.1 Types and benefits of activities 204

5.2 The planning and implementation of activities 228

5.3 Evaluation of activities 246

Unit 6 Public Health

6.1 Public health: origins, aims and data 256

6.2 Current issues in public health 280

6.3 Promoting and protecting public health in the UK 300

Answers to assessment sections 208

Glossary 315

Index 320

18-09-09
219097
361
MOO

Introduction

This book has been written to support students who are studying for the double award AS level GCE using the course structure designed by Edexcel. The book is designed to support the six AS level Units:

Unit 1 Human growth and development (externally assessed)
Unit 2 Communication and values (internally assessed)
Unit 3 Positive care environments (internally assessed)
Unit 4 Social aspects and lifestyle choices (externally assessed)
Unit 5 Activities for health and well-being (internally assessed)
Unit 6 Public health (internally assessed)

This book has been organised to cover each of these units in detail. Headings are designed to make it easy to follow the content of each unit and to find the information needed to achieve a high grade. As well as providing information, each unit is designed to stimulate the development of the thinking skills needed to achieve an Advanced level award.

Assessment

Each unit will be assessed by coursework or by an external test set and marked by Edexcel. Detailed guidance for coursework assessment and external test requirements can be found in the unit specifications and at Edexcel's website: for access to this use www.heinemann.co.uk/hotlinks express code 370XP. This book has been designed to support students to achieve high grades as set out in the guidance from Edexcel available during 2004/2005.

Special features of this book

Throughout the text there are a number of features that are designed to encourage reflection and to help students make links between theory and practice. In particular this book has been designed to encourage a depth of learning and understanding and to encourage students to go beyond a surface level of descriptive writing.

The special features of this book include:

Think it over

Think it over...

This feature is designed to provide thought provoking questions that will encourage reflective thinking, or possibly reflection involving discussion with others.

Did you know?

* DID YOU KNOW?

Interesting facts or snippets of information included to encourage reflective thinking.

Scenario

SCENARIO

This term is used in place of the more traditional term 'case study' because the idea of people being perceived as 'cases' does not fit easily with the notion of empowerment – a key value highlighted by government policy and by Edexcel standards. Scenarios are presented throughout the units to help explain the significance of theoretical ideas to Health, Social Care and Early Years settings.

Consider this

A 'Consider this' feature is provided at the end of each section of each unit. Each 'Consider this' involves a brief scenario followed by a series of questions. The first questions ask you to identify issues; if you can do this then you are likely to be able to describe key issues. The next questions ask you to go into greater depth and analyse using theory. These questions are designed to challenge your thinking skills to go beyond simply remembering information. Finally, there are questions that ask you to evaluate. At this level we are challenging you to access a wider range of learning in order to make an appropriate judgment or evaluation about an issue. The ability to evaluate is the 'thinking skill' that will enable students to achieve an A grade at Advanced level.

Key concept

Because the development of analytic and evaluative skills requires the ability to use concepts, the authors have identified key concepts and offered a brief explanation of how these terms might be used.

Key issue

The authors have identified key issues students should be aware of and consider.

Assessment guidance

At the end of each unit there is a 'How you will be assessed' section that provides either sample test material for externally assessed units or outline guidance and ideas designed to help students achieve the highest grades when preparing internally assessed coursework.

Glossary

This book contains a useful glossary to provide fast reference for key terms and concepts used within the units. Glossary terms are highlighted in **bold** throughout the book.

References

There is a full list of references used within each unit together with useful websites at the end of each unit.

Author details

Neil Moonie, former Deputy Director of the Department of Social Services, Health and Education in a College of Further and Higher Education. Chartered psychologist, part-time lecturer and contributor to a wide range of textbooks and learning resources in the field of health and social care. Editor of Heinemann's GNVQ Intermediate and Advanced textbooks on health and social care since 1993 and editor of the 2000 Standards AVCE textbook.

Beryl Stretch, former Head of Health and Social Care in a large College of Further Education. Currently part of the senior examining board for Edexcel, GCE and GCSE Health and Social Care. Former external and internal verifier for VCE, GNVQ, NVQ programmes and examiner for GCSE Human Biology. Contributor to several bestselling textbooks on health and social care at all levels.

Anne Bates has worked in statutory social work since 1977 in a range of settings including child care, mental health, adult services and inspection and monitoring of day care services with under 5's. Anne is currently working part-time as a social services team manager with a community dementia team and also as a lecturer and tutor on a social work degree programme in outer London.

Dee Spencer-Perkins began her social services career in research, moving on to become a trainer and then a training manager. She now works as an independent trainer, consultant and writer, and specialises in language and communication. Dee also has a keen interest in disability issues.

Jo Irvine has worked in health visiting and nursing and in further education for a number of years. She currently works as a consultant in health, social care and child care.

UNIT 1

Human Growth and Development

This unit covers the following sections:

1.1 Life stages and aspects of human growth and development

1.2 Factors affecting growth and development

1.3 Promoting health and well-being

Introduction

Every health and social care practitioner needs to acquire a working knowledge of the ways in which people grow and develop between conception and later adulthood. Key periods (or life stages) are characterised by distinctive patterns of growth and the development of a range of skills and abilities. The rate of growth and development in individuals is influenced by a range of factors including their genetic inheritance, environmental factors and lifestyle choices. This unit focuses on human growth and development across the whole lifespan and includes an exploration of the influence of different factors and health experiences.

How you will be assessed

This unit is externally assessed through a written examination.

1.1 Life stages and aspects of human growth and development

Key concept

Human growth: This refers to an increase in physical size, both mass and height. This occurs because the number of body cells increases and individual cells get bigger as they contain more material and become more sophisticated in their range of functions.

Key concept

Development: This refers to increasing skills, abilities and capacities and can be physical, social, intellectual and emotional. People can continue to develop throughout their lifetime although at different rates.

Life stages

It is traditional to see human lives as involving certain definite periods of development. Terms like infant, child, adolescent and adult have been used for centuries to classify the age-related status of individuals. One individual might believe that an 18-month-old girl is an infant whereas another might say she is a child; so agreeing the chronological boundaries for life stages is an important first step in studying this unit.

FIGURE 1.1 *Identifying life stages from appearance can be difficult*

Think it over...

Are the two individuals shown in Figure 1.1 two children, infant and child, infant and adolescent, or child and adolescent?

In fact, they are infant and adolescent, but it is difficult to tell from appearance alone.

You should understand, however, that other workers and researchers in this field, and other qualification specifications and their associated text references, might not use exactly the same age boundaries or titles for life stages as those given in this unit (see Figure 1.2).

LIFE STAGE	CHRONOLOGICAL AGE BOUNDARIES IN YEARS
Infancy	0–2
Childhood	2–8
Adolescence	9–18
Early adulthood	18–45
Middle adulthood	46–65
Late adulthood	65+

FIGURE 1.2 *Chronological age boundaries for life stages*

During the last century, it was common to assume that there was a universal pattern to both physical and social development. From infancy through childhood to **adolescence**, a person would grow physically and learn the knowledge and skills needed for a working life. Adulthood was a time when people would work, marry and bring up their own families. Children would be grown up when their parents reached middle age, and rearing their own families when their parents became retired in old age.

An American theorist has described the developmental tasks of the different life stages and some examples are given in Figure 1.3.

Later theorists argue that life has changed so much that the notion of life tasks fitting into specific life stages is no longer relevant for many people. We now live in a rapidly changing world in which, increasingly, it is the norm for many people to choose their own style of living and

INFANCY AND EARLY CHILDHOOD	MIDDLE CHILDHOOD	ADOLESCENCE
Learning to take solid foods Learning to walk Learning to talk Learning bowel and bladder control Learning sex differences and sexual modesty	Learning physical skills necessary for ordinary games Learning to get along with peers Learning appropriate gender role Developing basic skills in reading, writing and numeracy Developing concepts necessary for daily living Developing conscience, morality and a scale of values	Achieving new and more mature relationships with peers of both sexes Achieving a masculine or feminine role Accepting one's physique and using the body effectively Achieving emotional independence of parents and other adults Preparing for marriage and family life Preparing for an economic career

EARLY ADULTHOOD	MIDDLE AGE	LATER MATURITY
Selecting a mate Learning to live with a marriage partner Starting a family Rearing children Managing a home Getting started in an occupation	Assisting teenage children to become happy and responsible adults Reaching and maintaining satisfactory performance in one's occupation/career Relating to one's spouse as a person Accepting and adjusting to the physiological changes of middle age Adjusting to ageing parents	Adjusting to decreasing physical strength Adjusting to retirement and reduced income Adjusting to the death of one's spouse Establishing satisfactory physical living arrangements

FIGURE 1.3 *Developmental tasks ascribed to life stages by Havinghurst (1972)*

plan social roles, families and careers with less reference to age. There are, however, still some generalisations about social, biological and emotional development that will help care workers to understand their service users' needs.

Principles of growth and development

Every individual has a unique pattern of growth and development because of his or her genetic

Think it over...

Discuss the relevance of the developmental tasks listed by Havighurst for early adulthood, middle age and later maturity to adults living in the twenty-first century.

For example, it is not unusual for adolescents and people in their forties (and older) to start families in or out of marriage.

inheritance and the large number of other environmental factors influencing his or her progress.

After the mother's ovum is fertilised by the father's sperm the resulting zygote undergoes many divisions to form the new human being, the placenta (to supply nourishment) and the coverings such as the amnion. During the first 8 weeks of life in the uterus, the **zygote** becomes the **embryo** and all major organs are formed by the end of this period. For many of these weeks, the female may not be aware of the pregnancy so exposure to harmful substances can damage the formation of major organs, resulting in reduced health experience. For the remainder of the pregnancy (about 32 weeks) the embryo becomes the **foetus** and although major organs are formed, their further growth and development can also be affected by many factors, such as smoking.

*** DID YOU KNOW?**

If a pregnant mother catches Rubella (German measles) in the first 3 months of pregnancy, the foetus may be aborted, stillborn or have defects of the nervous system, particularly affecting vision and hearing.

There is, however, a great deal of controversy over the time when a foetus is said to be a human being and this is largely fuelled by the debate around legal abortion.

In Britain, the Abortion Act (1967) allowed termination of pregnancy up to the 28th week of gestation (the period of the pregnancy); in 1990, the time limit dropped to the 24th week of gestation. But advances in medical technology and images from a revolutionary new ultrasound scan showing a foetus 'walking' after just 12 weeks in the womb have re-ignited the debate about abortion. Most people now feel that there is a need to update Abortion Act legislation. There is now a one-in-five chance of survival for babies born at 23 weeks and this doubles for those born one week later. However, such babies could legally be aborted under the current laws.

Some religious and pressure groups (such as Life) as well as many individuals consider that all abortion is wrong and that human life is sacred from the date of fertilisation.

Think it over...

Discuss the pros and cons for having abortion legislation. What change, if any, would you propose to the time limit for abortion?

A newborn infant, often called a **neonate**, is a helpless individual needing the care and protection of parents or carers to survive. The nervous system, which coordinates many bodily functions, is immature and needs time to develop. The digestive system is not able to take and/or absorb food that is not in an easily digestible form, such as that found in breast milk. There is no control over bladder and bowel function and locomotion is purposeless or based on automatic reflexes. The circulatory and respiratory systems have undergone major changes at birth due to physical separation from the mother and air breathing for the first time. The neonate can be susceptible to hypothermia because of an immature temperature-regulating system and because a reproductive capacity is totally lacking.

Patterns of development

Development, despite being a continuous sequential process, is also an uneven one that affects parts of the body differently. The upper part of the body, chiefly the head and brain, grows and develops rapidly compared to the rest of the body, particularly the lower limbs. This is known as **cephalo-caudal development**, which really means head to tail. Similarly, the organs in the mid-line of the body progress faster than the arms and legs at the extremities. The reason for this is not hard to find, as the vital organs are controlled by the brain and protected by the head and trunk. Limbs are not vital at this stage, as the neonate is dependent on the mother for nourishment and protection (see Figure 1.4).

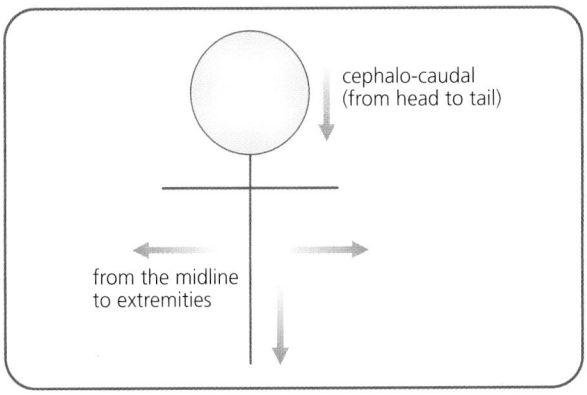

FIGURE 1.4 *The sequence of development*

There are characteristic patterns of development in the different life stages; for example, gross motor skills progress most rapidly in infancy than in any other life stage, and **social development** starts slowly in infancy but continues through all other life stages.

The rate of growth throughout the remaining life stages is never as rapid as that of the embryo and foetus. The average neonate comes out of the womb weighing around 3.5 kg and is approximately 50 cm in length. By the child's second birthday his or her height/length has nearly doubled and this is mainly due to the increasing length of long bones in the limbs.

During the remainder of childhood, there is a steady growth rate with boys just 2–3 cm taller than girls. Adolescence begins 2–4 years earlier in girls than boys, so for a short period their adolescent growth spurt makes them taller and heavier. The boys soon recover and overtake the girls once their **puberty** kicks in and they remain taller and heavier for the rest of their lives.

Key concept

Adolescence: This incorporates all the social, emotional, intellectual and physical changes associated with this life stage. Puberty refers only to the physical changes associated with sexual maturation.

Growth in bone takes place from plates of cartilage (known as epiphyses) sandwiched between the ends of bones and the shaft. When the epiphyses of differently named bones turn into bone (ossification), further growth is impossible and these dates can be useful in determining the age of an individual when this is unknown. They are visible as clear areas on X-ray.

Consider this

Using the figures given in the table below, plot growth curves for boys and girls on graph paper.

AGE IN YEARS	AVERAGE HEIGHT IN CM	
	BOYS	GIRLS
0	51	50
2	95	92
4	104	103
6	117	115
8	130	128
10	140	138
12	149	151
14	162	159
16	171	162
18	174	162

FIGURE 1.5 *Increase in height of boys and girls up to 18 years*

Write explanatory notes comparing the growth curves of boys and girls.

Mass (or weight) follows similar patterns of general increase in childhood and adolescence to that of growth. There is also increased weight gain during the adolescent spurt.

Although growth curves reflect the growth of the trunk and the limbs, not all parts of the body grow at the same rate in childhood. The graph overleaf (see Figure 1.7) shows the rapid expansion of the head and brain, which is almost full adult size by the age of 8 or 9 years.

The different rates of growth between the head and the torso from infancy to adulthood produce marked proportionate changes in growth profiles (see Figure 1.6). The figures are sketched to the same height to demonstrate the change in proportions. You will notice how small the head of an adult is in comparison with the newborn

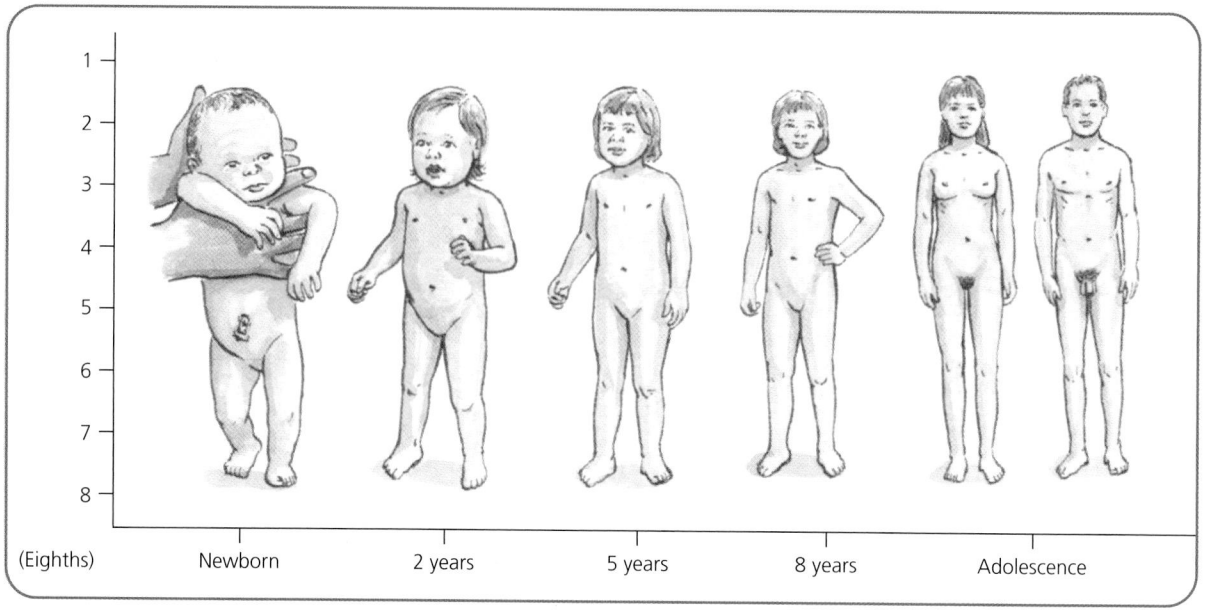

FIGURE 1.6 *Growth profiles from birth to the end of adolescence*

and, conversely, how long the length of the lower limbs of an adult are compared to those of the newborn. The intermediate age figures demonstrate the gradual shift in proportions.

By contrast, the reproductive organs remain small and undeveloped until adolescence, when there is a massive increase to adult size over a 4–5 year period. An endocrine gland called the thymus gland (not shown), located in the upper chest and lower neck, is large in infancy and continues to grow to a maximum at puberty, after which it declines slowly. It is associated with the immune system (see Figure 1.7).

Growth in height ceases in early adulthood but some individuals can increase in mass as they progress through adulthood. This is largely due to both increases in the number of fat cells and the volume of fat contained in each cell.

In early and middle adulthood there is no change in height as the skeleton has completely ossified. However, in later adulthood there is often some height reduction because the cartilaginous discs between the vertebrae of the spine become compressed over time.

Frequently, weight does change and middle-age spread is a well-recognised phenomenon, although there is no physiological reason for an increase in weight at this time. It is probably the result of maintaining the same pattern of eating from early adulthood with reduced levels of activity.

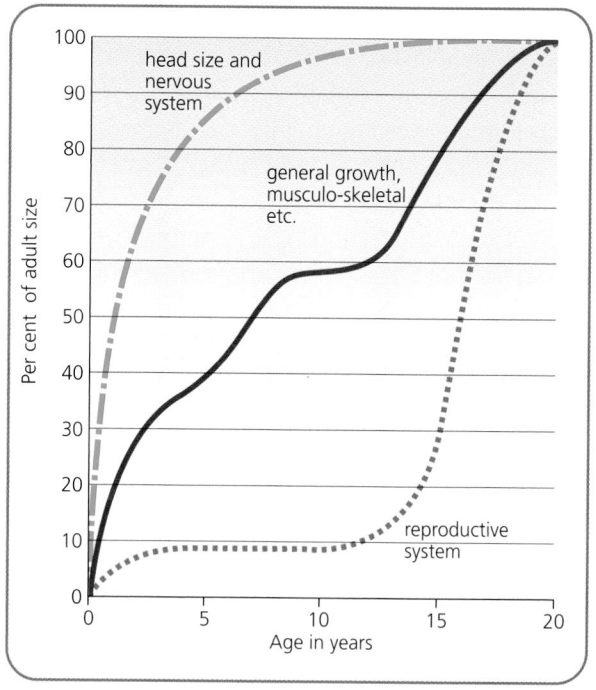

FIGURE 1.7 *Graph to show the differential growth of different body parts*

Although some individuals remain large in later adulthood, many become thinner possibly due to reduced appetite and less efficient absorption of food from the digestive tract.

Key concept

Control of growth: This is largely due to inherited characteristics, hormones, dietary patterns and health experience.

There are a large number of factors causing variations in the patterns of growth described above and you will find further information about some of these in Section 1.2.

✱ DID YOU KNOW?

The tallest man in the world was an American (who died in 1940) who was 2.62 m tall. The smallest is Chinese (still living) at a mere 0.70 m!

Development of physical skills

Infancy (0–2 years)

The neonate (newborn infant) is uncoordinated in movement and only **primitive reflexes** are present. Reflexes are automatic responses to stimuli and the most important are the rooting, suckling, grasp, Moro (startle) and walking reflexes.

✱ DID YOU KNOW?

The **paediatrician** Ernst Moro (1874 –1951) was the first to describe the defensive reflex seen in babies in the first six months of life.

Primitive reflexes disappear in the early months of life and are replaced some time later by voluntary movements. Some theorists believe that any reflex that persists longer than its allotted span interferes with learning at a later date.

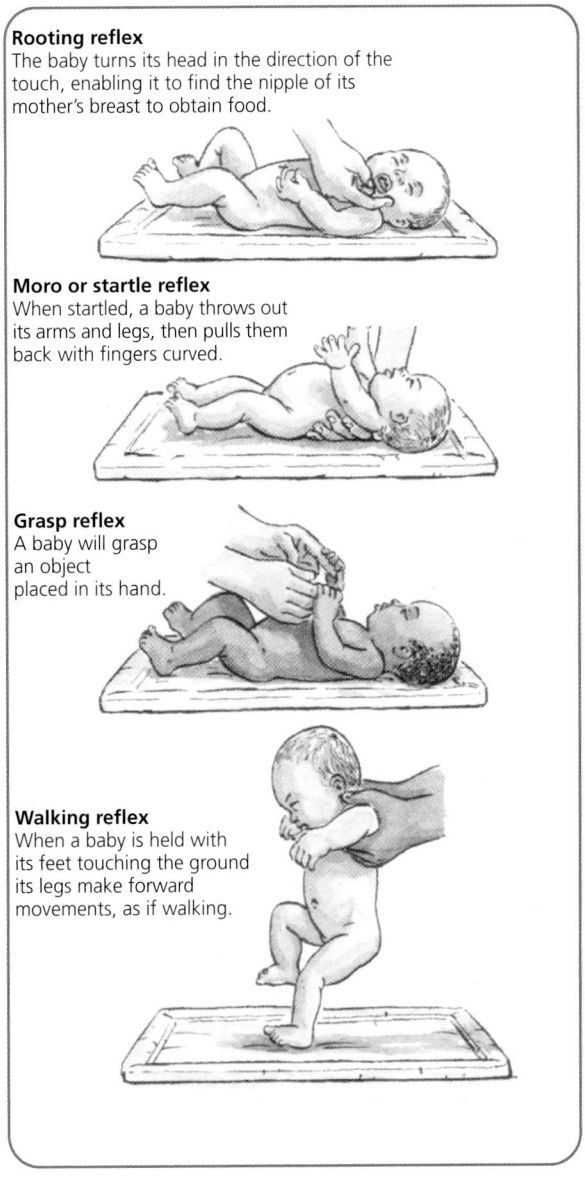

FIGURE 1.8 *Primitive reflexes*

Neonates can also smell, taste and hear as well as automatically blink their eyes.

NAME OF REFLEX	STIMULUS	RESPONSE
Rooting	Touch on cheek	Turns head towards breast and nipple
Suckling	Touch on the mouth	Starts to suck
Moro (startle)	Sudden noise or movement	Arms flung outwards and legs straightened, often with a cry. Limbs bend inwards as if trying to catch hold of something.
Grasp	Object placed in palm of hand	Strong grasp of object
Walking	When held upright with feet	Forward movements by legs, mimicking walking

FIGURE 1.9 *Primitive reflexes of the neonate*

Key concept

Gross motor skills: Using large muscle groups to accomplish tasks is called developing gross motor skills. Crawling or walking are good examples.

Key concept

Fine motor skills: These involve the more precise control of small muscles such as those found in the fingers when picking up a small object like a pea. Fine motor skills are more difficult to acquire and take longer to develop.

FIGURE 1.10 *Using gross motor skills*

Not surprisingly (see 'Patterns of development' on page 4) head control begins first. When the newborn infant is held in a sitting position, his or her head falls forward, but towards the end of the first month an infant can lift his or her chin for a few seconds. At 2 months of age an infant can hold his or her head up, and at 4–5 months will support and control his or her head when pulled to the sitting position. At age 3 months, infants will turn their heads to follow an adult, reach out for things, grasp a rattle for a few moments only and become fascinated by their own hands.

Infants can sit supported at 4–5 months of age, but around 6–7 months they can sit without support.

Key concept

'Milestones': The significant events described above are often termed 'a **milestone of development**', which means the average timing of the event for that particular infant or child. 'Milestones' (or norms) are useful tools for checking the progress of one child against many other children. A norm is a similar term that means a recognised standard. Health professionals will monitor growth and development throughout infancy and childhood and record milestones of development so that the progress of each child can be monitored.

FIGURE 1.11 *Sitting without support*

Around 2 months of age, babies lie flat or prone on the floor with their legs extended and can raise their head for only a second or two. By 3 months of age, they can lift their head for much longer and support their body weight on their forearms. Gradually, infants learn to tuck their knees under the body and turn over, such that by 9 or 10 months of age they can crawl quickly. Some infants never crawl but instead use their arms to bump the bottom around in a rapid 'shuffling' movement.

Around 6 months of age, babies can support their weight if held upright and by 10 months they can stand without support but holding onto furniture. Baby's first birthday is always an important occasion and he or she can celebrate by walking whilst holding onto an adult's two hands, gradually becoming steadier and needing only one hand. Between 13–15 months of age, an infant takes the important first steps alone without support, gradually increasing in confidence to carry toys around and climb steps.

Infants usually go up stairs in a crawling mode and come down backwards on their tummies.

For most infants, their walking has progressed so well by 18 months of age that running and kicking a ball are possible by their second birthday. Infants fall down regularly and this is part of the learning process; however, safety gates, guard rails, safety locks and fireguards should be used by parents or carers to ensure that no serious falls or escapes take place.

FIGURE 1.12 *Becoming more adventurous*

Fine motor skills are more pronounced after the age of 6 months, beginning with transferring objects from one hand to the other and picking up dropped toys. From the age of 9–12 months the 'pincer' movement develops, i.e. using the thumb and forefinger to pick up small objects; this is also the time for great fun for infants as they drop and throw toys from their buggy or high chair.

FIGURE 1.13 *Enjoying looking at pictures together*

Between 18 months and 2 years of age, the infant learns to hold small objects such as chubby crayons for drawing and a spoon for eating. At this stage, infants love action songs like pat-a-cake, turning the pages of books and building towers of blocks up to six blocks high.

Early childhood (2–8 years)

Children are now very mobile, with the ability to run, climb, kick a ball and go up and down stairs, placing one foot at a time on each step. A sense of balance develops and a child may take great pleasure in skipping, jumping, standing on tiptoes, balancing on one leg, using climbing frames, slides and roundabouts and riding (first a tricycle and then a bicycle). Fine motor skills have also progressed to threading beads, picking flowers for making a 'chain', drawing and painting, copying shapes and using scissors. Fastening shoelaces and buttons can still be challenging for a child at school entry, but by 6 or 7 years of age a child is usually competent at these tasks. School children become increasingly coordinated in their physical activities and by the end of this life stage they enjoy playing games of tennis, football, netball and other sports.

FIGURE 1.14 *Becoming competent with motor skills*

Growth in height and weight still increase steadily but not as rapidly as in infancy.

Both boys and girls are usually in control of complete bowel and bladder function during the day and night by the time they start school at 5 years of age.

Adolescence (9–18 years)

Anytime from 8 years old, a girl's breasts start to enlarge; this occurs well before the start of menstruation (called the **menarche**) and is usually the first outward sign of adolescence. Girls show major changes associated with puberty between 10–13 years of age, with boys following about 2 years later.

Key concept

Hormones: The pituitary gland at the base of the brain secretes hormones (gonadotrophins – follicle stimulating hormone (FSH) and luteinising hormone (LH) that stimulate the production of oestrogen and testosterone (the sex hormones) from the ovaries and testes respectively.

These sex hormones cause the growth of body hair, genital organs, the skeleton and muscles, and secondary sexual organs. They also cause the onset of menstruation, ovulation (about one year later) and sperm production.

Figure 1.15 lists the major physical changes associated with adolescence.

Early adulthood (18–45 years)

At the beginning of this life stage, people are said to be at the peak of their physical powers and considerably fertile. Towards the end, however, many people have begun to thicken around the waistline and become less physically active. Head hair in males starts to thin and recede, and hair colour in both sexes begins to fade as grey or white hairs appear. The ability to fine focus deteriorates, so many people need reading glasses

PART OF BODY	IN MALES	IN FEMALES
Breasts		Start to enlarge becoming glandular after ovulation has started
Body hair grows	Underarm (axillary) hair Pubic hair Chest hair Facial hair	Underarm (axillary) hair Pubic hair
Primary genital organs grow and become productive	Testes and scrotum enlarge and begin to produce sperm	Ovaries get larger and ovulation starts
Secondary sexual organs grow	Penis and accessory glands grow and start to secrete – giving rise to 'wet dreams'	Uterus, vagina and associated glands enlarge Menstruation becomes established
Skeleton	Growth spurt in height and weight Shoulders widen, hips remain slim	Growth spurt in height and weight Hips widen causing body shape to alter and a different walk with swinging gait
Voice changes	Rapid growth of voice box or larynx causes voice to change and become deeper in pitch	Voices tend to become less shrill, but not usually considered a significant change
Shape alters due to changes in soft tissues	Significant muscle development	Fat deposited under the skin and around the breasts leads to a curvaceous shape
Tonsils, adenoids, thymus and other lymphatic tissues	Having grown rapidly during childhood, they begin to shrink	Having grown rapidly during childhood, they begin to shrink

FIGURE 1.15 *Physical changes in males and females during adolescence*

as they become increasingly long-sighted (presbyopic). This is due to the eye lens becoming less elastic through age. A few wrinkles may appear as the elastic fibres in the skin begin to age.

Women still menstruate at this stage and increasingly, more women are having babies in their forties. Males produce sperm and can father children.

Middle adulthood (46–65 years)

People in this life stage do not think of themselves as middle-aged or old as they lead independent, fulfilling lives. The ageing process is subtle and the changes so tiny at first that they usually occur without notice.

The main physical event occurring in this life stage is the **menopause** for females. This is the gradual cessation of menstruation and may take between 1–2 years to complete. Because there are no more viable eggs left in the ovaries, the gonadotrophins are produced in greater quantities as they try to stimulate egg production. The high levels of these hormones causes symptoms such as irritability, night sweats and hot flushes. With the consequent decline in oestrogen and progesterone from the ovaries, the primary and secondary organs of the reproductive system shrink and become less glandular. In some women, this is accompanied by a loss of interest in sexual intercourse and some emotional turbulence.

Other symptoms that begin in the forties and continue throughout this phase include further loss of hair in males, long-sightedness, reduced skin elasticity and possibly early difficulties with mobility as a result of wear and tear on the joints.

Some people may experience further decline in the senses: their balance may not be as good, they may not hear high-pitched sounds as well as they once did, and their sense of smell may also decline.

Later adulthood (65+ years)

People in the early stages of later adulthood still do not think of themselves as old. Most live healthy and fulfilling lives and, with the right support and help, their quality of life can be good. People live longer than they used to, particularly women, and many are physically active until their late seventies and eighties.

FIGURE 1.16 *Many people in late adulthood are physically active*

Key concept

Ageing: Reduced functions of most organs takes place as a result of the ageing process, leading to the characteristic traits of later adulthood, although many service users may suffer from one or two effects only.

CHARACTERISTIC TRAITS OF LATER ADULTHOOD	
Skin	Thinner and less elastic so more wrinkled in appearance and acquires blemishes; less sensitive to temperature fluctuations so more likely to develop hypothermia in cold weather
Bones	Less dense therefore more likely to fracture, particularly in females
Muscles	Weaker therefore less power
Joints	Stiffer, reduced range of movements; may be painful; ligaments weaker
Height	Shrinks due to disc compression; spine may become rounded

CHARACTERISTIC TRAITS OF LATER ADULTHOOD	
Balance	Impaired, particularly when turning around
Heart	Less efficient at delivering and draining blood from tissues, so functions less well
Blood pressure	Rises with age due to reduced elasticity of vessel walls and calcium deposits; more risk of stroke or haemorrhage, particularly in brain
Breathing	Less efficient as muscles are weaker; gaseous exchange affected due to decline of elasticity in alveolar walls
Hormone production	Reduces due to ageing cells and resistance; lack of insulin gives rise to diabetes; lack of thyroxine leads to lowered metabolism
Alimentary canal	Muscles controlling peristalsis are weaker so constipation more likely; nutrients in food not absorbed so well, so anaemia and other deficiency diseases occur more often

FIGURE 1.17 *Effects of the ageing process*

It is also worth remembering that while the list of declining physical faculties shown in Figure 1.17 seems long and awesome, it can be counteracted by the acquisition of wisdom and peace of mind, especially when there is a support network of family and friends.

Development of intellectual skills

Infancy (0–2 years)

Soon after birth, infants appear to be ready to form relationships with parents and carers; they show interest in human faces and voices from a few weeks old and soon recognise their mother by sound and appearance.

Language development

Between the age of 6–9 months, infants respond to certain vocal instructions such as 'wave bye-bye' and 'clap hands', although they cannot yet say words. Babbling sounds that may seem like words are common around one year of age and some children will manage about three whole words; other children will be able to use sounds, facial and eye movements to communicate their needs to carers. Nearly all 2-year-old infants can put two words together such as 'Jane garden' or 'Sam milk'.

Thinking or cognitive development

Many psychologists have studied cognitive development and **Piaget** is one of the best known. Piaget believed that thinking was at first limited to repeating actions. The teat of the breast or bottle was placed in the mouth so the baby placed a rattle in his or her mouth. Young infants rely on in-built mental patterns for sucking, crawling and watching. Later, babies explore further by sucking toys, fingers, and clothes, for example, to develop an understanding of objects. The tongue contains thousands of sensory receptors and the baby uses these to explore texture, shape, hardness, and so on.

Piaget thought that up to the age of 18 months or 2 years an infant could not understand that his or her mother existed once she had left the room if the infant remained there. Piaget called this the **sensori-motor** stage of development and it ended when the infant could understand the existence of objects and people even when they could not be seen, heard, smelled or touched. Many people now believe that this stage is much shorter (probably 8–9 months) and infants are more capable than Piaget believed.

*** DID YOU KNOW?**

The psychologist Jean Piaget (1896–1980) studied the development of thought processes in children.

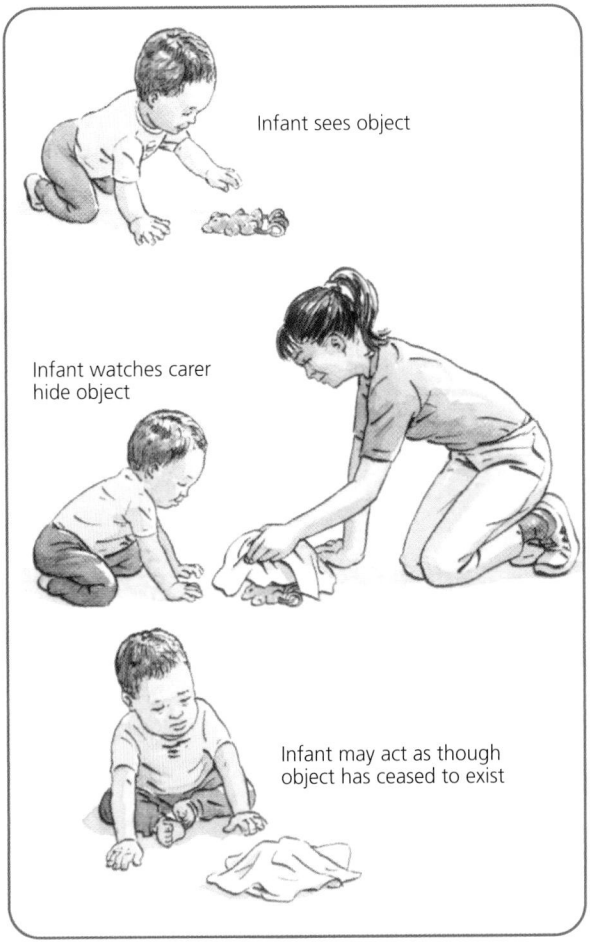

FIGURE 1.18 *The sensori-motor stage*

Early childhood (2–8 years)

Language

As children progress through childhood, they use their own pattern of language communication.

STAGE	NATURE OF STAGE	EXAMPLE
First (around two years)	Two-word statements	John comed
Second	Short phrases	John come play
Third	Being able to ask questions	Where John go?
Fourth	Using sentences	John come play and Sally come play
Fifth (around five or six years)	Adult sentences and fair vocabulary	John and Sally have come to play with me
Sixth (eight years and upwards)	Understanding and use of speech together with increasing vocabulary	John and Sally have come to play with me today and I will be delighted to go to their house tomorrow

FIGURE 1.20 *Development of language*

Young children do not use adult language and are best left uncorrected. The probable list of stages after 2 years of age is given in Figure 1.20

Thinking skills

Children in this stage still tend to base their thinking on what things look like rather than the logic of newly acquired counting skills. They also learn to weigh things but may believe that a large

FIGURE 1.19 *Understanding the concept of* ***object permanence*** *(18 months)*

pile of feathers will weigh more than one iron bar. Piaget called this stage the '**pre-operational**' period, meaning pre-logical.

Children may begin to use logic before 8 years of age providing that they can see things to help them.

Adolescence (9–18 years)

Piaget described the next stage as the 'concrete operational' period, extending from 7–12 years of age, in which children and adolescents can work out problems logically, providing that they have images, graphics or real life situations to assist them. From 12 years of age onwards, Piaget moved to the '**formal operational**' (or formal logical) stage, in which adolescents can imagine and think about things that they have never seen or done before. They are able to imagine and plan for future achievements and can solve problems in the same way as adults, although a lack of experience may not produce the right decisions. Decision-making skills are something that we acquire throughout the course of our entire lives.

Early adulthood (18–45 years)

Intellectual skills and abilities will increase during adulthood providing that the opportunities exist to exercise those skills.

Middle adulthood (46–65 years)

Older adults may be slightly slower in working out logical problems, but this reduction in speed may be compensated for by increased knowledge. Using knowledge gained from many years of experience helps people to make better decisions and judgements than those with more limited experience. As a consequence, they are often said to be wise or learned.

Later adulthood (65+ years)

Older people who stimulate their minds and enjoy good health can continue to develop their store of knowledge and wisdom even if they take longer to respond to situations.

Some people may suffer from ill health that interferes with mental activities, particularly illnesses that result in poor oxygenation of brain tissues such as respiratory and circulatory difficulties. This may result in confusion, poor decision-making, memory loss and difficulties in solving problems.

> **✱ DID YOU KNOW?**
>
> In the UK 1 per cent of adults over 60 years of age are afflicted with **dementia** and the rate doubles every 5 years after 60. The most common form of dementia is Alzheimer's disease.

The main signs and symptoms of dementia are:

- ✱ difficulty in communication, expressing thoughts and understanding other people
- ✱ reduced ability to control emotions
- ✱ difficulties in recognising people, places and things, coupled with loss of memory
- ✱ being unaware of where you are and what is going on around you
- ✱ problems with daily living, such as personal hygiene and dressing.

It is important to remember that most people in later adulthood do not suffer from dementia although they may have periods of confusion and difficulties with daily activities. The causes of dementia are not fully known and are probably multi-factorial (i.e. many influences may be involved). Causes of dementia will include genetic inheritance and environmental factors such as heavy smoking, alcoholism and infections such as HIV.

Emotional development

Emotional development considers how people develop a sense of themselves and how they develop feelings towards others.

> **✱ DID YOU KNOW?**
>
> **Self-concept** is said to be part **self-esteem** and part **self-image**. Self-esteem is how you value (or feel about) yourself and self-image is how you see yourself.

Infancy (0–2 years)

It seems that infants enter the world with an in-built ability to recognise and react to basic feelings in other people. Infants use this ability to attract attention and build emotional attachments with their parents and carers. By one year of age, infants can recognise and react to emotional expressions of happiness, distress and anger, and be guided by the emotions shown by their parents and carers.

Young infants probably do not have a sense of being an 'individual' but by 2 years of age, they have become aware of 'self' with a fixed gender.

During the first 18 months of life, the infant forms a loving bond that ties him or herself emotionally to parents or the main carers. There is general agreement among theorists that if the bonding process fails to develop, then a child's social and emotional development will be impaired.

Early childhood (2–8 years)

Children who have been able to bond well now start to feel safe in getting to know other children and adults, although starting school or playgroup may still be a daunting prospect even at the age of 5 years. From two and a half years onwards, children can use their imagination, particularly in copying what others do. As imagination develops in play with dolls, watching characters on TV, interaction with parents and others, so children come to understand who they are and have an idea of 'self'. Children need to feel valuable to family and friends and build up their self-esteem or self-worth in order to grow up feeling emotionally secure.

Children as young as 3 years will describe themselves as small or big, tall or short, but they can progress to a much fuller picture that includes hair and eye colour, school, family, and so on, by the time they are aged 8.

Adolescence (9–18 years)

Towards the end of their primary school life, adolescents can describe their self-worth in terms of what makes them happy. They will say, for example, what makes school good or bad, or which friends they like and why. A year or so later, they start to compare themselves with others. For example, 'Holly is better at Maths than I am, but Sally is better than both of us'. As they grow older, friends gradually take the place of family in being the major influence on self-concept.

As the sex hormones 'kick in' during the teens, the adolescent experiences huge physical, emotional and social changes. Adolescents are renowned for being 'touchy' with rapid mood swings, rebelliousness and anger, and their friends become the main emotional support rather than parents. Many suffer from depression, lack of **self-confidence** and low self-esteem as they struggle to come to terms with so many changes at a time of important educational and life decisions.

During this period, people will have to acquire a concept of themselves that guides them through leaving home, obtaining work and learning to live with a partner of their choice. These life events can cause a loss of self-esteem, conflict and stress.

Adolescents often develop a strong sense of self in terms of beliefs such as vegetarianism, religion, animal rights or other things seen as right or wrong; this has been termed the idealistic phase and it merges into developing an adult self-concept that helps to build confidence for future life changes.

Key concept

Self-concept: The understanding that we have of ourselves. A learned idea of how we are distinct from other people.

*** DID YOU KNOW?**

Self-concept is said to be positive or negative, not high or low. A person's self-concept can change as he or she progresses through life.

When you have a positive self-concept you are:

* self-confident
* keen to accept new challenges
* more likely to be successful
* motivated to do things
* good at mixing with other people
* happy in your life.

Early adulthood (18–45 years) and middle adulthood (46–65 years)

Our self-concept does not usually settle down until we are ready to undertake full-time work or leave home and live with a sexual partner. Such adult commitments may perhaps force us into making decisions about ourselves. A clear sense of what you are like and what you are good at may be necessary to be happy, confident and successful in work and in love; such clarity is more likely to be achieved in an individual's early twenties.

Research has suggested that many adults feel more satisfied with the quality of their lives in their thirties and forties than in their twenties. Young adults can experience a lot of stress in trying to establish a satisfactory lifestyle for themselves.

Adults can explain how they see themselves and the quality of their lives in much greater depth and detail than when they were adolescents. Adults will be aware that their sense of self can be influenced by events that happen in their lives.

You may hear an adult say, ' I became a stronger person after I lost my job' or 'I had to make all the decisions after Ted died'. Equally, a person's self-concept can be changed negatively after a life event, such as 'I lost all confidence after losing my job' or 'I felt that I was never the same person after that'.

Some people are able to change their self-concept as they get older. Success in an occupation or business career, having children, and gaining professional qualifications and experience are all likely to enhance self-concepts positively.

Think it over...

Think of circumstances that might change a person's self-concept negatively.

Some theorists have suggested that older adults may lose interest in other people and socialising once their families have grown up and left home; they become very settled in their ways – in a 'rut'.

The menopause, with the consequent hormone reduction, can cause emotional problems for some women, who may become depressed, tearful (often with rapid mood swings) and irritable, also affecting the males who are their partners. Some women feel 'down' because the menopause marks the end of the child-bearing years; they feel less feminine and unwanted as their children have grown up and left home. This is often called the 'empty nest' syndrome.

Successful ageing, therefore, might be regarded as the ability to remain socially engaged with people in an emotionally satisfying way.

*** DID YOU KNOW?**

Loss of skills and abilities resulting from trauma such as a stroke or accident can lead to feelings similar to those experienced in bereavement – namely fear, anxiety, frustration, anger, sadness and grief. In time, acceptance may follow, allowing the individual to undergo rehabilitation to achieve the best possible quality of life and independence.

Later adulthood (65+ years)

Older people can develop problems with their health which can affect their self-concept in a negative way; confusion, depression and loss of self-confidence are relatively more common in elderly people. As well as coping with their health problems, they also have to cope with the way in which society treats older people. Stereotyping of people in later adulthood is common. Others tend to treat older people as being less able than they actually are, causing their self-esteem and self-image to reduce.

Some theorists have suggested that the main challenge of later adulthood is to retain a strong sense of one's own self-esteem despite the problems that can arise with age. Some older adults may have more self-knowledge than during early adult life and show 'wisdom' in the way they explain their self-concept.

✱ DID YOU KNOW?

A person with a negative self-concept may:

- dislike trying new things because of fear of failure
- feel life is fraught with difficulties
- feel unhappy with life
- lack self-confidence
- dislike meeting new people
- lack motivation.

Development of social skills

Key concept

Social skills: These include the ability to communicate and make relationships with others; they are closely allied to and overlapped by emotional development, particularly in the early life stages.

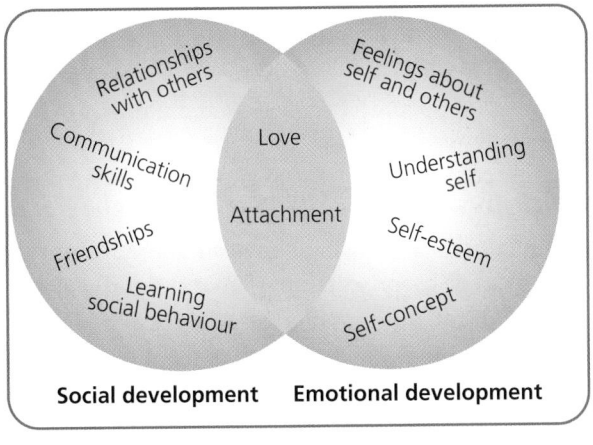

FIGURE 1.21 *Social and emotional development overlap*

Infants (0–2 years)

It seems that babies come into the world prepared to make relationships and learn about others because they are able to:

- follow a moving person with their eyes during their first month of life
- start to smile at human faces and may recognise their mother at age 2 months
- at 3 months of age, smile and make a noise when an adult or child goes by
- at 5 months of age, distinguish between familiar and unfamiliar people
- smile at a mirror image by age 6 months.

Infants may have an in-built need to form a close emotional relationship or bond with their primary carer. '**Bonding**' was originally emphasised by Bowlby (1953), who felt that separation of a baby from its mother at a critical period would produce psychological damage. Later researchers have doubted that separations, such as going to work or into hospital, cause very much damage and they feel that it is making the bond of love that is important, not whether temporary separation occurs. As the infant gets older, the bonds forged with parents are less intense but still important; bonds with siblings, grandparents and other members of the extended family follow closely behind.

Early childhood (2–8 years)

Children begin to be interested in other children from the age of 2 years. Initially, they are content to play by themselves alongside another child (called **parallel play**). Then one or two years later, the children actually play together (**cooperative play**).

✱ DID YOU KNOW?

There are different types of play as outlined in Figure 1.22 below.

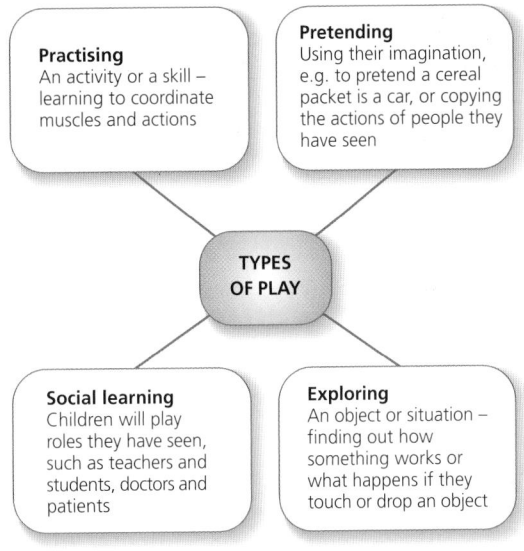

FIGURE 1.22 *Different types of play*

Think it over...

Looking at Figure 1.22, consider how the four types of play can develop children's:

* physical abilities
* emotional skills
* social skills
* learning or intellectual skills.

Children aged 3–4 years prefer to be with their parents than with friends, but by age 7 years this preference is reversed. Older children seek friendships based on trust rather than on the availability of others to play, and this continues through life. Up to the ages of 7 and 8 years, children's social groups are likely to be of mixed gender, but after this age they tend to be of the same gender. They will also choose friends with similar attitudes and values.

Relationships in the family setting provide opportunities for children to learn from others by copying what they do. They learn attitudes, behaviours and beliefs from parents, siblings and relatives in a process called **primary socialisation**. Families and other social groups develop attitudes about the right things to do, or norms. Some families have their evening meal together while sitting at a table; others would be surprised at this and eat from a plate on their lap while sat in front of the TV – both are norms for those families.

Think it over...

Make a list of the social and behavioural norms in your family and compare your results with others.

Adolescence (9–18 years)

Friendship groups now become more important than family groups and this is known as **secondary socialisation**. Adolescents (12+ years) explore relationships and sexual behaviour and begin to take on job responsibilities in the home, such as washing up and cleaning the family's car. Taking on adult responsibilities and trying to achieve more independence tends to cause most adolescents to become rebellious, bringing them into conflict with their parents.

Think it over...

Which is more important to you – family or friends? Would you stop seeing someone because your parents disliked him or her? Explain your answers.

Early adulthood (18–45 years)

Networks of personal friends become more extensive and most young adults experience sexual encounters and more or less permanent partnerships. Some plan to concentrate on gaining qualifications and career progression, putting ideas of marriage and family on hold.

Many people find coping with a partner, being a parent and an employee extremely stressful, and if they are experiencing financial problems as well, this can create emotional and social problems at home. Some older adults may find it difficult to support their grown up children at university, both socially and emotionally, or to help with accommodation costs once they have left home. As well as the effect on the family finances, they may feel that they have lost part of their social purpose because their children are no longer living with them.

Middle adulthood (46–65 years)

Many adults in this stage have smaller groups of long-lasting friendships that have stood the test of time and difficulties. New friendships can be made often as a result of holiday meetings, but they tend to fade away with time. Just as their children begin to start their own lives, new pressures appear as support for their own parents in later adulthood is required. Increasingly, grandparents take on the burden of childcare at some point in the week, so that their children can acquire and enjoy the luxuries of life without extra costs.

Later adulthood (65+ years)

In their sixties and early seventies, many adults lead varied and interesting lives. Long-distance travel, often to see siblings and other relatives, and new leisure pursuits such as painting and writing are common. The opportunities for older people to meet new friends can be extensive when their health is good and they have sufficient money. There are, however, many older people who find it difficult to make ends meet and tend to withdraw from socialising, due to feelings of shame. In addition there are those who suffer from ill-health and impairments, which results in their social isolation. A network of family and friends can provide vital and practical support, physically, socially and emotionally.

Summary of Section 1.1

The following key areas of theory have been considered in this section:

Infancy	Physical skills
Early childhood	Intellectual ability
Adolescence	Growth and development
Early adulthood	Emotional development
Middle adulthood	Social skills
Later adulthood	

Consider this

Su-Li is working in a local council day nursery looking after infants (aged 0–2 years) whose mothers have to go to work, as they are the sole wage earners for the family. As the infants start arriving early, each day rapidly becomes very busy. Su-Li is concerned about the four infants in her care and the small amount of time that she can spend with each one. She is also aware that she sees the infants more than their mothers do during the daytime.

Using concepts, can you identify?
How can Su-Li ensure that each infant in her care is growing satisfactorily?

How can Su-Li ensure that each infant is developing satisfactorily?

Go further – can you analyse issues using theory?
Freddy's mother is very young, and as she has learning difficulties she attends a local centre to continue her education. Su-Li thinks that Freddy is not thriving as much as the other infants and has not bonded with his mother or herself. How can Su-Li manage this situation sensitively?

Go further – can you evaluate using a range of theory?
Can you think how, 6 months later, Su-Li could judge whether Freddy is beginning to catch up on the other infants or whether he needs to be referred to a specialist?

1.2 Factors affecting growth and development

Genetic inheritance

The nucleus of every cell in the human body contains 23 pairs of chromosomes and each chromosome, made of DNA (deoxyribonucleic acid), carries units of inheritance known as genes.

Key concept

Genes: Genes control the chemical reactions in the cells and, therefore, inherited characteristics such as gender, hair and eye colour, height, skin colour and much more. Although scientists have made enormous advances in genetics in the last 20 years, each person is still a product of the genetic inheritance from his or her parents.

The mother donates one of each pair of chromosomes to the fertilised egg and the remainder comes from the father's sperm. It is the father's donation of the Y chromosome in the 23rd pair (called the sex chromosomes) that determines the sex of the child. For a person to have a genetic disorder, the abnormal genetic material must be present in every cell of the body, meaning that it must have been present in the egg cell or the sperm cell (known as gametes) or both. For this to happen, either one or both of the parents must have the faulty genetic material, or the fault initiates during one of the many cell divisions that preceded the formation of the gametes (the most likely) – this is known as a mutation.

Chromosome abnormalities

About one in 200 babies born alive has chromosome abnormalities, but there is a much higher incidence in spontaneous abortions (about one in two) suggesting that babies with such conditions are less likely to survive.

*** DID YOU KNOW?**

The physician Longdon Down (1828–1896) linked certain learning disabilities with a particular genetic disorder where three chromosomes (trisomy) appear at pair 21.

Abnormalities of chromosomes can and do occur, the best known being Down's syndrome (or trisomy 21); the name derives from the presence of three chromosomes instead of two at pair 21. This results in striking changes in the development and health of a person who happens to receive this extra chromosome. The incidence of Down's syndrome (about one in 650 babies born) increases with rising maternal age and pregnant women in their late-thirties and forties are offered screening tests to detect this and other genetic abnormalities. The invasive tests of sampling foetal cells from amniotic fluid (**amniocentesis**) or **chorionic villus sampling** carry risks to both mother and foetus and follow indicative blood tests.

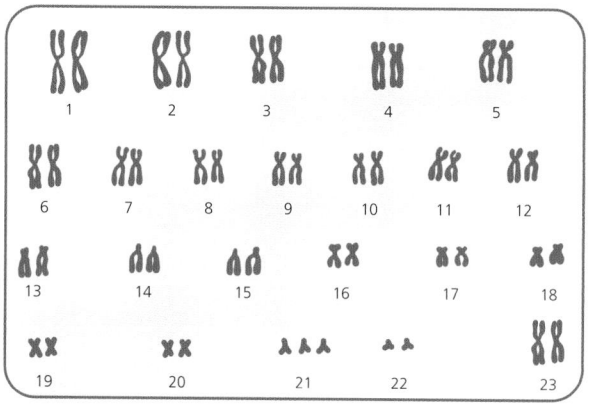

Note: trisomy at pair 21

FIGURE 1.23 *Karyogram depicting a chromosomal abnormality*

However, conclusive blood tests are currently being implemented throughout the UK that can provide results as early as 11 weeks of gestation without invasive investigations. Parents are offered counselling and the possibility of termination if the test is positive for Down's syndrome. Most people with Down's syndrome have distinctive small facial features with eyes that slope upwards at the outer corners and skin folds covering the nasal corners. Their hands are short and broad with unusual palm creases and the back of the head is flat. The tongue is large and often protruding. Many service users with Down's syndrome choose to have cosmetic surgery to alter their facial features.

Down's syndrome children are loving, cheerful and friendly, and they mix well with other children and adults.

FIGURE 1.24 *Young people with Down's syndrome enjoying life*

People with this condition have varying degrees of learning disability, but all are capable of some learning. Many individuals hold down useful jobs, live independently and have a good quality of life. Less than a generation ago, many Down's syndrome children did not live beyond adolescence or early adulthood because of the associated multiplicity of birth defects and susceptibility to infection. However, with advanced medical and surgical techniques, life expectancy has risen to middle adulthood.

Birth defects associated with Down's syndrome are:

* congenital heart disease
* congenital deafness and susceptibility to ear infections
* narrowing of intestines
* increased risk of atherosclerosis (narrowing of arteries by plaques of fatty tissue)
* general increased risk of infections.
* some neck joint problems.

Clearly, growth and development as well as the health experience for children and adults with trisomy 21 can be fraught with difficulties.

Other trisomies are rare, causing multiple physical defects and early death; but other abnormalities including missing or extra parts of chromosomes are more common. Abnormalities of the 22 pairs of 'ordinary' chromosomes are called *autosomal abnormalities* but those of the sex chromosomes are referred to as *sex chromosome abnormalities*; the former are slightly less common and are associated with physical defects and learning disabilities. The latter, not surprisingly, are linked to defective sexual development and infertility.

*** DID YOU KNOW?**

A syndrome is a group of signs and symptoms that occur together and characterise a particular medical abnormality.

When the genetic faults lie with genes rather than chromosomes, they may be unifactorial or multifactorial disorders.

Unifactorial disorders

These cause considerable disability. They result from one defective gene controlling a particular protein production and, therefore, forming the start of a metabolic error. They can be divided into autosomal and sex-linked disorders, nearly always associated with the X chromosome.

Autosomal disorders

In each cell there are 23 pairs of chromosomes. The gene controlling a particular factor is composed of two units called alleles, each one of which is on a single chromosome. Put more

AUTOSOMAL ABNORMALITIES	SEX CHROMOSOME ABNORMALITIES
Down's syndrome or trisomy 21 – presence of three chromosomes (i.e. an extra chromosome) at pair 21	*Turners's syndrome* – affects 1 in 2,500 females; one X chromosome instead of two; do not have proper ovarian development; typically short height
Cri du chat syndrome – part of chromosome missing results in severe birth defects, small head and brain, small larynx with a cat-like cry	*Klinefelter's syndrome* – affects 1 in 500 males; one or more extra X-chromosomes along with Y; affects learning disability is common

FIGURE 1.25 *Chromosome abnormalities*

simply, a gene consists of two alleles controlling a particular factor, each allele originating from one parent. It follows then, if there are two different alternative forms of alleles, usually indicated by letters, there are three variations that can occur.

For example, in the case of the gene for black hair, indicated by the letter B or b (two alternative forms), the gene could be composed of 2 alleles BB, bb or Bb (bB is the same effect):

* BB indicates alleles for black hair received from both parents
* bb indicates alleles from neither parent for black hair so the recipient will be fair-haired
* Bb (or bB) signifies one allele from each parent, only one of which is for black hair.

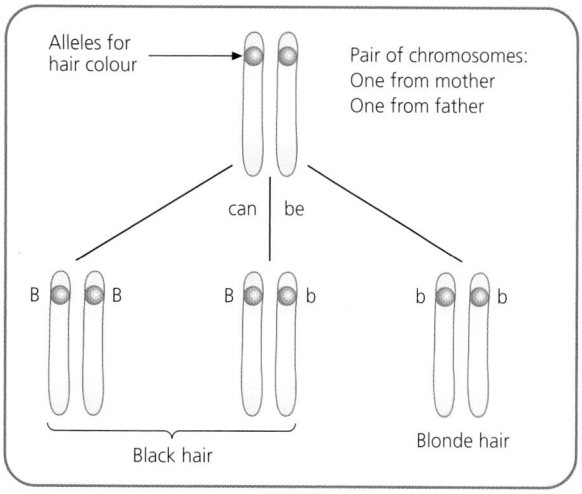

FIGURE 1.26 *Genetic inheritance of hair colour*

The recipient of the Bb inheritance is also black haired indicating the *dominance of the black-haired allele*, traditionally written with a capital letter. The allele B is said to be the **dominant** allele and allele b is the recessive allele for hair colour.

Autosomal disorders are also caused by dominant and recessive alleles, just as for hair colour. Only one parent has to possess and pass on a dominant allele for a disorder, but two parents must pass on two recessive alleles for an affected child, the normal allele being dominant and absent. Many of us carry recessive alleles for characteristics and disorders and are totally unaware of their existence because normal genes dominate them. We are said to be carriers of the conditions. When two carriers have children, there is a one in four chance of producing a child with an autosomal recessive condition and this may come as a complete surprise to the family. Autosomal disorders tend to affect both sexes in equal proportions.

Figure 1.27 shows some autosomal dominant and recessive genetic disorders affecting growth and development.

Sex-linked genetic disorders

In these genetic disorders, the faulty recessive gene is on the X-chromosome; a female has two X-chromosomes so the normal X dominates the affected allele and the female is normal, although

AUTOSOMAL DISORDERS	
AUTOSOMAL DOMINANT ALLELES CAUSE:	**AUTOSOMAL RECESSIVE ALLELES CAUSE:**
Achondroplasia – short stature	Albinism – lack of pigment in skin, hair and eyes
Familial polyposis – multiple polyps of the bowel eventually becoming cancerous	Cystic fibrosis – thick sticky mucus that predisposes to chronic lung infections
Huntington's chorea – early onset (age 35–40 years) of **dementia** and rapid jerky movements	Phenylketonuria – blond, blue-eyed babies lacking a vital enzyme that leads to severe learning disabilities unless placed on a special diet
Polycystic kidneys – multiple cysts in both kidneys that destroy kidney tissue	Sickle-cell anaemia – deformed red blood cells leading to severe anaemia, mainly in those of Mediterranean and African origins

FIGURE 1.27 *Examples of autosomal dominant and recessive disorders*

a carrier. When the female carrier has sons, one X-chromosome is passed on together with the normal Y-chromosome from the father and this may be either X. Statistically, 50 per cent of sons are normal and 50 per cent affected, as they do not have the normal dominant X. Similarly, this happens to daughters as well, although in this case there will be a normal X-chromosome from the father to mask the affected allele; 50 per cent of daughters are normal and 50 per cent are carriers. It is theoretically possible for a female carrier to have children with an affected male and produce an affected daughter, but the chances of this happening are very remote.

Probably the two most well known examples of sex-linked inheritance are haemophilia and colour blindness.

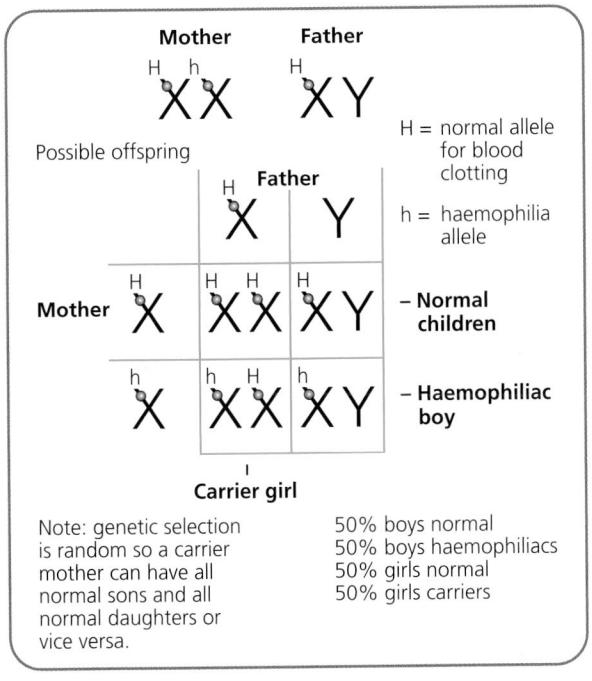

FIGURE 1.28 *Inheritance of haemophilia*

Haemophilia

Haemophilia, almost exclusively a condition of males, is a bleeding disorder due to the lack of a particular protein known as Factor VIII. Sufferers experience severe bleeding into muscles and joints even after very minor injuries. Such bleeding can lead to deformities of knees, ankles and other joints, and painful arthritis. In the past, many haemophiliacs were transfused with unscreened, donated plasma containing Factor VIII and as a result many clients and their sexual partners became infected with viruses such as HIV and viral hepatitis. Today, genetically engineered Factor VIII is available and it is virus-free. Donated plasma Factor VIII is screened for HIV, but there is still a risk of hepatitis.

Women who are known to be carriers often have brothers who are haemophiliacs and may choose to have termination in the case of male foetuses during early pregnancy rather than give birth to affected sons, although 50 per cent of male foetuses will be normal. (Few women choose to do so). Nowadays, the sex of an unborn child can be determined by ultrasound scanning and the appropriate treatment planned well in advance; if thought inconclusive, more invasive techniques (see page 20) can be employed, although the risks to the mother and baby are more significant.

Colour blindness

This is a sex-linked recessive disorder; however, it would pose very little influence on an individual's growth and development or health experience providing that person was careful in terms of hazards.

Duchenne's muscular dystrophy

Another sex-linked genetic condition is Duchenne's muscular dystrophy, which causes progressive deterioration in muscle fibres. It affects about one in 3,000 boys and there is no effective cure. A blood test looks for the enzymes released from damaged muscles

*** DID YOU KNOW?**

The **physician** Guillaume Duchenne (1806–1875) described a disease of the muscle resulting in dystrophy.

Multifactorial disorders

Large numbers of disorders are caused by the additive effects of certain genes together with various environmental factors, but the actual pattern of inheritance is complex; these are called multifactorial disorders. Asthma, insulin-dependent (Type 1) diabetes mellitus, schizophrenia and some congenital birth defects such as cleft palate are classed as multifactorial disorders.

Generally speaking, genetic faults cause serious effects on growth, development and health experience and the individual can only receive **palliative** treatment of symptoms. Genetic counselling and DNA sampling (through **amniocentesis** or **chorionic villus sampling**) can help in reducing the chances of a child being born with a serious genetic disorder.

Environmental factors influencing growth, development and health experience

There is a large range of environmental factors that impinge on the growth, development and health experience of all humans and research studies constantly supply more evidence of this on a daily basis. Basically, environmental factors can be divided into four groups:

* *lifestyle factors* such as substance abuse, diet, exercise and stress
* *social and community support factors* such as family, friends, health services, social class, cultural beliefs
* *physical environment factors* such as various types of pollution, safe neighbourhoods, access to employment, education and income
* *psychological factors* such as self-esteem, self-concept, relationships with family and partners, and stress.

Lifestyle factors

Diet

The Acheson report (1998) refers to 'food poverty' and notes that people in low socio-economic groups 'spend more on foods rich in energy and high in fat and sugar, which are cheaper per unit of energy, than foods rich in protective nutrients, such as fruit and vegetables' (1998: 65). 'People on low incomes eat less healthily partly because of cost, rather than lack of concern or information. Therefore increased availability of affordable 'healthy' food should lead to improved nutrition in the least well off'. (1988: 66.) The same report found that people in low socio-economic groups:

* consumed more processed food with high levels of salt, sugar and fat, thereby increasing the risk of cardio-vascular disease
* were less likely to breastfeed their babies and thereby protect them from infection
* were more likely to have low birth-weight babies than higher income groups, this being linked to the risk of cardio-vascular disease in later life
* had a greater risk of ill-health, generally due to obesity.

People on low incomes find it more difficult to travel to supermarkets to stock-up on cheaper food and 'special offers' and instead tend to shop on a daily basis at the local 'corner shop' where prices are higher. The Acheson report found that so-called 'healthy' food, therefore poverty may push people into choosing less healthy options.

Recommendations to consume five helpings or pieces of fruit and vegetables each day may have to be ignored when there is only a small amount of money available each week with which to purchase food to feed the family. Processed pies, chips and tinned beans will fill the family's stomach and lead to less complaint. Such a meal once in a while is all right, but day after day with little variation leads to obesity, heart disease, strokes, problems with mobility and, in some cases, cancer.

FIGURE 1.29 *Some children are in danger of becoming 'couch potatoes'*

Middle-class families frequently consist of overweight members too; children's sedentary leisure activities such as watching TV and playing computer games have taken the place of football in the park and skipping. Walking to school has been replaced by car journeys and, as increasing numbers of school playing fields are sold off, there is little physical activity in school. In the national press there are daily reports and articles about slimming diets for all, schools' attempts to try different school-meal options, and the poor health practices of multinational food industries. The British public is overwhelmed by food information and yet very little has changed. Overweight children are now suffering from cardiovascular disease. One study in Dundee, Scotland (1999) revealed that one-quarter of Scottish 11–14 year olds were beginning to show signs of heart disease not normally seen until middle age. One study in Glasgow by Reilly (1999) found childhood obesity between 2–15 years had doubled in 10 years: 'We found obesity was much more common than we expected – especially amongst children of a pre-school age'.

In February 2004, the World Heart Federation's World Heart Day had the theme 'Children, Adolescents and Heart Disease'. It noted that, globally, the number of obese adults has reached over 300 million and that about 22 million children under 5 years of age are obese, with and many more overweight. Common descriptions of this situation include phrases such as 'a time-bomb waiting to go off' and 'an epidemic of obesity'. It would seem that finally Western governments are waking up to the certainty that health services will collapse, when today's children reach early and middle adult life because their health problems will be colossal.

Possible actions:

* increase awareness through media activity especially during children's programmes
* develop improved food content information and labelling on packaging and restaurants
* develop and promote physical activity programmes, such as skipping skills

FIGURE 1.30 *Skipping together!*

* have cheap fruits and vegetables more readily available
* replace less healthy foods in vending machines with healthy options
* have healthy options near the cash points in supermarkets
* minimise the sale of fizzy drinks and high calorie foods in schools
* produce more healthy school meals
* increase physical activity by providing more sports facilities
* decrease salt and sugar content in foods and substitute fat
* encourage healthy cooking skills and the consumption of traditional food rather than processed or 'fast food'
* adopt price policies to make healthy foods more affordable and energy-rich foods more expensive, e.g. 'Fat VAT could save lives'
* make healthy choices more easy
* use legislation where voluntary actions fail to deliver.

Clearly, changes like these will not happen in a few months, but collective action is essential to advance public health and reduce the hazards of this global epidemic of obesity.

Exercise

Exercise, or the lack of it, has been mentioned several times in connection with diet since body weight is a balance between the input of food and

FIGURE 1.31 *Adults enjoying exercise*

the output of energy. This relationship becomes self-perpetuating because the lower the energy output, the more weight the body acquires (assuming food intake remains the same) and the inclination to exercise reduces further and so on.

There are many ways to enjoy physical activity, from simple walking to cycling in the Olympic games, and most also involve intellectual, social and emotional skills. People feel good after exercise and become more relaxed and confident. Exercise helps to combat the effects of stress in our daily lives, assists us to make relationships with others and encourages cooperation between individuals. A lack of exercise leads to a reduction in strength, suppleness and stamina, poor circulation and respiratory functions, and a build-up of fatty deposits in the arterial system. People who exercise regularly in adult life tend to live longer and have a better quality of life.

Stress

There are many occasions in our lives when we experience physical or mental tension and we might say that we are stressed.

Key concept

Stress: A physiological reaction to perceived threat. In other words, if a person believes that he or she is threatened, the stress reaction is set off.

The signs of tension received by the brain cause it to respond by secreting a hormone called adrenaline and increasing the activity of the sympathetic branch of our nervous systems. Both these activities 'switch' on the same actions around our bodies, but the outpouring of adrenaline boosts and sustains the actions more than the increased activity of the nervous system.

Figure 1.32 shows the different actions of adrenaline on the body.

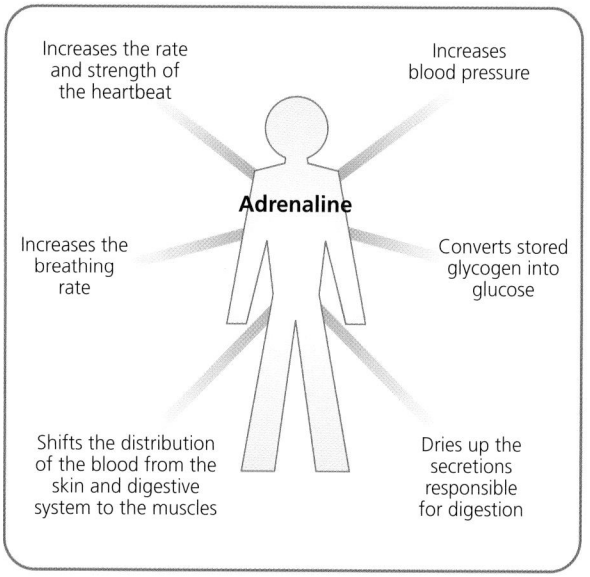

FIGURE 1.32 *The effects of adrenaline during stress or fright*

Large amounts of energy are released almost instantaneously into the blood and, together with increased oxygen, this is pumped rapidly around the body, chiefly to the muscles. From an evolutionary perspective, this response was designed to help an individual run away fast from enemies or stand up and fight. Adrenaline is therefore known as the fright, flight or fight hormone. Whilst some stress can liven up the body and help us to meet new challenges, some people in today's society experience stress on a continuous and long-term basis. The responses that adrenaline produces are often not helpful in the 21st century, as we are unable to run away or physically fight today's stressors, such as pollution, traffic jams, examinations and office hassle, for example. In fact, adrenaline-induced responses in the long-term can be positively harmful as they can lead to high blood pressure and increase the risk of coronary thrombosis, strokes and respiratory problems.

Think it over...

There are many symptoms of stress. The following list contains only a few; try to add more to this list:

Anxiety, heart disease, irritability, sleeplessness, diarrhoea, . . .

Mental and social problems arise with continuous stress, relationships break down, depression is common and suicidal or violent periods occur.

Use of drugs

A single or a mixed course of antibiotics or associated drugs can cure many infections that once might have caused death, disability or long-term illnesses in people. These prescribed drugs have revolutionised medical treatments although we have now reached the situation where scientists are struggling to maintain this supremacy over infections. This is because of the development of 'superbugs' resistant to the standard antibiotics – the infamous MRSA being one such strain.

Think it over...

Find out what words the initials MRSA stand for and their significance.

Surf the Internet to discover the causes and effects of MRSA infection on clients who need care.

An increasing number of drugs can now be bought in a pharmacy or supermarket and these are known as 'over-the-counter' drugs, with those for headache, toothache, coughing, influenza and colds being the most common. These types of drugs help people to avoid pain and other

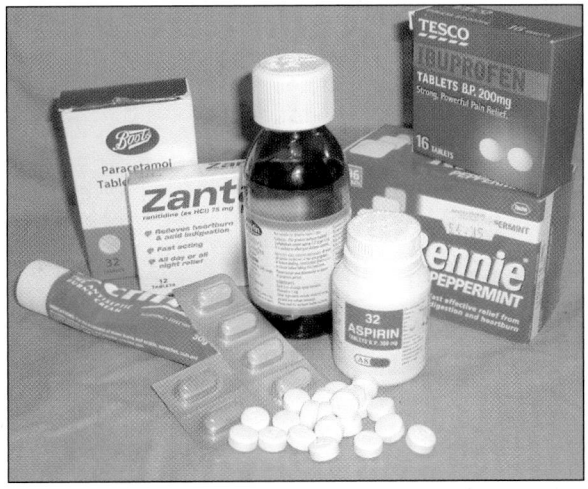

FIGURE 1.33 *Some common over-the-counter drugs*

symptoms almost instantaneously, so have to be mainly good for health and development. On the other hand, such drugs, being easily and widely available, can be a source of harm; all drugs carry the risk of side effects and over-use of most will result in liver and kidney damage, skin rashes, blood disorders and gastro-intestinal problems.

Illegal or controlled drugs are those taken by people to achieve a change in mood or behaviour. Only in a small number of special cases are these substances legally prescribed. Some drugs are called recreational or 'dance' drugs as they are taken to achieve a state of excitement at parties or raves. It is important to understand that many of these drugs arrive from foreign countries in very dubious circumstances, (some are even transported inside the living bodies of individuals) and hardly any are manufactured under safe, controlled laboratories. Before sale, they are often diluted or 'cut' with other materials that are often unsafe. The dose of each drug is not calculated accurately and people react to them in different ways. Taking illegal drugs once only can be dangerous, and taking them regularly can produce addiction. Addiction leads to tolerance whereby a higher dose of the drug is required to achieve the same effect, so the situation becomes more dangerous. As more research studies on the misuse of drugs report, there seem to be an increasingly large number of side effects emerging.

✱ DID YOU KNOW?

- ✱ 10 per cent of all those who have tried cannabis develop some form of psychological dependence.
- ✱ Cannabis remains the most widely taken illegal drug.
- ✱ Girls experiment with drugs almost as much as boys; young 'middle class' adults take drugs as much as people from poor social backgrounds; rural areas are affected as much as inner cities.

The range of illegal drugs is extensive and the side effects wide-ranging. You will find more specific details in Figure 1.34.

Alcohol

Deciding to drink alcohol can, in moderation and over the short term, confer some benefits such as a feeling of well-being and protection against coronary heart disease (in men and post-menopausal women). Recent research has demonstrated that alcohol raises the level of steroids in the body, which may increase the risk

MISUSED DRUG	APPEARANCE AND USE	EFFECTS OF USE	POSSIBLE RISKS TO HEALTH
Cannabis or hash, grass, marijuana, Black Leb, rocky, weed	Like dried herbs, a dark brown block or sticky and treacle-like; usually smoked but sometimes eaten	Feeling of sickness, hunger or worry More alert and talkative Imagine things (hallucinations)	Bronchitis and damage to lungs Raised pulse rate and blood pressure Inactivity and loss of memory Mental illness
LSD or acid, trips, tabs	Blotters and micro-dots that are swallowed (e.g. impregnated rice paper)	Greater self-awareness Disorientated in time and place Altered hearing, panic Depression and feeling that everyone and everything is against them (paranoia)	Never quite returning to previous normal state and needing more and more to achieve the same effects (tolerance) Flashbacks Anxiety Disorientation and depression
Heroin or H, Henry, smack	White or brown powder that is injected, sniffed up the nose or smoked	Feel sleepy and loved	HIV / AIDS and Hepatitis B when it is injected Thrombosis of veins or abscess at the injection sites Blood infection (septicaemia) Heart and lung disorders Can be fatal if impure
Ecstasy or E, xtc, M25s, lovedoves, Adam	Flat, round tablets that are swallowed	Confidence, calmness and alertness Thirst, anxiety Symptoms of heat stroke Sexual feelings	Nausea, headache and giddiness Raised body temperature with no sweating Muscular cramps Collapse Mental illness including paranoia
Cocaine, coke, snow or Charlie	White powder that is injected or sniffed	Anxiety, thirst and heat stroke symptoms	HIV / AIDS and Hepatitis B when it is injected Thrombosis of veins or abcess at the injection sites
Crack	Crystals that are smoked	Feel on top of the world, could do anything Panic, worry or hostility	Blood infection (septicaemia) Heart and lung disorders Highly addictive Raised body temperature with no sweating, muscular cramps Lack of appetite (anorexia)
Amphetamines or speed, sulph, whizz	White powder in tablets or screws of paper that is swallowed, sniffed or injected	Palpitations (increased force and rate of heart beat), weakness, hunger Lots of energy and confidence Depression and worry	HIV / AIDS and Hepatitis B when it is injected Raised blood pressure and risk of stroke Mental illness Tolerance develops
Solvents or glue, Evo, aerosols, petrol, lighter fluid	Various fluids or sprays that are sniffed	Heightened imagination, depression, happiness or sadness, hostility Fatigue, confusion	Liver and kidney damage Increased risk of accidents during the abuse Heart failure, suffocation, vomiting / choking, death

FIGURE 1.34 *The effects and risks of some commonly misused drugs*

of breast cancer in adult women up to the menopause. Anyone who consumes more than the current alcohol recommendations increases the risks to his or her health.

✱ DID YOU KNOW?

In the UK, daily alcohol recommendations are 3 units for women and 4 units for men.

15 per cent of men and 27 per cent of women drink more than the recommendations.

1 unit = one half-pint of beer or similar or
one small glass of wine or
one measure of spirits

The effects of alcohol consumption are shown in Figure 1.35. Short-term effects will continue until all the alcohol has been broken down by the liver and eliminated through the kidneys. Approximately one unit is metabolised per hour, but this varies from person to person. Women have smaller livers than men so are more susceptible to the effects. Both sexes will also be more prone to accidents as their self-control is impaired; women are less likely to protect themselves against unwanted pregnancies.

Over 10 units of alcohol per day in pregnancy can lead to foetal alcohol syndrome in babies, resulting in facial deformities, stunted growth, heart and joint abnormalities and learning disabilities.

Smoking

Significant changes in social attitudes to smoking have occurred in the last few years and further progress is planned for the near future. Some countries, including Ireland, have already banned smoking in public places and the government in the UK is being urged to follow suit.

The director of the Tobacco Control Resource Centre states that 'tobacco smoke is a potent cocktail of over 4,000 toxins (poisons) – more than 50 of which cause cancer.'

The Acheson report (1998) points out major class differences in smoking behaviour. 2 per cent of men and 16 per cent of women in the professional classes smoke, compared with 41 per cent of men and 36 per cent of women in the unskilled classes. Other theorists have noted that smoking rates increase with poverty and that women, in particular, find it difficult to give up. Some social groups will say that smoking is the only way to manage the stress of living on a low income and that it is the only luxury they allow themselves.

EFFECTS OF ALCOHOL CONSUMPTION	
SHORT-TERM EFFECTS	**LONG-TERM EFFECTS**
Increased heart rate	Raised blood pressure
Palpitations	Coronary heart disease
Increased skin temperature	Pancreatitis and cirrhosis of the liver
Diuresis – enhanced urine formation	Weakened immune system
Increased happiness and reduced inhibitions	Decreased sex drive
Slurring of speech	Irregular menstrual cycles, some sterility Foetal alcohol syndrome
Tendency to be argumentative	Increased risk of strokes
More accident prone	Increased risk of some cancers e.g. oesophagus
Muscle weakness	Obesity
Facial flushing	Brain damage and depression

FIGURE 1.35 *Effects of short- and long-term alcohol consumption*

Think it over...

In groups, consider the arguments you might use in trying to encourage a young single parent on benefits to stop smoking 40 cigarettes a day.

✱ DID YOU KNOW?

More than 1,000 people die every year as a result of diseases linked to passive smoking.

The home is now the most common place where children are exposed to tobacco smoke, and some places in the UK are taking part in an initiative called *Smoke-free homes* to tackle this problem. The biggest barrier that prevents people from making their homes smoke-free is the fear of harming important relationships with family and friends who smoke. More than 17,000 children are admitted to hospital each year in the UK because of the effects of inhaling tobacco smoke.

*** DID YOU KNOW?**

In 2000, the EU spent over £650 million on subsidies (i.e. grants of money) to tobacco producers and £1.3 million on smoking prevention! Under the common agricultural policy, tobacco is the most heavily subsidised and the only non-food product to be subsidised.

So, why is smoking so harmful to people? The pattern diagram below (Figure 1.36) shows the most serious effects of smoking.

Social and community support factors

An individual needs social and community support if his or her development is to proceed without problems or difficulties. We need to develop relationships with others to advance our social skills, and emotional development is likely to be affected if there is no one to share our 'highs' and 'lows' with. Intellectual stimulation is often dependent on good social and emotional development as well as the stimulation of exchanging views with others. Growth, development and health in childhood and adolescence are closely dependent on the groups to which we belong.

Family support

Key concept

Family: A family is a social group made up of people connected to each other by blood or marriage. Families in Britain usually consist of adults acting as parents or guardians to children.

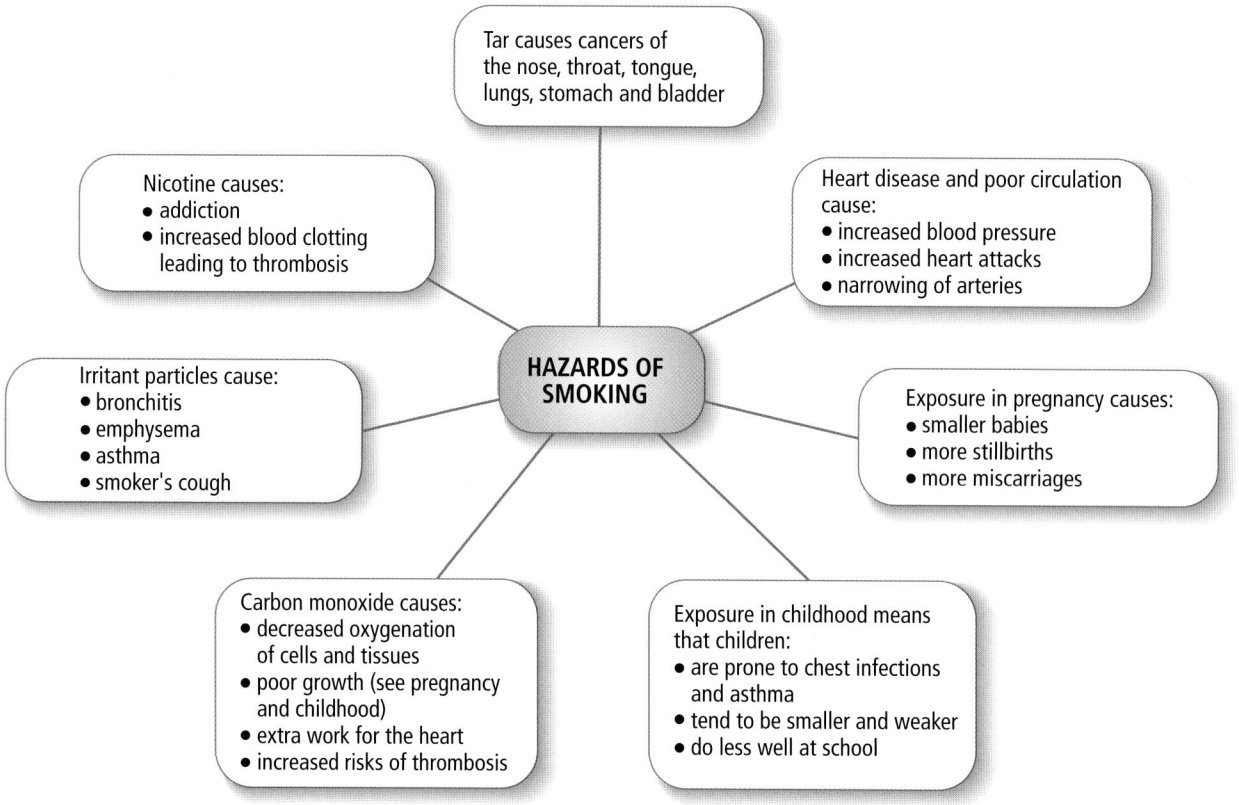

FIGURE 1.36 *The hazards of smoking*

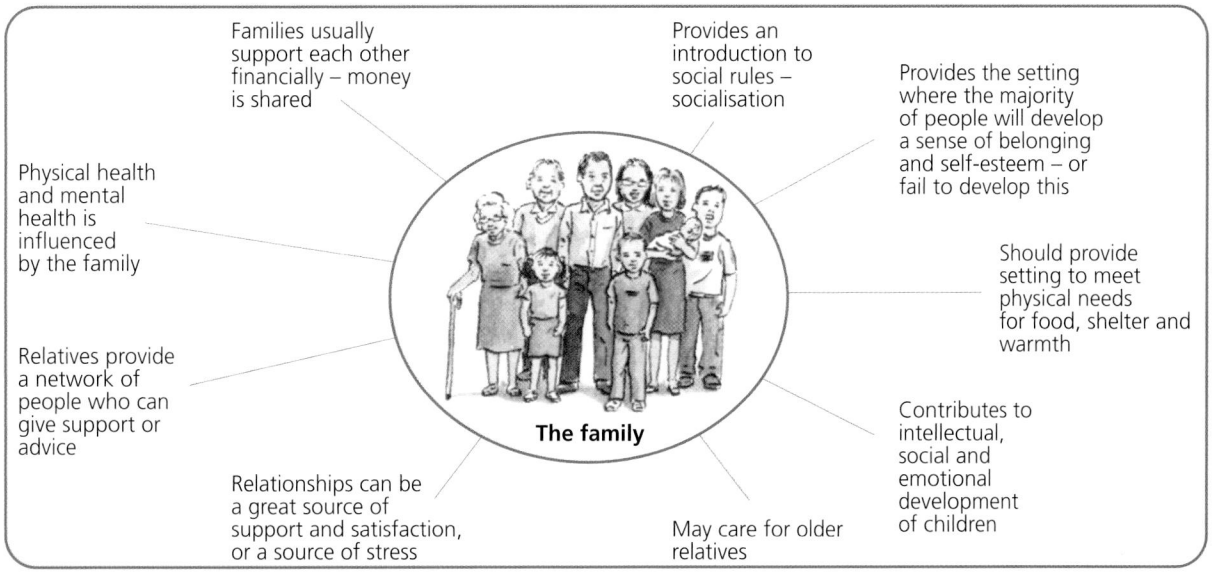

FIGURE 1.37 *Advantages of belonging to a family group*

Belonging to a family can have many advantages – such as safe, care settings for children; education and guidance for children and adolescents; and social and emotional support for older people. (See Figure 1.37.)

Sociologists have identified four types of families, which are classified as:

* extended
* reconstituted
* nuclear
* lone-parent.

Extended families

An extended family is where parents, children, grandparents and sometimes aunts and uncles live in close proximity so that they are in constant contact. The extended family provides a network of people who care and financially support each other. Families used to live this way in the 19th century so that everyone could help with feeding animals and working in the fields. However, industrialisation caused many people to travel to cities to work and live in much smaller houses.

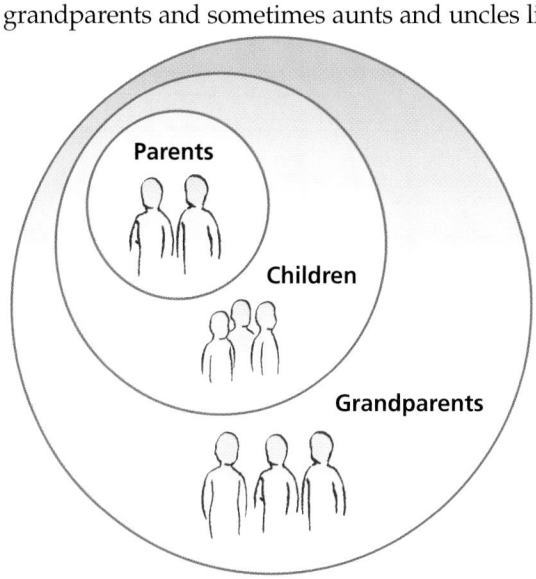

FIGURE 1.38 *The extended family*

Nuclear families

This term is used to describe the smaller family unit of husband, wife and children. In the past, the husband worked to earn money and the wife shopped, cooked, cleaned and looked after the children. In today's society, many families consist of two working parents, with nurseries, child-minders or nannies caring for the children except at weekends. Men and women share more of the household tasks although women still tend to undertake the biggest share.

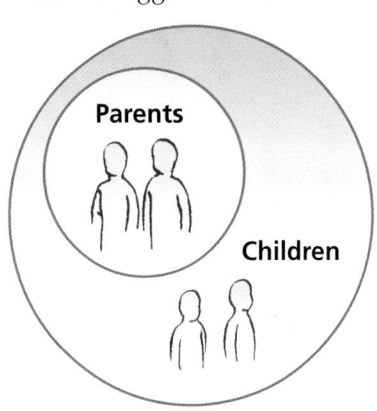

FIGURE 1.39 *The nuclear family*

✱ DID YOU KNOW?

The proportion of women aged 18–49 who were married dropped from 74 per cent in 1974 to 49 per cent in 2002. Over the same period the proportion of single women rose from 18 per cent to 38 per cent.

Reconstituted families

Approximately one marriage in three ends in divorce and more people are now cohabiting than ever before. Some of these couples will eventually marry whilst others will also split up. Around one-quarter of children under the age of 16 will experience their parents divorcing. A reconstituted family is one in which the partners are not both the biological parents of each child in the family.

✱ DID YOU KNOW?

The proportion of non-married women cohabiting in 1974 was 11 per cent compared with 29 per cent in 2002. Cohabiting single women rose from 8 per cent in the same period to 31 per cent in 2002. (Non-married women include divorced or separated women.)

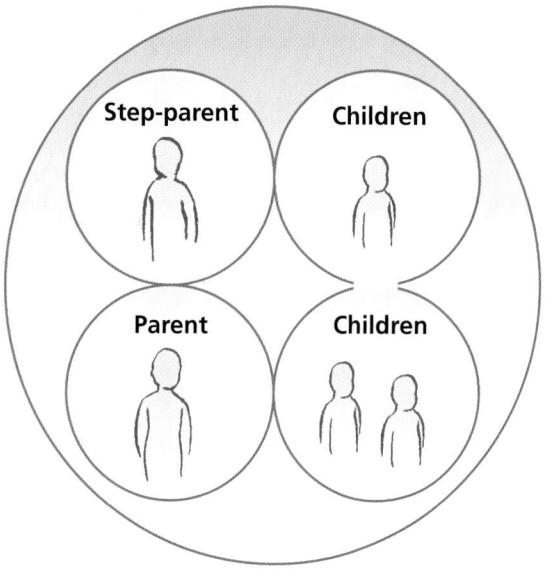

FIGURE 1.40 *The reconstituted family*

Lone-parent families

The proportion of families containing a married or cohabiting couple with dependent children declined from 31 per cent in 1979 to 21 per cent in 2002; by comparison, families headed by a lone parent rose from 4 per cent in 1979 to 7 per cent in 1993. Nearly one-quarter of all families with dependent children are now lone-parent families; most are led by the mother as the lone parent. While some lone-parent families are in satisfactory financial circumstances, most are disadvantaged because they survive on benefits or low incomes.

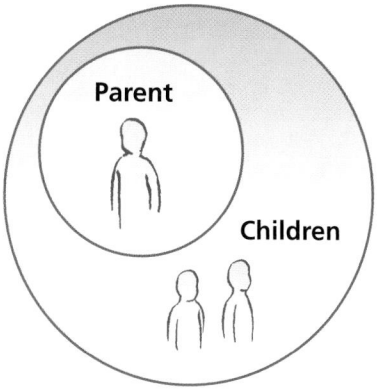

FIGURE 1.41 *The lone-parent family*

Insufficient family support

Insufficient support, however, may arise from dysfunctional, incomplete, undisciplined or over-large families, often as a result of circumstances beyond their immediate control. When there are large numbers of siblings born close together, an over-worked parent or carer, lax rules and low income, then there is often disregard for education, more aggression and slower cognitive progression. It is important to recognise the dangers of stereotyping for there are many entertainers, sports personalities, academics and authors who describe such backgrounds and have performed extremely well. Some wealthy entrepreneurs admit to disinterest in school and education during childhood and adolescence and to fending for themselves in a wider world. It might seem as if 'hunger' would drive some people onwards in a dynamic and exceptional way, but the majority of people lacking appropriate family support and/or income might find life increasingly difficult.

In recent years, we have recognised the importance of family support and instituted **holistic** treatment when an individual finds life difficult. Children and young people with psychological and/or behavioural problems might therefore be treated as part of the family rather than as individuals. Family therapy is becoming increasingly important and regular meetings with a therapist help to expose the feelings between family members. The therapist then works with the family to promote greater understanding and harmony.

Family is the setting in which we first learn social values. This is called primary or first socialisation.

Friends

Key concept

Socialisation: The process by which we learn the norms, values and behaviour that makes us a member of a particular group. Learning to socialise or be a social member of a group.

As childhood advances into adolescence and early adulthood, we find that friendship groups create a process called **secondary socialisation**. This is where friends influence our beliefs and values. A life without friends is likely to be very difficult indeed, for we call upon our friends to assist us in a variety of ways.

The same life-stage friends can be particularly important as experiencing the same or similar joys and difficulties forges a strong bond between people. Individuals from different life stages can also make firm friendships but often of a different nature, the elder listening to the younger person's problems and offering advice in an objective way.

Recent studies have shown, however, that children and adolescents who go about in 'gangs' do less well than those who have a few strong friendships. Gangs tend to move progressively

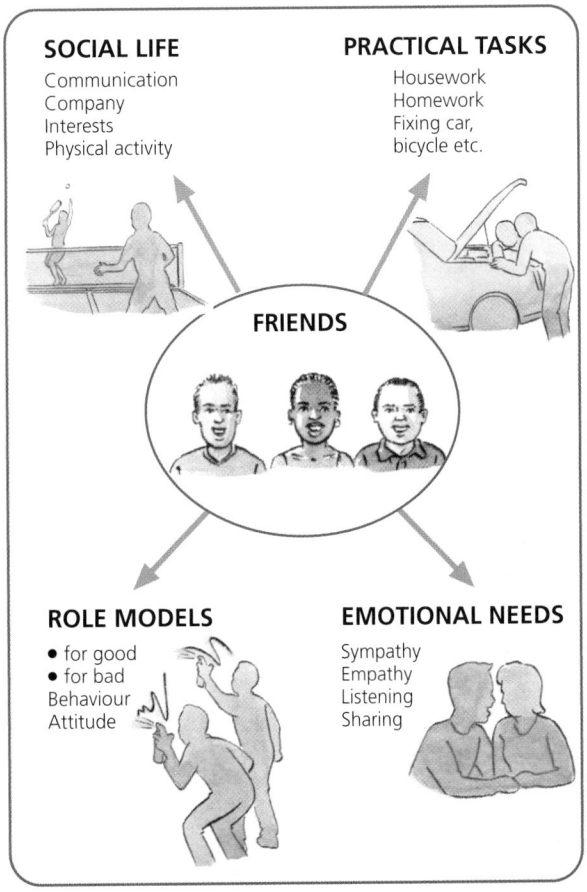

FIGURE 1.42 *Ways of friendship*

towards increasingly risky pastimes and the member who wants to withdraw is subjected to ridicule, bullying and even violence. In many communities, it is much safer to conform and belong to a gang than to be outside it.

FIGURE 1.43 *It is safer to belong to a gang than to be outside it*

Health services

The Acheson report (1998) identified an 'inverse law' in some areas of care. Communities with the greatest need receive the lowest level of service, whilst those with the lowest need receive the highest level of resource. In the field of preventive medicine, communities at the most risk of ill health often experience the least satisfactory access to the full range of preventive services. For example, the lack of a female general practitioner in a practice may deter Asian women from cervical cytology and other essentially female services. Deprived areas have increasing difficulty in recruiting GPs, health visitors and practice nurses. Dentists in the NHS have become extremely scarce in many areas of the country and several local populations, including children, have experienced several years of dental neglect.

New methods of booking appointments to see GPs and telephone consultations have disadvantaged people who do not have a private telephone, dislike using the instrument or have communication difficulties. The proportion of GP consultations at home fell from 22 per cent in 1971 to 5 per cent in 2002, but this coincided with increases in telephone (4 to 9 per cent) and surgery consultations (73 to 86 per cent). Clients in rural districts, who need to travel long distances to see GPs must to some extent appreciate new arrangements for telephone consultations.

Doctors spend more time with middle-class patients (social classes 1 and 2) and there is evidence that NHS expenditure is 40 per cent greater than on those in classes 6 and 7 because the former can manipulate the health systems to their advantage. (See Figure 1.45.)

Community groups

There is a wide range of groups serving different needs in the community. The primary focuses of these groups can be broadly categorised into serving these needs of its members as in Figure 1.44. Members of each group might also serve as friends and intimate relationships can be formed through shared interests.

FIGURE 1.44 *Community groups*

Think it over...

Some examples of community groups have been added to Figure 1.44. Make a list of community groups in your locality and add them to the relevant branch of a similar diagram.

Social class

In the UK we divide society into different levels according to the degree of wealth and power possessed by individuals. Historically, there was an upper class consisting of aristocrats who did not work for a living; middle classes who were in trade (shopkeepers, wholesalers, businessmen) or professions; and the working classes who worked for the middle and upper classes and generally had to manage on low incomes.

Key concept

Social class: The status given to different types of occupation or work.

Occupations are chosen because they are linked to a level of income, behaviour, lifestyle and standing in a community. The new system of

THE NATIONAL STATISTICS SOCIO-ECONOMIC CLASSIFICATION – ANALYTIC CLASSES	
1	Higher managerial and professional occupations Large employers and higher managerial occupations, e.g. chief executives of major organisations Higher professional occupations, e.g. doctors, lawyers
2	Lower managerial and professional occupations Middle management in bigger organisations, departmental managers, e.g. physiotherapists, teachers, police
3	Intermediate occupations, e.g. clerks, bank workers
4	Small employers and own account workers, e.g. painters, decorators, small manufacturing company owners, taxi drivers
5	Lower supervisory, craft and technical occupations, e.g. plumbers, builders, joiners, train drivers
6	Semi-routine occupations, e.g. shop assistants, hairdressers, labourers
7	Routine occupations, e.g. cleaners, refuse collectors, assembly workers
8	Never worked or long-term unemployed

FIGURE 1.45 *The National Statistics Classification*

classification shown in Figure 1.45 is now used in research into health and social issues.

Countries with the smallest income differences between the classes have the best health status; in the UK, where the income difference between classes is large, there is likewise inequality in health status. Accidental deaths in children are five times greater in the lowest social classes than in the higher classes. Infant mortality, lung cancer, stroke and heart disease rates are all several times greater in the lowest social classes.

Argyle (1987:189) states, 'The lower social classes are affected by most illness, more often, take more days off from work, and die a little sooner because of them (the illnesses). This is partly due to inequalities in the conditions of life – smaller homes, less heating, larger families, less good food and so on.' Argyle argues that middle-class people make more use of preventive health services such as antenatal clinics, vaccination programmes and cervical screening, than do working class people. There is evidence that social classes 1 and 2 smoke less, weigh less and exercise more than classes 6 and 7.

A study by Blaxter (1990) found that there is a close link between poverty and ill health and that there might be more ill health for the very wealthy than for those who are just well off.

Think it over...

There are over three-and-a-half times more suicides and four times more accidents in social class 7 than in class 1. What possible reasons can you think of for this?

Socialisation

A child learns a great deal from copying the activities of members of its family, but characters on TV, in books, in computer games, on DVDs and on radio also influence him or her. **Primary socialisation** then, occurs from experiences learned at an early age in the home and through the media. Children learn the 'norms' or beliefs of the family. When father goes to work every weekday to earn money to satisfy the needs of the family, this becomes the norm, and a family whose male parent does not work is outside that norm. Similarly, when appointments for clinics, surgeries or hospitals are largely ignored or complained about, the child rapidly picks up that such arrangements are not important and the indifference becomes perpetuated in their families in the future.

Secondary socialisation comes from a wider field of influence when the child becomes older. Between the ages of 11–15 adolescents become very involved with their own group of friends and the influence of the family wanes (but doesn't disappear) while that of the friendship group increases. This is particularly noticeable in music styles, sports enthusiasms, eating and drinking habits, substance abuse and fashions. Popular culture often does not include healthy lifestyles but fortunately, most of these lapses are temporary.

Cultural beliefs

Key concept

Cultural beliefs: Families and small social groups are influenced by the culture that surrounds them. This culture is influenced by ethnicity, religion, lifestyle, social class and geographical location. Different assumptions will be made within the group and these become the norms for the behaviour of the group.

Culture remains a strong influence on individuals during their lifespan. Different people have different beliefs about what is morally right and wrong and these can extend into aspects of care as well as in the home.

Physical environment factors

Air quality

Local authorities control air pollution from about 20,000 small industrial processes and the Environment Agency regulates the release of pollutants from over 2,000 major, more complex industries. The EU is legislating to bring a wider range of processes into regulation. Major sources

POLLUTANT	MAIN SOURCES	MAIN EFFECTS ON HEALTH
Particulate matter	Transport exhausts Burning of fossil fuels	Tiny particles enter and remain in the lungs; may cause inflammation and be a source of allergy and asthma. Can cause ground ozone (with carbon monoxide)
Carbon monoxide	Transport exhausts Burning of fossil fuels Furnace gas	Combines more powerfully with haemoglobin than oxygen so results in less oxygen available to the tissues. Headaches, faintness, nausea and dizziness result. In large quantities will cause brain damage and even death. When combined with soot particles in the presence of sunlight makes smog and ozone at ground level – a lethal mix of gases that causes breathing problems and asthma. Common in some cities in sunny climates, e.g. Los Angeles, Tokyo
Carbon dioxide	All combustion including gas fires, gas central heating	Transmits sunlight but partially resists the outward flow of infrared radiation from Earth to space, resulting in 'the greenhouse effect' and preventing the Earth from cooling at night. Consequently, the Earth's surface is warming up – so-called global warming with freak storms and hurricanes increasing the number of deaths and injuries
Sulphur dioxide	Coal-burning power stations, industrial processes	Causes the finer bronchioles in the lungs to contract making breathing more difficult and irritation of the upper respiratory tract. Largely responsible for 'acid rain'
Nitrogen oxides	Burning of fossil fuels Transport exhaust gases	Also forms 'acid rain' and ground ozone (see carbon monoxide) Damages stratospheric ozone layer, causing increased skin cancer and genetic mutations from extra radiation
CFCs chloro-fluoro-carbons	Chiefly aerosols	Damages the stratospheric ozone layer (see under nitrogen oxides)
Moulds	Decaying organic matter	Spores from moulds can cause allergies, hay fever and asthma

FIGURE 1.46 *Main sources and effects of air pollutants*

of pollution such as transport (chiefly cars) are controlled by a combination of actions at European, national and local levels.

Main pollutants of air are **noxious** gases and small particles (particulate matter PM10). You can check out their main sources and effects in Figure 1.46.

The good news is that levels of air pollutants are falling. However, the fall may not be fast enough to prevent large numbers of people suffering problems with their health.

Falling pollution levels are attributable to:

* regular monitoring of industrial processes and heavy fines for non-compliance with regulations
* catalytic converters fitted to cars
* reduction in coal-fired power stations
* regulations about the sulphur and lead content of fuel
* more 'lean-burn' engines in cars which reduce nitrogen oxide levels.

Water quality

There is sanitation, sewage treatment, waste disposal and water treatment in the UK and most developed countries. Water is sterilised and tested before it is supplied to homes; consequently, tap water is considered very safe. Accidents happen only very rarely when some contaminant enters the water system and correction or shutting down occurs quickly. Most of our sanitation systems are many decades old and modernisation is urgently needed in some parts of the country. Rats are a problem in our sewers and waterways, and if rats bite people there is always the possibility of diseases such as Weil's disease, typhus and plague.

*** DID YOU KNOW?**

The **physician** Adolf Weil (1848–1916) isolated rats as the cause of a particular disease he had described in humans.

Certain diseases, such as typhoid fever, cholera and viral hepatitis A, can transmit through water, so it is always prudent to boil or otherwise sterilise water in developing countries. Bottled or canned water is usually safe too, although there have been some incidents of too many salts in commercial preparations. Many of the diseases hitherto mentioned are potentially fatal diseases so it is very important to maintain water safety.

Noise pollution

Exposure to a very loud noise such as a jet engine at 30 metres can cause immediate and permanent damage to the ears; but, more commonly, hearing loud noise for a long time results in high-pitched tones becoming lost. Loud music or pneumatic drills can cause pain and temporary deafness, lasting minutes or hours. Regulations exist in workplaces to ensure that noise levels do not rise above certain levels and that those people exposed to loud noises in their occupations wear ear protectors. A common complaint, especially from those living in inner cities, is about traffic noise. Although regulations exist for minimising such noise, it can be extremely stressful, cause sleeplessness and eventually ill health. Similar experiences happen to people who live near busy airports, and night flights are particularly troublesome.

Access to employment

Worthwhile employment is one of the few ways to improve lifestyle, income, housing and health prospects. However, if an individual suffers from ill health and is deemed unreliable by employers, he or she is less likely to retain a job or get good references to obtain a new one. Maternity leave and the care of small children can also disadvantage women of childbearing age. Lone parents find it particularly difficult to find work that allows them to care for school-age children because of school hours and long holidays. Part-time work is usually low-paid and having to combine part-time work, school hours and holidays makes worthwhile employment almost impossible, even if a willing employer can be found. In such circumstances living on benefits becomes more attractive. Such a lifestyle also carries with it the enormous stress of dealing with being punctual, sudden child sickness, or school closures for elections and teacher training days. Many couples paying for childcare, either pre-school or after-school, find that the costs almost equate to one salary or wage packet.

As manufacturing declines in the UK there are fewer social class 7 jobs available, particularly in the North, and the cost of living in the South prohibits people from moving. This leads to frustration, anger, stress and ill health for the long-term unemployed and their families. Unemployment affects the way we treat other people, the treatment we receive from others, the services we are entitled to and our attitude to life generally. Unemployment also contributes to the decline of areas, as people have little money with which to purchase commodities, so shops close down, vandalism is rife and dereliction becomes the norm. People who live in the poorest areas tend to have low self-esteem and this is a significant deterrent to potential employers when being interviewed for all but the lowliest of jobs. Unemployment has a profound effect on self-esteem and motivation; there is no point in working hard to gain qualifications if there are no jobs to apply for.

Unemployment in the UK (measured by the International Labour Organisation, ILO, 2002) is running at 4.7 per cent or just under one and a half million people. This figure relies on the Labour Force Survey of the number of people without employment who have made recent efforts to find it.

There has been marked growth in employment in the UK in the recent past, but most jobs are part-time and low paid. In 1996, just over a quarter of a million people entered employment of which 63 per cent were part-time, and a quarter of employed people earned less than £4 per hour.

People *not* counted as unemployed but who want to work include those:

* who informally care for others – children, elderly or disabled people
* working part-time because they cannot get a full-time job
* young people on training schemes like New Deal and Modern apprentices
* people who have moved on to sickness or disability benefit rather than the 'dole'
* students in full-time education
* adolescents under 18 years who are not allowed to register as unemployed.

The Trades Union Congress (TUC) has reported that as many as two million people not counted as unemployed want full-time work. If these people were added to the 'official' ILO figures, then the UK would have a higher unemployment total than France or Germany.

People most likely to be unemployed are lone parents, disabled people, those without many skills or qualifications, those over 50 years and people from ethnic minorities.

Many people are multi-disadvantaged; for example, a lone parent from an ethnic minority and with low qualifications. If we removed people in these areas of society from the unemployment register, we would have only 4 per cent unemployed.

Unemployment is mainly concentrated in deprived areas where the rate can be many times the national average.

Key concept

Income: Money that an individual or household gets from wages, benefits, investments or other sources.

Many families who are well off tend to have the best of everything, including rich food. Too much of the wrong kind of food, rich in fat and salt content, is harmful to the cardiovascular system and causes obesity, with all its problems. Such families are usually regularly monitored by their physicians and given the correct advice and attention. They can afford designer-wear clothes, to go to private gymnasia or even to have a personal trainer to take them in hand. Many families in the social classes 1 and 2 tend to drink too much alcohol, particularly on holiday, which is the main occasion for so-called 'binge-drinking'. Young adults, particularly females, regularly drink more than the recommended allowance, putting their physiological health at risk, together with possible accidents and unwanted pregnancies.

Despite the Welfare State, the gap continues to widen in life expectancy and health experience between those who are well off and those who are poorer. Several studies have reported on the number of unnecessary deaths, particularly of those under 65 years of age, which take place in the poorest areas of Britain. It has been estimated that if full employment could be achieved some 2,500 deaths would be prevented each year.

The UK has the second highest proportion of full-time workers on low pay of all major economies in the West; only the United States has more. People on low pay are also more vulnerable to unemployment and after losing a job are more likely to be paid even less on re-entering work. The longer someone has been on a low income, the more likely they are to remain so and this especially applies to older workers and women.

Levels of dental decay and rates of infant mortality, teenage pregnancy, and suicide are all increased in deprived areas. Suicides are strongly linked to poverty and depression and are two to three times higher among the unemployed. The suicide rate in Scotland is twice as high as in England and Wales and a serious cause for concern. Teenage pregnancies, linked to poverty and unemployment, in Scotland are the highest in Western Europe.

The lower the income of an individual or family the more risks they suffer throughout all life stages.

Education

Education levels in the poorest areas are lower than for the rest of the country. The government believes the improvement in primary and secondary schools is vital to give people the necessary skills to achieve jobs and careers. Schools in deprived areas suffer more vandalism, rubbish accumulation and lack of resources than more affluent schools. This produces stressful working conditions for staff and pupils, who are less likely to take full advantages of learning opportunities. Children arrive at school hungry, without energy-sustaining breakfasts, tired and minus homework, or even simple writing instruments. The start of the school year is particularly difficult for teachers, as many children may have had to fend for themselves over the long summer break, while parents are at work, or worse, on holiday. Parents who continually hear about the difficulties and behavioural problems of their children soon cease to be interested in parents' evenings or education generally. Stress, depression and social exclusion reduce the interest level even further.

Acheson (1998) reports that education has a link with health in that low levels of educational achievement are associated with poor health in adult life. Poor health and poor educational achievement are caused by **poverty**. It is likely that the combined effects of poor resources, low expectations and the need to earn money often influence young people from low-income families to give education a low priority.

New initiatives from the government to increase participation in higher education are likely to be offset by the student loan debate and the almost certain legacy of incurring a large debt. The effects of maintenance allowances, which aim to encourage students from low income families to achieve university entrance qualifications, are likely to be countered by the pressure from the family to work and provide extra income.

Safe neighbourhoods

The Rowntree Report (1995) drew attention to the fact that some neighbourhoods were particularly stressful to live in because of high levels of poverty, unemployment, crime and vandalism.

The Social Exclusion Unit Paper 'Opportunity for all' (1999) explains that some communities are 'trapped outside mainstream society'. High levels of crime form one of the main problems in such communities; people are afraid to venture out, principally in darkness, as they are afraid of becoming victims of crime. Growing up and living in the most deprived neighbourhoods may greatly restrict an individual's chance of developing his or her full intellectual, social or emotional potential.

Much of the crime on estates is drug-related, as individuals search for money or valuables to pay for their next 'fix'. Gun crime is increasing in the UK and most of this is also drug-related. Innocent people have been gunned down in Liverpool, Manchester, Nottingham and London while carrying out their day-to-day business or leisure activities. High levels of crime also facilitate gang formation, as individuals feel safer in the company of several friends.

Unemployment, low income, poor educational opportunities, high crime levels, poor health, poor services, neglect and abuse of all types 'feed' off each other, creating housing estates that undermine all but the very strongest.

Psychological factors

Health can be strongly influenced by the way individuals feel about things, particularly themselves.

Self-concept is a term used to incorporate both self-esteem and self-image. Self-concept is defined as an understanding of self, gained from how we feel about or value our self and the reactions of others towards us.

Key concept

Self-esteem: How highly we value our skills and abilities.

Self-image: How we see our self and the reactions of others towards us.

Self-esteem

This is the regard individuals have for themselves, which can influence behaviour and moods. Having a high self-esteem increases self-confidence and makes an individual more able to cope with the difficulties he or she might face. It also might mean that a person is popular with peers and more likely to be successful. A child having high self-esteem is more likely to be content and happy in his or her adult life. It would seem that a close, loving relationship with his or her mother, a fair, constant framework of discipline and the ability to express individuality provides a good foundation for the development of self-esteem through childhood.

Self-esteem and the development of self-concept

As children grow they become socialised into the beliefs, values and norms of their initial family or care-giving group. Later, the beliefs, values and norms of their friends with whom they mix and play will influence them. Children adopt other values and norms in order to be accepted into social groups, to be liked and to be popular. Mead (1934) believed that children learn general social rules and values during childhood. He believed that children might learn to display emotion as expected in their social roles and the cultural context of their home. They do not simply do what others teach them, however; they internalise values from the world around them, built into a sense of self that becomes part of their self-concept and social identity.

This sense of self will guide the individual to exaggerate, suppress or even substitute emotional expression. In some geographical areas and social classes, boys may learn to exaggerate feelings of anger and aggression to achieve social status. In a different social class, boys may learn to express anger in terms of clever verbal behaviour with little hint of emotion. Some girls may learn to hide feelings of distress in order to look in control. Mead's theory explains how social influences work on an individual. It is the idea of 'self' or 'me' that explains how social values influence individual behaviour.

During adolescence this sense of self becomes of central importance. Erikson (1963) believed that biological pressures to become independent would force adolescents into a crisis, which could only be successfully resolved if the individual developed a conscious sense of self or purpose. He wrote, 'In the social jungle of human existence, there is no feeling of being alive without a sense of ego identity.'

Other theorists have regarded the development of the self-concept as more gradual and less centred on biological maturation. A clear sense of self might provide a person with the ability cope with changes in life and lead to a feeling of self-worth.

The psychologist Donaldson (1986) believes that a child can only develop a strong or positive self-concept when he or she feels effective, independent and competent.

The benefits conferred by a positive self-concept can be to:

* make effective social and sexual relationships with others

* cope with decision-making, especially in work environments
* develop self-confidence in social and work settings
* accept new challenges with enthusiasm
* cope with own feelings to arouse motivation
* cope with complex interpersonal situations by using appropriate skills, e.g. assertion.

Consider this

With a good friend to help you, draw up a list of questions to investigate the strength of a person's self-concept. You can use the following phrases to get you started:

* physical attraction
* intelligence or cleverness
* athletic or sporting ability
* popularity
* fitness
* problem-solving
* decision-making.

When you have completed the list, devise a method of scoring, say, from 0–5, where 0 represents no ability at all and 5 represents excellence. If you have 9 questions, then 45 is the top score. You can also devise a means to interpret the score in terms of self-concept – for example, 35–45 is a positive self-concept and 0–20 is a negative self-concept. Some individuals will be positive in some aspects and more negative in others. Try your system out on each other and analyse the results in terms of effectiveness for you.

FIGURE 1.47 *The development of self-concept begins with self-awareness*

Think it over...

Using your 'home-made' self-concept from the last exercise, explore the ways in which your self-concept has been influenced by the factors in Figure 1.47. Talk your answers through with the person who previously partnered you.

AGE	STAGE OF DEVELOPMENT
1½–2 years	Self-awareness develops – children may start to recognise themselves in a mirror
2½ years	Children can say whether they are a boy or a girl
3–5 years	When asked to say what they are like, children can describe themselves in terms of categories, such as big or small, tall or short, light or heavy
5–8 years	If you ask children who they are, they can often describe themselves in detail. Children will tell you their skin colour, eye colour, about their family and to which school they belong
8–10 years	Children start to show a general sense of 'self-worth', such as describing how happy they are in general, how good life is for them, what is good about their family life, school and friends
10–12 years	Children start to analyse how they compare with others. When asked about their life, children may explain without prompting how they compare with others. For example: 'I'm not as good as Zoe at running, but I'm better than Ali.'
12–16 years	Adolescents may develop a sense of self in terms of beliefs and belonging to groups – being a vegetarian, believing in God, believing certain things are right or wrong
16–25 years	People develop an adult self-concept that helps a great deal as they grow older
25+ years	People's sense of self will be influenced by the things that happen in their lives. Some people may change their self-concept a great deal as they grow older
65+ years	In later life it is important to be able to keep a clear sense of self. People may become withdrawn and depressed, without a clear self-concept

FIGURE 1.48 *Overview of the developmental stages of the self-concept*

General factors influencing self-concept are displayed in Figure 1.48.

An overview of the developmental stages of self-concept might be summarised as in Figure 1.49.

Relationships with family and partners

Blaxter (1990) discovered that stressful life events such as widowhood, bereavement, divorce, unemployment and moving home were associated with increased morbidity (incidence of disease) and mortality (death). She reported that people were protected or 'buffered' against these effects of stress when they had a close social support network of friends, family, partners and/or community links.

As well as protection against stress, support will also maintain self-esteem, self-concept and identity when these may be threatened. Argyle (1987) maintained that the quality of support was important and that both sexes preferred to have meaningful dialogue with females, who are more pleasant and open to self-disclosure than men.

Blaxter (1990) noted that family relationships and close bonds were strongly protective against stress, perhaps through positive effects on self-esteem and feelings of control. The relationship between social networks and health is so strong that it can be used predictively in relation to mortality. People with poor social networks run a greater risk of dying from illness than those with close relationships. In terms of support, marriage

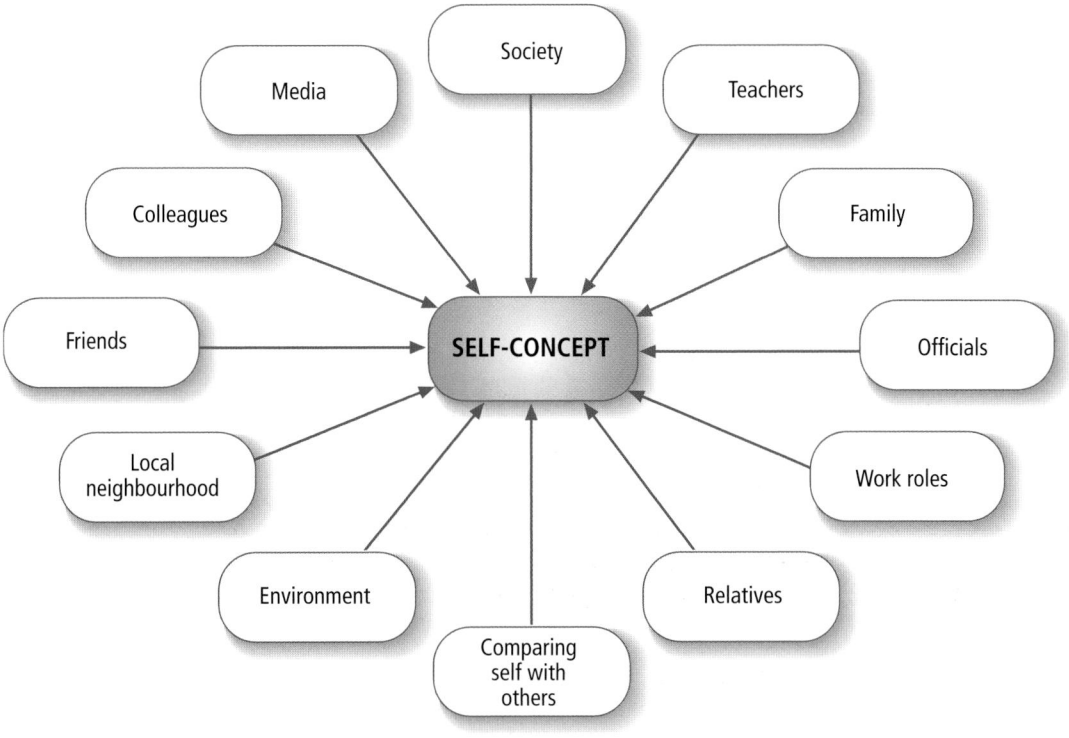

FIGURE 1.49 *Influences on self-concept*

produced the strongest protection, followed by friends and relatives – even more than belonging to church or other organisations.

Argyle further contends that stress impairs the immune system – the natural defence against disease. Social support might restore the immune system by replacing negative emotions such as depression and anxiety with the positive emotions of hope and belief. Those with good relationships are more likely to seek support and help than turn to drinking and smoking.

Blaxter's study (1990) provided evidence that marriage and cohabiting have a more positive relationship on health than being single. This is significant for men generally and older men in particular, as living alone is associated with more illness and poorer psychological and social well-being. Socially isolated people may lack a buffer to protect themselves against anxiety, strain and threat.

Stress

There are many ways to define stress, but one expression that fits life generally is 'any interference that disturbs a person's healthy mental and physical well-being'. Some people are more susceptible than others to stress-related problems, but most people find the death of a loved one, the birth of a baby, moving house, divorce, violence and conflict, and other significant life events, cause them stress.

The physiological responses to adrenaline and cortisol outpourings produce changes in heart rate, blood pressure, respiratory rate, metabolism and physical activity designed to improve overall performance; however, such responses also reduce the individual's ability to cope. Long-term stress reduces the ability of the immune system to protect against disease, produces depression and anxiety, indigestion, palpitations, hypertension (and resulting heart disease) and muscular aches and pains.

Nature–nurture debate

The debate about inherited and environmental influences on behaviour, health and well-being is sometimes referred to as the nature (inherited influences) or nurture (environmental influences) debate. The argument has been going on between

GOOD RELATIONSHIPS CAN PRODUCE:	POOR RELATIONSHIPS CAN PRODUCE:
Infancy Secure attachment between the infant and parents A rich learning environment A safe, loving environment which meets a child's emotional needs	A failure to make a secure or safe emotional attachment between parents and the child Neglect, rejection of the child
Early childhood A secure home from which to develop slowly Parents who can cope with the stressful behaviour of young children Friendships with other children	A stressful home situation Neglect or rejection of the child Inconsistent attempts to control a child Parents who become angry or depressed because of the child Isolation from other children
Later childhood Membership of a family or care group Socialisation into a culture Friendships with others at school Increasing independence from parents A feeling of being confident and liked by other people A feeling of being good at things	Stress and change if parents fight each other or separate No clear feeling of belonging with a group or culture Limited friendships Feelings of not being liked by others Feelings of not being good at anything or not as good as others
Adolescence Independence but still with the support of the family A network of friends, a sense of belonging with a group of friends A culture shared by friends A positive environment that has opportunities for the future	Conflict and fighting with parents and family Few friends, feeling depressed and rejected No feeling of belonging with other people No clear sense of who you are The feeling that life is not worth much
Adulthood A network of friends and family who help and support you A secure, loving, sexual relationship Good relationships with work colleagues The ability to balance time pressures between work, partner and other family relationships A feeling of being secure and safe, with other people to help you	Feelings of isolation, loneliness, rejection and no feeling of belonging with friends No support Changing relationships No social protection from stress Low self-esteem
Old age A network of family, friends and partner to provide emotional support Control of own life A sense of purpose	Few friends, no social support No social protection from stress Isolation No sense of purpose

FIGURE 1.50 *The effects of personal relationships at different life stages*

theorists for decades – long before genes and chromosomes were discovered.

Bateson, quoted in *The Independent* (18th February 1995) argued that human development is a process like baking a cake: the end result of which is nothing like the ingredients that were used to make it, and the process of mixing and baking produces something quite different. Similarly, the contribution of environmental factors on human growth and development are impossible to separate from the contribution of genetics. Human beings are infinitely more complex than cakes, which become finished products, whereas human learning and development continues until death. A useful conclusion is that neither nature nor nurture can be abstracted from the process of development, but that they both interact throughout the lifespan. At some times, it appears that genetic influences are more dominant and, at others, environmental factors override the inherited component.

Recently, the leader of the private effort to decode the human genome, Venter, said, 'genetic determinism, the idea that a person is controlled by their genes, is a fallacy.' He made his remarks after stating that humans had far fewer genes than expected – only 30,000 – and suggested that environmental influences play a larger role in development than was previously thought.

Researchers predict that soon the data will unlock the secrets of how genes influence behaviour. Other theorists have argued that the (relatively) small number of genes does not indicate the larger role of environmental influences at all. The nature–nurture debate, as old as it is, just will not go away!

Summary of Section 1.2

The following key areas of theory in nature versus nurture have been covered in this section:

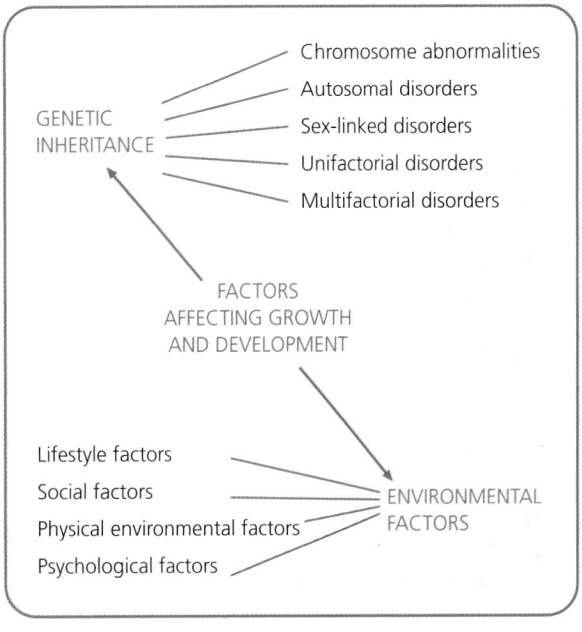

Consider this

Tom's family has a history of coronary heart disease due to a high level of blood cholesterol. Several close members of his family have died in early and middle adulthood, making it necessary for him to have regular checks by the family doctor.

Tom used to be both a heavy smoker and drinker and he works long hours with disadvantaged children. His frail mother now lives with Tom, his wife and four children ranging in age from 4–15 years. The house is fairly crowded and the older two children go out most evenings to their friends. Tom worries that he is losing touch with the teenagers and that they might get into trouble but is anxious to help out with the younger children and his mother, who he feels has not long to live.

Using concepts, can you identify?

1. Genetic factors that have an impact on Tom's experience of health and well-being?
2. Environmental factors that have an impact on Tom's experience of health and well-being?

Go further – can you analyse issues using theory?

Discuss the relevance of the nature versus nurture debate with particular reference to Tom's experience of health and well-being.

Go further – can you evaluate using a range of theory?

Using a range of concepts, can you make judgements on the factors influencing Tom's health that were under his control and those which he would not be able to change.

1.3 Promoting health and well-being

Defining '**health**' is a difficult task as it means many different things to people, rather like 'stress' or 'happiness' does. These words are almost indefinable except in the most general terms. We must, however, have some idea of the meaning of 'health' as we use the word in titles such as 'health visitor', 'health education' and '**health promotion**'.

Understanding 'health'

If you asked friends or members of your family what they understand by 'health' or 'being healthy', you will collect varied responses.

Most people will respond in terms of 'not being ill' indicating a rather negative view that health is something that you don't think about until you have not got it. In other words, health is something that you have until your daily life is disturbed by illness and you are unable to carry out your normal programme. Other people might produce a more wholesome or '**holistic**' view of health as being in the peak of physical, mental and emotional fitness. Some people might provide you with a very personal notion of health, such as 'when my rheumatism isn't giving me trouble'. Personal views like this might

FIGURE 1.51 *'Health' means different things to people; some associate it with decent accommodation*

SCENARIO

A state of health

Simin is 22 years old and uses a wheelchair after a road accident left him paralysed 4 years ago. He has totally recovered from the accident and travels by car to his local leisure centre to play basketball with other wheelchair users. Simin hopes to take part in national events next year and international competitions in a year or two. When asked, Simin replies that he is in excellent health.

Mary and her four children have lived in bed and breakfast accommodation for 2 years. Before that, Mary was homeless and the children were in residential care. Last month, Mary and her family moved into a partly furnished council house. Mary obtained two nursery places for her pre-school children and managed to get a part-time job in the local supermarket. When Mary met her friend yesterday she told her that she felt 'on top of the world'.

Stan is a 68-year-old ex-miner who is a widower, living alone. He smokes 20 cigarettes a day and enjoys a few pints at the local with his friends when he can manage the walk. Stan has chronic bronchitis and moderately severe arthritis, a legacy from his working days. On the days when he can meet his friends and spend a few hours chatting about old times, Stan says that 'he is in great shape'; on other days he will say that he is 'soldiering on'.

Simin probably links the perception of his health to his basketball prowess and considers himself 'ill' if he cannot attend practice sessions due to physical ailments.

Mary associates health with decent accommodation and being with her family. She is unlikely to worry about minor problems of physical health, like colds.

Stan is likely to concentrate on meeting his friends. It is likely he will dismiss his bronchitis and arthritis as being natural because of his age and previous occupation. When he cannot manage to get out to see his friends then life is more of a burden.

depend on age, social background, culture, circumstances and experience, as seen in the mini-case studies on page 46.

The scenerios show how each person's view of 'health' is different and closely linked to feelings, moods and being able to cope with daily activities, jobs or events.

Other people, especially those with different cultural inheritances, may view health as a spiritual form of well-being; for example, consuming alcohol is seen as an unholy thing to do as it leads to loss of self-control.

Think it over...

At this stage, you might like to think about how *you* might define health, bearing in mind the difficulties with care terminology already referred to.

Defining 'health'

The World Health Organisation (WHO), part of the United Nations Organisation, was set up in 1948 and at that time defined 'health' as being 'a state of complete physical, mental and social well-being and not merely the absence of disease or infirmity.' Later on, criticisms about the idealistic nature of 'complete state of well-being' and the unreal, implied view that health is static throughout one's lifespan, led to an expansion of this definition by several groups and individuals in the mid-1980s.

Seedhouse (1986) proposed health *'as a foundation for achieving a person's realistic potential'*, whereas WHO offered a revised concept of health as *'the extent to which an individual or group is able, on the one hand, to realise aspirations and satisfy needs, and on the other hand, to change or cope with the environment.'*

Key concept

Health: Health is now seen as a positive concept that focuses on personal and physical capacities, together with social resources, adaptability and responsibility.

It is worth considering now the meaning behind 'health education' and 'health promotion'.

Health education and health promotion

Health education is now seen as a very important part of a wider 'umbrella-type' concept of health promotion. It involves trying to influence or direct a change of attitude or behaviour in people as a result of giving information about health.

When a group of people is informed about the dangers of cigarette smoking through statistics on smoking-related deaths and the potentially lethal composition of cigarette smoke, they are being given health education.

FIGURE 1.52 *Health education*

Rather like the original WHO definition of 'health', it became evident that while health education involved vital information that needed to be distributed, a wider, less individual initiative involving more activities was required. The umbrella term was 'health promotion' is therefore used to describe a process involving a wide range of activities to improve the health of individuals.

Key concept

Health Promotion: The WHO explanation of 'health promotion' is the process of enabling people to increase control over, and to improve, their health.

Health promotion campaigns

Special interest groups, organisations or national government frequently mount health promotion campaigns to enhance this process. Campaigns can be short-lived and locally focused, such as endeavouring to keep a community-based special needs playgroup open in opposition to planned closure, or long-term and nationwide, such as a 'don't drink and drive' campaign.

Planning is an essential part of any campaign, which should have a *purpose* (intention), stated *aims* (general statements of achievement) and *objectives* (specific outcomes within a time period).

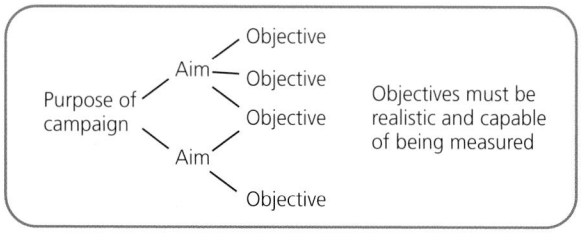

FIGURE 1.53 *Analysis of a campaign*

Think it over...

'Don't drink and drive' campaigns are familiar to most of us as they appear on TV, radio and hoardings. Individually or in a small group, try to work out the purpose, aims and objectives behind a recent campaign.

Aims of health promotion campaigns

What is any health promotion campaign trying to achieve?

* Is it trying to get people to be more knowledgeable about issues relating to healthy living? This is raising heath awareness.
* Is it trying to get people to generally improve their fitness?
* Is it trying to prevent people becoming ill?

The aims, as they exist in Figure 1.54, do not exist in isolation, for they are interconnected. Informing a group of school leavers about the reasons for continuing to take regular exercise in their leisure time means that you are raising their awareness about a health issue, thereby improving fitness levels and helping to prevent obesity, heart disease and respiratory problems in later life.

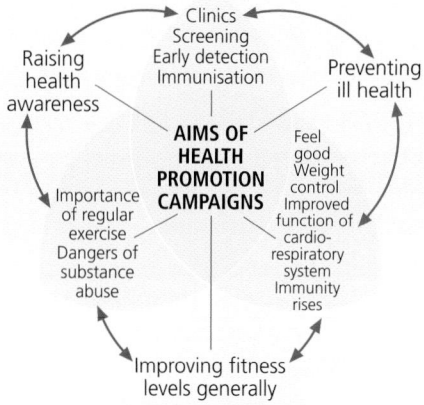

FIGURE 1.54 *The aims of health promotion campaigns and their links*

Different approaches to health promotion

Biomedical approach or model

This approach focuses on the prevention of disease or disability through intervention by medical (or other caring) professionals. It is important when using this model to have a group of clients who will act in accordance (be compliant) with medical advice and the use of preventive measures.

Examples of health promotion using a biomedical model include immunisation schedules,

SCENARIO

Biomedical approach

The West Piptree Group practice is located in an area favoured by retired people and those in later adulthood. Dr Wright, the senior partner in the practice, has sent letters to all his clients over the age of 65 years inviting them to the local community centre on a specific Friday in October to have 'anti-flu jabs'. The clerical assistants have telephoned all clients over 75 years of age as well, to reinforce the letter of invitation.

Influenza can have serious effects on older people and secondary bacterial infection is common, resulting in respiratory and circulatory problems that can be fatal.

FIGURE 1.55 *Service users receiving their 'flu jabs' (biomedical approach)*

cervical cytology, mammography, X-ray screening of the chest, family planning clinics, etc.

Giving 'flu jabs' is an example of health promotion using the biomedical approach. The biomedical approach can be seen to be 'expert-led', as in the scenario above, as far fewer people in later adulthood would have remembered to make appointments to protect themselves against influenza. This approach is also popular because it relies on medical science and, generally speaking, clients place great faith in such techniques. However, structures and resources need to be in place for this model to be successful.

Finally, the biomedical approach helps to avoid disease and prevents people becoming ill in the first place.

Educational / behavioural approach or model

This model emphasises information giving to promote better knowledge and understanding of health matters so that individuals, or groups, can adopt healthier lifestyles. The relevant, accurate information should be delivered at the right level to an audience capable of making informed decisions. Health promoters using this model will also believe in the rights of individuals to choose their own lifestyle.

Examples of the educational or behavioural approach include the distribution of leaflets explaining the dangers of all types of substance abuse, talks on the dangers of smoking, and advice on birth plans.

SCENARIO

Educational approach

Josh will soon be 16 years old and plans to leave school in the summer. He has no idea what he will do, as he doesn't expect to achieve any worthwhile qualifications. His best times have been spent in the local youth club, where he has made friends with Sam, one of the youth workers. Josh often smokes cannabis and sees no harm in it. Sam is aware of Josh's habit and they have talked about it several times. Sam has allowed Josh to continue attending the youth club, providing that he never encourages anyone else to use cannabis and never smokes in the club. Sam has invited a worker from the local drugs council to talk to the members about the dangers of substance abuse, particularly cannabis. Sam is sure that Josh is not aware of the mental health problems recently highlighted in the press and hopes that new information will encourage Josh to get 'clean' now that he is searching for work.

In this scenario Sam is using the educational/ behavioural model of health promotion.

The behavioural aspect of this approach puts health firmly in the hands of the individual rather than the expert. The downside of this approach is that it places the blame for a poor lifestyle choice on the individual, especially if they are not yet ready to make 'healthy judgements' for other reasons such as peer pressure, life stage, environment and low income. The educational aspect of this approach assumes that the more an individual knows and understands about the health issue, the more likely he or she is to adopt a different way of thinking and consequently behave differently. This may take place with some clients and the resulting change in behaviour may not be the desired one; for example, information on the dangers associated with substance abuse may result not in the cessation of the habit but of a different substance being abused. Many smokers are fully aware of the dangers of tobacco consumption but continue to smoke cigarettes; some clients will change to cigars or pipe smoking, which are generally perceived to be less harmful.

Societal approach or model

This concentrates on changing society rather than the individual, so for the most part it encompasses either national or local political decisions to change physical, social or economic environments for the greater health of inhabitants. People using this model are not afraid to politicise health issues to improve the health of society.

Examples of the societal approach or model include imposing a ban on smoking in public places; making it illegal to purchase fireworks, tobacco and alcohol products under a certain age; banning the display of fireworks between 11.00 p.m. and 7.00 a.m. and permitting it only on certain dates.

In November 2004, the Secretary of State for Health unveiled a public health white paper, *Choosing health – making healthy choices easier.* It announced that all workplaces would be smoke-free by the end of 2008 except for private membership clubs and pubs, bars and clubs that do not prepare and serve food on the premises. These will have the freedom to allow smoking under licence, except at bar areas.

This partial ban on smoking in public places is an example of health promotion using the societal approach.

Which approach or model?

To differentiate between societal, biomedical and educational/behavioural approaches, decide whether the model affects society as a whole, individuals or groups of individuals. If it is the former and implementation has arisen through local or national political decisions then the approach is societal. When the improved health is likely to arise from medical intervention (using scientific methods) to large numbers of people to prevent ill health, disease or disability then the biomedical approach is being used. Lastly, when information has been dispatched to single individuals or groups and this is trying to persuade the recipients to change to healthier lifestyles, the educational/ behavioural approach is being followed.

Summary of Section 1.3

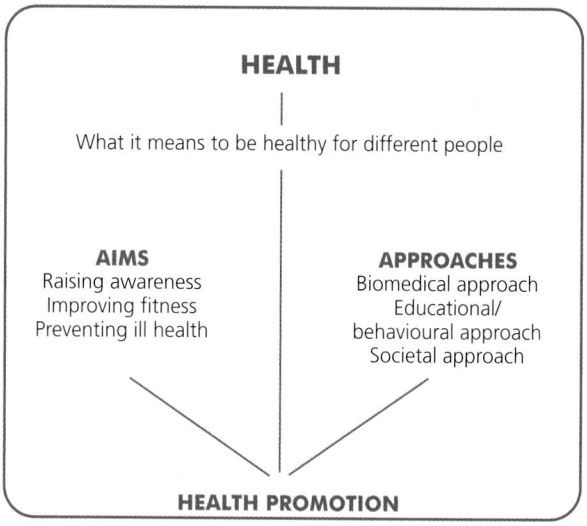

2190971361 M00

Consider this

Tony wants to join the Army. In fact he really wants to become one of the elite SAS but knows that he will need experience in a regiment first. At the moment, Tony is still on holiday but he has his starting date for the Army. He enjoys leisure times with his friends in the snooker room of his 'local', playing snooker and billiards, smoking and having one or two pints of beer. In the evenings, he works behind the very busy bar serving drinks and collecting empty glasses. He likes the smoky, cosy atmosphere in the pub, but he also knows that it can only be for a limited time as he also likes the outdoor life. Tony has already had most of his immunisations brought up to date and picked up several leaflets on stopping smoking in the surgery, as he is beginning to think he needs to get fitter. The landlord has told him that he will be happy to have Tony back to work if the army life doesn't suit him and that the pub will not change, as he is applying for a smoking licence. Tony feels happy to know he has this safeguard.

Using concepts, can you identify?

1. When Tony becomes involved in the biomedical approach to health?
2. How the practice managers use the educational/behavioural approach to health promotion?

Go further – can you analyse issues using theory?

How might the practice managers know whether the educational/behavioural approach was being successful?

Go further – can you evaluate using a range of theory?

Feeling happy about the landlord's compliments, Tony begins to think around the issues of getting fitter and the landlord applying for a smoking licence. Imagine using a range of concepts to judge the values behind a partial smoking ban and to encourage the population to get fitter.

UNIT 1 ASSESSMENT

How you will be assessed

The external assessment is through a $1^1/_2$ hour written examination consisting of structured questions based on case studies. The material will include:

* aspects of growth and development throughout the different life stages
* environmental and genetic factors that can influence growth, development and health
* what it means to be healthy and how health can be promoted.

The examination will test your understanding and the ability to apply the knowledge you have gained from studying the units. You will be expected to analyse the issues and problems presented in the case studies as well as evaluate the evidence, make judgements and draw conclusions from the material. Remember to look carefully at the number of marks allocated to each question and try to make the same number of points in your answer.

Do not waste time or effort repeating the question or part of it, as this will gain zero marks. Read through each question in total before attempting to answer it. Candidates frequently answer a part of a question with an answer that belongs to another part that they haven't yet read. You will not be required to give the same answer twice; if you are tempted to do so, you are missing another point. Unless the question clearly needs a one- or two-word answer, write your answer in a properly constructed sentence or paragraph. The space allotted to each question is for guidance and you should not write either a great deal less or a great deal more.

Assessment preparation

FIGURE 1.56 *Sarah, her son and her daughter-in-law*

1 a) Sarah is 72 years old. She lives alone because her husband died six months ago, but her son John, 51 years old, and daughter-in-law Sue live only twenty miles away. Sue is 49 years old and is going through the menopause.

(i) Name Sarah's current life stage. (1)

(ii) How many life stages has Sarah passed through *before* this current life stage? (1)

(iii) Name the life stage that Sue is in now. (1)

(iv) Identify and explain the likely effects of the menopause in Sue's life. (4)

b) John was made redundant last year but they manage financially because Sue runs a corner shop in a deprived area on the edge of town. The shop is "a lock-up" and gets regularly vandalised. Sue visits her GP regularly with complaints related to stress.

(i) Identify and explain the likely effects of redundancy on John's social and emotional development. (4)

(ii) Identify three possible reasons why Sue feels stressed. (3)

(iii) Explain the possible effects of long-term stress on Sue's health. (5)

2. Sue often feels guilty about her ailments as she has many customers in the shop who suffer more stressful life events than she does. She also has support from her doctor who has encouraged her to join a gymnasium. There are no surgeries, medical or dental, on the estate so people buy a lot of over-the-counter drugs to treat their disorders. An hourly bus service runs through the estate in the daytime but drivers have refused to travel at night because of the number of aggressive youth gangs in the locality.

a) (i) Name three other life events that can lead to stress. (3)

(ii) Discuss why large estates like this one frequently have no medical services. (3)

(iii) Explain why Sue has been advised to do more physical exercise. (4)

(iv) Discuss the advantages and disadvantages of purchasing over-the-counter drugs to treat your own health. (6)

b) (i) How can living in a deprived area affect an individual's growth, development and health experience? (6)

(ii) Why do some young people prefer to travel around in 'gangs'? (2)

(iii) Minor gang members often have low self-esteem. Explain what is meant by self-esteem. (2)

(iv) Give reasons why self-esteem is important. (3)

3. Sue and John have a 17-year-old daughter, Melanie, who is a single mother with a 1-year-old son, Boris. She has left the parental home and is living with Sarah so that she can go to the college nearby. Sarah looks after Boris during the day and some evenings when Melanie wants to go out with her friends. Boris's father plays no part in supporting the child financially or in any other way.

a) Name the life stages of:

(i) Melanie (1)

(ii) Boris (2)

(iii) Identify and explain the likely effects of these changes on Sarah. (5)

(iv) Explain why it is important for Melanie to continue seeing her friends. (3)

b) A few days after being born, Boris had a 'heel prick' test and this showed that he had a genetic condition known as Phenylketonuria or PKU. As a result, his health is carefully monitored and he has to take a special diet.

(i) What is a genetic condition? (2)

(ii) Explain how genetic factors can influence the health of an individual. (5)

(iii) State three *other* factors that can influence the health of an individual. (3)

(iv) Choose one of the named factors and give a precise account of the way it can affect the health of an individual. (5)

(v) Explain what is meant by the nature – nurture debate. (6)

4 a) Sue tried to sell fresh produce, especially fruit and vegetables, in her shop as she is enthusiastic about healthy eating, but she had too much wasted produce as people preferred cheaper frozen and tinned goods. Bread, cigarettes and sweets sell well and all types of meat products such as sausages, burgers and pies are popular.

(i) Explain why Sue can no longer sell fresh produce in the shop. (2)

(ii) What are the disadvantages of eating only processed food? (4)

(iii) Discuss the harmful effects of smoking on the women and children of the estate. (6)

(iv) Comment on the expected state of children's teeth on the estate. (4)

b) The health promotion unit in the nearby town has recently distributed information leaflets on 'Looking after your teeth' through people's letterboxes and in Sue's shop, hoping to see an improvement in dental hygiene in the area.

(i) Explain which approach is being used to promote a change in dental health. (2)

(ii) Which approach is being used if all the primary schools in the area are instructed (by the local authority) to provide at least one piece of fruit daily for each child? (2)

(Total marks = 100

References and further reading

Acheson, D. (1998) *Independent enquiry into inequalities in health* (HMSO)

Argyle, M. (1987) *The Psychology of Happiness* (Methuen)

Bateson, ? (1995) (Independent Newspaper)

Blaxter, M. (1990) *Health and Lifestyles* (Routledge)

Bowlby, J. (1953) *Child care and the growth of love* (Penguin)

Dorling, D. et al. (1999) *The Widening gap: health inequalities and policy in Britain* (The Policy Press)

Erikson, E. (1963) *Childhood and Society* (Norton)

Ewles, L., Simnett, I. (2003) *Promoting Health – a practical guide* (Bailliere Tindall, London)

Havinghurst, R. J. (1970) *Developmental tasks and education* (David McKay)

HM Government (1997) *Saving Lives: Our Healthier Nation* (HMSO)

HM Government (2004) *Choosing Health – Making Healthier Choices Easier* (HMSO)

International Labour Organisation (2002) *Unemployment in the UK*

Naidoo, J., Wills, J. (2000) *Health Promotion – Foundations for Practice* (Bailliere Tindall, London)

Mead, G.H. (1934) *Mind, self and society* (ed. Morris, C.) (University of Chicago Press)

Moonie, N. (2000) *Advanced Health and Social Care* (Heinemann, Oxford)

Public Health News monthly magazine (Chadwick House Publishing)

Social Exclusion unit (1999) *Opportunity for all* (HMSO)

Unemployment unit (March 2000) *Working Brief*

Unemployment unit (May 1996) *Three Quarters of Job Growth is Part-Time*

Relevant websites

Please see www.heinemann.co.uk/hotlinks (express code 370XP) for links to the following websites which may provide a source of information:

* Joseph Rowntree Foundation findings online

UNIT 2

Communication and Values

This unit contains the following sections:

2.1 Communication

2.2 Care value base

2.3 Transmission of values

Introduction

This unit is designed to explore the importance of communication in all caring activities. When you have completed this unit you will understand a range of communication skills, the care value base and the transmission of values through communication. Your communication work might involve either people in health care settings, children in Early Years settings, older people in care settings, or people who have specific needs.

How you will be assessed

This unit is internally assessed. You must produce a written report.

2.1 Communication

Different types of communication

There are many different ways in which people communicate with each other. These can include language, body language, signs and symbols, written communication, art and music. Recorded information also enables communication to take place.

Many animals and insects communicate information between individuals, but no other species can communicate in the complex range of ways used by humans. Ways in which people communicate with each other are set out below.

Language

Spoken, signed, or written communication can communicate complex and subtle messages between individuals or groups of people. Language not only enables people to communicate information, but it also provides a basis for people to develop concepts. Concepts:

* influence the way individuals think
* enable us to group experiences together to help us understand events that we have experienced
* enable us to predict the future.

Human civilisation has developed because of our ability to classify experience using language.

Body language

Facial expressions, body posture and muscle tone all provide messages as to how we feel and perhaps what we are thinking. Mime and drama use body language to communicate complex ideas and emotions.

Signs and symbols

Gestures made with hands or arms, written symbols or diagrams such as traffic signs all communicate messages to people.

Signed languages

Language does not have to be based on sounds that are heard. Signing systems, such as British Sign Language, provide a full language system for people who do not use spoken language.

Visual, electronic and written communication

Humans can communicate across distance and time by using books, email, text messages, and so on. Recorded information such as books, magazines, newspapers, films, videos, tapes, CDs and other electronic mediums enable us to re-experience events or messages from the past. But recorded communication does not have to be visual.

Braille

Braille (a system of raised marks that can be felt with your fingers) provides a system of written communication based on the sense of touch for people who may have limited vision.

Arts and crafts

Paintings, photographs, sculptures, architecture, ornaments and other household objects can communicate messages and emotions to people. People often take photographs or buy souvenirs to remind them of happy experiences. Many individuals earn their living by designing and developing artwork.

Music

Music can provide an effective communication system for expressing emotion. Music is sometimes called the language of emotion.

Exchange of information

Some forms of communication involve simply sending a message within a fixed unambiguous system of meaning. An example might be an airline pilot trying to park an aircraft. But most communication between people is not simple and unambiguous. A lot of spoken and written communication is like music and artwork – rarely communicating straightforward information. It is normal for people to experience completely different messages from the same music or picture. Some communication is designed to stimulate thoughts and emotions in people.

Within care settings a great deal of communication is complex. It is important to understand that each person will have his or her own way of interpreting what they see and hear. Communication is not just about passing on information. Effective communication will depend on engaging in a 'communication cycle', which takes into account the way information is being received by the other person.

Listening skills and the communication cycle

When we communicate with people we become involved in a process of expressing our thoughts and interpreting the other person's understanding of what we are communicating. This process should usually involve the steps set out in Figure 2.1.

Communication needs to be a two-way process whereby each person tries to understand the viewpoint of the other. The **communication cycle** (see Figure 2.2) requires professionals (at least) to have advanced listening skills and the ability to check their understanding of the responses of others.

Listening is not the same as hearing the sounds people make when they talk. Listening involves hearing another person's words – then thinking about what they mean – then thinking what to say back. Some people call this process '**active listening**'. As well as thinking carefully and remembering what someone says, good listeners will also make sure their non-verbal communication demonstrates interest in the other person.

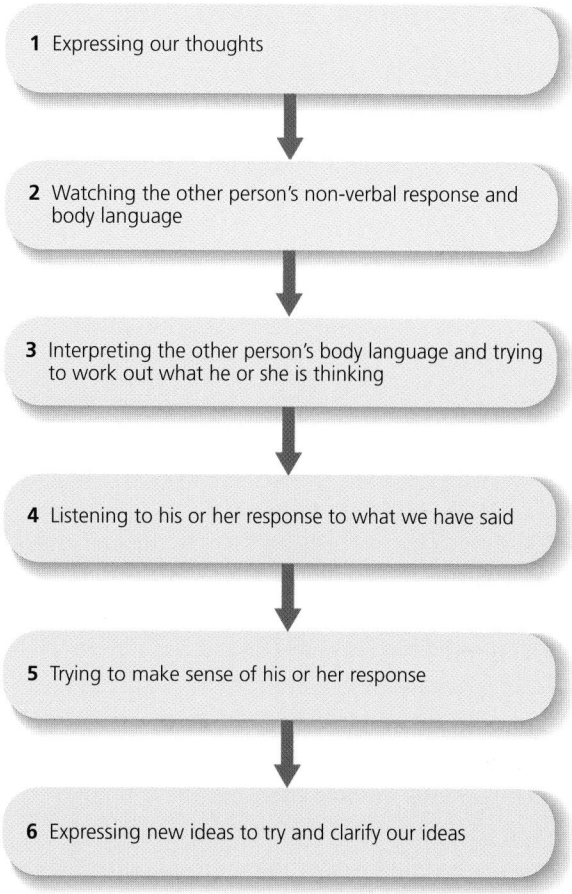

FIGURE 2.1 *The process of expression and interpretation*

Key concept

Active listening: Active listening involves more than hearing – it also involves using the communication cycle and being able to demonstrate what you have understood when you listen to another person.

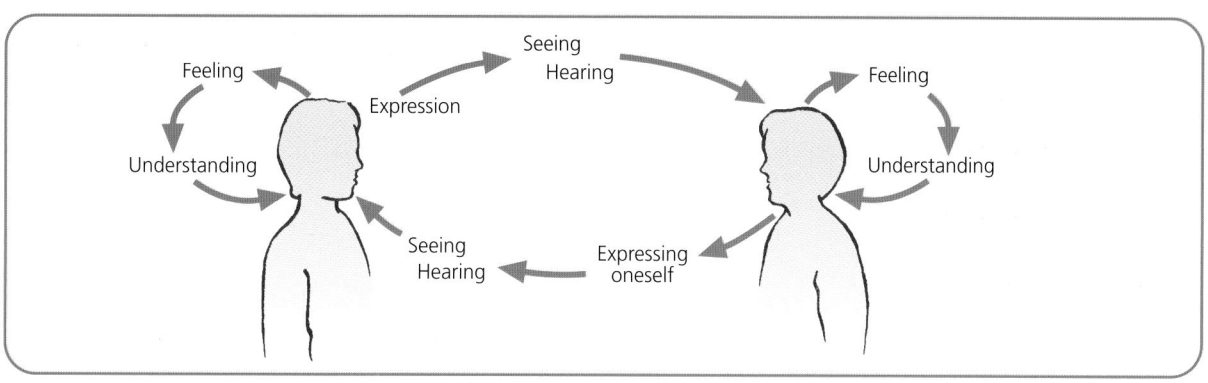

FIGURE 2.2 *The communication cycle*

So, skilled active listening involves:

* looking interested and ready to listen
* hearing what is said
* remembering what is said
* checking understanding with the other person.

It is usually easier to understand people who are similar to ourselves. We can learn about different people by checking our understanding of what we have heard.

Checking our understanding involves hearing what the other person says and asking them questions. Another way to check our understanding is to put what a person has just said into our own words and to say this back to them. This technique is called paraphrasing. Paraphrasing enables us to find out if we did understand what another person said.

When we listen to complicated details of other people's lives, we often begin to form mental pictures based on what they are telling us. Listening skills involve checking these mental pictures to make sure that we understand correctly. It can be very difficult to remember things accurately if we don't check how our ideas are developing.

Good listening involves thinking about what we hear while we are listening and checking our understanding as the conversation goes along. Sometimes this idea of checking is called 'reflection' because we reflect on the other person's ideas (see Figure 2.3).

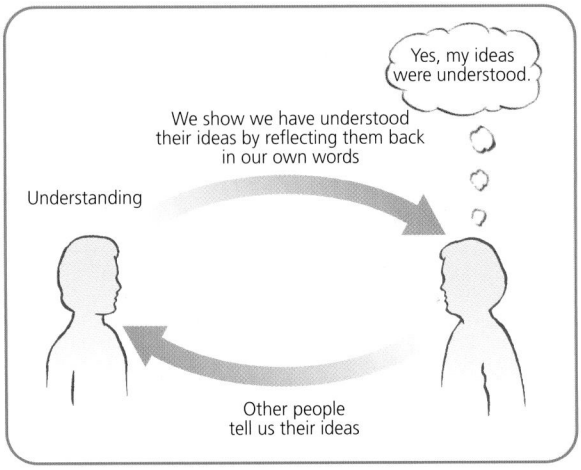

FIGURE 2.3 *Reflection*

The importance of cultural variation

Both words and non-verbal signs have to be understood in a particular context. For example, the word 'wicked' can have different meanings. If an older person used this phrase to describe his or her experience of World War II it would mean 'horrific' or 'terrible'. In a TV comedy made during the past 15 years the phrase would mean 'cool' – something very desirable. In a religious context 'wicked' might relate to the concept of sin.

Making sense of spoken language requires knowledge of the context and intentions of the speaker. Understanding non-verbal communication involves exactly the same need to understand 'where the person is coming from'; or, to put it more formally, the circumstances and cultural context of the other person.

*** DID YOU KNOW?**

Both spoken and non-verbal communication is influenced by culture. For example, in the UK the hand gesture with palm up and facing forward means 'Stop, don't do that.' In Greece it can mean, 'You are dirt' and is a very rude gesture.

Why do the same physical movements have different meanings? One explanation for the hand signs is that the British version of the palm-and-fingers gesture means, 'I arrest you, you must not do it'; whereas the Greek interpretation goes back to medieval times when criminals had dirt rubbed in their faces to show how much people despised them.

Using care values means that carers must have respect for other people's culture. People learn different ways of communicating, and good carers will try to understand the different ways in which people use non-verbal messages. For instance, past research in the USA suggests that white and black Americans may have used different non-verbal signals when they listened. It suggests that some black Americans may tend not to look much at the speaker. This can be interpreted as a mark of respect – by looking away it demonstrates that you are really thinking hard about the message.

Unfortunately, not all white people understood this cultural difference in non-verbal communication. Some individuals misunderstood and assumed that this non-verbal behaviour meant exactly the same as it would mean if someone from their own cultural background had done it. That is, it would mean they were not listening.

Key concept

Cultural variation: Communication is always influenced by cultural systems of meaning. Different cultures interpret body language differently.

There is an almost infinite variety of meanings that can be given to any type of eye contact, facial expression, posture or gesture. Every culture develops its own special system of meanings. Carers have to understand and show respect and value for all of the different systems of sending messages. But how can you ever learn them all?

No one can learn every possible system of non-verbal message – but it is possible to learn about those the people you are with are using! It is possible to do this by first noticing and remembering what others around you do, i.e. what non-verbal messages they are sending. The next step is to make an intelligent guess as to what messages the person is trying to give you. Finally, check your understanding (your guesses) with the person.

Skilled interpersonal interaction involves:

* watching other people
* remembering what they do
* guessing what words and actions mean and then checking your guesses with the person
* never relying on your own guesses, because these might turn into assumptions
* understanding that assumptions can lead to discrimination.

Using care values involves getting to understand people – not acting on unchecked assumptions. So non-verbal messages should never be relied on; they should always be checked.

Think it over...

Imagine you are working with an older female person. Whenever you start to speak to her she always looks at the floor and never makes eye contact. Why is this?

Your first thought is that she might be depressed. Having made such an assumption, you might not want to talk to this person. But instead you could ask, 'How do you feel today? Would you like me to get you anything?' By checking out what she feels, you could test your own understanding. She might say she feels well and is quite happy, and then suggest something you could do for her. This would suggest that she cannot be depressed.

Why else would someone look at the floor rather than at you?

Age and gender

Perceptions of age-appropriate behaviour and gender-appropriate behaviour are strongly influenced by culture. People are socialised into the norms and values of a culture. Group norms and values – the 'rules' for behaviour – vary between different religious, ethnic, class, gender and age groups.

Group expectations of speech vary between social groups, but they also change with time within a particular group. People of different age groups have usually been socialised into different norms with respect to interpersonal behaviour.

Interpersonal interaction

Body language

When we meet and talk with people, we will usually use two language systems. We will use verbal or spoken language and non-verbal or body language. Effective communication in care work requires care workers to be able to analyse their own and other people's non-verbal behaviour. Our body sends messages to other people – often without us deliberately meaning to send these messages. Some of the most important body areas that send messages are outlined overleaf.

Think it over...

Florence Tucknell was born in 1922. When she was young there was a cultural norm that only close friends and family would call her by her first name. She was Miss Tucknell to everyone else. For a stranger to call her 'Florence' would be a sign of disrespect, a sign that they thought they were socially superior to her. When Florence went into care for a week she was upset that everyone used first names. She knows that this is common practice nowadays, but this was not how she was brought up to behave.

Miss Tucknell was very pleased to be greeted by her carer who introduced herself as, 'I'm Anthea Shakespeare, may I ask your name?' Miss Tucknell replied, 'I'm Miss Tucknell, please.'

Martin Howarth was born in the north of England in 1956. Some years ago he moved to the south-east of England and took a job as a care worker. Martin was surprised to find that many of his younger female colleagues were complaining about his behaviour. Martin had been socialised into the norm of calling women 'Flower' or even 'Petal.' When Martin used these terms he was expecting to communicate approval, comradeship and warmth. Martin believed that these were universal terms of endearment, i.e. 'You are likeable, we're all working together; we get on – don't we?'

His new colleagues in the south had never been referred to as 'Flower' before and saw it as sexist. Individually, Martin's colleagues' view of him was 'You are saying that I am weak, short-lived and that all that matters about my existence is my degree of sexual attractiveness!'

Can you think of other examples where age, gender and region influence how words are understood?

Key concept

Body language: The way we use our body can communicate messages to other people. People communicate using words and also by using body language.

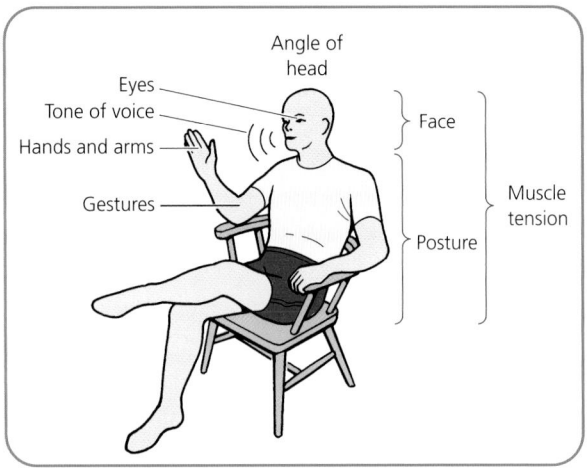

FIGURE 2.4 *Areas of the body that we use in communication*

We can guess the feelings and thoughts that another person has by looking at their eyes. One poet called the eye 'the window of the soul'. We can sometimes understand the thoughts and feelings of another person by eye-to-eye contact. Our eyes get wider when we are excited, attracted to, or interested in someone else. In European culture, a fixed stare may send the message that someone is angry and looking away is often interpreted as being bored or not interested.

The face

The face can send very complex messages and we can read them easily – even in diagram form (see Figure 2.5).

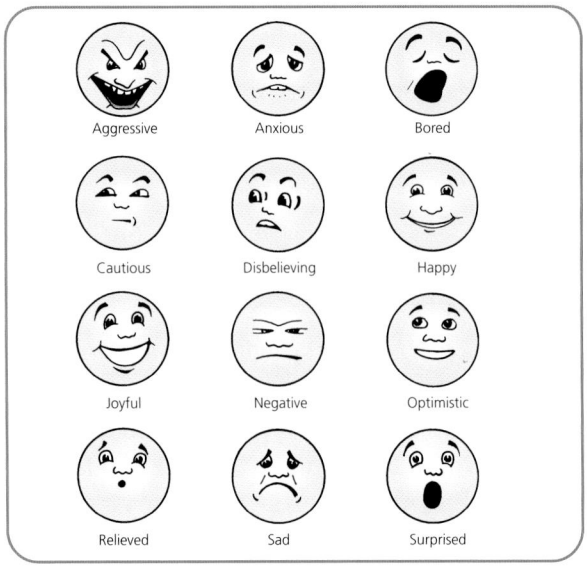

FIGURE 2.5 *The face expresses emotion*

Our face often indicates our emotional state. When a person is sad they may signal this emotion with eyes that look down, there may be tension in their face and their mouth will be closed. The muscles in the person's shoulders are likely to be relaxed but their face and neck may show tension. A happy person will have 'wide eyes' that make contact with you – their face will smile. When people are excited they may move their arms and hands to signal their excitement.

Voice tone

It's not just what we say, but the way that we say it. If we talk quickly in a loud voice with a fixed voice tone, people may see us as angry. A calm, slow voice with varying tone may send a message of being friendly.

Body movement

The way we walk, move our head, sit, cross our legs and so on, send messages about whether we are tired, happy, sad or bored.

Posture

The way we sit or stand can send messages. Sitting with crossed arms can mean 'I'm not taking any notice'. Leaning can send the message that you are relaxed or bored. Leaning forward can show interest. The body postures in Figure 2.6 below send messages.

Muscle tension

The tension in our feet, hands and fingers can tell others how relaxed or how tense we are. When people are very tense their shoulders might stiffen, their face muscles might tighten and they might sit or stand rigidly. A tense face might have a firmly closed mouth with lips and jaws clenched tight. A tense person might breathe quickly and become hot.

Gestures

Gestures are hand and arm movements that can help us to understand what a person is saying.

FIGURE 2.7 *Some gestures common in Britain*

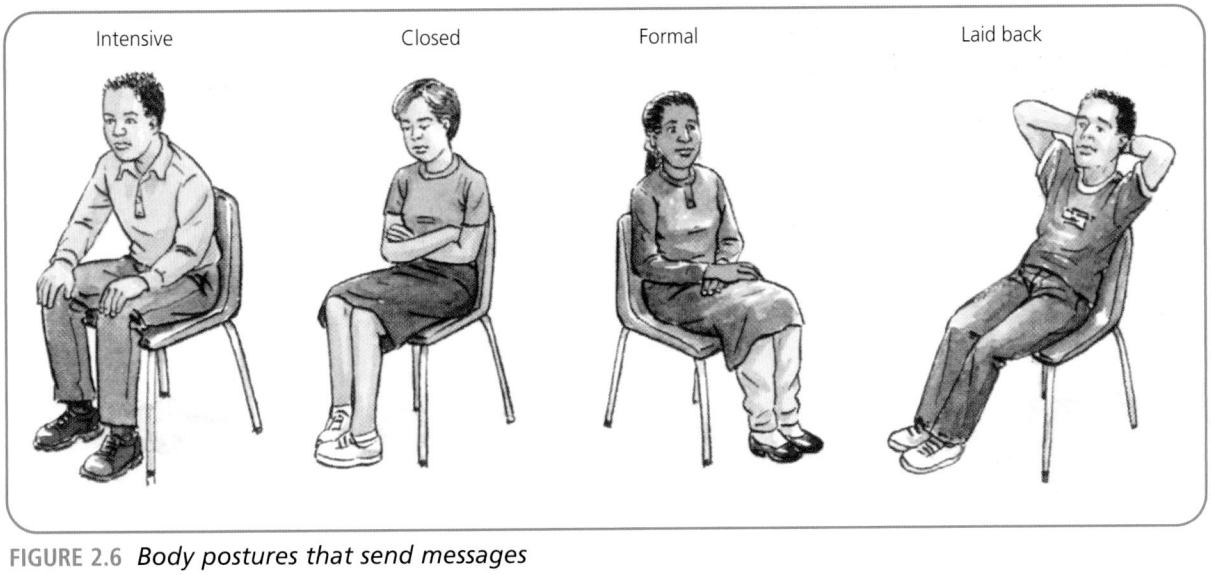

FIGURE 2.6 *Body postures that send messages*

Some gestures carry a meaning of their own. Some common gestures are shown in Figure 2.7.

Touch

Touching another person can send messages of care, affection, power over them, or sexual interest. The social setting and other body language usually help people to understand what touch might mean. Carers should not make assumptions about touch. Even holding someone's hand might be seen as trying to dominate them!

Proximity and personal space

The space between people can sometimes show how friendly or 'intimate' the conversation is. Different cultures have different assumptions about how close people should be (proximity) when they are talking.

In Britain there are expectations or 'norms' as to how close you should be when you talk to others. When talking to strangers you may stand an arm's-length apart. The ritual of shaking hands indicates that you have been introduced – you may come closer. When you are friendly with someone you may accept them being closer to you. Relatives and partners may not be restricted in how close they can come.

Personal space is a very important issue in care work. A care worker who assumes it is all right to enter a service user's personal space without asking or explaining, may be seen as being dominating or aggressive.

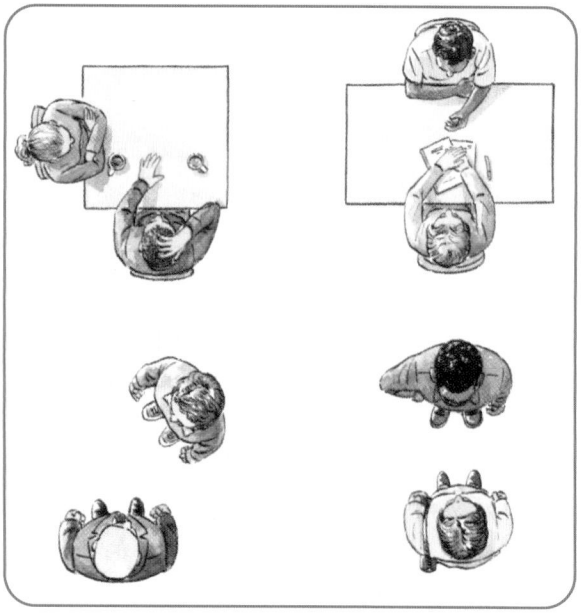

FIGURE 2.8 *Face-to-face interaction*

Face-to-face positions (orientation)

Standing or sitting eye-to-eye can send a message of being formal or being angry. A slight angle can create a more relaxed and friendly feeling. Examples of face-to-face interaction are shown in Figure 2.8.

Using appropriate language – degree of formality

Speaking is about much more than just communicating information between people. For a start, many people can speak with different degrees of formality or informality. The degree of formality or informality is called the language 'register'.

For example, suppose you went to a hospital reception area. You might expect the person on duty to greet you with a formal response, such as, 'Good morning, how can I help you'. An informal greeting of the kind used by white males in the south-east of England might be, 'Hello Mate, what's up then?' or 'How's it going?'

FIGURE 2.9 *Informality and informal humour may be perceived as disrespect*

It is possible that some people might prefer the informal greeting. An informal greeting could put you at ease; you might feel that the receptionist is like you. But in many situations the informal greeting might make people feel that they are not being respected.

The degree of formality or informality establishes a context. At a hospital reception you are unlikely to want to spend time making friends and chatting things over with the receptionist. You may be seeking urgent help. Your expectations of the situation might be that you want to be taken seriously and put in touch with professional services as soon as possible. You might see the situation as a very formal encounter. If you are treated informally, you may interpret this as not being treated seriously, or in other words 'not being respected'.

Speech communities

Another issue is that informal speech is very likely to identify a specific speech community. Different localities, different ethnic groups, different professions and work cultures all have their own special words, phrases and speech patterns. An elderly middle-class woman is very unlikely to start a conversation with the words 'Hello Mate'. Some service users may feel threatened or excluded by the kind of language they encounter. However, just using formal language will not solve this problem. The technical terminology used by social care workers may also create barriers for people who were not part of that 'speech community'.

Structuring a conversation

When we talk to people we have to start the conversation off. Usually we start with a greeting or ask how someone is. Conversations have a beginning, a middle and an end. We have to create the right kind of atmosphere for a conversation at the beginning. We might need to help someone relax by showing that we are friendly and relaxed. We then have the conversation. When we end the conversation we usually say something like 'See you soon'. When ending a conversation we have to leave the other person with the right feelings about what we have said. The conversation sandwich shown in Figure 2.10 illustrates this point.

Think it over...

Consider the following conversation between a service user and a service worker.

Service user: "I've come about getting some help around the house, you know, 'cause it's getting 'ard' nowadays, what with me back an' everything."

Service worker: "Well you need to speak to the Community Domiciliary Support Liaison Officer who can arrange an assessment in accordance with our statutory obligations."

The two statements above use different levels of formality, but they also represent speech from different speech communities. Can you work out what each person is saying? How do you think the service user will feel given such a response? Will the service user feel respected and valued?

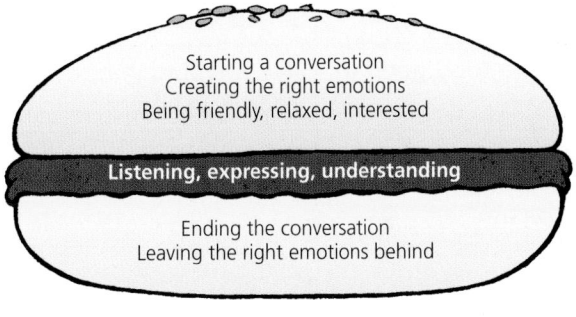

FIGURE 2.10 *The conversation sandwich*

Asking questions

Some questions don't really encourage people to talk – these are called 'closed' questions. Questions like 'How old are you?' are closed. They are closed because there is only one, right, simple answer the person can give, for example, 'I'm 84', and so on. Closed questions don't lead on to discussion. 'Do you like butter?' is a closed question as the person can only say yes or no. 'Are you feeling well today?' is a closed question. Again, the person can only answer yes or no.

Open questions are 'open' for discussion. Instead of giving a yes or no answer, the person is encouraged to think and discuss their thoughts and feelings. A question like, 'How do you feel about the food here?' means that the other person has to think about the food and then discuss it.

✱ DID YOU KNOW?

Open questions help to keep the conversation going. Sometimes closed questions can block a conversation and cause it to stop.

In some formal conversations it can be important to ask direct closed questions; but the best way to ask closed questions is to ask open questions beforehand. There is an old saying that if you really want to find out what someone else thinks then 'Every closed question should start life as an open one'. Some examples of open and closed questions are given in Figure 2.11.

CLOSED QUESTION	OPEN QUESTION
Do you like your teacher?	What do you think about your teacher?
Is the food good in here?	What would you say the food is like here?
Do you like rock music?	What kind of music do you enjoy?
Do you sometimes feel lonely?	How do you feel about living on your own?
Do you enjoy drawing?	What are your favourite activities in school?

FIGURE 2.11 *Open and closed questions – some examples*

Silence

One definition of friends is 'people who can sit together and feel comfortable in silence'. Sometimes a pause in conversation can make people feel embarrassed. It may look as if you weren't listening or interested. Sometimes a silent pause can mean 'let's think' or 'I need time to think'. Silent pauses can be all right as long as non-verbal messages that show respect and interest are given. Silence doesn't always stop the conversation. Some carers use pauses in a conversation to show that they are listening and thinking about what a service user has said.

Probes and prompts

A probe is a very short question such as 'Can you tell me more?' This kind of short question usually follows on from an answer that the other person has given. Probes are used to 'dig deeper' into the person's answer; they probe or investigate what has just been said.

Prompts are short questions or words, which you offer to the other person in order to prompt them to answer. Questions such as 'So, was it enjoyable or not?' or, 'would you do it again?' might prompt a person to keep talking. Sometimes a prompt might just be a suggested answer. 'More than 50?' might be a prompt if you had just asked how many service users a carer worked with in a year and they seemed uncertain.

✱ DID YOU KNOW?

Probes and prompts are both useful techniques to improve questioning skill, or to use when you are trying to keep a conversation going.

Here are some ideas for preventing unwanted silence:

- ✱ Use non-verbal behaviour like smiling and nodding your head to express interest.
- ✱ Use short periods of silence to prompt the other person to talk.
- ✱ Paraphrase or reflect back what the other person has said so that they will confirm that you have understood them.
- ✱ Ask direct questions.
- ✱ Use probes and prompts to follow-up your questions.

Assertive skills

Some people may seem shy and worried; they say little and avoid contact with people they don't know. Others may want people to be afraid of them; they may try to dominate and control others. Fear and aggression are two of the basic emotions that we experience. It is easy to give into our basic emotions and become either submissive or aggressive when we feel stressed. Assertion is an advanced skill that involves controlling the basic emotions involved in running away or fighting. Assertion involves a mental attitude of trying to negotiate, trying to solve problems rather than giving in to emotional impulses.

Key concept

Assertion: Assertion is different from both submission and aggression. Assertion involves being able to negotiate a solution to a problem.

Winning and losing

During an argument an aggressive person might demand that they are right and other people are wrong. They will want to win while others lose. The opposite of aggression is to be weak or submissive. A submissive person accepts that they will lose, get told off, or be put down. Assertive behaviour is different from both these responses. In an argument an assertive person will try to reach an answer where no one has to lose or be 'put down'. Assertion is a skill where 'win-win' situations can happen because no one has to be the loser. For example, suppose a service user is angry because his or her carer is late. Look at Figure 2.12 to compare the possible responses of a carer.

Assertive skills enable carers to cope with difficult and challenging situations. To be assertive a person usually has to:

* understand the situation that they are in – including the facts, details and other people's perceptions
* be able to control personal emotions and stay calm
* be able to act assertively using the right non-verbal behaviour
* be able to act assertively using the right words and statements.

Some verbal and non-verbal behaviours involved in assertion are summarised in Figure 2.13.

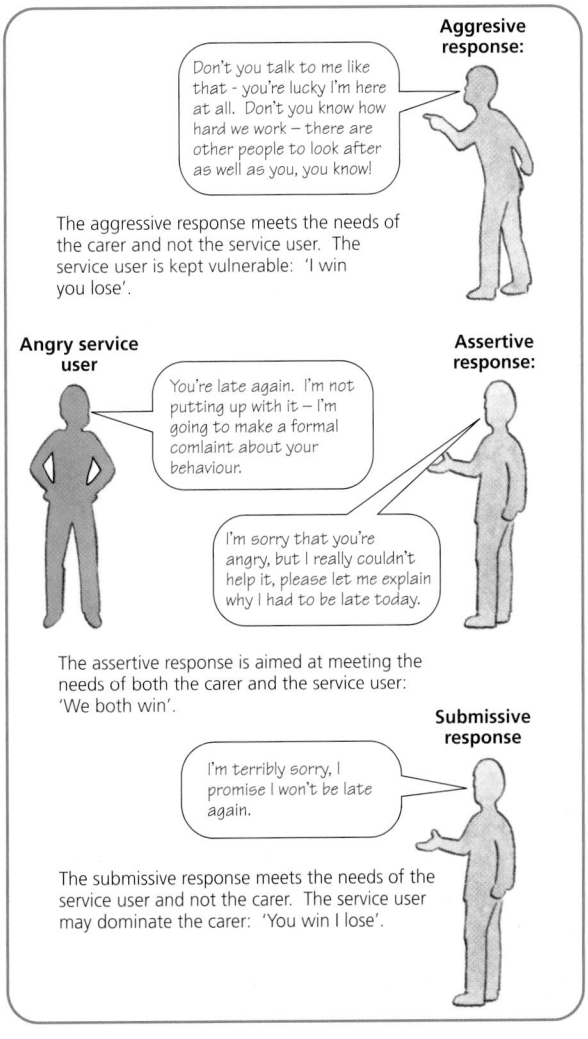

FIGURE 2.12 *How assertion enables both people to win*

Professional relationships

People who are good at communication and assertive skills are likely to be good at building social relationships. Professional relationships may be regarded as different from ordinary social relationships and friendships because:

* professionals must work within a framework of values (see Section 2.2)
* professional work always involves a duty of care for the welfare of service users (see Section 2.3)
* professional relationships involve establishing appropriate boundaries.

AGGRESSIVE BEHAVIOUR	ASSERTIVE BEHAVIOUR	SUBMISSIVE BEHAVIOUR
Main emotion: anger	*Main emotion*: staying in control of actions	*Main emotion*: fear
Wanting your own way Making demands Not listening to others Putting other people down Trying to win Shouting or talking very loudly	Negotiating with others Trying to solve problems Aiming that no one has to lose Showing respect for others Keeping a clear, calm voice	Letting others win Agreeing with others Not putting your views across Looking afraid Speaking quietly or not speaking at all
Threatening non-verbal behaviour including: fixed eye contact, tense muscles, waving or folding hands and arms, looking angry	**Normal non-verbal behaviour** including: varied eye contact, relaxed face muscles, looking 'in control', keeping hands and arms at your side	**Submissive non-verbal behaviour** including: looking down, not looking at others, looking frightened, tense muscles

FIGURE 2.13 *Some verbal and non-verbal behaviours involved in assertion*

A boundary is a line that must not be crossed. In care work the metaphor of a boundary means that there are limits to the degree of emotional involvement and commitment within a relationship. Although professionals care about what happens to service users, professionals do not form an emotional bond in the way that parents and children do.

Please see Section 2.2 for theory on confidentiality and Section 2.3 for theory on empathy.

Barriers to effective communication

Communication can become blocked if individual differences are not understood. There are three main ways that communication becomes blocked, and these are shown in Figure 2.14.

Key concept

Barriers: Effective communication depends on identifying barriers that may block understanding. Barriers can exist at a physical and sensory level, at the level of making sense of a message, and at a cultural and social context level, whereby the meaning of a message may be misunderstood.

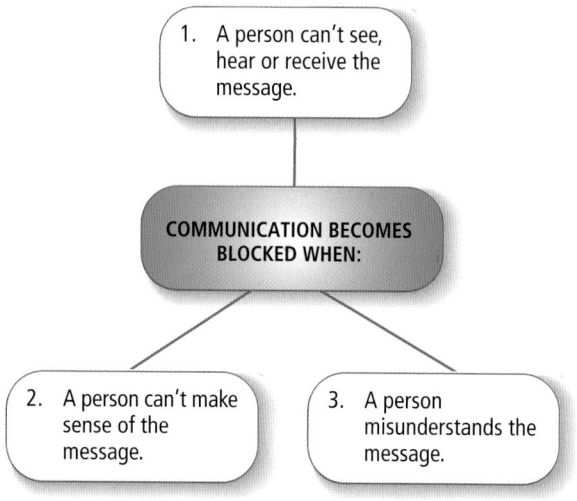

FIGURE 2.14 *Three main ways in which communication becomes blocked*

Examples of the first kind of block, where people don't receive the communication, include visual disabilities, hearing disabilities, environmental problems such as poor lighting and noisy environments, and speaking from too far away.

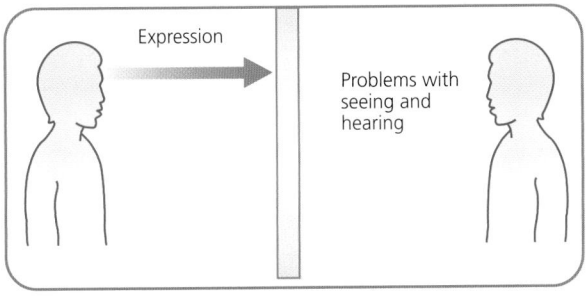

FIGURE 2.15 *Environmental problems like noise and poor light can create communication barriers*

Examples where people may not be able to make sense of the message include:

* the use of different languages, including signed languages
* the use of different terms in language, such as jargon (technical language), slang (different people using different terms), or dialect (different people making different sounds)
* physical and intellectual disabilities, such as dysphasia (difficulties with language expression or understanding) aphasia (an absence of language ability), being ill, or suffering memory loss or learning difficulty.

Reasons for misunderstanding a message include:

* cultural influences – different cultures interpret non-verbal and verbal messages, and humour, in different ways
* assumptions about people, e.g. about race, gender, disability and other groupings
* labelling or stereotyping of others (please see Section 2.2 for details of these concepts)
* social context – statements and behaviour that are understood by friends and family may not be understood by strangers
* emotional barriers – a worker's own emotional needs may stop them from wanting to know about others
* time pressures can mean that staff withdraw from wanting to know about others
* emotional differences – these can sometimes be interpreted as personality clashes or differences. Very angry, or very happy, or very shy people may misinterpret communication from others.

The psychologist Maslow (1970) explained human needs in terms of the five levels set out below. More detail of this theory can be found in Section 2.3 (page 96). Barriers to communication might block human need as shown in Figure 2.16.

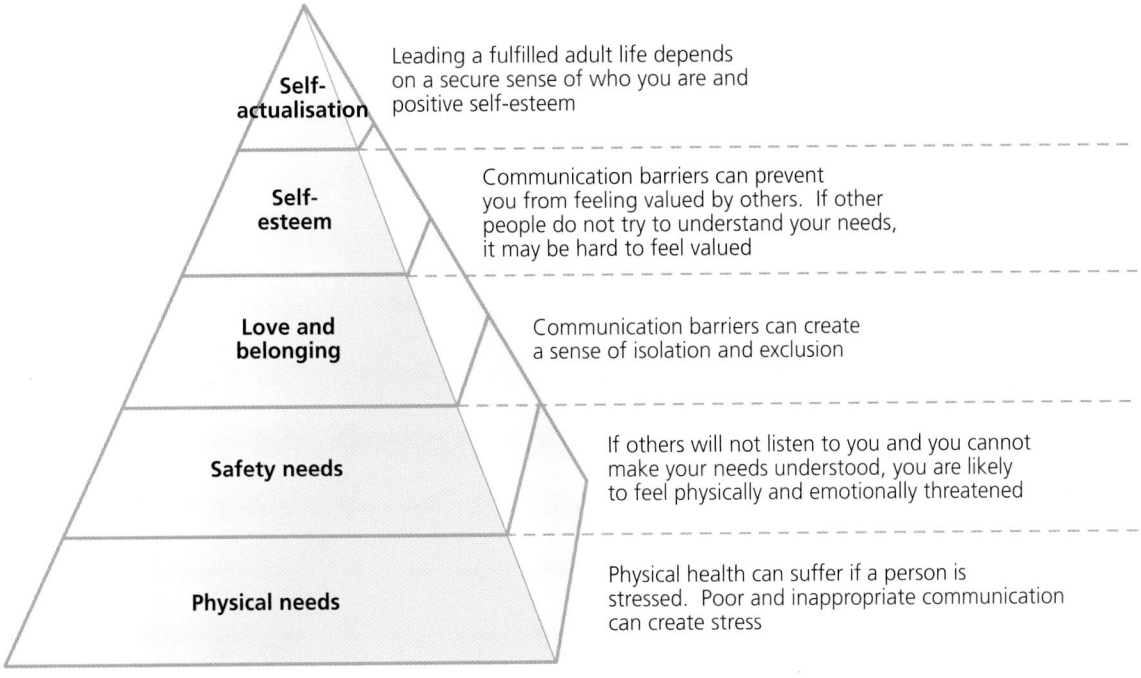

FIGURE 2.16 *Communication barriers can damage a person's quality of life*

Ways of overcoming difficulties in communication

It is always important to learn as much as possible about other people. People may have 'preferred forms of interaction'. This may include a reliance on non-verbal messages, sign language, lip-reading, use of description, slang phrases, choice of room or location for a conversation, and so on. Everyone has communication needs of some kind.

Some ideas of how you may overcome barriers to communication are given in Figure 2.17.

OVERCOMING BARRIERS TO COMMUNICATION	
BARRIERS	**TIPS**
Visual disability	Use language to describe things Assist people to touch things (e.g. touch your face to recognise you) Explain details that sighted people might take for granted Check what people can see (many registered blind people can see shapes, or tell light from dark) Explore technological aids such as information technology that can expand visual images Check glasses, other aids and equipment
Hearing disability	Don't shout, keep to normal clear speech and make sure your face is visible for people who can lip-read Show pictures, or write messages Learn to sign (for people who use signed languages) Ask for help from, or employ, a communicator or interpreter for signed languages Check that technological aids such as hearing aids are working
Environmental constraints	Check and improve lighting Reduce noise Move to a quieter or better-lit room Move to smaller groups to see and hear more easily Check seating arrangements
Language differences	Communicate using pictures, diagrams and non-verbal signs Use translators or interpreters Be careful not to make assumptions or stereotype (see Section 2.2 on stereotyping) Increase your knowledge of jargon, slang and dialects Re-word your messages – find different ways of saying things appropriate to the service user's 'speech community' Check your level of formality; speak in short, clear sentences if appropriate
Intellectual disabilities	Increase your knowledge of disabilities Use pictures and signs as well as clear, simple speech Be calm and patient Set up group meetings where people can share interests, experiences or reminiscences Check that people do not become isolated Use advocates – independent people who can spend time building an understanding of the needs of specific individuals to assist with communication work
Cultural differences	Try to increase your knowledge of different cultures and speech communities Watch out for different cultural interpretations Avoid making assumptions about, or discriminating against, people who are different Use active listening techniques to check that your understanding is correct Stay calm and try to create a calm atmosphere Be sensitive to different social settings and the form of communication that would be most appropriate in different contexts Check your work with advocates who will try to represent the best interests of the people that you are working with

FIGURE 2.17 *Some ways of overcoming barriers to communication*

Emotional barriers to communication

Service users often have serious emotional needs; they may be afraid or depressed because of the stresses they are experiencing. Sometimes service users may lack self-awareness or appear to be shy or aggressive. Listening involves learning about frightening and depressing situations. Carers sometimes avoid listening to avoid unpleasant emotional feelings.

Emotion can create barriers because care workers:

* are tired – listening takes mental energy
* believe that they do not have sufficient time to communicate properly
* are emotionally stressed by the needs of service users
* react with negative emotions towards the culture of others
* make assumptions about, or label or stereotype others.

Interpreters and translators

*** DID YOU KNOW?**

Interpreters are people who communicate meaning from one language to another. Translators are people who change recorded material from one language to another.

Translating and interpreting involve the communication of meaning between different languages. This is not just a technical act of changing the words from one system to another. Many languages do not have simple equivalence between words or signs. Interpreters and translators have to grasp the meaning of a message and find a way of expressing this meaning in a different language system. This is rarely a simple task even for professional translators.

Interpreters can be professional people, but they may also be friends or family members. For example, a mother might learn sign language in order to communicate information to a deaf child. It is possible for family members to interpret for each other.

Interpretation and translation are vital in any setting where communication is blocked due to different languages or communication systems. For example, many people may not use English as their first language. When these people need to access health care or social services, or legal support, the services of translators and interpreters are likely to be needed.

*** DID YOU KNOW?**

People who are deaf from birth often develop a signed language such as British Sign Language. British Sign Language is not a version of the English language; it is an independent language system, which is as different from English as Spanish is.

Issues surrounding interpretation

Interpretation raises a number of important issues. These are outlined below.

Interpretation can disrupt the communication cycle

It will often be important that the interpreter can confirm that he or she has understood things correctly before attempting to pass that understanding on to another person. Much interpretation in care and social work settings is consecutive interpretation. Consecutive interpretation is when the first person pauses to allow the interpreter to make sense of what they have communicated. When the interpreter is clear about the message, he or she then communicates it to the second person.

Another kind of interpretation is called simultaneous interpretation; this occurs when an interpreter explains what the first person is saying while they talk. Because of the need to clarify subject matter and emotions, this kind of interpretation is likely to be more difficult to use in care settings. Interpretation makes the communication cycle more complicated.

Knowledge of the subject matter

An interpreter is likely to be more effective when he or she understands the issues involved. Professional interpreters may be able to explain details of legislation or procedures for claiming benefit because they understand the issues. If relatives or friends act as interpreters they will have to make sense of the technical details before they can communicate clearly. Knowledge of languages alone is not always sufficient to enable clear and effective communication.

Trust

It is important that people have confidence in somebody who is acting as an interpreter. People from specific communities may find it hard to trust a member from a different community. Many women may not feel safe and confident discussing personal issues using a male interpreter. The issue may not be about the interpreter's language competence, but about the interpreter's ability to empathise with or understand and correctly convey what a person wants to say.

Social and cultural values

Many people may wish to use a professional interpreter or a specified member of their community or gender group because of social norms. Many people may feel that it is inappropriate to discuss personal details using an interpreter of the opposite sex. Some deaf people do not feel confident using interpreters who have not experienced deafness themselves. Choice of an interpreter must support the self-esteem needs of people who need to access interpretation services.

Confidentiality

Confidentiality is a right enshrined in the 1998 Data Protection Act as well as an ethical duty on professional staff. Professional interpreters are likely to offer guarantees of confidentiality. Using a relative or volunteer may not necessarily provide people with the same guarantee of confidentiality.

Non-judgemental support

A professional interpreter who has trained in social work is likely to offer advanced interpersonal skills which include the ability to remain non-judgemental when undertaking interpretation work. Volunteers, relatives and friends may have language competence, but they may not necessarily be able to interpret meaning without biasing their interpretation.

Advocates

Sometimes, when people have a very serious learning disability or an illness (such as **dementia**) it is not possible to communicate with them. In such situations, care services will often employ an advocate. An advocate is someone who speaks for someone else. A lawyer speaking for a client in a courtroom is working as an advocate for that client. In care work, a volunteer might try to get to know someone who has dementia or a learning disability. The volunteer tries to communicate the service user's needs and wants – as the volunteer understands them. Advocates should be independent of the staff team so they can argue for a service user's rights without being constrained by what the staff think is easiest or cheapest to do.

Advocacy is not straightforward, as volunteers may not always understand the feelings and needs of the people that they are advocating for. Some people argue it would be better if service users could be supported to argue their own case. Helping people to argue their own case is called self-advocacy. Self-advocacy may work very well for some people, but others may need very considerable help before they can do this.

Another kind of advocacy is called group advocacy. This is where people with similar needs come together and receive support to argue for their needs as a group. Different people may need different kinds of advocacy support.

Communication in groups

In everyday language 'group' can mean a collection or set of things, so any collection of people could be counted as a group. For example, a group of people might be waiting to cross the road. They are a group in the everyday sense of the word, but not in the special sense of 'group' that is often used in care work.

The stages groups may go through

Working with a group is usually taken to imply that the individuals identify themselves as belonging to a group. Groups have a sense of belonging that gives the members a 'group feeling'. This could be described as a group identity. Social scientists sometimes use the term 'primary group' and 'secondary group.'

Primary groups usually share the following features:

* people know each other
* there is a 'feeling of belonging' shared by people in the group
* people have a common purpose or reason for coming together
* people share a set of beliefs or norms.

The term 'secondary group' is used when people simply have something in common with each other.

Many theorists have studied the way people start to work together in a group. Before a sense of belonging can develop, people need to learn about each other. Most groups seem to go through some sort of struggle before people finally unite and work effectively together.

One of the best known theorists to explain group formation stages is Tuckman (1965). Tuckman suggests that most groups go through a process involving four stages before they can become effective (see Figure 2.18).

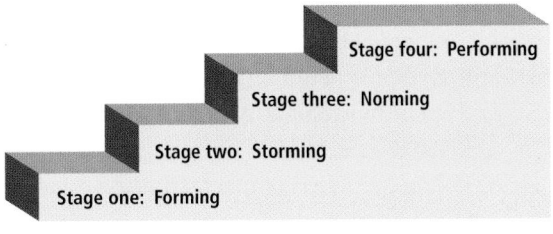

FIGURE 2.18 *Tuckman's four stages of group formation*

An outline explanation of Tuckman's four stages of group formation is shown in Figure 2.19.

PROCESS OF GROUP FORMATION	
STAGE	**BEHAVIOUR**
Stage one: Forming	When people first get together there is likely to be an introductory stage. People may be unsure why they are attending a meeting. The purpose of the group may not be clear. People may have little commitment to the group and there may be no clear value system. Stereotyping and prejudice may be expressed.
Stage two: Storming	There may be 'power struggles' within the group. Different individuals may contest each other for leadership of the group. There may be arguments about how the group should work, who should do tasks and so on. Groups can fail at this stage and individuals can decide to drop out because they do not feel comfortable with other people in the group. Staff teams sometimes split into sub-groups who refuse to communicate with each other if they become stuck in the storming stage.
Stage three: Norming	At this stage group members develop a set of common beliefs and values. People are likely to begin to trust each other and develop clear roles. Norms are shared expectations which group members have of each other. Norms enable people to work together as a group.
Stage four: Performing	Because people share the same values and norms the group is able to perform effectively. People may feel that they are comfortable and belong in the group. There may be a sense of high morale.

FIGURE 2.19 *An explanation of Tuckman's four stages of group formation*

Key concept

Group values: For a group to perform effectively, group members will need to share a common system of beliefs or values relevant to the purpose of the group. It may be very important to identify the extent to which a group does share a value system when planning to run an activity.

Turn-taking

Working in a group can be more difficult than holding an individual conversation. If a group is worth belonging to, people must take turns in listening and speaking. Once everyone is speaking, no one is listening! Turn-taking between two individuals is easy, but turn-taking in groups is not so easy.

Turn-taking involves complicated non-verbal behaviour. When a speaker is finishing, he or she usually signals this by lowering and slowing the voice and looking around. Who speaks next depends on eye-contact around the group – not just with the speaker. Group members have to watch the faces and eyes of everyone else in order that just one person takes over and speaks in turn. If people get excited or tense, then they usually add gestures to their other non-verbal messages to signal forcefully that they want to speak next. Sometimes people will put their hand out or nod their head to say (non-verbally): 'Look, it's my turn next!'

Eventually turn-taking goes wrong, and two or more people start talking at once. This is called a failure to 'mesh'. Meshing means that conversation flows easily between people around the group. People link together in conversation, like the linking in 'wire mesh'. When two people talk at the same time, one person has to give way. A group leader can act as a 'conductor' to check that turns are taken.

Managing group activity

Most care groups have a purpose or task to work on. Children get together to play games, adults may get together in recreational groups. Groups often need a focus – a game to play, an activity to join in or a topic to discuss. Consider the observations on group behaviour shown overleaf in Figure 2.20.

As well as performing their tasks, groups have to be 'maintained'. Group maintenance consists of encouraging a sense of belonging and keeping the whole meeting enjoyable. The following list includes ideas of some behaviours that might be useful for maintaining group discussion:

* A bit of laughter can help to relieve tension and create a warm, friendly feeling that everyone can join in.
* Show interest in the people in the group – be prepared to negotiate and discuss different views.
* Be 'warm' and show respect and value when listening to people who are different from yourself or who have had different life experiences. This behaviour makes it safe to be in the group.
* Express feelings honestly and with sincerity. This will help others to understand your identity. Help others to understand you as well as trying to understand others.
* Take responsibility for ensuring that everyone has a chance to speak and contribute. Some people may need to be encouraged or invited to speak and some people may need organising, so that turn-taking works!
* If necessary, get people to explain what they have said, and to talk through – or negotiate – disagreements. Group members need to feel that their shared values will make it possible to arrive at solutions when people disagree.

A group leader must keep thinking about what is happening in the group. Do I need to guide the group back to the task? Is this the right time for a funny story? Should I make it clear that I am listening and that I value what is being said by this person? Every other group member who really wants the group to work will also monitor how the group is getting on with its task.

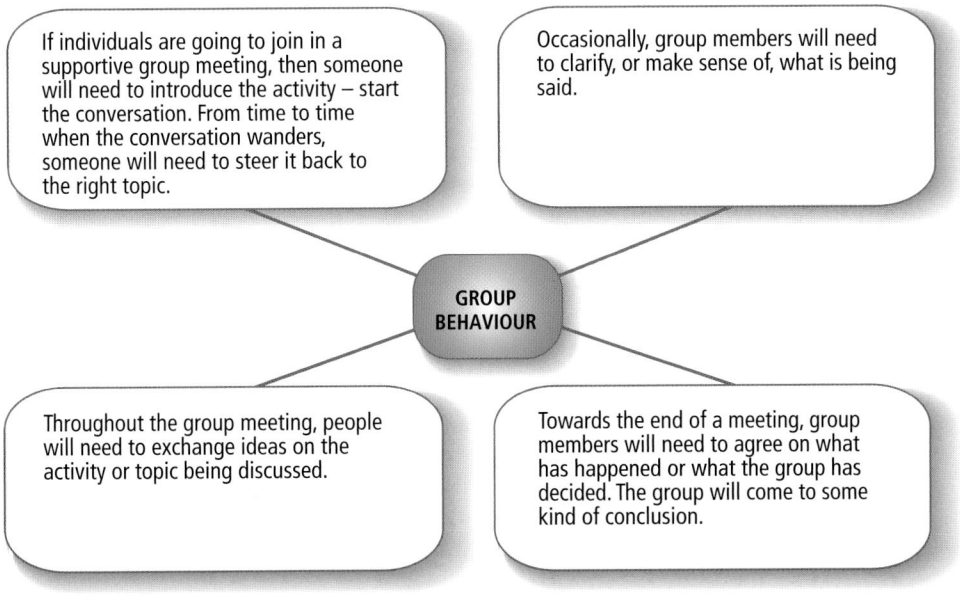

FIGURE 2.20 *Some observations on group behaviour*

Communication in a group might work best when groups:

* keep working on a task or discussion activity
* create a feeling of shared identity or belonging
* make sure each individual is supported and valued.

The dynamics of a care group are illustrated in Figure 2.21.

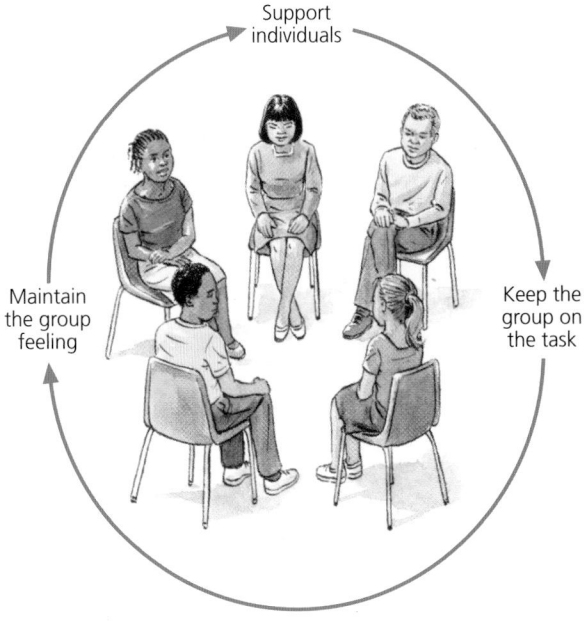

FIGURE 2.21 *The dynamics of a care group*

Group values

In care work the 'value base' should provide a basis around which groups can develop their 'ground rules' or norms. In practice, sharing the care value base is likely to mean that group members will encourage one another to speak, since everyone has an equal right to speak and be included in the group. Group members will try to understand and value differences between people. People will show respect and value for one another.

If people do not share caring values then it is quite likely that some people may try to dominate the group. Sometimes people 'pair' with others who think the same way, to fight for control of a group. Sometimes people can block the progress of a discussion with irrelevant or other deliberate distractions aimed at disrupting the discussion. Sometimes people may become withdrawn and ignore the group if they don't feel they belong. Groups have to develop shared beliefs and a feeling of 'belonging' if they are to work effectively.

Group discussion can sometimes be difficult. Some reasons for finding discussion difficult are listed below:

* not knowing the beliefs and values of others in the group

* not understanding the purpose of a meeting
* feeling different from others in the group
* not feeling confident of communication skills
* feeling threatened by other members (perhaps they may stereotype or label)
* feeling powerless and believing that others control the group.

Where individuals are not clear about the purpose of the group, or do not feel they belong, they may engage in disruptive behaviours such as:

* irrelevant talking
* trying to dominate other people
* changing the subject
* other kinds of behaviour that block the group from working such as splitting into pairs and excluding others.

Observing and evaluating group behaviour

The idea of classifying the behaviour of people in groups was put forward by Bales (1970). He suggested that observers could understand and analyse what was happening in a group by using an interaction analysis of individual member's behaviours. An interaction analysis involves classifying the way people behave using defined categories. Bales' categories are outlined in Figure 2.22.

Using categories can be a useful way of getting insight into how an individual is influencing the work and the emotional maintenance or feeling involved in group communication. It is possible to design a grid that can be used minute by minute to try to categorise the task and maintenance behaviours occurring in groups. An example relevant to the standards in this unit is offered in Figure 2.23.

A process of planning, doing and reviewing may enable individuals to understand how their own skills influence others (see Figure 2.24 on page 78). The ability to imagine and understand how an individual's behaviour will influence outcomes lies at the heart of getting a group activity to work.

CATEGORY	ANALYSIS
Group task	Gives suggestion (including taking the lead) Gives opinion (including feelings and wishes) Gives information (including clarifying and confirming) Asks for information Asks for opinion Asks for suggestion
Group maintenance (called 'Social-emotional Area' by Bales)	Seems friendly Dramatises Agrees Disagrees Shows tension Seems unfriendly

FIGURE 2.22 *Bales' categories of how people behave in groups*

Concluding group activity

When a group of people have worked together for a long period of time, there can be a feeling of loss when the group finishes. An example might be that a class of students who have worked together for a year might feel sad when the course comes to an end.

Benson (2001) offers a range of advice on a practical, emotional and intellectual level. This advice includes the need to feel that tasks have been completed. A group of students would need to feel that their course was over. Group members need to prepare to say goodbye and work through the emotions involved in parting. Most importantly, Benson stresses the need to encourage 'ritual and celebration'. Student groups might organise a farewell party – and this would be an example of celebrating the conclusion of belonging to a group.

In care settings the conclusion of a group activity might involve a period of time at the end of the session. When working with young children this might be a quiet time following practical work – perhaps listening to a story. When working with adults, group members

	Behaviour seen in each individual									
	1	2	3	4	5	6	7	8	9	10
Group task:										
Starting discussion										
Giving information										
Asking for information										
Clarifying discussion										
Summarising discussion										
Group maintenance:										
Humour										
Expressing group feelings										
Including other people in discussion										
Being supportive (using supportive skils)										
Behaviour which blocks communicaton:										
Excluding others										
Withdrawing										
Aggression										
Distracting or blocking disscusion										
Attention seeking and dominating discussion										

FIGURE 2.23 *A profile to monitor group behaviour*

SCENARIO:

Planning, managing and concluding a group activity

Alesha wants to involve a small group of adults who have learning disabilities in a cookery class. Alesha's idea is not to train the group to make cakes, but to provide an enjoyable social experience that the group can join in with to maintain their social skills. Before she can start, Alesha needs to plan. She needs to plan what ingredients to buy, and her own preparation of the ingredients, before the session begins. She also needs to organise the use of an oven for baking cakes, and so on.

As well as this, Alesha needs to plan how to support the group. Who does or doesn't get on with others? Who might be able to help with tasks? How could she interest and motivate the individuals? How will she keep the atmosphere enjoyable? All this planning depends on Alesha's ability to use her imagination, perhaps to picture the group and to work out how to organise the session.

Alesha will need to ensure that the tasks are enjoyable and appropriate to each individual. Before moving on to the activity, she could also get advice on the plans from a senior member of staff – just to check that the activities are appropriate.

Doing the session would not necessarily be straightforward. Alesha will need to monitor how the session is going. Do the verbal and non-verbal messages from her group suggest that they are enjoying themselves? Alesha will need feedback, so she could ask the group members what they thought. Another member of staff might help her by joining in and providing feedback. Whilst leading the cookery session Alesha will also be observing or taking in what is happening.

After the session is over Alesha will need to evaluate what has happened. Evaluation will depend on imagination. The evaluation will enable Alesha to make recommendations to improve her work in the future by thinking her work over before, during and after the cookery session. Alesha will thus be able to develop her own self-awareness and sense of skill.

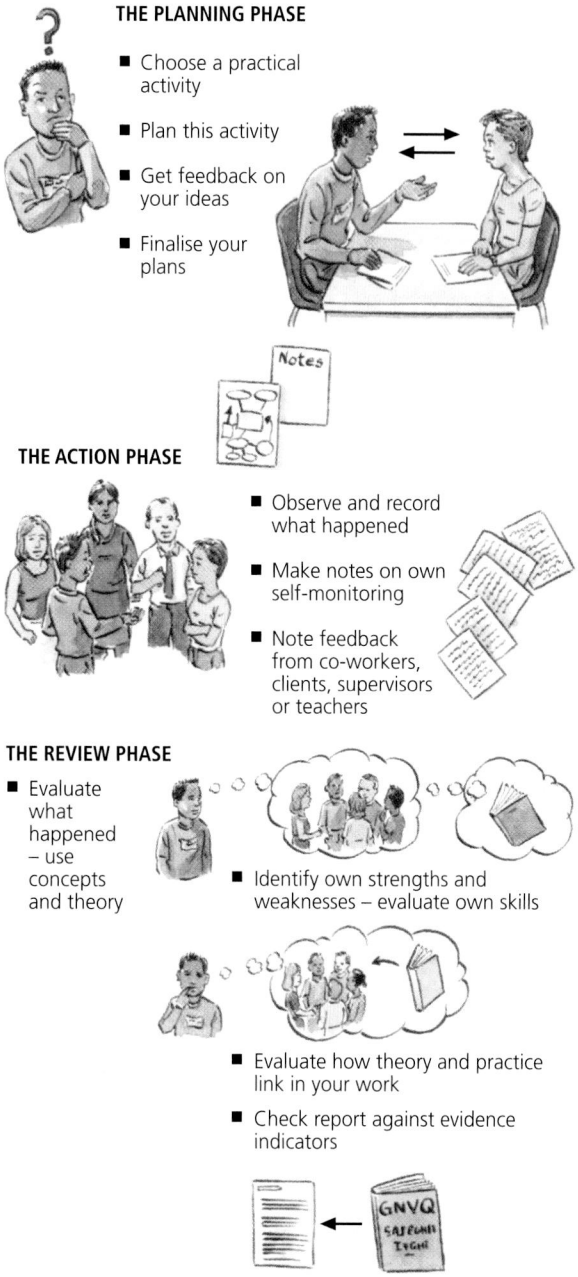

FIGURE 2.24 *Three phases in getting an activity to work*

might be invited to talk through their feelings about the day's activity, or to talk through their feelings at the end of the day. Leaving a group for good might require more in-depth emotional work.

Summary of Section 2.1

The following key areas of theory have been covered in this section:

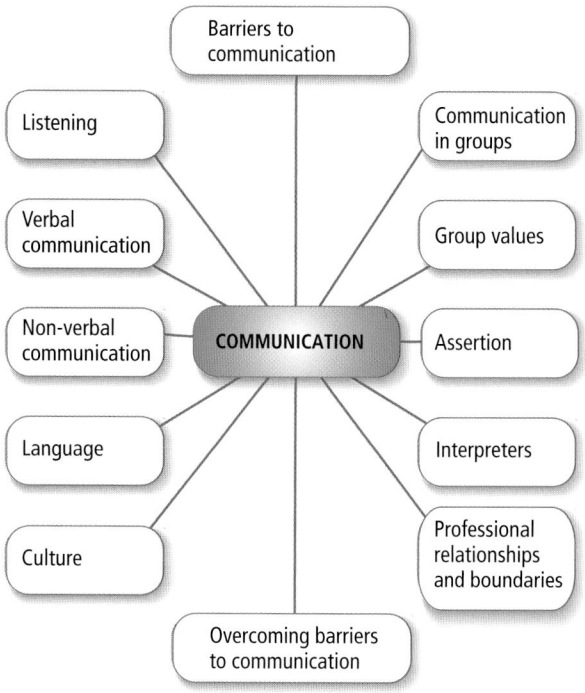

Consider this

Chloe works at a day nursery. Parents sometimes make an appointment to see the nursery and to talk to the staff in order to decide whether the nursery would be appropriate for their children. Chloe expects to meet some parents in order to show them around the nursery and talk about the work they do. These parents do not live locally; they are from different ethnic and age groups to Chloe and have well-paid professional jobs.

Using concepts, can you identify?

1. What communication skills Chloe is likely to need in order to provide an appropriate welcome and to clearly explain the work of the nursery?

2. What barriers to communication Chloe should be prepared for as she takes the parents around the nursery?

Go further – can you analyse issues using theory?

How could Chloe know whether she was communicating clearly and effectively with the parents? How could Chloe know if she was successful at providing a warm and friendly welcome?

Go further – can you evaluate using a range of theory?

Chloe feels confident that she was highly skilled at holding the conversation with the parents. As she remembers how the conversation went, she can check what she did using the range of theory in this section. Can you imagine how you could use a range of concepts in order to judge the value of a conversation you have had?

2.2 Care value base

Principles that underlie care practice

The first standards for National Vocational Qualifications (NVQs) in care, published in 1992, included a unit of study that was called the 'value base'. Skilled caring is not simply about knowing the right techniques; a carer also needs to 'value' the service users that he or she works with. The 1992 value base stressed the importance of anti-discriminatory practice, confidentiality, rights, choice, effective communication and the importance of service users' personal beliefs and identity. Later standards in 1998 simplified these principles and emphasised equality and diversity, together with confidentiality and other rights and responsibilities. Proposed 2005 standards no longer specify a unit of study as a value base but do require that workers demonstrate an embedded framework of values. These values include the promotion of equality and diversity, the ability to challenge discrimination and an understanding of the rights and responsibilities of people involved in care settings.

Key concept

Care values/value base: Occupational standards and the GSCC code of practice identify a framework of values and moral rights of service users that can be referred to as care values or a value base for care.

In 2002 the **General Social Care Council (GSCC)** published a **code of practice** for both employees and employers. A summary of the code of practice for employees is set out in Figure 2.25.

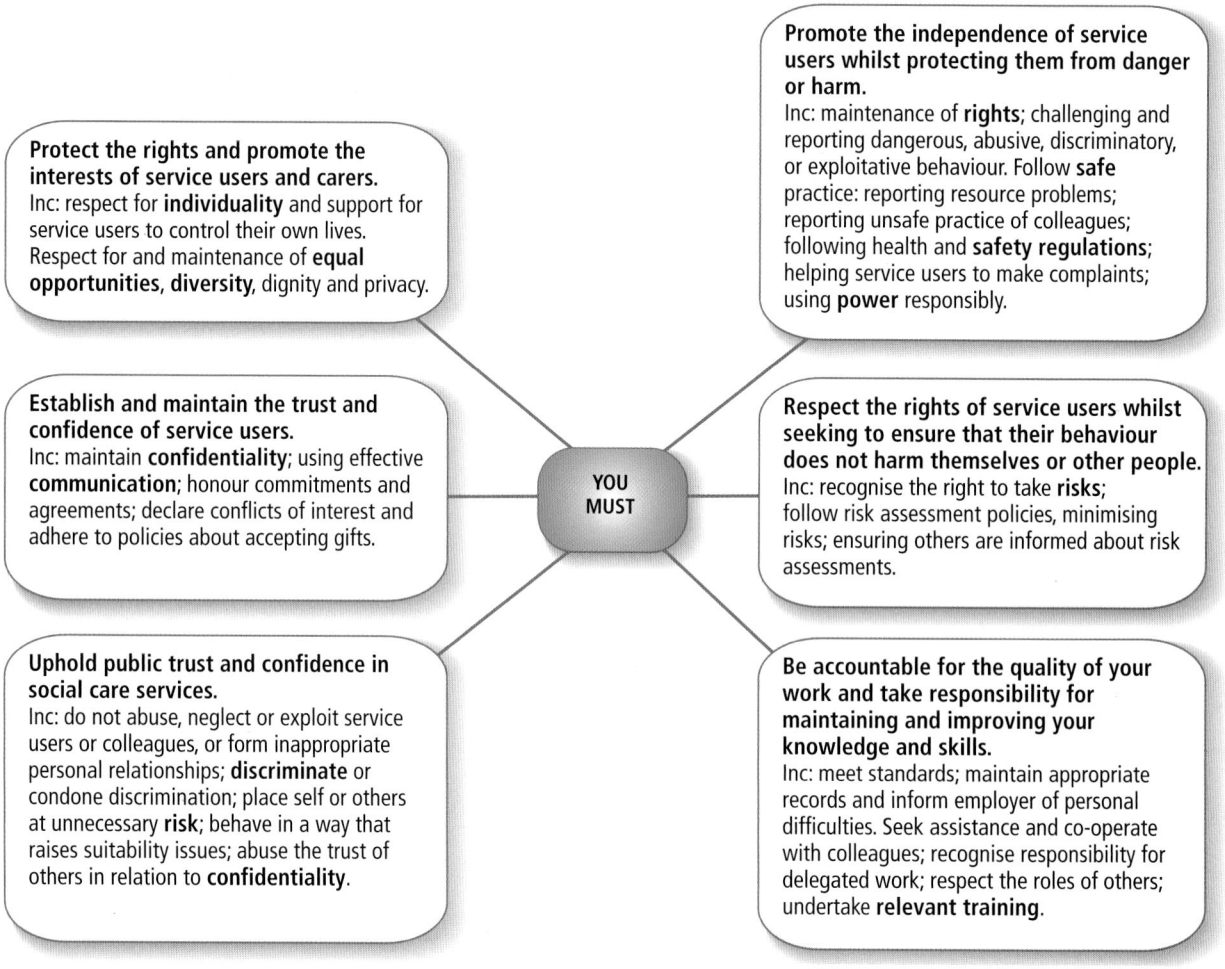

FIGURE 2.25 *The GSCC code of practice for social care workers: an outline summary*

Value base principles and moral rights

Figure 2.26 lists key value base principles that might also be considered to be service users' moral rights, together with other rights that are specified within the GSCC code of practice.

Legislation standards and policies

It is important to know about legislation, such as the Care Standards Act 2000, because laws create a framework for the development of good practice. Laws can create commissions that develop standards and check that standards are being met. Each Care Service will develop its own written policies and procedures in order to monitor that service users' rights are respected. Figure 2.27 illustrates how law, standards and policies influence practice.

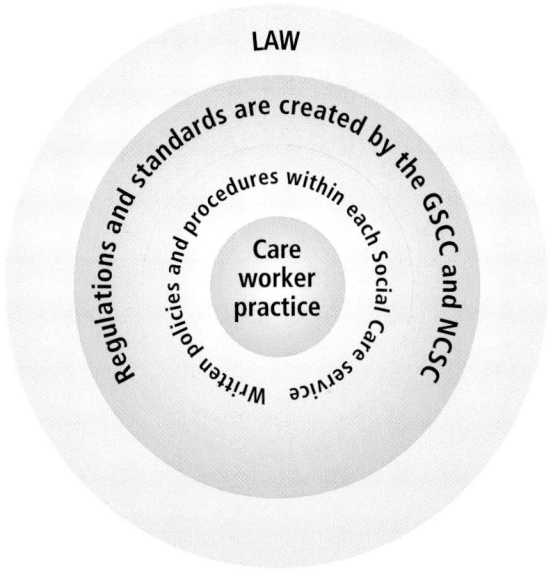

FIGURE 2.27 *How law, standards and policies influence practice*

MORAL RIGHTS OF SERVICE USERS	GSCC STANDARDS
Diversity and respect for differences	1.1 treat each person as an individual 1.2 respecting and promoting individual views 1.6 respecting diversity and different cultures and values
Equality in care practice	1.5 promoting equal opportunities
Anti-discriminatory practice	5.5 care workers must not discriminate 5.6 care workers must not condone discrimination
Confidentiality	2.3 respecting confidential information
The right to take control over one's own life – the right to choice and independence	1.3 supporting service users' rights to control their lives and make informed choices 3.1 promoting the independence of service users 3.7 helping service users and carers to make complaints 3.8 recognising and using power responsibly
Dignity and privacy	1.4 respecting and maintaining the dignity and privacy of service users
The right to effective communication	2.2 communicating in an appropriate, open, accurate and straightforward way
The right to safety and security	Principle 3: promote independence while protecting service users, including health and safety policies, appropriate practice and procedures. 4.2 / 4.3 follow risk assessment policies, take steps to minimise risk 5.2 must not exploit service users 5.7 must not put self or others at risk
The right to take risks	4.1 service users have the right to take risks – help them to identify and manage risks

FIGURE 2.26 *A summary of the GSCC code of practice for employees*

Laws provide the background to policy making, and policy and standards guide managers when they design procedures.

Equal opportunities legislation

The main Acts of Parliament covering discrimination are shown in Figure 2.28.

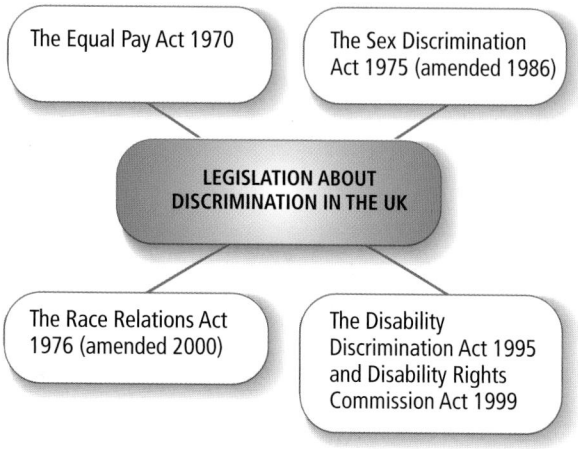

FIGURE 2.28 *Main Acts of Parliament covering discrimination in the UK*

The Equal Pay Act 1970

This Act made it unlawful for employers to discriminate between men and women in terms of their pay and conditions of work. Before this law was passed it was possible for an employer to pay men more than women – even though doing the same job!

Equal pay legislation was updated in 1975 and 1983 to make it possible to claim equal pay for work that was considered to be of 'equal value'.

The Sex Discrimination Act 1975

This Act made it unlawful to discriminate between men and women in respect of employment, goods and facilities. The Act also made it illegal to discriminate on the grounds of marital status. The Act identified two forms of discrimination: direct discrimination and indirect discrimination.

The Act tries to provide an equal opportunity for both men and women to get jobs and promotion. In order to make sure that people's rights were protected the government set up the **Equal Opportunities Commission** to monitor, advise and provide information on men and women's rights under the law. People can ask the Equal Opportunities Commission for help and advice if they believe they have been discriminated against because of their gender. The law was updated in 1986 so that it also applied to small businesses.

The Race Relations Act 1976 (amended 2000)

This Act makes it unlawful to discriminate on 'racial grounds' in employment, housing or services. 'Racial grounds' means according to colour, race, nationality, ethnicity or national origins. The Act makes it an offence to incite or encourage racial hatred. As in the law against sex discrimination, both direct and indirect discrimination are made unlawful.

The Commission for Racial Equality was set up in 1976 to make sure that the law against racial discrimination works. The Commission can investigate cases of discrimination and give advice to people who wish to take legal action because of discrimination. The Race Relations Law was strengthened and widened by an amendment in 2000 in order to prevent discrimination in any public situation.

The Disability Discrimination Act 1995

This Act is designed to prevent discrimination against people with disabilities, covering employment, access to education and transport, housing and obtaining goods and services. Employers and landlords must not treat a disabled person less favourably than a non-disabled person. New transport must meet the needs of disabled people and colleges; shops and other services must ensure that disabled people can use their services.

The Disability Rights Commission was set up by the **Disability Rights Commission Act** of 1999. This commission has the power to conduct formal investigations and to serve non-discrimination notices, make agreements, and take other actions to prevent discrimination against people with a disability. The commission can give advice to people who believe they have experienced discrimination.

CONFIDENTIALITY

Confidentiality is an important right for all service users. Confidentiality is important because:

* service users may not trust a carer if the carer does not keep information to him or herself
* service users may not feel valued or able to keep their self-esteem if their private details are shared with others
* service users' safety may be put at risk if details of their property and habits are shared publicly
* a professional service which maintains respect for individuals must keep private information confidential
* there are legal requirements to keep personal records confidential.

The Data Protection Act 1998

The Data Protection Acts of 1984 and 1998, Access to Personal Files Act 1987, and Access to Health Records Act 1990 made it a legal requirement to keep service user information confidential. The 1998 Data Protection Act establishes rights to confidentiality covering both paper and electronic records. This Act provides people with a range of rights including:

* the right to know what information is held on you and to see and correct information held on you
* the right for you to refuse to provide information
* the right that data held on you should be accurate and up to date
* the right that data held on you should not be kept for longer than necessary
* the right to confidentiality – that information about you should not be accessible to unauthorised people.

See Unit 3 for more detail on confidentiality, and the recording and storage of records.

Key concept

Confidentiality: Confidentiality involves keeping information safe and only passing it on where there is a clear right and a clear need to do so. Confidentiality is an important moral and legal right, promoting safety and security of service users and their property. The maintenance of confidentiality is vital in order to maintain a sense of trust.

Other important laws relevant to care

The Children Act 1989 outlined 'parental responsibility' and established children's right to be protected from 'significant harm'. The NHS and Community Care Act 1990 established that all people who are in need of community care have the right to have their needs assessed and to have services if their needs meet criteria. The Care Standards Act 2000 created a new framework for defining and controlling quality within care work. (See Unit 3.)

Codes of practice charters and policies

Healthcare workers such as nurses follow a code of professional conduct published by the Nursing and Midwifery Council (NMC). The code has similar principles to the GSCC code for social care. Full details of the code can be found at the NMC website through www.heinemann.co.uk/hotlinks (express code 37185). A summary of the key principles are listed below.

In caring for patients and clients, you must:

* respect each service user as an individual
* obtain consent before you give any treatment or care
* protect confidential information
* cooperate with others in the team
* maintain your professional knowledge and competence
* be trustworthy
* act to identify and minimise risk to patients and clients.

The majority of Early Years services are inspected by Ofsted and do not involve the Commission for Social Care Inspection (CSCI) or the GSCC code of practice. Instead, Early Years National Vocational Qualifications have a set of Underlying Principles; in outline these specify:

* that the welfare of the child is the most important issue
* that children must be kept safe
* workers must work in partnership with parents and families
* children's learning and development are centrally important
* that the principle of equality of opportunity is critically important
* that anti-discriminatory practice is vital
* that care practice must 'celebrate diversity'
* the principle of confidentiality must be followed
* workers must work with other professionals in the best interests of children and families
* early years workers must learn to reflect on their practice and principles.

After 2005 it is proposed that these principles should be revised and embedded within NVQ awards rather than being found as a separate set of principles.

Charters

Charters are another source of policies that define the values and principles of caring. Many health services – such as doctor's surgeries – may have a 'Charter' that specifies the quality of service that a patient may expect. Originally the idea for these charters may have come from the Patient's Charter, launched by the government in 1992. The Patient's Charter set out some general rights and quality standards that the public could expect from the National Health Service. This charter was replaced in 2001 by a lengthy publication called 'Your Guide to the NHS: Getting the Most from your National Health Service'.

National Minimum Standards of Care

The Care Standards Act 2000 established the National Care Standards Commission (NCSC). The NCSC produces a set of regulations and National Minimum Standards that care services must achieve. There are different sets of standards for different care services. The Standards provide very detailed guidance on how services must be delivered. Care services are now inspected by 'The Commission for Social Care Inspection'(CSCI) to make sure that they are providing high quality care. Further detail of National Minimum standards can be found in Unit 3.

Equality and respect for difference

Historically in the UK there have been major tensions between different social groups, such as religious groups. One idea for reducing conflict is the concept of 'tolerance'. This word was widely used two centuries ago to argue that different religious groups could co-exist without needing to fight each other. Tolerance and respect are values that could be argued to lay a foundation for anti-discriminatory practice. Celebrating diversity and anti-discriminatory practice involves much more than tolerance, however. Celebrating diversity involves being interested in and willing to learn about other cultures and belief systems. Anti-discrimination involves providing the same quality of service for everyone. If everybody is treated the same – if everyone were given the same dinner, for instance – then some people would be discriminated against. Vegetarians might not get the food they need, for example. Equality is about everybody getting the same *quality* of service – not the same service!

Anti-discriminatory practice

Some groups of people that are at risk of being discriminated against are listed in Figure 2.29. Discrimination may take the forms identified in Figure 2.30.

Key concept

Discrimination: In care work, discrimination means to treat some types of people less well than others. People are often discriminated against because of their race, beliefs, gender, religion, sexuality or age.

Direct and indirect discrimination

Direct discrimination is where the discrimination is open and obvious. In the 1950s and 1960s, properties for rent in London would sometimes have signs which read 'no blacks, no dogs, no Irish'. Such offensive and obvious discrimination is 'direct'; the

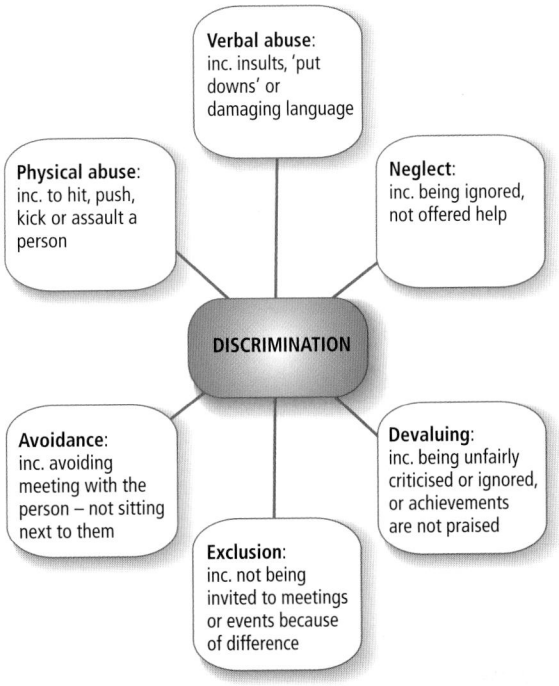

FIGURE 2.30 *Examples of some forms of discrimination*

FOCUS OF DISCRIMINATION	EXAMPLES OF RISK OF DISCRIMINATION DIFFERENCE IS SEEN AS A PROBLEM RATHER THAN AS SOMETHING POSITIVE
Race	People might not be included in activities, chosen as friends, or selected for a job because they are seen as 'not like us' and 'not to be trusted'
Religious belief	Assumptions are made that everybody follows the same cultural traditions. For example, Christmas is celebrated, but the festivals of other religions are not
Gender	Assumptions are made that male workers are the most reliable 'because they don't have to look after children'
Disability	People with a disability are thought of as being defective or damaged people who deserve pity because they are not 'normal'
Culture	A person from a different ethnic or even a different social class might be seen as inferior, 'having bad habits' and so on
Health status	HIV positive people are seen as 'untouchable' and a risk to others because of fears of **contagion**
Cognitive ability	People with learning difficulty being assumed to be 'children' who need everything decided for them
Mental health background	Assumptions that all people with a history of mental health problems are a risk to others
Place of origin	Assumptions that only people 'like us' can be trusted – even people from different geographical areas may be 'outsiders'
Marital status	Assumptions that only married adults are 'normal'. Alternatively, assumptions that married women will want to leave a job in order to have children
Sexuality	People might be avoided or made 'fun of' because they are seen as 'not normal'

FIGURE 2.29 *Groups of people that are at risk of being discriminated against*

advertisements were openly committing racial discrimination.

Indirect discrimination may do equal harm but it is less clear. On one occasion an employer produced an advert stating that applicants for a job must live in certain local areas. At first this sounds all right, but it became obvious that the areas had been carefully chosen to avoid the black and Asian communities. The advert was indirectly discriminating by identifying areas where only white people lived. Indirect discrimination involves unequal treatment that may not be obvious at first.

Receiving a worse service than others because of your age, gender, race, sexuality, or ability, could strike at the heart of a service user's sense of self, self-esteem and feelings of self-worth. Discrimination can damage a person's ability to develop and maintain a sense of identity.

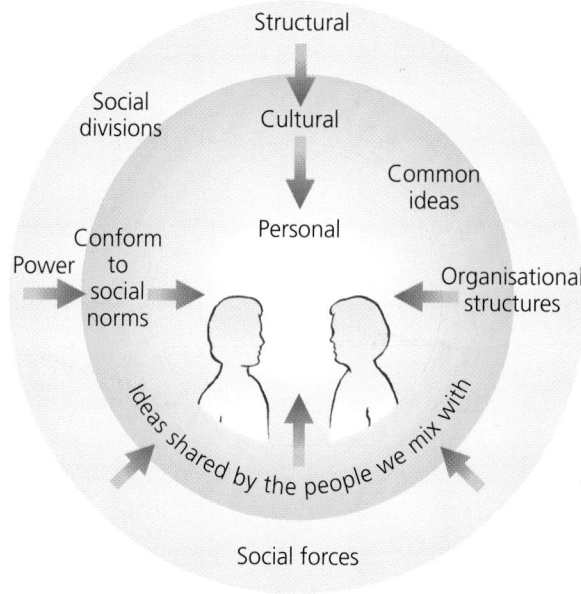

FIGURE 2.31 *Different levels of discrimination (P, C and S)*

Thompson's PCS Model for understanding discrimination

Thompson (1997) identifies three levels where discrimination and anti-discrimination practice can take place. These three levels are analysed as being P, C and S levels.

P – personal and psychological
C – cultural and conformity to norms
S – structural and social forces

Discrimination can work on any of the three levels (see Figure 2.31). On a structural level, historical beliefs about gender role and about the superiority of ethnic groups influence the assumptions that surround us. Some organisations may still value male employees more highly than women. Men may find it easier to gain promotion because organisations have built-in or 'structural' systems that make it easier for men to succeed. Structural economic systems may result in some black communities living in more deprived housing conditions. Stressful housing conditions may represent one factor that can reduce life chances and opportunities.

On the cultural level, we mix with groups of people who share values and ways of behaving. A great deal of discrimination happens because people conform to the expectations of others. People might, for instance, join in with jokes about a particular minority, not because they hold personal prejudices but because they want to fit in with others. On a personal level our own beliefs are often translated into our verbal and non-verbal behaviour. Our personal practice has a direct and immediate effect on others.

On an individual level, Thompson (1997) makes the point that carers can make a major difference to the quality of a service user's life by checking their own assumptions and their own behaviour. On a personal level, discrimination may result from emotional reactions as well as resulting from prejudice. Building an understanding of each service user's life and respecting service users' rights might enable a carer to avoid negative reactions to service users. Every carer has the power to develop his or her own skills and to employ appropriate skills when interacting with others. Lack of time may limit personal effectiveness, but there is nearly always something that could be achieved within person-to-person communication.

On a wider cultural level, individuals can 'make a difference'. Individuals can analyse what is happening and can challenge others to try to change group norms and values. Organisations must introduce management and quality systems, which aim to ensure that workplace norms and expectations conform to national standards and codes of practice for care.

Think it over...

In the past, people with a disability have been thought of as being damaged or limited types of people. 'Handicap' has sometimes implied 'less than normal'. Assumptions like this might result in discrimination. On a personal level, what could you do in order to challenge these assumptions?

On the very widest structural level, individuals may feel that they have little influence. Setting up quality standards and systems is a government function and the standards and the resources which services have to operate within are strongly influenced by political views and values. Individuals may need to join pressure groups, or become involved in political debate in order to influence the structural level of discrimination.

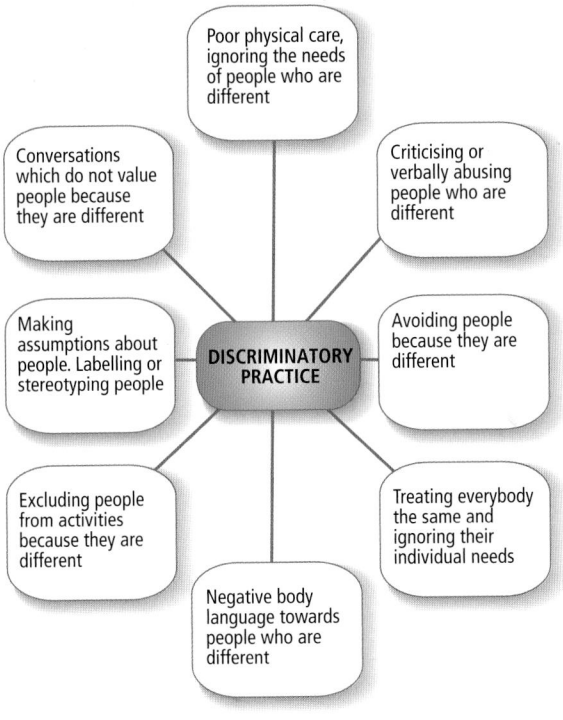

FIGURE 2.32 *Some types of discriminatory practice*

Some obvious types of discriminatory practice are listed in Figure 2.32. It should be possible to monitor one's own and other's behaviour in order to minimise such risk.

Stereotyping and labelling

Sometimes people try to save mental energy and just make the assumption that groups of people are 'all the same'. Perhaps a younger person meets an 80 year old who has a problem with his or her memory. Perhaps they have seen someone with a poor memory on TV – it's easy then to think that 'all old people are forgetful'. This would be a stereotype.

A stereotype is a fixed way of thinking. People may make assumptions based on stereotyped thinking. For example, a carer working with older people might say 'I'll just go in and wash and dress this next one. I won't ask what she would like me to do because she's old – old people don't remember – so it doesn't matter what I do'. Stereotyped thinking may cause us to discriminate against people.

Key concept

Stereotyping: Stereotyping is a fixed way of thinking involving generalisations and expectations about an issue or a group of people.

When people say 'All women are ...,' or 'all black people are ...,' or 'all gay people are ...,' they will probably go on to describe a stereotype or label for these groups.

Another way in which thinking can lead to discrimination is labelling. Labelling is similar to stereotyping but labels are simple. Instead of having a set of fixed thoughts about a group, a person gets summed up in just one word or term.

Think it over...

Many years ago there was a care setting for children with learning difficulties. Some children were not very skilled with holding plates, and so on. They were labelled 'clumsies.'

What effect do you think describing these children as 'clumsies' would have on their development of self-esteem?

Labels may be words such as 'aggressive', 'emotional', or 'naughty.' They can also be words that create a category of assumptions. Historically, a word like 'paranoid' was a medical term, but today it can be used as a label that neatly categorises and ignores another person's worries.

Labels are often used in order to categorise and discriminate against ethnic groups, women or old people. Labels may say that people are only one thing, such as aggressive, emotional or worthless. When individuals are labelled, it's almost as if they stop being people; they are just mentally ill, for example. That's all they are, no other details matter. Labels can reduce people's self-esteem, dignity and individuality.

Language differences often result in labelling or stereotyping. For example, people who have difficulty hearing or seeing are sometimes assumed to be 'awkward' or mentally ill. Older people are sometimes seen as 'demented' or 'confused' if they do not answer questions appropriately.

People can also be labelled or stereotyped when they use different language systems. Sometimes people shout at others who speak a different language, as if increasing the volume would help. People who sign to communicate are sometimes thought to be odd or to have learning difficulties, because they don't respond to written or spoken English.

The effects of discrimination

Discrimination that results in abuse can have permanent and extremely damaging effects on people. All forms of discrimination will harm people.

Discrimination may result in the outcomes shown in Figure 2.33.

FIGURE 2.33 *Some effects of discrimination on people in care settings*

Empowerment

When a conversation takes place between a professional worker and a service user, who is the most powerful? Half-a-century ago, expert professionals held the power and made the decisions about what kind of treatment or care people would receive. For example, a person with learning difficulty might be sent to a specialist hospital that provided residential care. Within this institution, staff would decide the daily routine that each 'inmate' would follow. People with learning difficulty might not be consulted about their lifestyle – everything was decided for them. In this situation, the staff hold all the power; the service users have no power to choose how they would like to live or what they would like to do.

Half-a-century ago a visit to the doctor would involve the patient explaining his or her problem and accepting the advice received in return. The term 'doctor's orders' was sometimes used to describe a treatment plan that a patient had to follow. Patients often thought of doctors as being senior officers who were entitled to give them orders, rather like officers in the army.

The theory of empowerment is that health and care staff should not make decisions and take control of service users' lives. Care staff should communicate their knowledge to service users and enable service users to make their own decisions and choices about care plans or medical treatment. Empowering communication is communication that aims to give service users choice and control of the service that they receive.

Key concept

Empowerment: Empowerment enables a service user to make choices and take control of his or her own life.

An example of empowerment

In 2001, the government launched the 'Expert Patient Initiative'. The idea of an 'expert patient' is that a person with a long-term, or chronic, illness such as arthritis can learn to take control of the management of his or her condition. Expert medical staff can provide advice and guidance, but the patient is the expert on his or her own body. The patient works in partnership with medical staff in order to build his or her own treatment plan.

The 'expert patient' is empowered to take control of his or her own medical condition. The expert patient does not simply have to comply with the treatment prescribed.

FIGURE 2.34 *A service user taking on the management of her health*

Bringing about empowerment

The idea that health and care workers should work in partnership with service users is closely associated with the value base of care work. But there are pressures that may limit the degree to which service users are empowered, as shown in Figure 2.35.

Descombes (2004: 94) provides evidence that within medical practice 'It is still the doctor who controls the whole patient–practitioner encounter. It is the doctor who decides just what information will be given and how much use can be made of it'. Establishing an empowering approach will require much more than simply giving clear information to service users.

Balancing the rights of individuals with the rights of others

Rights of individuality, freedom from discrimination, confidentiality, choice, dignity, independence, effective communication, and safety, all protect individual well-being and encourage self-esteem. Rights usually carry responsibilities with them. An individual can expect respect, but he or she has the responsibility not to interfere with or damage other people's rights. You have a right to be free from discrimination but a responsibility not to discriminate against others.

Think it over...

Nasil argues that he has a right to smoke – it's his life and he has a right to choose how he lives and dies. Nasil attends a day centre that has a no smoking policy inside the building. Nasil will often go outside to have a cigarette, but he complains that the cold damp air is unpleasant and bad for his health. 'Us smokers are discriminated against', he says. 'Why should we have to put up with being cold just because other people have got different habits?'

What are Nasil's rights and what are his responsibilities in relation to smoking?

Some care workers may enjoy a sense of prestige and power that might come from making decisions for other people. In reality, some care staff may be reluctant to share their expert status.

SERVICE USERS' EMPOWERMENT MAY BE LIMITED BECAUSE:

Lack of time may represent a problem for some care workers – working in partnership may require longer conversations than a more directive approach.

Some service users may resist 'working in partnership'. Some service users may find it preferable to delegate responsibility for meeting their needs to others. Taking responsibility for your own life may require a well-organised self-concept, a degree of confidence in your own abilities and perhaps some energy and enthusiasm for being in control. Many vulnerable people may initially prefer 'to be looked after' by professionals.

FIGURE 2.35 *Limitations of service users' empowerment*

Adults have a right to choose to smoke even though smoking usually damages health and might shorten a person's life. Smokers have a responsibility not to put other people's health at risk because people have a right to health. Other people, including care staff, should not have to breathe in tobacco smoke. This means that in most places today, smoking is only allowed in specially designated areas.

In the past, service users' responsibilities may not have been a major focus because service users generally have less power than staff. Service users are generally vulnerable, whilst care workers generally have a degree of control over their own lives. But just because a person is vulnerable, it doesn't mean that he or she has a right to interfere with other people, or for instance, threaten people with racist or sexist behaviour.

Some ways of understanding rights and responsibilities are set out in Figure 2.37.

FIGURE 2.36 *Rights do not work without responsibilities*

Key concept

Rights and responsibilities: All moral rights also involve responsibilities towards others. Rights are part of a social system involving a two-way process of rights and responsibilities within UK society.

SOME MORAL RIGHTS OF SERVICE USERS	RESPONSIBILITIES OF SERVICE USERS
Diversity and the right to be different Including an individual's right to express his or her own identity / self-narrative and interpretation of life from the standpoint of different social group memberships	**To respect diversity in others** Including an acceptance that other people have a moral right to interpret life differently. A moral responsibility not to discriminate against others on the basis that own identity / social group membership is morally superior to that of others
Equality and freedom from discrimination Including freedom from discrimination on the basis of race, sex, ability, sexuality, religion	**Respect for the equality of others** Including respect for and not discriminating against members of other social groups
Control over own life, choice and independence Including the freedom to choose own lifestyle, self-presentation, diet and routine	**Respect for the independence, choice and lifestyle of others** Including arriving at a balance between the impact of own choices and the needs of other people who may be affected by the service user's choices – including care staff
Dignity and privacy Including the right to be responded to in terms of own interpretation of dignity and respect	**To share or disclose own assumptions about dignity and negotiate boundaries with others** Including boundaries associated with the health and safety or the identity needs of other users or carers
Confidentiality Including rights as established in law and local codes of practice	**Respect for the confidentiality of others** Including others' legal rights, and rights established in local codes of practice
Effective communication Including appropriately clear and supportive communication that minimises vulnerability	**Communication that does not threaten others** Including appropriate respect
Safety and security Including physical safety, living in an environment that promotes health and emotional safety. Security of property, and freedom from physical, social, emotional or economic threat	**Contributing to the safety and security of others** Including to behave in a way that does not compromise or threaten the physical or emotional safety and security of others
The right to take risks Including taking risks as a matter of choice, in order to maintain own identity or perceived well-being	**Not to expose self or others to unacceptable risks** Including a willingness to negotiate with respect to the impact of risk on others

FIGURE 2.37 *Rights and responsibilities of service users*

Inequalities within society

People have very different opportunities in their lives. The general income level a person has is likely to influence his or her expectations and assumptions about life.

✱ DID YOU KNOW?

Just over one-sixth of Britain's population (17 per cent) were estimated by the Institute for Fiscal Studies to be living in relative poverty (low income) in the period 2001/2002 (Social Trends 2004). People who get less than 60 per cent of the level of income that an average person expects may be considered to be at risk of poverty and 'social exclusion'.

Key groups of people who have to live on very little money include: one-parent families, people who are unemployed, elderly people, people who are sick or disabled, a single earner, unskilled couples (where only one person works in an unskilled job).

People on low income may have enough money for food, for some clothes and for heating, but poverty means that there is little money for the interesting purchases that buy into exciting lifestyles. People who depend on benefits have limited life choices.

The government's 'Opportunity for all' (1999) publication states that:

* the number of people living in households with low incomes had more than doubled since the late 1970s
* one in three children lived in households with below half average income
* nearly one in five working-age households had no one in work
* the poorest communities had much more unemployment, poor housing, vandalism and crime than richer areas.

The problems which prevent people from making the most of their lives are characterised in the publication as:

* **Lack of opportunities to work** – work is the most important route out of low income but the consequences of being unemployed go wider than lack of money. It can contribute to ill health and can deny future employment opportunities.
* **Lack of opportunities to acquire education and skills** – adults without basic skills are much more likely to spend long periods out of work.
* **Childhood deprivation** – with its linked problems of low income, poor health, poor housing and unsafe environments.
* **Disrupted families** – the evidence shows that children in lone-parent families are particularly likely to suffer the effects of persistently low household incomes. Stresses within families can lead to exclusion; in extreme cases to homelessness.
* **Barriers to older people living active, fulfilling and healthy lives** – too many older people have low incomes, lack of independence and poor health. Lack of access to good-quality services are key barriers to social inclusion.
* **Inequalities in health** – health can be affected by low income and a range of socio-economic factors, such as access to good-quality health services and shops selling good-quality food at affordable prices.
* **Poor housing** – this directly diminishes people's quality of life and leads to a range of physical and mental health problems, and can cause difficulties for children trying to do homework.
* **Poor neighbourhoods** – the most deprived areas suffer from a combination of poor housing, high rates of crime, unemployment, poor health and family disruption.
* **Fear of crime** – crime and fear of crime can effectively exclude people within their own communities, especially older people.
* **Disadvantaged groups** – some people experience disadvantage or discrimination, for example, on the grounds of age, ethnicity, gender or disability. This makes them particularly vulnerable to **social exclusion**.

The cycle of disadvantage

When children are born into an environment in which they experience discrimination, poverty, poor housing and lack of opportunity they are less likely to develop the social and academic skills of more advantaged children. They are, therefore, unlikely to get the best jobs. Very often children who are born 'poor' are likely to stay 'poor'. This situation is called a 'cycle of disadvantage', because the disadvantage is recycled to each new generation.

Think it over...

Living on a low income might lead to a whole range of other problems that are not just about debt. For example, if you have a low income, you might live in a poor neighbourhood; if you live in a poor neighbourhood you may experience more fear of crime.

Can you think of any other issues that might link with a low income?

Identifying own beliefs and prejudices

We all learn to simplify our world in order to make it easier to cope with. It is easy to make assumptions that people who are different are perhaps bad, frightening or 'best avoided'. Skilled care work might depend on identifying ways of coping with our own emotions. Some brief examples of prejudiced beliefs and reactions are set out in Figure 2.38, together with some ideas for avoiding discriminatory reactions.

Think it over...

Can you think of other examples where you can challenge assumptions that you might make?

Celebrating diversity

Equality between different groups in society cannot happen if some groups are seen as being superior to others. Differences between people such as race, gender, class, sexuality and age, must be valued. Learning about differences and trying to understand individual beliefs and needs is an essential skill for promoting equality.

One advantage of celebrating diversity is that it will help to create a fairer and more just society. But valuing diversity might also make your own life more interesting and exciting. If you are open to understanding other people's life experience and differences you may be able to achieve the benefits shown in Figure 2.39 for yourself.

Employers are likely to want to employ people who value diversity because:

* effective anti-discriminatory care depends on staff valuing diversity
* GSCC codes of practice require workers to respect diversity and employers to provide training to assist workers to develop skills
* people who value diversity are likely to be flexible and creative
* people who value diversity may make good relationships with one another and with service users
* diverse teams often work very effectively. If everyone has the same skills and interests then team members may compete.

SITUATION	RISK OF PREJUDICE	ALTERNATIVE
A service user comes from a different culture	Not understanding the service user's needs Avoidance, stereotyping and labelling	Using skilled conversation and listening in order to build an understanding of the other person
A service user has a learning difficulty	Thinking that the service user is a damaged or 'sad' individual	Using appropriate values and communication skills to learn about the unique individual nature of this person
A service user has different beliefs from you	Labelling difference as 'mad' or 'bad'	Thinking of difference as an interesting experience rather than a threat to one's own beliefs

FIGURE 2.38 *Some examples of prejudiced beliefs and reactions*

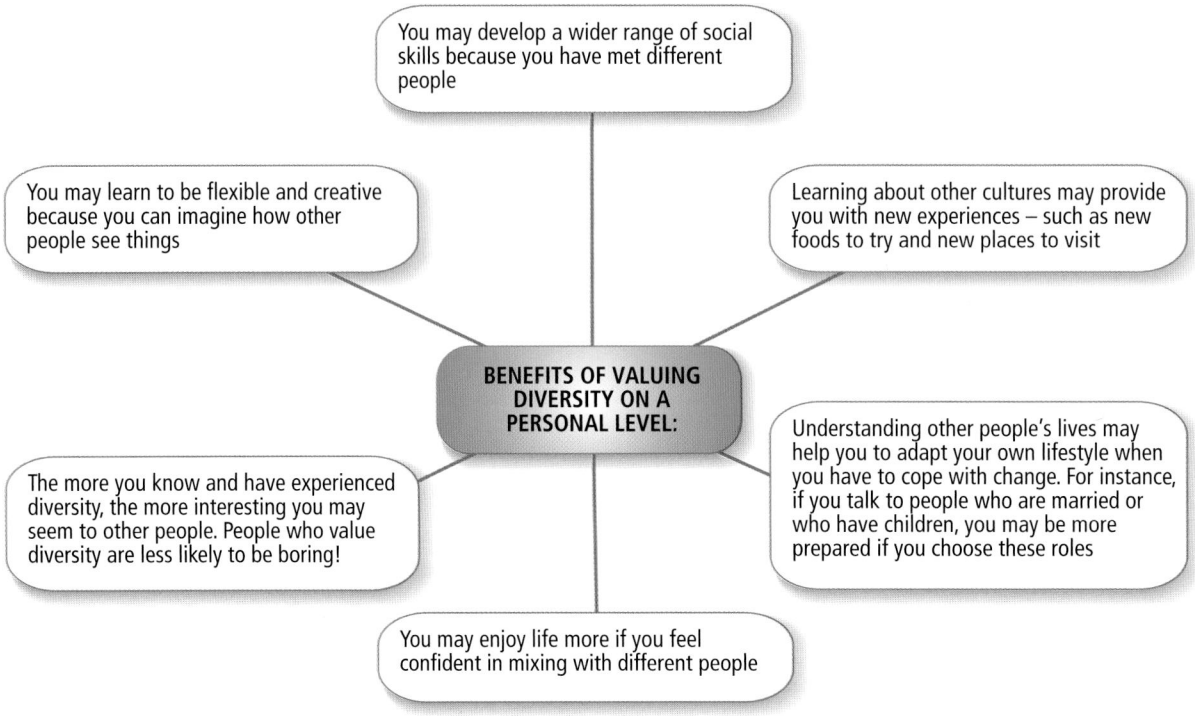

FIGURE 2.39 *Benefits gained through understanding other people's life experiences and differences*

Summary of Section 2.2

The following key areas of theory have been covered in this section:

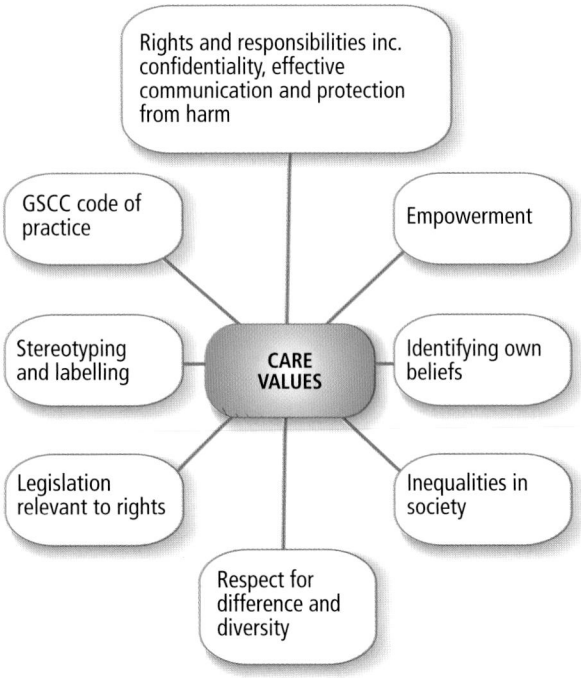

Consider this

Palvinder grew up in a low-income family on a housing estate. Palvinder was often ill and missed a great deal of school when he was young. Palvinder has bad memories of the school that he attended; he says that he was bullied and called names. Palvinder now lives in a housing complex with people who have a learning difficulty. He is happy there and says that the people who work in the housing complex are 'nice'.

Using concepts, can you identify?

1. Examples of the kind of discrimination that Palvinder may have experienced.
2. Examples of care worker values that might contribute to Palvinder feeling happy at the housing centre.

Go further – can you analyse issues using theory?

Staff in the housing complex say that they work in an anti-discriminatory way and that they try to empower service users. What might this mean for Palvinder?

Go further – can you evaluate using a range of theory?

Palvinder experienced a range of disadvantage and discrimination when he was young. In what way can care values expressed in codes of practice, and legislation that provide rights contribute to a better quality of life for service users?

2.3 Transmission of values

Awareness of needs

Care workers often work with people who have experienced abuse, are afraid, or who do not understand what might happen next. They are often vulnerable people who feel threatened by what they are experiencing. Care staff must use effective communication skills if they are to meet the needs of the people they work with.

Human needs are complex. In the past it was sometimes assumed that physical needs should always take priority over other social and cultural needs. Today physical needs are often seen as the foundation for working with people, but not always the most important issue to address. One way of understanding human needs is through the work of Abraham Maslow (1908–1970). Maslow's theory was that the purpose of human life was personal growth. That is, the quality of a human life can be understood in terms of an individual's development of his or her own ability and potential. Before a person can fully develop his or her potential, there are levels of need (called deficiency needs) which first have to be met. **Maslow's hierarchy** of needs is often set out as a pyramid, as shown below on the left-hand side of Figure 2.40. The role of communication in meeting human needs is described on the right-hand side of the diagram.

Effective communication needs to operate at every level of the triangle. It is important to give and receive clear information about physical needs in order to respond to those needs. A lack of clear communication may result in a person's physical needs being unmet.

Listening skills are vital in order to create the basis for psychological safety and to reduce the threat that members of the public may feel. If people do not feel that they have been listened to they may feel disrespected. A lack of respect may create a feeling of low self-esteem and emotional vulnerability. As well as this, individuals may feel that they are physically at risk because their needs have not been understood. Effective body

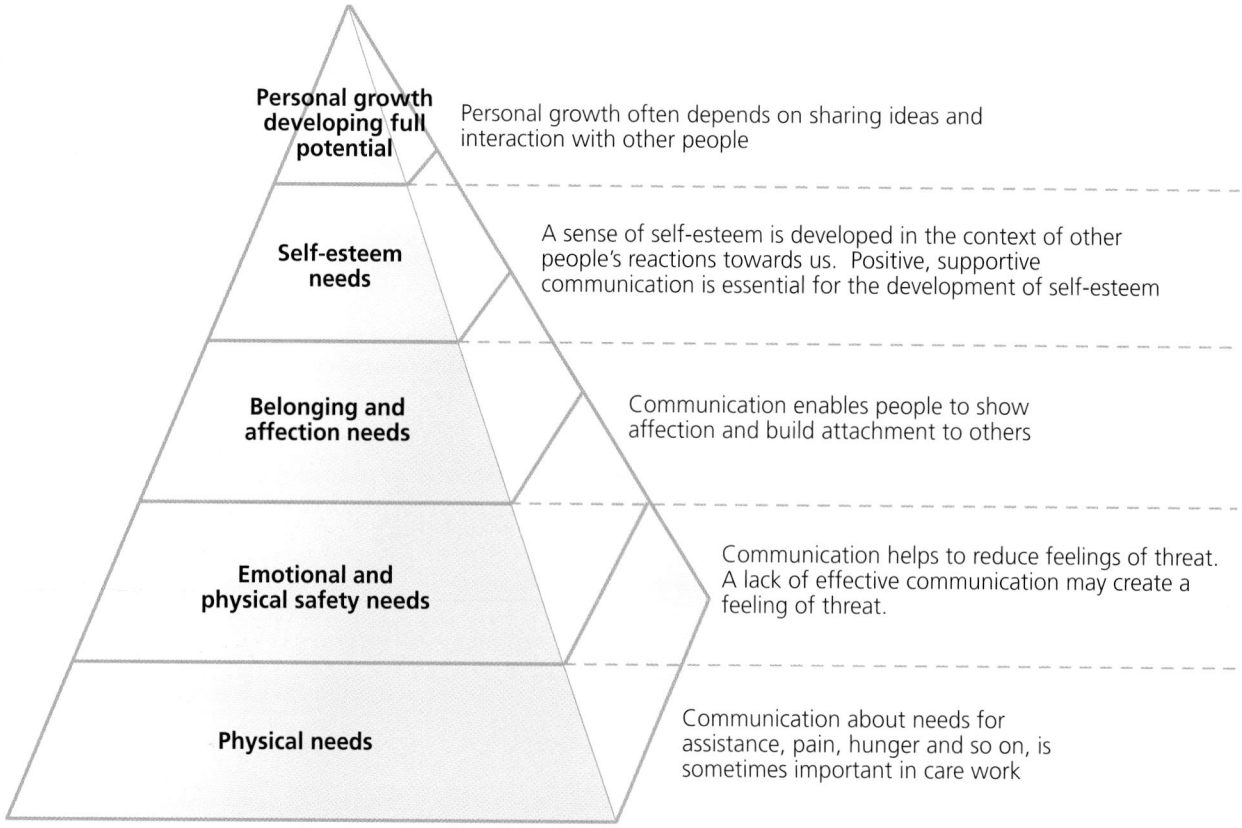

FIGURE 2.40 *Communication within Maslow's hierarchy of needs*

language is vital to establish professional relationships and create a sense of safety and belonging with people in care.

Establishing and maintaining relationships

Being good at establishing relationships may require supportive behaviour.

Supportive body language

Muscle tone, facial expression, eye contact and posture can send messages of being friendly. When meeting a person it is usually appropriate to smile, to express interest through eye contact and to maintain a relaxed posture – free of muscle tension. This indicates a readiness to talk and listen. It is difficult to define a simple set of rules for supportive body language because each individual will have his or her own expectations about what is appropriate and normal. The settings in which conversation takes place can influence how people should behave. The most important thing about supportive body language is to learn to monitor the effects that our behaviour is having on another person. Being supportive involves being aware of your own non-verbal behaviour and monitoring how your non-verbal behaviour is affecting others. Section 2.1 explores the components of non-verbal communication in more depth.

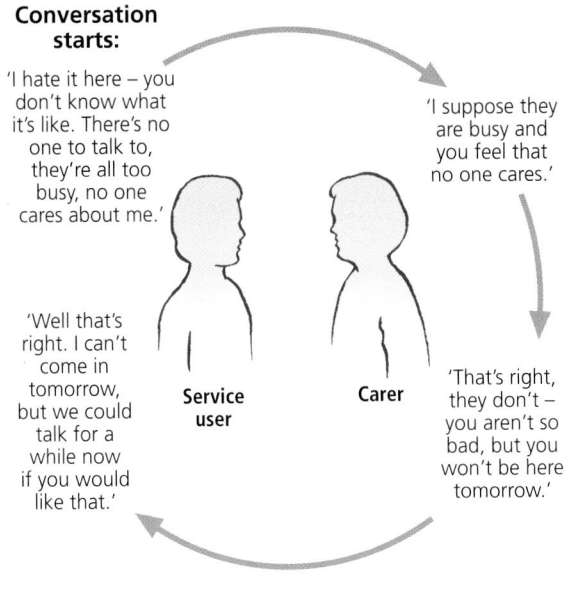

FIGURE 2.41 *Developing a supportive sense of warmth involves being non-judgemental*

As well as the communication skills outlined in Section 2.1, it is important that service users feel emotionally safe and able to share experiences. The skills for creating a sense of emotional safety were first identified by Carl Rogers (1902–1987). Originally these skills were seen as a basis for counselling relationships, but they have since become adopted as a basis for any befriending or **supportive relationship**. There are three conditions for a supportive conversation and these are that the carer must show (or convey) a sense of warmth, understanding and sincerity to the other person. These conditions sometimes have other names:

* warmth (sometimes called acceptance)
* understanding (originally called empathy)
* sincerity (originally called genuineness).

Showing warmth

The ideal is to get to know the service user in a sensitive manner and share experiences.

Warmth means being seen as a warm, accepting person. In order to influence another person to view you this way, you will need to demonstrate that you do not stereotype and label others. You will need to demonstrate that you do not judge other people as good or bad, right or

Think it over...

Imagine that you feel sad about something and that you explain your problems to a friend. How would you feel if your friend did not look at you and instead seemed interested in what was happening outside the window? How would you feel if your friend just 'parroted' things you said back to you? How would you react if he or she just said things like 'I know', or 'Yes' all the time – without sounding sincere or interested?

Being a good friend involves supportive behaviour. How good are you at showing others that you understand their feelings?

wrong. This is sometimes referred to as a non-judgemental attitude.

Conveying warmth means being willing to listen to others. It means being able to prove that you are listening to a person because you can remember what he or she has said to you. Warmth involves using **active listening**. That is, you give your attention to the person when talking, and remember what he or she said. You can then reflect the words back again.

In Figure 2.41, the carer is able to show the service user that she is listening by repeating some of the things that the service user has said. The repetition is not 'parrot fashion'; the carer has used her own way of speaking. The carer also avoids being judgmental. When the service user says that no one cares, the carer does not argue. The carer might have felt like saying, 'How can you say that – don't you know how hard we work for you? You want to think yourself lucky – there's plenty of people who would be pleased to be here; other people don't complain'. This advice to think yourself lucky and comparison with other people is judgmental. The statement does not value the other person, and it is not warm. If the carer had said these things it would have blocked the conversation. Warmth makes it safe for the service user to express his feelings. Warmth means that the carer can disagree with what the service user has said, since the service user feels safe that he will not be put down.

In developing the skill of showing warmth, it is important not to judge. Carers should accept that people have the right to be the way they are, and to make their own choices. While you may disapprove of a person's behaviour, you must show that you do not dislike him or her as an individual. This is particularly important when working with people with difficult behaviour. It is essential that individuals know it is the behaviour which is disliked, not them as a person.

Conveying understanding

Understanding means learning about the individual identity and beliefs that a person has. Carl Rogers saw the idea of understanding or empathy as the ability to experience another person's world as if it was your own world. The key part being the 'as if'. We always understand our own world and we know that other people have different experiences from our own. It is important to try to really understand others' thoughts and feelings.

Active listening provides a useful tool to enable carers to learn about people. If a person is listened to, he or she may experience a feeling of being understood. If the carer is warm and non-judgemental, it becomes safe for a service user to talk about his or her life. If the carer checks that he or she understands the service user, that person may feel valued. As the person feels that they are valued, so he or she may talk more. The more the person talks, the more the carer has a chance to learn about the service user.

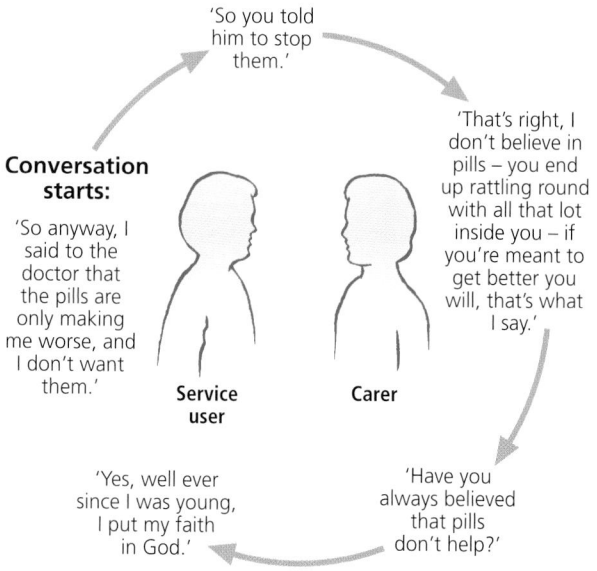

FIGURE 2.42 *Developing a supportive sense of understanding involves active listening*

In Figure 2.42, listening and conveying warmth the carer is being given the privilege of learning about the service user's religious views. Understanding can grow from a conversation that conveys value for the other person. A sense of trust may develop out of a sense of understanding. If you feel you are understood then you may feel it is safe to share your thoughts and worries.

Conveying sincerity

Being sincere means being open about what you say and the way that you speak. It means not acting – not using set phrases or professional styles that do not reflect your true self. In some ways being sincere means being yourself – being honest and real. Being real has to involve being non-judgemental though – trying to understand people rather than trying to give people advice. If being honest means giving other people your advice – don't do it! However, when you listen and learn about other people, do use your own normal language. Think about ways you might describe yourself and occasionally share details of your own life with the people you are helping. Sometimes it is necessary to share your thoughts to keep a conversation going. Sharing information from your own life might help to convey sincerity or genuineness in some situations.

FIGURE 2.43 *Sharing information about your own life may help to convey sincerity*

Understanding, warmth and sincerity have to be combined in order to provide a safe, supportive setting.

Learning to create a supportive relationship with people will involve practice and a great deal of self-monitoring and reflection. If you practise conveying warmth, understanding and sincerity, it will be important to get feedback from colleagues, supervisors and most importantly service users.

You may be able to tell if your communication is effective because the other person may reflect your behaviour. That is, if you are warm and understanding the other person may come to trust you; then you may find that this person is warm and friendly toward you. If you are honest and sincere, people may be honest and sincere with you. The quality of a supportive relationship should become a two-way process.

Establishing and maintaining relationships

Think it over...

You could try the following ideas for developing your relationship skills.

1. Work with a friend. Take turns in imagining that you are upset or sad whilst the other person uses reflective listening skills. Tape-record the conversation. Play the tape back and evaluate your performance in terms of warmth, understanding and sincerity.
2. Watch videos of conversational skills or counselling situations where warmth, understanding and sincerity are demonstrated. Discuss how this is effective and how you might develop your own conversational skills.
3. Think about your own conversations with service users – keep a logbook to reflect on your skills development.
4. Write up examples of being warm, understanding and sincere and discuss your examples with your tutor – ask for feedback.

The importance of identity and the worth of others

In order to enjoy life, it is very important that adults develop a sense of personal identity. If you feel confident that you understand your own abilities and your relationships with others then you may feel in control of your life.

Self-esteem and feeling that life is worthwhile depend on the development of a secure **identity**. Children develop a sense of self through the quality of their relationships with other people. If you work with children you may influence their development of identity in terms of the relationships that they experience.

If you work with adults or older adults it is very important that communication work shows respect for identity. One of the main ways to 'promote a person's identity' is to listen and build an understanding of his or her life. Listening and understanding skills are explained in Section 2.1. Listening and showing that you understand usually creates a feeling that you have been respectful.

Respect for difference

It is very important that people are not 'treated all the same'. Each person in care will be different from other people in terms of his or her ethnicity, gender, age group, religion, social class and chosen lifestyle. Together with these differences each person will have a unique set of personal characteristics, attitudes and emotions. If you get to know each person as an individual and you make it clear that you can remember some personal details, then you can show that you are working with or 'transmitting' care values.

Sometimes, listening involves switching into a store of knowledge and understanding. For some people, this is a conscious 'switching on' process. We switch on by remembering details of another person; perhaps we can recall when we last talked to this individual and what he or she said. Transmitting respect for individual differences may depend on being able to remember these important details; for example, greeting another person using a word of welcome in his or her own first language, remembering a recent event such as a visit of grandchildren, or discussing an interest that you know that person has, such as music.

Some key ideas for transmitting care values are set out in Figure 2.44.

Consider this

Sarah works as a home care worker with older people in their own homes. Sarah takes time to learn and remember the personal likes and dislikes of each person that she works with. Many service users feel safe to talk about their life histories and their current interests and worries with Sarah. Although service user plans specify the work that Sarah is supposed to do, Sarah always asks how service users would like tasks such as cleaning to be done. Service users are full of praise for Sarah, saying things like 'Oh you couldn't want for a better person – she is so kind and thoughtful.'

Using concepts, can you identify?

1. Evidence that suggests that Sarah is good at building supportive relationships with service users.
2. Examples of respect for service users' rights.

Go further – can you analyse issues using theory?

Service users say that Sarah is kind and thoughtful. Sarah might achieve this response because she is good at transmitting care values. What care values might guide Sarah's work?

Go further – can you evaluate using a range of theory?

Sarah is using a range of skilled communication, values and supportive skills in order to build successful caring relationships. Can you imagine how the theory in this unit can be used to explain successful caring relationships?

COMMUNICATING CARE VALUES THROUGH:	KEY IDEAS
Awareness of needs	It is very important to understand the self-development, self-esteem and belonging needs of service users and not be limited to understanding only the basic physical and safety needs of people
Relationships	Use the supportive skills of 'understanding', 'warmth' and 'sincerity' in order to build appropriate caring relationships
Understanding a service user	Learning about others is a key way to show that you value them. Formal techniques for understanding a service user's life history include: life story work with children and adults; life review and reminiscence work with older people
Respect for differences	Never 'treat everybody the same' – this is not equal opportunity. Alter your verbal and non-verbal behaviour to show respect for each different service user
Maintaining personal dignity	Giving physical care such as washing, dressing, feeding and cleaning should focus on making the service user feel that he or she is respected. Feeding someone should not be just about putting food in his or her mouth, it should also meet emotional and social needs
Providing choice	Always offer choices – when service users cannot do things for themselves they can still be offered a choice of how they would like you to do things for them. How would a service user like to be fed? When would he or she like to eat?
Encouraging independence	A sense of self grows out of the choices and decisions that we make. Learning to travel, learning independent living skills, learning to operate a computer helps to create a sense of self-esteem. Care workers often focus on helping people to be independent rather than being dependent on others
Confidentiality	Each work setting will have policies and procedures to follow in order to ensure confidentiality. Check out the procedures that you need to follow in relationship to a given care setting
Praise	Praise can be very effective in influencing children, but adults will interpret praise as patronising if it does not seem genuine. It is important to establish an understanding of another person's identity in order to be supportive and sincere when offering praise
Promoting identity	One theory of identity (Glynis Breakwell, 1986) suggests that identity involves self-esteem, a feeling of being special and a sense of own history or life journey. If you listen to service users and communicate the care values set out in this table, you will contribute to the development and maintenance of a service user's identity

FIGURE 2.44 *Some ideas for transmitting care values*

UNIT 2 ASSESSMENT

How you will be assessed

In order to achieve this unit you must produce a report of an interaction with at least one other person in a care setting. The person you are interacting with should be either a child, an older person, someone who is ill, or someone with specific needs such as learning or hearing difficulties.

If you want to work towards a higher grade your report will need to cover more than one interaction and might include communication with groups of people.

You will be given instructions regarding the structure of the report, but your report will need to include evidence for each of the following:

ASSESSMENT OBJECTIVE		DETAILS
A01	Types of Communication Used and Care Values	You must explain the types and range of communication skills you have used. Your discussion of communication must show that you are aware ofthe 'care value base'.
A02	Transmission of Care Values	You must explain how you have used and transmitted care values in the way you have communicated with other people.
A03	Barriers to Communication	You must explain possible barriers to communication that might have existed and explain how you overcame any barriers that you identified.
A04	Evaluation of your report	You must evaluate your interactions, explaining how well the interactions proceeded, and draw conclusions from the evidence of the interactions that you have collected. You must also discuss the features of a group, or individual situation that you would need to take into consideration when evaluating the success of your interaction(s).

Assessment preparation

A01 Communication skills

You need to produce a report that explains the types and range of communication skills that you have used in interactions with others. The Rating Scale below may help you to identify and then to evaluate some of the skills that you have used.

The rating scale

How good were different aspects of non-verbal communication?

How to rate behaviour

Place a circle around the number that fits your observation:

1 Very effective and appropriate use of a skill.
2 Some appropriate use of the skill.
3 The skill was not demonstrated or it does not seem appropriate to comment on the area.
4 Some slightly ineffective or inappropriate behaviour in relation to the area.
5 Very inappropriate or ineffective behaviour in relation to the area.

Eye contact	1 2 3 4 5
Facial expression	1 2 3 4 5
Angle of head	1 2 3 4 5
Tone of voice	1 2 3 4 5
Position of hands and arms	1 2 3 4 5
Gestures	1 2 3 4 5
Posture	1 2 3 4 5
Muscle tension	1 2 3 4 5
Touch	1 2 3 4 5
Proximity	1 2 3 4 5

How good were verbal communication and listening skills?

Appropriate language (speech community and register)	1	2	3	4	5
Encouraging others to talk	1	2	3	4	5
Reflecting back what others have said	1	2	3	4	5
Using appropriate questions	1	2	3	4	5
Use of prompts	1	2	3	4	5
Using silence as a listening skill	1	2	3	4	5
Clarity of conversation	1	2	3	4	5
Pace of conversation	1	2	3	4	5
Turn taking	1	2	3	4	5

(Use the same rating instructions as for non-verbal communication above.)

This grid may help you to analyse and provide examples of your communication skills. In order to achieve the highest marks your report will need to go beyond a description of skills and you will need to provide comparisons and contrasts between different interactions. You will also need to explain some of the theory that helps you to understand what is happening as you interact with others. Your analysis of interaction will also require an analysis of how effectively you transmitted care values (see below).

VALUE	WHAT EVIDENCE CAN YOU FIND THAT YOU TRANSMITTED THESE VALUES?
Respect for individual identity	
Valuing diversity and equality	
Preventing discrimination	
Maintaining confidentiality	
Respecting individual rights to make choices	
Empowering others rather than expecting them to be dependent	

A02 The transmission of care values

Thinking about your interactions, how far were you able to maintain care values? The grid above identifies some issues that you may wish to comment on in your report in order to evidence your awareness of the care value base.

In order to achieve the highest marks you should identify how your interaction has protected and maintained the self-esteem and identity of others. You will also need to discuss the importance of the care value base in relation to other care settings and not just in terms of your own analysis of interaction.

A03 Barriers

You must produce a report that explains possible barriers to communication within your interactions and how you overcame any barriers that you identified. The grid overleaf provides a starting point that might help you to identify barriers and analyse your interaction.

The barriers to communication grid

Rating scale:

1 Good – there are no barriers.
2 Quite good – few barriers.
3 Not possible to decide or not applicable.
4 Poor – barriers identified.
5 Very poor – major barriers to communication.

BARRIERS					
In the environment					
Lighting	1	2	3	4	5
Noise levels	1	2	3	4	5
Opportunity to communicate	1	2	3	4	5
Language differences					
Appropriate use of language:(terminology and level of formality)	1	2	3	4	5
Carer's skills with different languages	1	2	3	4	5
Carer's skills with non-verbal communication	1	2	3	4	5
Availability of translators or interpreters	1	2	3	4	5
Assumptions and/or stereotypes	1	2	3	4	5
Emotional barriers					
Stress levels and tiredness	1	2	3	4	5
Carer stressed by the emotional needs of others	1	2	3	4	5
Cultural barriers					
Inappropriate assumptions made about others	1	2	3	4	5
Labelling or stereotyping present	1	2	3	4	5
Interpersonal skills					
Degree of supportive non-verbal behaviour	1	2	3	4	5
Degree of supportive verbal behaviour	1	2	3	4	5
Appropriate use of listening skills	1	2	3	4	5
Appropriate use of assertive skills	1	2	3	4	5
Appropriate maintenance of confidentiality	1	2	3	4	5

Once you have identified potential barriers you need to research other people's perception of these issues. You might discuss your analysis of your interaction with a tutor or colleague. If possible it would be ideal to discuss your work with a member of staff in the care setting where your interactions took place.

The views of service users are vitally important when evaluating a service; and it might be possible for you to ask service users about language and environmental barriers. It will be important to plan any questioning work carefully and to check your plans with a tutor before undertaking any research.

In order to achieve the highest marks you will need to take the initiative in obtaining feedback from others. You should analyse why people have responded in the way that they have. You will need to gain information from different sources and to provide an analysis of the issues you have identified.

A04 Evaluation of your report

You must provide an evaluation of how well your interactions went and draw conclusions from the evidence you were able to gather. To achieve the highest marks you will need to evidence independent thinking and initiative. You will need to be able to show that you have fully understood what took place during your interactions and what impact you had on others. You will need to be able to give reasons for any conclusions you make and these conclusions will need to be supported with evidence.

Unit test

1 Identify five examples of areas of the body that can send messages to other people as body language

2 Identify three verbal (including para-language) and three body language behaviours associated with assertive behaviour

3 If you talk to a four-year-old child, skilful verbal and non-verbal communication is likely to involve different skills compared with adult communication. Identify four verbal or non-verbal aspects of communication that you would adapt for creating a friendly conversation with young children.

4 If you plan to interview a care worker about values in care identify two issues that you would need to think about and plan before starting the interview.

5 List three ways in which you could help to 'promote a service user's identity.

6 Identify three communication skills that you believe would be important for a care worker to use in order to maintain a conversation about an older person's past life.

7 Explain how you could identify whether or not care values were being effectively transmitted within a conversation between an adult service user and a care worker.

8 Explain three different types of barriers to communication that you might identify within a day service for people with learning difficulty.

9 Why is it important to understand cultural differences in communication?

10a When service users receive a service they will have certain rights and responsibilities - where do these rights are responsibilities come from?

10b Why is it important that service users have rights?

The answers to these questions are provided on page 157 of this book.

References and further reading

Bales, R. (1970) *Personality and Interpersonal Behaviour* (New York: Holt, Rinehart & Winston)

Benson, J.F. (2001) *Working more creatively with Groups (2nd Ed.)* (London and New York: Routledge)

Breakwell, G. (1986) *Coping with Threatened Identities* (London and New York: Methuen)

Descombes, C. (2004) *The smoke and mirrors of empowerment: a critique of user-professional partnership* in *Communication, Relationships and Care,* Robb, M.,Barrett, S.,Komaromy, C., and Rogers, A. (eds) (i.e.) (London & New York OU & Routledge)

Maslow, A.H. (1970) *Motivation and Personality (2nd Edition)* (New York: Harper & Row)

Rogers, C.R. (1951) *Client Centred Therapy* (Boston: Houghton Mifflin)

Thompson, N. (1997) *Anti-discriminatory Practice* (Basingstoke and London: Macmillan)

Tuckman, B. (1965) *Development Sequence in Small Groups,* in Psychological Bulletin, Vol 63, No 6

Key resources

Johnson D. and Johnson F. (1997) *Joining together: group theory and group skills (6th Ed.)*(Allyn & Bacon)

Pease, A. (1997) *Body Language* (London: Sheldon Press)

Thompson N (1996) *People skills* (Basingstoke and London: Macmillan)

Thompson N. (2001) *Anti-Discriminatory Practice (2nd Ed.)* (Basingstoke and London: Macmillan)

At a more advanced level:

Hargie, O. (ed.) (1997) *The Handbook of Communication Skills (2nd Ed.)* (London and New York: Routledge)

Relevant websites

Please see www.heinemann.co.uk/hotlinks (express code 370XP) for links to the following websites, which may provide a source of updated information:

* Commission for Racial Equality
* Equal Opportunities Commission
* General Social Care Council
* The Nursing and Midwifery Council

UNIT 3

Positive Care Environments

This unit contains the following sections:

3.1 Values and individual rights

3.2 Barriers to access

3.3 Creating a positive environment

3.4 How society promotes service users' rights

Introduction

This unit addresses the main issues involved in achieving and maintaining a positive care environment. It begins by exploring the importance of values and beliefs in creating a positive care environment. An explanation of the different barriers to access is given, and the nature and dangers associated with discrimination are explored in detail. The third section considers the ways in which institutional policies, practices and culture can both hinder and promote service users' rights. Finally, the role of law in promoting service users' rights and the mechanisms that exist to enable service users to challenge unfair or discriminatory actions are examined. A discussion of current law and policy in relation to service user rights is also included.

How you will be assessed

This unit is internally assessed. You must produce a written report.

3.1 Values and individual rights

The nature of values and ethics

Positive care environments make an enormous difference to the quality of life of both the service users and the staff. It takes a lot of work to create and maintain a good care setting but the effort makes it a much more rewarding place to work. Consider the example below.

SCENARIO

The Mansion

Staff spend the majority of time in face-to-face contact with the residents. Meal times are flexible and there is a choice of menus to ensure people's dietary and religious food needs are followed. The furniture is up to date and clean. Residents have activities arranged to suit their preferences and interests. The television is only put on when the residents request to watch it. There are often trips out to places of interest. A hairdresser and beautician visit every week. The manager speaks to the residents every day to check how they are feeling. Records are filled in three times per day with action points, which are ticked off when they have been completed. The staff get on well with each other and are keen to go on training courses to update their skills and knowledge. People enjoy their life in the Mansion.

How should carers behave? Make a list of at least five values that might guide the staff in 'The Mansion'.

Today, a great deal of care is provided in people's own homes, but wherever care is provided it is important to understand that positive care environments do not just happen: they have to be created and require ongoing maintenance. This demands key skills of self-awareness and a commitment to the rights of others. Care environments reflect the **values** held by society in general, as well as the aims and goals of the organisation. The personal values of the manager and care workers also are very important in setting the atmosphere of the care environment.

Values involve a judgement that is made about the worth or importance of a particular action, attitude, behaviour, person or situation. These judgements are made on the basis of unconscious and conscious views that we hold. Some views may reflect our upbringing and the values we have learned from our parents. Other values may be shaped by public attitudes as expressed in the media. In health and social care environments, values relate to the judgements made about the moral worth and acceptable standards of behaviour in other people. Values have a fundamental effect on how a care environment is run. The values held by society and individuals change over time. In some cases the change is radical.

* DID YOU KNOW?

One hundred years ago values and attitudes towards people with psychiatric illness were very negative. People with a mental illness were viewed as dangerous and therefore the care environments created were like massive hospitals, built in remote rural areas separated from the rest of society.

Even just 80 years ago a homeless, single mother could be deemed to be 'mentally defective' for having a child. This was because of a belief that all children should be born within marriage. Some single mothers were held in hospitals for the remainder of their lives.

So, although values may be held on an individual basis, general social values and attitudes also influence the type of care environments that are created.

Key concept

Values: Values are beliefs that identify 'something that is valued' or 'valuable' in a situation. Beliefs and values can influence what people do and the choices and decisions that they make.

Key concept

Ethics: **Ethics** are formally stated principles that can guide professional decision making.

Because health and social care workers take on a paid professional role they have a high level of responsibility towards service users. There must be a bond of trust between a professional carer and a service user; this principle is stated in the GSCC code of practice (see Unit 2). Workers also have a duty to act for the benefit of service users. These responsibilities and duties are recognised in law and as a result the courts view abuse of a service user by a professional worker very seriously.

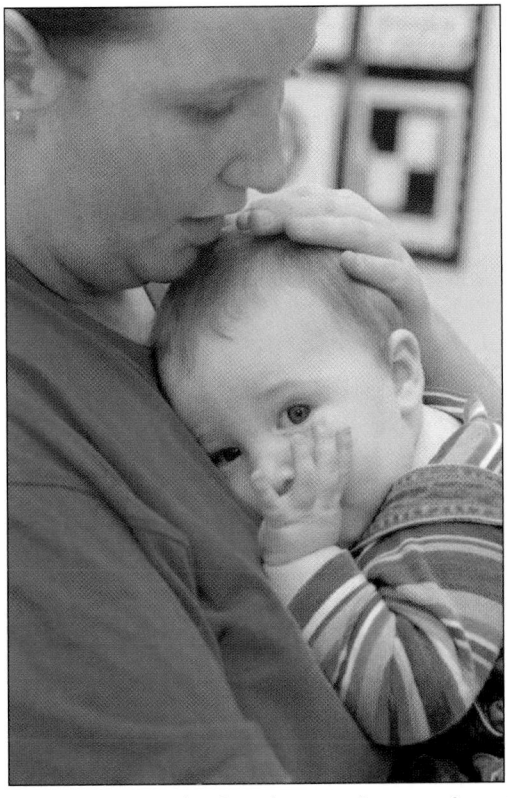

FIGURE 3.1 *Professional carers have a duty to act for the benefit of service users*

Within health and social care there are different approaches to the definition of values. Biestek (1961) compiled a list, which includes those shown in Figure 3.2.

Shardlow (1998) describes understanding values and ethics in social care as 'picking up a live, large and very wet fish out of a running stream. Even if you are lucky enough to grab a fish, the chances are, that just when you think you have caught it, the fish will vigorously slip out of your hands and jump back in the stream' (1998: 23). In this extract, he is referring to the different views and opinions in the areas of values and ethics. Often workers in this field might focus on practical tasks and not think more deeply about why they are working in a particular way.

Vulnerability

Values are very important because service users are vulnerable. Many service users are at high risk of experiencing harm. This may be from others in the form of abuse, or it may be that their health is more at risk because of the poor conditions they live in. People can also be vulnerable where they

DEFINITION OF VALUES	
Individualisation	This means that what is done with a service user and how is made to fit his or her individual needs and wishes. One size does not fit all situations and the need for an individual approach is essential
The purposeful expression of feelings	This means that for people to have a good quality of life they need to be able to express their thoughts and feelings and for these to be understood
Emotional acceptance	People need to feel that they belong and are accepted by others
A non-judgmental attitude	This refers to people's need to be understood and their views and feelings not being condemned
Self-determination	People need to feel they have choices and some control over their own lives
Confidentiality	When someone talks about private or sensitive information he or she needs to know that it is safe to do so

FIGURE 3.2 *Biestek's definition of values (1961)*

are ignored and have few services or people to support them. This is often referred to as being vulnerable. Many service users experience high levels of stress when care services are needed. They might be in pain or experiencing **marginalisation** because of their age, race, sexuality or gender; this will also affect their sense of well-being and ability to deal with the particular problems they may be facing.

The rights of an individual cannot be upheld where there is no commitment to a shared set of values. Values must not only be reflected in the policies and procedures of the organisation but also used by individuals on a daily and ongoing basis. To fully understand the fundamental importance of values you need self-awareness of your own beliefs and how you react to different situations. If you are honest and open about your own beliefs and prejudices you can imagine the effect your values may have in a health and social care environment.

Having identified your values, think about how they compare with the values described below. In order to work effectively with vulnerable people it is centrally important that you value and work within the principles of:

* confidentiality
* effective communication
* anti-discriminatory practice
* **empowerment**
* respect for individual choice, identity, culture and beliefs

Together with the service user rights explained in Unit 2, these principles can be seen as forming a value base for care work.

Think it over...

How would you feel about carrying out the activities listed below?

1. Visiting someone who has admitted abusing a child.
2. Providing a care service for someone who has an alcohol addiction.
3. Telling a child they cannot return home.
4. Working with a teenager who tells you they don't want to know, as you will just let them down like everyone else.
5. Working with an asylum seeker who was actively involved in past war crimes.
6. Advising a pregnant teenager.
7. Working with a home owner who wishes to evict an older person because the local authority will not pay the home owner above a certain limit.

Give each activity a score ranging from 1–10 (where 1 equates to feeling confident to and 10 equates to feeling very uncomfortable).

Think about why you have given each score and list the main reason behind each of your answers.

Key concept

Care values/value base: Occupational standards and the GSCC code of practice identify a framework of values and moral rights of service users that can be referred to as care values or a value base for care.

The role of values in positive care

Equality does not happen automatically. Indeed, the source of the many barriers that prevent equality being achieved can be traced back to the values that are held by individuals and **groups**, both consciously and unconsciously. These values are translated into attitudes systems and institutions that make it easier for some groups and individuals to access services, goods and opportunities than others.

The key to developing a positive care environment is to acknowledge how crucial values are (see Figure 3.3).

THE RELATIONSHIP BETWEEN VALUES AND A POSITIVE CARE ENVIRONMENT	
Values affect behaviour	In health and social care, workers have particular relationships of trust and responsibilities for ethical behaviour towards service users
Vulnerability of many services users and carers	Many service users and carers come from vulnerable groups whose needs have been ignored or pushed to the edges of society. The absence of status and power has a major impact on the life chances and well-being of such groups and individuals
The UK consists of many different cultures and groups. Difference is often seen as a threat	In biology, richness and diversity of plant and animal life is seen as a good thing and a sign of health. However, in terms of human society the same value is not always placed on diversity
Self-awareness	Recognising your own values and ways in which you judge the worth of a person or group is essential
Understanding of inequalities in society	You need to be aware of the ways (past and present) that society has failed to treat everyone fairly
Experience of discrimination	Discrimination will be a common experience for many people in need of health or social care services
Anti-discriminatory practices	Good practice in care work will recognise and challenge inequality through anti-discriminatory working
Policies and procedures	Policies and procedures are important in setting standards of behaviour and protecting service users rights, but in themselves they are not sufficient to guarantee that good quality care is maintained at all times
Actively promote equality in social and health care	Equality in social and health care is a meaningless term unless actively promoted at an individual and organisational level

FIGURE 3.3 *The importance of values in developing a positive care environment*

Think it over...

Consider the list below. Which are the most important qualities / values to you personally? Give a maximum of 5 points to the most important area and 1 to the least:

* honesty
* fairness
* kindness
* understanding
* efficiency
* being well organised
* support
* authority
* respect.

What are the most important qualities in a care environment? Are they any different to your own views and, if so, why?

Confidentiality

In situations of stress or need, personal information often needs to be shared. In order to feel comfortable about discussing private concerns, a person needs to feel that there is an emotional climate of safety in which to do so. Information is therefore given in trust to the care worker. A key principle in positive care environments requires that permission is needed from a service user before such information can be shared. It is essential that a service user is confident that the worker can be trusted. Information can also be seen as the property of a person. Breaking confidentiality can cause considerable damage to people whose rights have been infringed.

For example, an older female resident tells a care worker that she was not married when she gave birth to her children. The next day a woman in the next chair leans across and says: 'I hear you had your children when you weren't married'. The care worker has clearly broken the confidence without a good reason and the person whose confidence has been broken will be upset – at the very least – by this loss of trust.

Boundaries to confidentiality

The British Association of Social Workers (BASW) states that confidentiality is, in essence, concerned with faith and trust. The BASW acknowledges a direct relationship between the principle of confidentiality and respect for people. However, confidentiality cannot be seen as an absolute right and might at times conflict with the equally valid rights of others to protection.

SCENARIO

Within boundaries

Ross is a child, aged 6 years, and he tells his teacher that his stepfather has hit him with a belt. He then tells the teacher not to say anything to anyone else, but shows his teacher his bruises. There is a clear duty to protect Ross from further harm and the teacher must break Ross's wish for the information not to go any further. However, suppose that Ross is aged 74 years and tells his care worker that his son has hit him; but he also says that he does not want any action taken. The situation may not be as straightforward, as an adult does have rights to choose what he or she wishes to do.

So there are many difficult areas around the limits of confidentiality, and, at times, it is not easy to balance the right to confidentiality with the right of a vulnerable individual to be protected from harm.

Service users have a right to confidentiality but a responsibility in relation to the rights of others. Confidentiality often has to be kept within boundaries or broken where the rights of others have to balance with the service user's rights. Keeping confidentiality within boundaries occurs when a carer tells his or her manager something that was learned in confidence. The information is not made public so it is still partly confidential. Examples of situations when information may need to be passed to managers are given in Figure 3.4.

A MANAGER NEEDS TO KNOW WHEN:	
SITUATION	**EXAMPLE**
There is a significant risk of harm to a service user	An older person in the community refuses to put her heating on in winter; she may be at risk of harm from the cold
When a service user might be abused	A person who explains that his son takes his money – he might be being financially abused
Where there is a significant risk of harm to others	A person who lives in a very dirty house with mice and rats may be creating a public health risk
Where there is a risk to the carer's health or well-being	A person is very aggressive, placing the carer at risk

FIGURE 3.4 *Examples of situations when information about service users may need to be passed by carers to their managers*

Confidentiality and the need to know

Good care practice involves asking service users if we can let other people know things. It would be wrong to pass on even the data of a person's birthday without asking him or her first. Some people might not want others to celebrate their birthday! Whatever we know about a service user should be kept private unless the person tells us that it is all right to share the information. The exception to this rule is that information can be passed on when others have a right and a need to know it.

Some examples of people who have a need to know about work with service users are:

* the manager – he or she may need to help make decisions, which affect the service user

* colleagues – these people may be working with the same person
* other professionals – these people may also be working with the service user and need to be kept up to date with information.

Giving information

When information is given to other professionals it should be passed on with the understanding that they will keep it confidential. It is important to check that other people are who they say they are. If you answer the phone and someone says they are a social worker or other professional, you should explain that you must phone them back before giving any information. By doing so you will be sure that you are talking to someone at a particular number or within a particular organisation. If you meet a person you don't know, you should ask for proof of identity before passing any information on.

Relatives will often say that they have a right to know about service users. Sometimes it is possible to ask relatives to discuss issues directly with the service user rather than giving information yourself.

Service users have a right to accurate recording of information about them.

FIGURE 3.5 *Sometimes it is possible to ask relatives to discuss issues directly*

The dangers of inaccurate information include:

* serious delays in meeting people's needs
* inability to follow up enquiries
* making mistakes with arrangements for people's care

SCENARIO

Confidentiality

Ethel is 88-years-old and receives home care. One day she says 'Keep this confidential, but I don't take my tablets (pain killers for arthritis and tablets for blood pressure) – I'm saving them so that I can take them all at once and finish my life if my pain gets worse.' Ethel manages to say this before you can tell her that some things can't be kept confidential.

Do you have to keep this information confidential? Ethel has a right to confidentiality, but she also has a responsibility not to involve other people in any harm she may do to herself. She doesn't have a right to involve you. The information about the tablets should be shared with managers and her GP, who can discuss the matter with Ethel.

Ethel's neighbour stops you as you are leaving one day. The neighbour asks 'How is Ethel, is she taking her tablets?'

Can you tell the neighbour of your worries? Before giving any information to anyone, carers have to ask the question 'Does this person have a need to know?' A need to know is different from wanting to know. Ethel's neighbour might just be nosy, and it would be wrong to break the confidentiality without an important reason. If Ethel's GP knows that Ethel doesn't take her tablets, he or she may be able to save Ethel's health or even her life. But the neighbour should not be told.

* missing meetings or important arrangements
* not providing a professional service to people
* failing to organise services for others properly
* other professional workers not having the right information.

Many organisations use printed forms to help staff to ask important questions and check that they have taken accurate information. Service users' personal records are likely to be written on forms that use headings.

The need for confidentiality is more than a moral right; it is a right that is made **law** by the **Data Protection Act 1998**.

The law set out in the Data Protection Act 1998 has been incorporated into the regulations set out by the NCSC and the GSCC. For example, Standard 10 of the **Commission for Social Care Inspection's National Minimum Standards** for Care Homes for Younger Adults is set out in Figure 3.6.

All services now need to have policies and procedures on the confidentiality of recorded information.

Effective communication

Principle 2.2 of the GSCC code of practice identifies that care workers must communicate in an appropriate, open, accurate and straightforward way. In many care situations this will involve the need for active listening skills (see Unit 2). Very often it is the little things that care workers do that will create a sense of trust and confidence when working with service users. Compare the two situations below:

TWO DIFFERENT SCENARIOS	
Scenario A	'Good morning. I'm afraid I haven't got long, just got to change this dressing like I've done before – won't take a minute – OK. All done – bye'.
Scenario B	'Good morning. How did your son get on with that job that you were telling me about yesterday? I'm afraid I can't stay long, I just called in to change the dressing, but I do enjoy our conversations. I often think about the things you tell me. So how does the dressing feel; is it OK? I do hope things work out for your son. I'll see you again in three days time.'

In both situations the technical work – changing a dressing – gets done. But the communication work in scenario A is very limited and might feel mechanical to the service user, who is being processed as though an object. The care worker only discusses the need to change the dressing –

	STANDARD 10
10.1	Staff respect information given by service users in confidence, and handle information about service users in accordance with their home's written policies and procedures and the Data Protection Act 1998, and in the best interests of the service user
10.2	Service users and their families have access to their home's policy and procedures on confidentiality and on dealing with breaches of confidentiality, and staff explain and / or ensure service users understand the policy
10.3	Service users' individual records are accurate, secure and confidential
10.4	Staff know when information given them in confidence must be shared with their manager or others
10.5	Information given in confidence is not shared with families / friends against the service user's wishes
10.6	The home gives a statement on confidentiality to partner agencies, setting out the principles governing the sharing of information

FIGURE 3.6 *Standard 10 of the Commission for Social Care Inspection's National Minimum Standards for Care Homes for Younger Adults*

quickly. In scenario B, the carer becomes involved with the service user, using a range of skills that will help to develop a bond of trust.

Think it over...

Using the theory in Unit 2 can you identify the communication skills that the carer is using in scenario B?

Anti-discriminatory practice

Anti-discriminatory practice means being able to recognise and identify the different levels of discrimination and disadvantage described in Unit 2.

A first step to developing anti-discriminatory practice is to be aware of the inner world that you believe is important and valuable. The beliefs of a person may affect how he or she understands the actions of other people. Generalised or **stereotyped** views about particular groups of people or types of behaviour will be reflected in your speech, language, decisions and actions. In health and social care, this explains why it is so important for workers to be self-aware of the views and attitudes they hold.

FIGURE 3.7 *Stereotyped thinking can result in discriminatory behaviour*

Anti-discriminatory practice firstly requires an understanding and recognition of what discrimination looks like. Secondly, it requires a willingness to change views and actions that disadvantage others. In practice, this means not only thinking about what happens on a day-to-day basis, but also thinking ahead. This will ensure that the rights of service users are being thought about in any future plans. An example of this might be a female Jewish service user. Is her diet in line with her faith? Does she have the opportunity to practise her faith on a daily and weekly basis? Might there be particular newspapers or television channels she might like? Do the staff understand about Jewish religious festivals that are important, and that the Jewish weekly day of worship is on a different day to that of Christians?

Key concept

Non-discrimination: Not discriminating – not damaging other people by providing some people with a better quality of service than others. Not stereotyping or labelling people (see Unit 2). Avoidance of assumptions associated with negative beliefs about disability, age, sexuality, gender, ethnicity, religion and other social groups.

Anti-discrimination: As for non-discrimination above, but with the added principle that you actively identify and challenge discriminatory behaviour – in yourself or in others – or systems that result in discrimination, within your work setting.

The main aim of anti-discriminatory practice is to value difference and to recognise that such differences do not mean that someone is of lesser worth or value. Honest self-awareness and understanding of social prejudice is the key to a lifelong approach to anti-discriminatory practice.

Empowerment

Global economic functioning involves assumptions about consumer choice. Worldwide, consumer behaviour often focuses on individuality and the assertion of individuality in the purchase of goods. European society operates within a framework of individual human rights. Within the United Kingdom there is an assumption that individuals have the right to choose their own lifestyle and make their own decisions as to how they wish to live.

Key concept

Empowerment: Empowerment enables a service user to make choices and take control of his or her own life.

(The opposite of empowerment is dependency, where a service user is expected to accept whatever services the State or his or her carer chooses to provide.)

The concept of '**empowerment**' identifies an individual's right to make choices and be independent. Historically, children and any adults who needed health or care services were seen as needing to be dependent on their carers. If a person was vulnerable then he or she needed to be 'looked after' by somebody, who would make choices and decisions for them. The idea of empowerment challenges this idea of dependency. Empowerment requires health and care services to support vulnerable people to make their own choices. A simple slogan for empowerment might be 'it's my life'. Principle 3 of the GSCC code of practice for social care workers requires workers to 'promote the independence of service users while protecting them as far as possible from danger or harm'. The principle of empowerment might be developed with different service user groups as shown in Figure 3.8.

Respect for individual choice, identity, culture and beliefs

Anti-discrimination and empowerment are not possible without respect for diversity, respect for individual dignity and privacy, and respect for the individual rights of service users. The first principle of the GSCC code of practice emphasises the importance of respect for service users. Without receiving respect from other people it is difficult to feel that you belong, and perhaps impossible to develop positive self-esteem. If you are to maintain a sense of self-esteem you will need to feel that other people respect you.

Think it over...

Imagine you go into a shop and you are ignored whilst people behind you in the queue are served before you. You will probably feel that you are not being respected, and that perhaps you are being discriminated against. How will this affect you?

Imagine that you are in a residential situation and the care staff have favourite people that they look after – but you're not one of them! Care staff ignore you; they prioritise other people's needs and you often can't get attention or help. How will this affect you?

USER	CONCEPT
Young children	Empowerment will stress the educational needs of young people – the need to develop **self-confidence** and **self-esteem**
People with health care needs	Empowerment will stress the person's involvement in the management of an illness, together with the right to make choices about the type and nature of treatment
People with a learning difficulty	Empowerment will stress supporting people to understand possible choices, and enabling people to make important choices
People with a physical disability	Empowerment will stress the importance of the person – the right to be independent and the right to self-esteem. A person should not be seen as a problem!
Older people	Empowerment will again stress the individual's right to maintain personal decision-making, make choices about care and maintain **self-concept** and self-esteem

FIGURE 3.8 *Developing the concept of empowerment with different user groups*

Respecting and valuing others is not just the first principle in the GSCC code; it is perhaps the most central value in any social situation.

Both situations might make you feel angry; both situations might make you want to complain. But you are much more vulnerable in the care situation – it will be much more difficult to walk away from this. A lack of respect may damage your self-esteem whenever this happens, but in a care situation the effects are likely to be amplified.

Policies and procedures

All care organisations will have written policies and procedures that need to be followed with respect to service users' rights. **National Minimum Standards (NMS)** for the different care services will require every organisation to have a documented complaints procedure and a policy on confidentiality. Services are inspected by the **Commission for Social Care Inspection (CSCI)** and this organisation will refer to National Minimum Standards as a basis for its report. Care organisations may have a range of other policy documents including a policy on **advocacy**. Advocacy is explained in Unit 2. Service users may need to work with an advocate in order to understand the choices available to them. Sometimes an advocate might need to make a case for the service user, when the service user cannot express his or her own wishes. Sometimes an empowering approach may not be possible without the services of an advocate.

Redress

Things can and do go wrong in health and social care. However, it is only in the last 30 years that the rights of service users and carers to challenge processes, events and policies have been developed. Redress means making good, or righting a wrong. It also has the idea of compensation and making good the balance within it. All local authorities must have a complaints procedure. This was required by the Local Authorities and Social Services Act 1970. Further directions and regulations have also been issued by the DOH (Department of Health). The Children Act 1989 requires a complaints procedure for actions involving children and families, as does the NHS and Community Care Act 1990.

Many care environments are privately owned or are in the voluntary sector. The requirements of the Care Standards Act 2000 have to be followed. Home Care agencies also now have to be registered. There are minimum standards for different areas as well as more detailed regulations. When the local authority buys a service from an agency the local authority is also responsible for that service as the agency is delivering services that in the past the local authority would have provided. Therefore, organisations like residential and nursing homes are required to have their own complaints procedures but have to follow additional regulations as well. For example, if a concern is raised about injury, ill treatment or neglect to a person in a care environment, the home must let the local Commission for Social Care Inspection know (under Regulation 37 of the Care Homes Regulations). The home must also advise the local authority social services under current Adult Protection Procedures.

Summary of Section 3.1

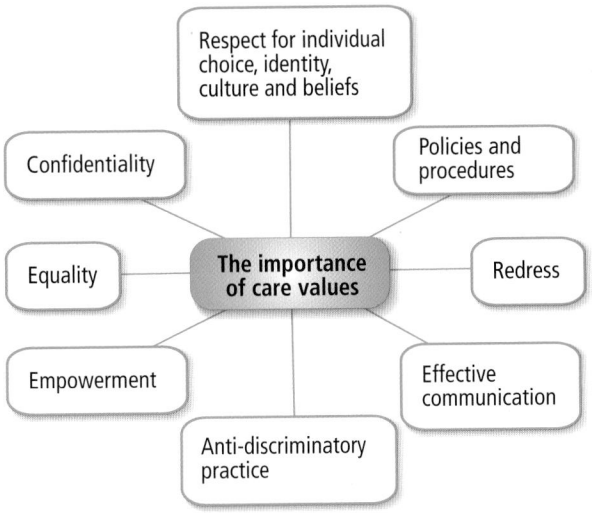

Consider this

You are talking to an adult man who has a degenerative illness that will cause increasing difficulty in coping with daily life. The man says, 'One of the main problems is the way other people see me. People say things like, "Oh, I am so sorry for you". And you know they're trying to help – but it doesn't help. At the moment I can cope with them and make them see me for who I am. I talk about all my achievements, so they start to think about me, instead of seeing me as a diseased body. But I'm so afraid that as I get weaker I won't have the energy to challenge them. They will just see me as a problem and I will start to see myself as a problem. I could lose the will to live.'

FIGURE 3.9 *Listening to the concerns of a service user*

Using concepts can you identify?

1 Examples of care values that are missing in the way that people treat this man.

2 What basic communication approaches might be needed in order to maintain this person's self-esteem.

Go further – can you analyse issues using theory?

What systems of support and redress should exist within a care service in order to help this person maintain personal choice and dignity and not see himself as a problem?

Go further – can you evaluate using a range of theory?

How might care workers use the value base of care in order to avoid assumptions and to communicate a feeling of being valued to this man?

3.2 Barriers to access

Some of the barriers that service users may encounter are identified below.

Language/communication barriers

People who do not speak English as a first language (or Welsh in Wales) may need the services of an interpreter or translator (see Unit 2) to be able to find out about, and be appropriately assessed for services. People who communicate using British Sign Language may also need an interpreter in order to access services. Having to access a different language system is an obvious barrier, but even within the same language, terminology can create a barrier to understanding. Words like 'assessment' may lead to misunderstandings about care services, causing people to ask 'Do I have to pass a test then?' The degree of formality in the communication (see Unit 2) may also have an impact on whether service users feel welcome and valued. The issues listed in Figure 3.11 provide a summary of communication barriers.

FIGURE 3.10 *Reception areas should be designed to assist communication*

Organisational barriers

Sometimes organisations have systems in place that unintentionally excludes certain people. Many organisations expect staff to work long hours and to put family commitments second to work commitments. Promotion to a senior post may depend on always being available to do overtime. But such an organisational culture

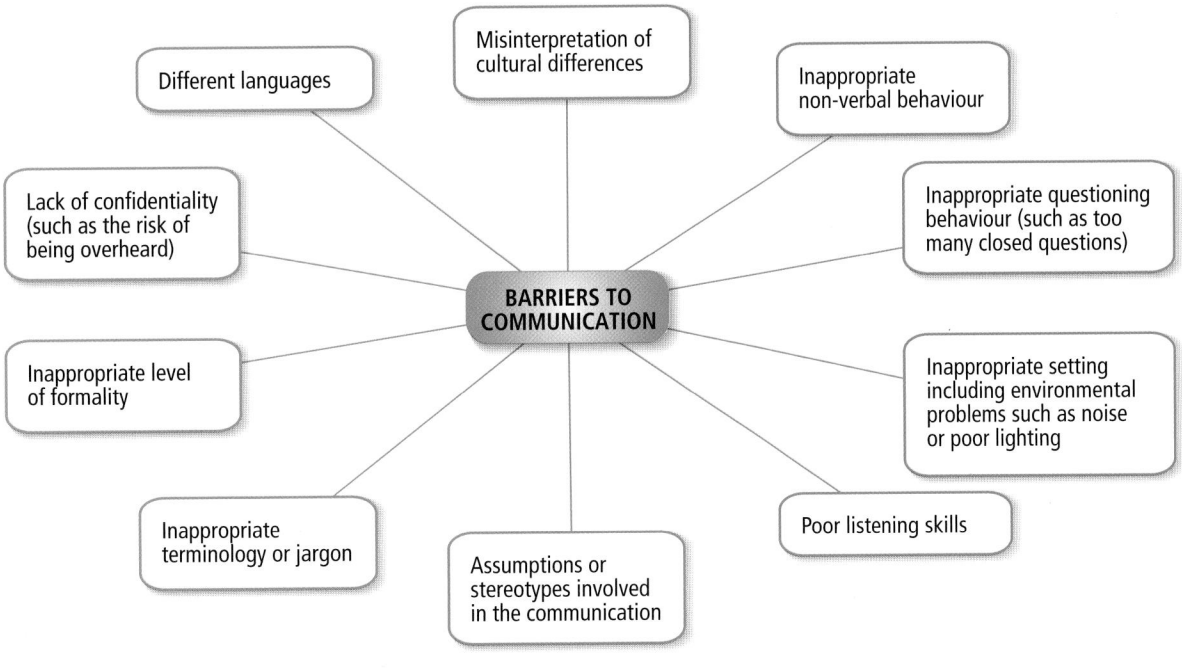

FIGURE 3.11 *A summary of barriers to communication*

might create a barrier for people (usually women) who have child-care responsibilities.

In many organisations 'invisible' organisational barriers exist. For example, less than 3 per cent of judges are black or Asian. Whilst there may well be bias in the selection process, there are underlying factors that place many black people at a disadvantage. For example, there is clear evidence of inequality in educational opportunities for minority communities. In addition, there are sustained high costs associated with entering the legal profession that some families may not be able to meet.

Many women complain of the 'glass ceiling' when it comes to career progression. They experience very real limits to their career, yet there are no obvious policies that are responsible for the lack of women in senior roles. In 2004 the Equal Opportunities Commission (EOC) published a paper entitled 'Sex and power: who runs Britain?' In a press release Julie Mellor, the chair of the Equal Opportunities Commission, stated: 'Almost 30 years since the Sex Discrimination Act was passed, women are still massively under-represented in positions of influence in Britain. No one can argue anymore that it's just a matter of time until more women make it to the top . . . Women are still often prevented from getting to the top because they take on more caring responsibilities than men. Until every organisation accepts that they can't capitalise on the talent available without taking account of people's caring roles, the profile of the people who run Britain will not change.'

Emotional barriers

Many people do not perceive themselves as carers or as in need of services. In practice, the level of services people request is relatively modest. One of the emotional barriers to accessing services is that people do not like to see themselves as needy or dependent.

The name of some benefits also sets up emotional barriers. For example, Attendance Allowance suggests that a claimant has to have someone attending to them. Likewise, until recently one benefit was called Invalid Care Allowance. Many people would not see themselves as an invalid – a term that can imply dependence and helplessness. Many older people do not feel they are 'elderly', associating that term with very frail people who have multiple impairments

Stereotypes exist around characteristics that particular **groups** are believed to show. These can impact and create barriers, sometimes with devastating consequences.

*** DID YOU KNOW?**

The fastest growing numbers of people with HIV are heterosexual. This is, in part, a reflection of the emotional barrier created by the false belief that only gay people have HIV.

Geographical and physical barriers

Rural areas are often very poorly served with services. This is often made worse by the lack of reliable and affordable transport. Often facilities may be many miles away and there are often difficulties in recruiting home care staff for rural locations. Public transport – including bus services, for example – is often limited.

Physical and geographical barriers were deliberately created in the past. People with

FIGURE 3.12 *A workhouse/psychiatric hospital*

disabilities and people with mental or physical health problems were segregated from mainstream society. Many large hospitals were built in remote locations. People who had no income were treated harshly since being poor was seen as a sign of laziness. The workhouse existed from the mid-Victorian times and the last workhouses only ceased to function as late as the 1940s. Some older people have memories of the workhouse and still associate residential care with 'the workhouse'. This can create real barriers to accessing care services.

Physical barriers also create problems in terms of accessing facilities. It is only in recent years that architects have thought about disabled access. There are still many stations without lifts and only a small proportion of buses that are suitable for wheelchair users. The Disability Discrimination Act has new regulations that came into force in 2004, which require that reasonable adjustments are made to meet the needs (including physical access) of anyone with a disability. Many cinemas and theatres limit the number of people in wheelchairs who can attend at any one time. Many shops have steps to the interior and often changing-cubicles are not large enough to allow wheelchairs inside. The processes that a person with a disability has to go through in order to access everyday facilities are significantly different to the majority of the population. For many, it proves to be too stressful and reinforces disabled people's sense of difference and isolation.

Discrimination

Discrimination and prejudice result in many vulnerable groups and individuals experiencing barriers to accessing the services and support they need. These barriers can be traced back to the attitudes, values and beliefs that affect behaviour and the way society is organised. Good practice in health and social care is based on recognising discrimination and how it creates barriers to services.

Some beliefs are based on assumptions that one group is superior to another group. One example of this was the apartheid scheme in South Africa.

*** DID YOU KNOW?**

South African society was based on the assumption that white people were superior. There where multiple barriers that prevented black people having equal chances, including physical and geographical barriers. Black people were not allowed on the same transport as white people and had to live in separate areas that had been designated by white people. Society was clearly separated to allow white people access to jobs, education, and housing, and to keep black people separate.

The direct discrimination experienced by people in South Africa has been outlawed in the UK by Acts of Parliament, such as the Race Relations Act 1976 (amended 2000). However, there are still major barriers for people who are in a minority. These barriers are often hidden and disguised as something else, making challenge very difficult. This type of indirect discrimination can be as intensely damaging as direct discrimination. This section looks at some of the barriers that are used on an everyday basis to reinforce prejudicial and discriminatory practices.

Types of discrimination

Anti-discriminatory law in the UK recognises different categories of discrimination:

* direct discrimination
* indirect discrimination
* victimisation
* harassment.

Some examples of discriminatory practices are shown in Figure 3.13.

Direct discrimination

This means treating one person or group less favourably than another on the grounds of race, disability, sexual orientation or gender.

Indirect discrimination

This refers to an organisation applying a general condition or requirement that is not justifiable in terms of the job requirements.

TYPE OF DISCRIMINATION	EXAMPLE
Direct discrimination	Phoning up for details of an advertised job. Any women who phone are told that the position has been filled, whereas an application form is sent out to any men who phone.
Indirect discrimination	A historical example of this was police recruitment policies that required a certain height for applicants. This had the effect of disadvantaging some ethnic groups. Being tall was not necessary for police work.
Victimisation	Not speaking to a colleague or sharing information with him or her because he or she had previously complained about discrimination.
Harassment	Anonymously sending rude or upsetting emails in order to make the victim feel threatened.

FIGURE 3.13 *Some examples of discriminatory practices*

Victimisation

This can occur where an individual has experienced difficulties and challenges the practices of an organisation, yet there is no protection for that employee. Employers may not make the working life of that employee more difficult and any such action is seen as unlawful discrimination. An employment tribunal can award damages if this takes place towards an employee involved in proceedings brought under anti-discriminatory legislation.

Harassment

This is defined as unwanted conduct that violates people's dignity or creates a hostile, degrading, humiliating or offensive environment. This has been introduced with recent changes brought in under the Employment Equality (Sexual Orientation) Regulations and the Employment Equality (religion and belief) Regulations 2003. In October 2004 the outlawing of discrimination and harassment of people with a disability came into force and extended the requirements of the 1995 Disability Discrimination Act.

Areas of protection under anti-discriminatory legislation

There are four main areas that discrimination legislation covers, regarding access to and opportunities within:

* education
* housing
* employment
* goods and services.

How do you recognise discrimination?

Often people are not honest or open about admitting that they hold views that disadvantage and diminish particular groups or individuals in society. Some of the ways in which you can assess whether unfair values or attitudes are being put into practice are shown in Figure 3.14. Although some of these areas do overlap they do provide an insight and a way of beginning to assess whether discrimination exists.

Effects of discrimination

Negative and judgmental attitudes have significant effects on both the person and group that express it and the group or individual on the receiving end. For those who express their views and prejudices, it often gives a false sense of superiority and power. Ultimately, labels and judgmental views are about avoiding change and favouring one individual or group over another. One group might be favoured in terms of power or access to resources.

For the person or group on the receiving end of discrimination there are several possible

ASSESSING WHETHER VALUES OR ATTITUDES ARE UNFAIR	
Subjective criteria used	This is when unfair decisions are made about the type of qualities or attributes needed for a particular job. One example would be not employing women as they are viewed as less reliable employees – in the event that they should have children
Ignorance	Ignorance is no defence in law and the fact that someone may argue that they did not realise an action or policy was discriminatory does not lessen the damage it may cause to the person at the receiving end
Pressure from others	Groups often develop shared 'cultures'. In other words, an agreed (although often unsaid) agreement about who is acceptable and who is not. An example might be arranging meetings at a time that undesirable group members will not be able to attend
Traditional criteria	A strongly held belief that has always been accepted and seems like good 'common-sense' may have its roots in a blinkered view of what roles and jobs people should do. For example, the idea that women make good carers and that men do not is based more on a world view than any objective evidence to support this
Unintentional discrimination	This refers to individuals and groups who are committed to equality, but have not evaluated their views or practices and realised that some practices have the effect of excluding certain groups. For example, arranging to meet in a pub, since setting that serves alcohol might be offensive to certain religious groups such as Muslims and Methodist Christians
Stereotyping	This refers to rigid and simplistic assumptions made about individuals or groups, the outcome of which is that they are viewed and treated less favourably than the group or individual making that judgement. An example of this is a generalised assumption that anyone with mental health concerns is a danger to others
Unsatisfactory procedures	For example, not making issues clear, assuming that everyone thinks the same way and knows the same information that you do
Personal prejudice	This means an opinion formed beforehand that is based on inadequate facts. Give-away phrases often used include 'those people' or 'people like that', which often indicate prejudice

FIGURE 3.14 *Recognising discrimination*

negative outcomes. This can be understood as a process that repeats itself as a circle or negative downward spiral.

A cycle of oppression

When a person experiences discrimination there will always be an effect, even if at a subconscious level. Over time, an individual or group may feel threatened or devalued. If this concern is not recognised or addressed by the organisation a negative spiral may result. The person on the receiving end will experience anger or **depression**. Either anger or depression can be interpreted as 'over-sensitivity' or 'proof that this person is aggressive or difficult' by the people responsible for the discrimination.

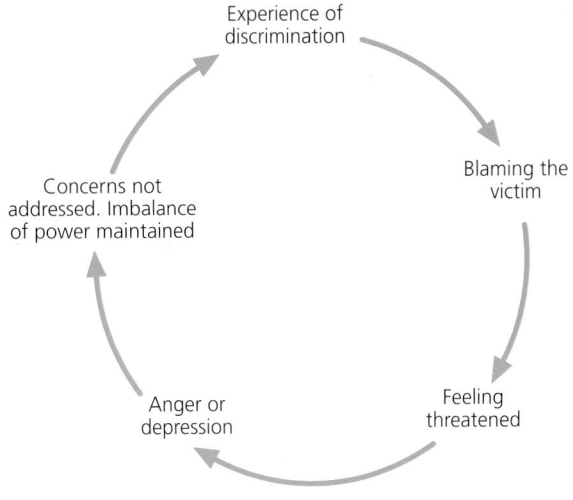

FIGURE 3.15 *The circular effects of discrimination*

For many people, the spiral of discrimination will be a daily experience. Individuals may feel that it is impossible to fight this process. This cycle also shows the injustice of expecting the victim of the discrimination to be the one to fight it (see Figure 3.15). It is the responsibility of everyone in social care to identify and challenge discrimination.

Approaches to equal opportunities

Three approaches to equal opportunities are shown in Figure 3.16.

Anti-discriminatory legislation

Some of the main Acts of Parliament covering discrimination are:

* The Race Relations Act 1976/2000
* Sex Discrimination Act 1975 and 1986
* Equal Pay Act 1970/1983
* Disability Discrimination Act 1995 and Employment Directive Regulations Article 13
* Employment Equality (Sexual Orientation) Regulations 2003
* Employment Equality (Culture and Belief) Regulations 2003.

However, there are many areas where there is no **law** about discrimination. For example, there are no laws about less favourable treatment on the grounds of size or class. Law on age discrimination is due in 2006

The law does provide a method of challenging discrimination, but, equally, some laws and practices are very discriminatory in themselves. For example, recent actions by the government regarding asylum seekers have been so harsh in proposing to leave people in total poverty, with no provision of money, that the courts have judged this to have broken the basic requirements of the Human Rights Act 1998.

Processes of discrimination – stereotyping and labelling

Stereotyping refers to generalised assumptions made about a particular group of people. The generalisations are usually negative and may identify a particular physical or social characteristic. These views are not usually flexible and are used as the basis for treating one group of people less favourably than another. Often these views are held very rigidly, even in the face of direct evidence that indicates their inaccuracy.

Stereotypes can lead to groups missing out on support and services that are really needed.

APPROACHES TO EQUAL OPPORTUNITIES	
Equal treatment	This is an inadequate approach that assumes that as long as there is no direct discrimination that will be enough. If there are barriers to access on the grounds of prejudice it is up to the disadvantaged group to 'assimilate' and adapt to the majority culture. This approach treats everyone as the same and does not recognise that there may be differences. This approach is not acceptable within the care value base.
Equal access	This approach focuses on removing barriers. All practices and procedures, therefore, need to be checked. Access to disadvantaged groups should be facilitated. One example is recruitment to the police force. The number of people applying from minority communities is very low. Previous poor experiences of policing may be one reason but the police are taking active steps to increase the number of minority police officers, to put right the imbalance and more fairly represent the community as a whole. This approach is the one that you are most likely to see in care organisations.
Equal share	This approach focuses on equality of outcome rather than any particular procedure for achieving this. It is the responsibility of the State to put right any unfairness and to redistribute resources more fairly. Some equal opportunities authors argue that this more radical approach would be best.

FIGURE 3.16 *Creating equal opportunities*

✻ DID YOU KNOW?

Words can often be associated with stereotypes. One recent example is that until 2002 the Carers Allowance was called Invalid Care Allowance. The word 'invalid' can work as a label and conjure up notions of helplessness and dependence. In this way stereotypes can be translated into institutional practices and reflected in the personal views of many care workers.

Key concept

Stereotyping: Stereotyping is a fixed way of thinking that involves generalisations and expectations about an issue or a group of people.

FIGURE 3.17 *Health Warning: Do not make assumptions about our lifestyles or needs. You will damage our health*

When labels are attached to people they carry with them strong meanings and views. This is nown as attaching a stigma.

The stigma of telling an employer or school that you are HIV positive is one example. Another example would be of letting it be known that you are gay or lesbian. Many people have experienced other people becoming more distant and being treated as though they do not belong. At worst there may be obvious unfair treatment. Attaching labels to people either as

✻ DID YOU KNOW?

The word 'stigma' comes from the Greek language. Particular types of criminals had to wear signs round their necks to tell other members of society what their crime had been. The effect is much the same today, although not always in such a direct and obvious way.

Key concept

Discrimination: Katz (1978) defined discrimination as prejudice plus power.

sense of their worth or value and creates a false sense of 'them and us'.

Katz's definition firstly draws attention to the fundamental influence of personal values but indicates that where this is combined with personal, institutional or organisational power, discrimination moves beyond the realms of personal views. Thompson (1997) identifies how discrimination can work at the personal, community or structural levels (see Unit 2). Senior people in an organisation have the power to prevent prejudice resulting in discrimination.

Consequences of discrimination

Behaviour and attitudes that exclude and reduce the worth of others do have serious consequences, both for the person expressing the attitude and for those on the receiving end. On a personal level, being constantly seen as inferior can be internalised, creating depression and low **self-esteem**, and it can cause withdrawal from the people or institutions who treat individuals in this way. Anger is another response to rejection. Often when this anger is expressed it may be that other people see this as a sign that the victim is 'oversensitive'; this feeds into the cycle of oppression (see Figure 3.15). Both the person who is discriminating and the person on the receiving end may, therefore, show the effects of discrimination in the form of an emotional reaction.

Discrimination can result in a failure to provide services that are suitable to minority groups. Discrimination also results in failing to make any effort to reach out to minority groups with services, employment, education or housing.

Marginalisation and exclusion

Marginalisation describes the process whereby individuals or groups are pushed to the fringes or edges of mainstream activity. Where minority groups are excluded from the opportunities available to the majority of people in the UK the term '**social exclusion**' is used. The effect of marginalisation is to disadvantage many people and to sideline any social, economic or moral concern for their well-being. The government in 2005 set up the Social Exclusion Unit to monitor progress on tackling poverty and disadvantage.

Disempowerment

Disempowerment refers to the loss of life chances and power. Many people are disempowered by the way society views them as a group and the absence of recognition or resources to enable them to improve their lives. Many parents of children with a disability describe their experience with social services as disempowering, or as 'being a fight'. Morally, it seems right that children or adults with a disability should have automatic entitlement to the services that they need. But in reality the experience is very different. The amount of help and services available are limited since local authorities have strict budgets that they have to work within. The reason for this is a political decision made by successive governments that the cost of health and social care must be limited and focused on those in most need.

Because people may be disempowered by the high cost of services they need, the government introduced a system called Fairer Charging in 2003. This means that the full details of each service user's financial situation is recorded. Adults who have savings over £20,000 are assessed as paying full cost for services. Many Social Services departments have a top limit to the contribution from the service user. Currently this may be around £125 per week.

The real cost of care may be around £400 per week in residential care and around £550 per week for nursing care, although prices do vary throughout the country. Many service users and their families feel financially disempowered by the cost of services. Scotland has made nursing and residential care services free, but in England the government felt that such a scheme would be too expensive.

Summary of Section 3.2

This section has looked at some of the different types of barriers that can prevent people from having the health and social care services and support they need; the key messages include:

Consider this

Davinder is an older woman who came to the UK 30 years ago. Davinder is disorientated and cannot communicate easily in English. She also has mobility problems and diabetes. Her close family have recently emigrated, and she is living temporarily at her local temple. The temple guardians have approached Social Services for help, as they can only support Davinder on a temporary basis. The message that Davinder receives is that there are no services available to her.

Using concepts can you identify?

1. Reasons why Davinder may be vulnerable that are associated with the bases of discrimination.
2. Potential barriers to services that may exist for Davinder.

Go further – can you analyse issues using theory?

What might be the consequences for Davinder if she believes that she is marginalised and excluded from the quality of life most people expect?

Go further – can you evaluate using a range of theory?

What kind of support and help might Davinder need in order to feel safe, supported and of value to other people?

3.3 Creating a positive environment

There are two key elements to creating a positive **environment**. The first is the responsibility of individual care practitioners to challenge behaviour and practices that discriminate against service users; the second is to understand the role of the organisation. The size, structure and practices of an organisation will have a major effect on the quality of the care environment.

The individual practitioner

Why do people have discriminatory beliefs? One explanation is that they are socialised into thinking this way. **Socialisation** in its boldest sense means to become social.

Key concept

Socialisation: Giddens (1997) explains that 'socialisation is the process whereby the helpless infant gradually becomes a self-aware, knowledgeable person, skilled in the ways of the culture into which he or she is born' (1997:25). Socialisation involves learning the social norms of your culture.

Theories put forward by both Vygotsky (1869–1934) and Bandura (b.1925) argue that people learn by copying others. This happens from a young age. When a child learns effective ways of behaving this encourages **self-confidence**. However, many people do not have such positive experiences and learn to see themselves as ineffective at changing or controlling what happens to them. This will be carried forward into adult life and make a significant difference to how people approach the problems that they face.

A child's parents or carers will be the main people who influence early socialisation. They pass on what they see as right or good, as well as what is not valued. Prejudice and discriminatory attitudes are, therefore, communicated at a very early age. Ethnic minority parents, for example, may have to ensure their children develop a positive **self-image** by trying to protect them from prejudiced views that other children have learned from their parents. Parents may have to act as a **'buffer'** to protect their children from discrimination and at the same time teach their children to be able to deal with prejudice.

The effect of experiencing constant negative responses has been described by Seligmann (1975) as 'learned helplessness'. When a child particularly experiences constant rejection or discrimination, he or she learns to withdraw and to give up trying. This can produce feelings of helplessness, which can further develop into anxiety and **depression**. These theories help to explain the devastating impact of prejudice on individuals and the lifelong consequences of prejudice.

Key concept

Prejudice: A prejudice is a 'pre' 'judgement' of an issue. The term is used to mean a negative judgmental attitude about an issue or about a **group** of people. Like **stereotypes**, prejudiced beliefs tend to be fixed rigid systems of thinking that are difficult to change.

Norms

A **norm** is a word describing the general standards of expected behaviour of a particular group or individual. Ideas about how people should behave vary over time. The generally held views of society are reflected in how institutions and systems are set up and run.

The importance of the care value base

When people work together they may develop a common group identity (explained in Unit 2) that involves shared values or norms. Tuckman (1965) argued that a group of people become a functioning group when they have been through the stage of 'norming'; this involves sharing beliefs and expectations about the purpose of the work of the group. Creating a positive care environment needs care workers to adopt the care value base (see Figure 3.18).

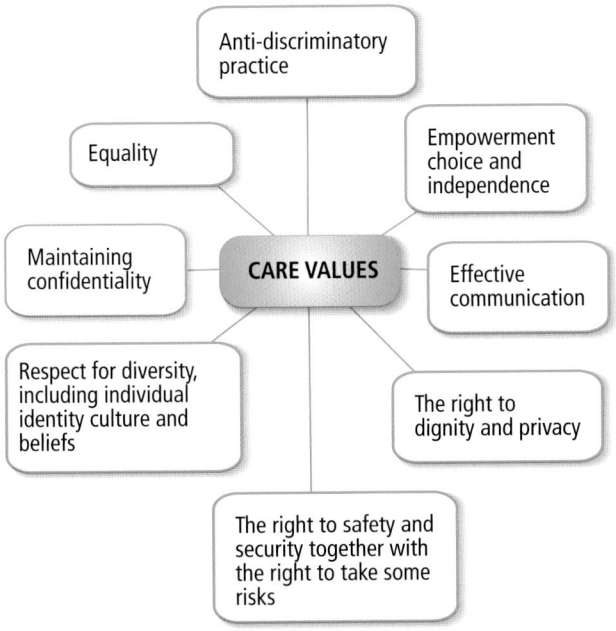

FIGURE 3.18 *Care values are important in creating a positive caring environment*

Think it over...

Consider the following statements made by two carers who work with different service users.

Early Years worker: 'I chose this job because I really enjoy working with young children. I know that I'm making a difference to their lives. I mean you can see the excitement in their faces when they are successful at an activity. And I think to myself that I'm helping them to develop as confident, successful people. Then that makes me feel that I'm valuable.'

Worker with older people: 'Yes, I know exactly what you mean. I get really interested in the life stories that some of the service users tell me. Just by listening to people, I think that I can make a difference to their quality of life and they value the work I do.'

Both workers look after different service user groups, but they work with similar values. Can you analyse how their experience relates to working within the value base? Can you see how the value base is associated with a general attitude towards people? Can you see how values are much more than just rules or procedures?

The terminology of the care value base provides a way of analysing the issues that care workers need to value. Most people develop their attitudes, **values** and beliefs by copying other people. To begin with we are socialised into beliefs. The main way in which care workers will begin to use the care value base will be by following the role models provided by senior care workers and managers. A truly positive care environment will be one in which care workers are treated with respect and valued by their employers. Care workers are likely to reflect this respect back to managers. The care value base then becomes a 'way of being', an attitude that affects every interchange between people whether they are managers, carers or service users. The GSCC combines the published code of practice for care workers with a code of practice for employers, and this emphasises that values are not just an issue for individual workers.

Aspects of care values – Empowerment

Many people's problems are rooted in the wider prejudices and disadvantages that exist in society. Historically, it was often assumed that individual people had problems as a result of their inability to cope. Radical social work argues that blaming service users for not coping was not only unfair but in fact 'blamed the victim' for his or her own misfortune.

Thompson (1991) explained the need to look at problems people face from a variety of different viewpoints. He argued that whilst it is important to look at the problems an individual is facing, it is also essential to understand the experience of different social groups. He argued that it is the interaction of individual and social factors that result in people's experiences of **marginalisation**, or being pushed to the edges of society. This theory opened the way to look at the bigger picture and to make it acceptable to point out where systems were causing injustice. Giving individuals and groups more power is referred to as **empowerment**, which includes harnessing awareness of unfairness to achieve social change. In recent years much more attention has been paid to disadvantaged groups such as ethnic minorities and older people.

Empowerment involves identifying areas of oppression and disadvantage then analysing biased policies and challenging these in order to achieve change. There is a need for any support and assistance given to individuals to be matched by a similar level of effort going into challenging institutions and society to change unfair views and practices.

*** DID YOU KNOW?**

Radical social work has its roots in a much older theory about society called Marxism. Marxism explained how the working people in society were made poor by the action of their employers (the ruling classes) in taking so much money for themselves. Radical (or empowering) social work has a much wider focus than money and looks at areas such as racism, sexism, sexual orientation, ageism and many others as areas of disadvantage that are created by the general actions of people in society as a whole.

However, although challenging unfairness and disadvantage may be seen as a noble and worthwhile cause, it is important to recognise that health and social care workers have control functions as well as having a responsibility to support people. For example, local authorities have clear legal duties to protect children from harm, following the requirements of the Children Act 1989. This may involve removing a child from home against a parent's wishes. Similarly, under the Mental Health Act 1983 a person with a mental disorder can be admitted by force to a psychiatric hospital if they are a danger to themselves or others. Balancing the need to control behaviour with the need to work in a supporting way can be very stressful for care workers. Law, policies, guidelines and procedures may be helpful in showing what good practice should be, but they do not provide all the answers for every situation.

Respect for individual choice

One of the main aims of the NHS and Community Care Act 1990 was to allow people to have choice over the services and care available to them. The purpose of this was to enable people to stay independent for as long as possible. The role of the social care worker was to provide clear and accurate information and to work together with people to identify their needs and the risks that threatened their independence. The law is also very clear in outlining the duties of local authorities to provide information.

There are three main acts that guide local authorities about providing information for adults. They are:

* The Chronically Sick and Disabled Persons Act 1970
* The Disabled Persons Act 1986
* The NHS and Community Care Act 1990.

The Children Act 1989 also makes requirements about providing information to children and families.

Choice and independence through Direct Payments

In recent years there has been a new way of encouraging choice and independence through the introduction of Direct Payments. Normally, once a social worker has assessed a person's needs the real cost of the care is worked out. Then the local authority might either provide the services themselves or buy in the services needed from a private or voluntary agency.

With Direct Payments, instead of the local authority buying the service, the money is given to the disabled person in order that he or she may purchase the services needed. Support is available for the disabled person to assist with the extra responsibilities of managing a direct payment. These include making tax and National Insurance payments. The Direct Payments scheme allows a person direct control over whom they employ and the hours they work. The current government strongly wants this scheme to be more widely used. The scheme started with the Direct Payments Act 1996 when only people between 18–65 years could apply. This was extended in 2000 to people over 65 years and also to parents with children under 16 years and carers. Since April 2003 all local authorities must have a Direct Payments scheme and must also assess anyone who asks to be part of the scheme.

The importance of identity

Identity means having sense of who you are. Feeling comfortable and happy with who you are is seen as a sign of good mental and physical health. For many years, how people felt about themselves was not seen as important in health and social care work, but in recent years the strong links between health and a secure sense of self have increasingly been recognised.

One example of this is that in the past many young black children were placed with white people who had no experience of any black communities. Many of these young people grew up to feel they did not belong in either white or black groups. Many people were found to have a very low opinion of themselves and often this reflected the views that black people were somehow less important than white people.

Thompson (2000) argues that identity is not a single and solid fact. A person's sense of self may change. Identity is not something that exists but is created by the way in which we interact with others. Thompson indicates that when these interactions with others feed back either negative or mixed messages this often results in people having a low opinion of their own worth and identity. Problems associated with identity can result in low **self-esteem** and this may be associated with poor relationships with other people. One crucial factor is the quality of the relationship of an individual with his or her parents or carers during the early years stage of life. Theorists such as Carl Rogers (1902–1987) argued that if a child did not receive love without conditions, his or her view of self could be severely affected. Mixed messages in childhood were seen to result in an inner uncertainty for the child about his or her own worth. These views would be carried through to adulthood. One saying has it that there are three causes to mental ill health: low self-esteem, low self-esteem and low self-esteem.

A further factor affecting identity relates to what is seen as 'normal'. Society makes value judgements around difference. This is reflected in generally held views about worth and value. For example, older people are often seen as dependent burdens. Likewise, **stereotypes** around race, sexuality, religion, and gender all play a major part in establishing identity.

A key value in social work focuses around the worth of the individual. Anti-discriminatory practice is based around avoiding generalisations and treating people as if they were all the same. It is easy in towns and cities for individuals to lose their importance as individual human beings, and become lost in health and social care systems. Therefore, in health and social care it is vital to look at each person as an unique individual with his or her own beliefs, wishes and views. This is called working in a person-centred way and has the effect of supporting and strengthening a person's sense of self-worth and identity.

The importance of culture and beliefs

Culture refers to the traditions, beliefs, values and ideas that are inherited or passed on within a group of people, and the way in which these affect their roles, activities and actions. Culture is, therefore, a major factor in establishing the identity of an individual or group of people. Linked with the understanding of identity is also the idea of difference. For many people, difference automatically means that a culture or way of relating to the world is not as good as their own way. Difference can often be seen as threatening. Threatened groups may develop ideas of one group being superior to another.

Culture, therefore, has a major impact on how people experience and interpret what happens to them. Therefore, all health and social care workers need to be aware of and sensitive to culture and race. Anti-racist practice will need to acknowledge the reality of racism and the fundamental way this will affect groups and individuals.

Effective communication

Effective communication requires a number of attributes on the part of the social or health care worker. Key elements of effective communication are shown in Figure 3.19.

Effective communication depends on a mixture of actions, behaviour and attitudes. In turn, these are strongly connected to the underlying value base held by the individual.

Effective communication is also related to using straightforward language and avoiding jargon or complicated language that may not be understood. One example of this is when care workers talk about 'eligibility criteria'. This has little meaning to many but, in fact, relates to the conditions set down about who may receive a service. Given the diversity of the population in the UK, it is also essential to ensure that information is available in a variety of languages and formats. People with sight impairment may need a guide in Braille. People with learning difficulties also need to receive and understand information about the services that may affect their lives.

An essential skill in communication is the manner in which it is carried out. In highly emotional situations it is essential for care staff to understand that it may be difficult for the other person to fully take in what is being said.

Language is very powerful in conveying underlying attitudes. In the UK, discriminatory comments are often justified by stating 'it was only a joke', then blaming the victim as someone who 'can't take a joke'. Terminology can also act as a label; for example, describing a group of people as 'the elderly' reflects underlying stereotypical generalisations. Thompson (1993) argues such terms are depersonalising and ageist.

SCENARIO

Arriving in a care home

John was aged 80 years and had memory problems when he was brought into a care home. His wife had just been taken into hospital. He could not look after himself at home. John was bewildered and kept asking if he had hurt his wife and whether it was his fault that she was ill. He couldn't understand that she had a heart problem and that he could not stay at home. The staff needed kindness and patience and their warmth and kindly manner helped John to settle rather than anything that they said.

Can you identify the aspect of effective communication that care staff used here?

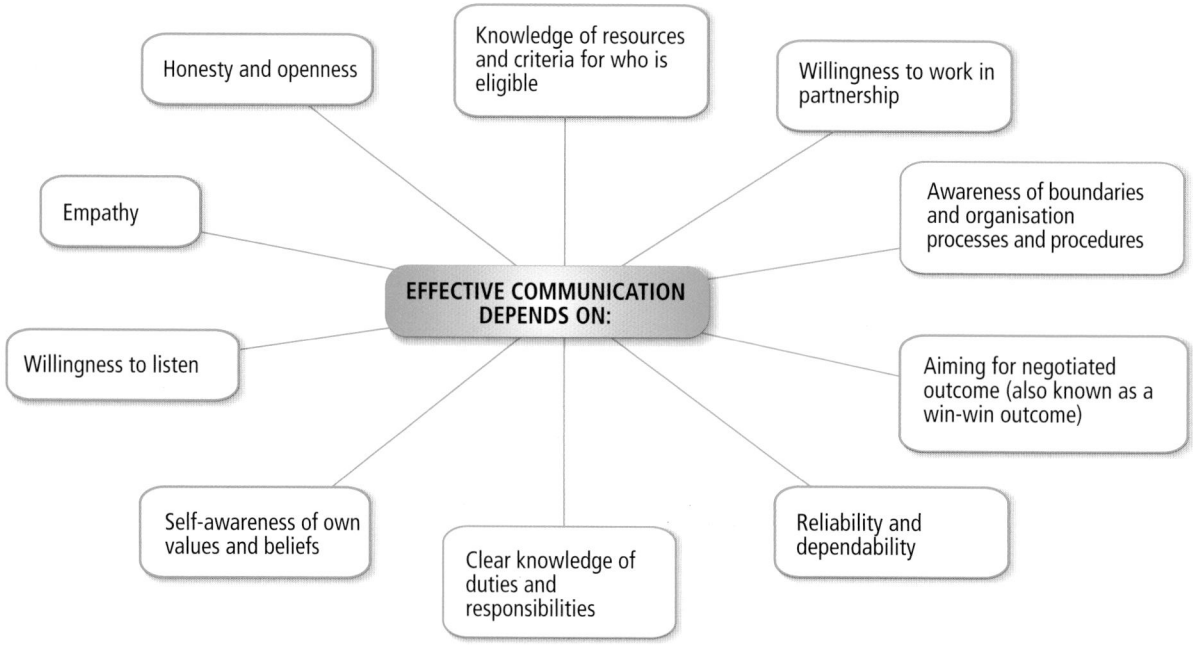

FIGURE 3.19 *Key elements of effective communication*

How to challenge discrimination or poor practice

The first step in challenging discrimination is to recognise its existence and the damaging effects it has on people. This also requires a degree of personal honesty and reflection about the views and prejudices that you may hold about particular situations or people. Training opportunities can really help to build your awareness of different types of discrimination and how it affects individuals, groups and organisations. Thompson (1993) argues that groups can have a much greater effect than individuals working alone, so change is much more likely to happen if staff develop group values and norms associated with the value base.

Challenging discrimination often involves challenging stereotypes or attitudes that fail to convey respect and value for service users. You may often need to challenge behaviour and assumptions that do not fit the value base for care. Some examples of discriminatory statements and possible challenges are set out in Figure 3.21.

Pressure groups can also play a major role in bringing issues to local and national awareness and are important factors in the process of change. Appreciating how crucial the role of **anti-discriminatory** practice is in social and health care will have a major impact on creating and sustaining a positive care environment. Awareness of discrimination is not an added extra or a separate area of learning, but is the bedrock of good practice and positive care environments.

The organisation

Some of the key organisational factors that impact on creating a positive environment are outlined below.

Policies and procedures

Policies reflect organisations' views about a particular area; this is usually combined with an expectation and procedures as to how staff working for that organisation will behave. Many organisations have policies on equal opportunities with a clear sequence of actions that staff must take if discriminatory language or behaviour occurs.

FIGURE 3.20 *Groups have a much greater effect than individuals in challenging discrimination*

Policies and procedures play a vital part in establishing the 'culture' of an organisation. This refers to a set of commonly held beliefs, values, and behaviours. The culture of an organisation will affect how things get done and will also affect the staff's views and attitudes to learning.

In order to be effective, policies need to be made clear and regularly updated. Having a first aid policy is of little use if no one knows the policy and the approved first aider is on holiday when help is needed. The same applies to fire procedures.

Policies and procedures do provide a clear structure for how to work and what to do in particular situations. They are essential in promoting the rights of service users and also define the limits of a worker's role or responsibilities. However, policies alone are not enough. Staff need not only to have knowledge of them but above all a commitment to implementing and maintaining policies and procedures; unless they are believed in and adopted into everyday behaviour, high quality care practice cannot be achieved or maintained.

SETTING OR SERVICE USER GROUP	DISCRIMINATORY STATEMENT	POSSIBLE WAYS OF CHALLENGING THE STATEMENT
Early years setting	'Children from this ethnic group never mix with others, do they?'	A statement like this is a generalisation/stereotype. There could be a variety of reasons for a child not mixing with others; for example, due to shyness or feeling unsafe. It is important not to blame the child – the problem may be with the attitude of the staff.
People with a learning difficulty	'There is no point in asking these people what they want. They haven't got the ability to know!'	This discriminatory statement labels people as having 'no ability'. All living people have some abilities. Skilled care workers must work with people and not see 'the person as the problem'. If there are communication barriers then an advocacy approach can be used.
Healthcare setting	'It's the lifestyle that these people live. They bring the problems on themselves. Why should we have to work with them?'	A judgmental statement that assumes that some people deserve help and others do not. There is an assumption that people who are socially disadvantaged automatically do not deserve help. The attitude is almost as absurd as the argument that only healthy people should receive health care.
A service setting for older people	'Well, these people have had their lives haven't they.'	A discriminatory statement that regards service users as 'non-people' valued as 'already dead'. A positive, value-base approach might emphasise the richness of life experience and the life story of each service user together with the communication skills needed to maintain the service user's self-esteem.

FIGURE 3.21 *Examples of discriminatory statements and possible challenges*

SCENARIO

Organisational culture

Care Home A has a strict rule-bound way of working. The manager constantly criticises the staff and has threatened to sack someone who was late because she had to take her daughter to hospital as an emergency. Staff have no choice other than to work double shifts and the manager rarely talks to the residents. The staff are afraid and resentful of the manager and only do what they are told to do. The manager sees herself as the expert in all areas of knowledge and does not like the staff having any training, as she knows what to do. The staff only hear about policies and procedures when the manager tells them that they have done something wrong. They do not know any of the written policies

In Care Home B the staff are encouraged to use their own ideas and common sense to deal with difficult situations, and receive support and back-up from their manager. They are often able to attend training courses and are encouraged to put new ideas into practice. The residents enjoy a laugh and a joke with the staff. The manager offers regular supervision to the staff and spends time with the residents every day. They have regular staff meetings and work together to solve problems. Policies and procedures are always looked at as part of the staff meetings.

The culture of Care Home B means that policies and procedures are seen as helpful tools to keep up good standards, whereas in Care Home A they are used negatively. Policies and procedures on their own are not enough to ensure that there is a positive care environment. The culture of each organisation will also play a major part.

Effect of organisational size, structure and culture

Many organisations providing social care are commercially run in order to make a profit. Many care homes have closed in the last 4 years, and in 2003 alone over 15,000 care home beds disappeared. Many smaller homes cannot survive financially and larger commercial groups are taking over ownership of many residential and nursing homes. The larger the home the more savings can be made (called economies of scale). There is a trend for homes to become larger, but this brings with it problems of keeping individual residents as the main focus.

Each home is required to meet **National Minimum Standards** as set down in the Care Standards Act 2000. There can sometimes be tensions as providing the best quality care would mean far higher costs in staff and supplies. Maintaining a balance between good standards of care and making a profit is not easy to get right.

Key organisational policies and procedures

Policies and procedures are vital elements in creating and maintaining a positive care environment (see Figure 3.22).

Equal opportunities policies

The Commission for Racial Equality recommends that equal opportunity policies should include a policy that covers recruitment, training and promotion. The policy should contain clear targets, following a thorough assessment of the organisation's current position on equal opportunities. Consideration should be given to pre-employment training that prepares job applicants for tests and interviews. In addition, applications from under-represented groups should be encouraged and effective links built with the community. The Commission also recommends that flexible working options should be considered and special equipment should be provided to meet the needs of people who are disabled.

Mission statement

This should be a clear short statement indicating the name and type of agency, its location, what it does, where and for whom. The vision and purpose of the agency also need to be included together with a statement of where the organisation wishes to go.

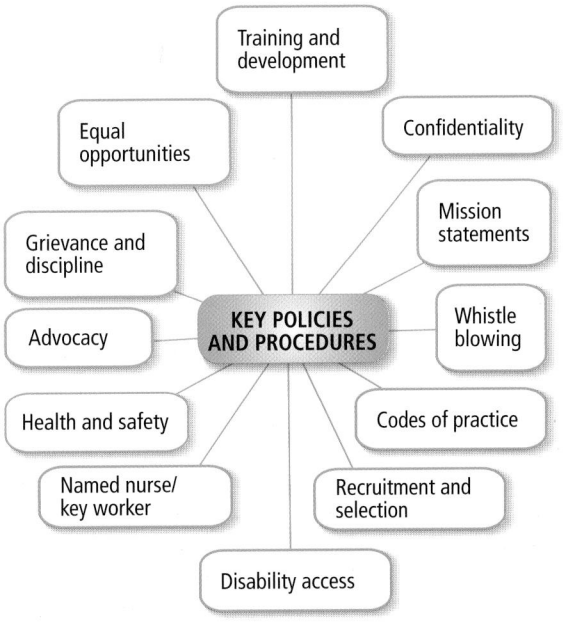

FIGURE 3.22 *Areas requiring clearly defined policies and procedures*

An example of a mission statement for a local authority social services department might be 'To provide accessible, quality services to the people of the borough'.

An example of a mission statement for an organisation working with people with learning difficulty might be 'To provide quality, **person-centred care** that values the individuality and potential of every service user'.

Codes of practice

These are statements of good practice and help to make clear what standards a service user can expect. They are useful for reviewing the quality of care. The Commissions that deal with areas of discrimination, such as the Disability Rights Commission, produce codes of practice to give guidance about good practice in the area of discrimination. They provide professionals with advice and guidelines and often can give detailed values relevant to a specific service. The codes of practice for nurses and the code of ethics for social workers can be found by accessing www.heinemann.co.uk/hotlinks (express code 37185) for the relevant websites.

FIGURE 3.23 *Codes of practice for care workers can be found on the Internet*

Recruitment and selection

Recruiting and selecting the right people is of the highest importance to a health or social care organisation and will affect its future success. The processes for recruiting and retaining staff must be free from bias and discrimination.

*** DID YOU KNOW?**

The Race Relations Amendment Act 2000 places the responsibility on organisations to prove they are not discriminatory and to monitor their practices.

Whistle blowing

This is the process whereby employees can safely state their concerns if bad practice occurs. The Public Interest Disclosure Act 1998 protects staff from victimisation provided they make their concern known 'in good faith'. An example of this would be if someone was being abused in a care home. The normal first step would be to talk to the manager. Where an employee cannot safely talk to someone within their own organisation, the organisation should provide a list of other people that can be contacted.

Confidentiality

As a result of legislation and National Minimum Standards all care organisations must have a policy about confidentiality including the safety and security of recorded information. There will be procedures to follow when accessing information about service users or when records are updated.

Advocacy

Advocacy developed from radical social work and focuses on increasing the control and power of service users and carers over their own lives. On one level, it could be argued that social care workers empower service users by enabling them to access and receive the services they need. In more recent years, advocacy has developed to provide support and a voice for people who may have a mental health problem or learning difficulty, enabling them to fully participate in decision-making over their own lives. Such occasions might be an appeal against compulsory detention in a psychiatric hospital. It might also involve enabling someone with learning difficulties to plan short- and long-term goals for their lives in a person-centred planning meeting.

The task of an advocate is to enter into the life of a service user and to identify the service user's view of the world and to represent those views, where the person may find it hard to state these for himself or herself.

Advocacy recognises the powerlessness of particular groups. One area of empowerment has focused on black communities in the UK, who have traditionally experienced lower levels of employment, access to health services and mental health.

Person-centred planning

There are five key features to person-centred planning, as shown in Figure 3.24.

The White Paper 'Caring for People' (1991) indicates that the views and wishes of people with learning difficulties as to how they wish to live must be listened to; this is called person-centred planning. For example, a person with learning difficulties who lives in a shared house with care staff might wish to live in his or her own flat and get a part-time job. Such an individual might like to learn to horse ride and would like to go abroad once a year for a holiday. He or she might also want to buy different

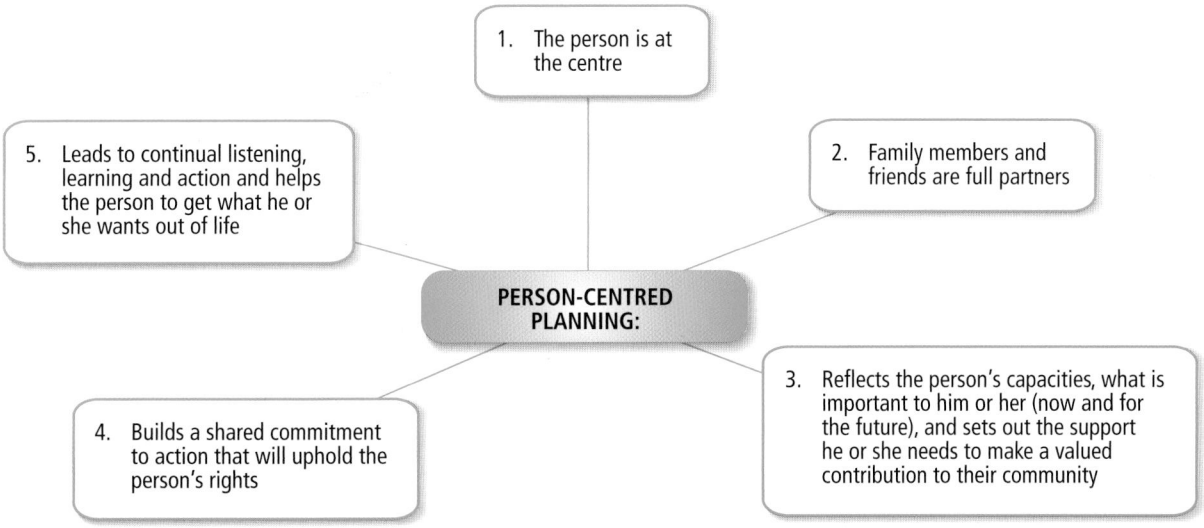

FIGURE 3.24 *Key features to person-centred planning*

Source: Planning With People: Guidance for Implementation Groups (Department of Health, 2002:13–14).

pictures for his or her room and change the wallpaper. So person-centred planning is about the little things as well as wider goals and ambitions. For people to have choices they need to know what is available, together with information about costs, as many services are chargeable. The provision of clear information is also essential.

Health and safety

Under The Health and Safety at Work Act (1974) both the employer and the employee are jointly responsible for safeguarding the health and safety of themselves and anyone using the premises. Each workplace must have a written statement of its health and safety policy with the name of the person responsible for implementing the policy. A list of hazards and risks should be put together and a clear procedure for recording accidents at work established. There should also be a clear statement about how the premises would be cleared in an emergency. All employers have to assess any risks under the Management of Health and Safety at Work Regulations 1992. Risk control measures must also be put in place.

Training and professional development

Under the Care Standards Act 2000 there are clear training requirements for social care workers. By 2005 at least 50 per cent of the workforce must have achieved NVQ qualifications at level 2/3. Eventually, all social care workers will be registered with the General Social Care Council. Training and professional development is an essential part of all health and social care work, in order to improve the standards and quality of care environments. In Early Years settings, 'Sure Start' estimates that the expansion of childcare services will require 175,000 to 185,000 new childcare workers, who will all need to be trained or retrained to meet current standards.

Named nurse and key worker

Effective care requires workers to know important information about service users. A named nurse or a key worker is a person who has a specific responsibility to get to know certain individual service users. A key worker will have a responsibility for coordinating the service user's plan of individual care. This may involve contact with relatives and friends in order to update and monitor the individual plan of care.

Grievance and discipline

The Labour Relations Commission has developed a code of practice to advise on how these procedures should be set up and operated. Grievance means a concern an employee has about the employer or another employee. Disciplinary procedures cover situations in which the employer has serious concerns about the professional behaviour of the worker. In the health and social care field, a list of those people considered unsuitable to be working with vulnerable adults was set up in June 2004 under the Care Standards Act 2000. If the result of the disciplinary procedure indicates concerns about a worker's suitability to work with vulnerable people, his or her name may be added to this list. However, there are very clear rules about the process of how this might happen.

Disability access

Part Three of the Disability Discrimination Act 1995 came into force in October 2004 and requires that reasonable adjustments are made to enable disabled people physical access to the buildings they need. Fines of up to £50,000 can be imposed on employers who do not make these adjustments. However, in practice the majority of stores are still not fully accessible for people in wheelchairs.

How organisations can promote positive practice

Promoting positive practice is the responsibility of every worker, but the organisation bears responsibility for ensuring that policies and procedures are in place to support and encourage good practice. Regular inspections by the Commission for Social Care Inspection do play a valuable role in monitoring the progress of an organisation. Care environments have to conform to clear standards. Inspection can monitor the quality of record keeping and other procedures. However, measuring the quality of care is not always so easy. Each organisation will develop its own culture and way of doing things.

It is important to become familiar with formal policy and legal requirements. Care environments operate where the personal and individual world of the individual overlaps with the legal and formal requirements of the law and guidance. Codes of practice and organisational policy documents give helpful guidelines about positive practice (see Figure 3.25).

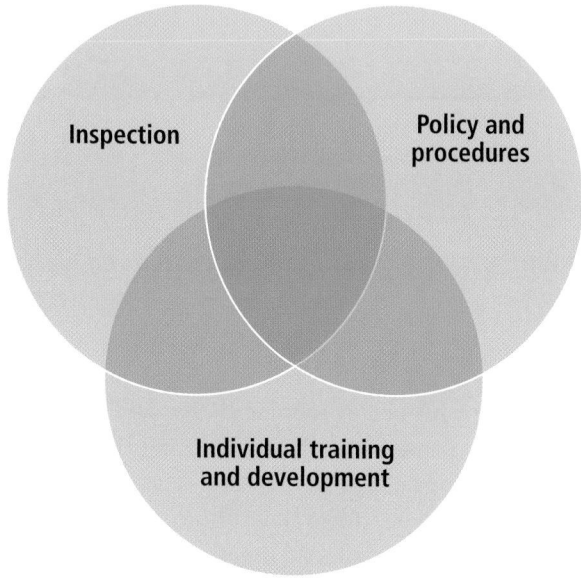

FIGURE 3.25 *The overlapping world of the individual and the legal and formal requirements in care environments*

It is also important to identify what changes are needed in order to improve the care environment. Whilst this can be done on an individual and personal basis, each organisation should have procedures whereby staff can become involved in changing and improving the practices of the organisation. Having clear goals and objectives is one of the most effective ways of achieving change.

Reviewing the position of the organisation and individuals on an ongoing basis is also a key to maintaining high standards. Training on a regular basis is also important in ensuring that consistently high standards are maintained. As part of the implementation of the Care Standards Act 2000 the goal is for at least 50 per cent of care workers to have achieved NVQ level 2/3 by 2005.

Summary of Section 3.3

Both the individual worker and the organisation must take an active part in creating and promoting a positive environment:

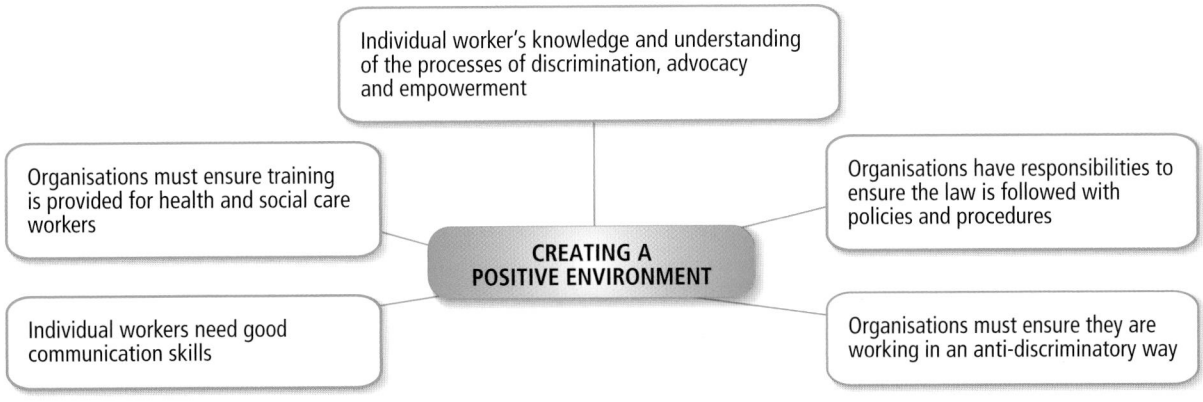

Consider this

You visit a care setting. The staff are welcoming and friendly; they seem to have good communication skills and no difficulty remembering important details relevant to the lifestyle of service users. You hear that staff meetings focus on positive attitudes about working together; the staff seem to value and support each other. The care workers you talk to enjoy working with the service users and clearly value diversity and difference. The staff enjoy team development days, and each full-time member of staff has a personal development plan of training.

Using concepts can you identify?

1 Some of the organisational policies and procedures that might support the good practice you have seen.

2 Some of the care values that care workers must be using.

Go further – can you analyse using theory?

Can you analyse some of the influences that might have resulted in the staff team adopting care values as part of their norms for working as a group. What part might staff training have played?

Go further – can you evaluate using a range of theory?

Can you evaluate the extent to which organisational policy may have contributed to good practice and the extent to which personal commitment to care values may have contributed to this good practice?

3.4 How society promotes service user's rights

This section looks at the rights of service users and how they are defined and protected in **law**. In working in the field of health and social care there are specific and general areas of law that affect people's rights.

Acts of Parliament are divided into parts (like chapters in a book) and they have sections (like paragraphs). At the end are schedules, which contain important principles about how the law should operate.

Essential general law

These are laws that underpin any work within the health and social care field. These can be seen as bedrock or underpinning law, as all actions must follow these general laws. This means that they are in force and are as important as particular laws such as the Children Act 1989, which cover special areas. The important basic laws include:

* Human Rights Act 1998
* Discrimination legislation
* Data Protection and Freedom of Information.

Human Rights Act 1998

FIGURE 3.26 *Rights are defined and protected in law*

The Human Rights Act 1998 adopted the European Convention of Human Rights. The Act is based on a commitment to individual rights and freedom from the State acting against groups or individuals in an illegal way. The Act came into force in October 2000 and is now part of UK law. Previously people had to apply to the European Court of Human Rights in Strasburg, but this is no longer the case as any legal proceedings in the UK must take account the Human Rights Act. The Act contains 16 Rights and is very clear that discrimination is not allowed.

Absolute Rights

There are four Absolute Rights (see Figure 3.27). This means there is no compromise or change and they must not be broken.

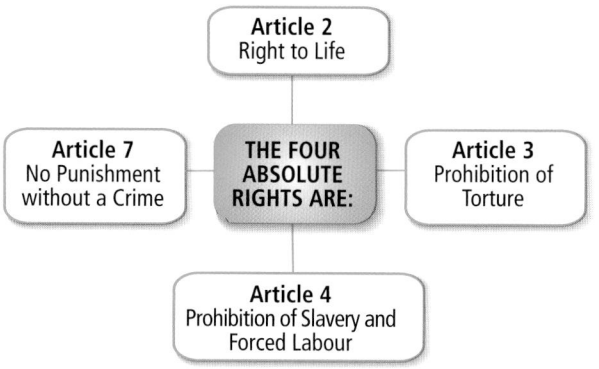

FIGURE 3.27 *The four Absolute Rights of the Human Rights Act 1998*

Limited Rights

Others rights, such as Article 8: Right to respect for Private and Family Life, are limited or qualified rights, so they need to be balanced with risks. This means that if a child were at risk of being hurt then the child could be removed, as his or her need for protection would override the family's right to respect for their privacy. This means that in certain situations these rights can be overridden.

The Human Rights Act applies to social care placements such as residential and nursing homes as well as voluntary organisations. This is because they provide services, which would otherwise be offered by the local authority. This means that social care establishments need to incorporate the principles of the Act into its policies and rules: how to make decisions, staffing and personnel procedures, how to run the establishment and also in the manner of relating to the public. Much of the Human Rights Act 1998 will apply in the social care field, as social care is very much involved with protecting and promoting people's mental and physical health.

Where it has been proved in court that any of a person's human rights has been broken, a range of legal **redress** is possible. These include damages, and the courts can also declare that the practice of an organisation is not legal.

Discrimination legislation

Sex Discrimination Act 1975 and 1986

Whilst pay was addressed in the Equal Pay Act (1970), other areas of discrimination against women were not covered. The Sex Discrimination laws cover discrimination and make direct and indirect discrimination illegal. The Equal Opportunities Commission plays the major role in helping individuals who experience discrimination, and they also have the power to issue a 'non-discrimination notice' to stop unfair practices. The notice can be enforced by injunction in the High Court. Compensation can be awarded by an employment tribunal and the employer may be ordered to change its practices. If there is discrimination in terms of provision of goods and services an individual can bring the matter before a county court, which have the power to award damages and issue injunctions (legal orders) to prevent further discrimination.

The Sex Discrimination Act also covers discrimination on the grounds of marital status as well as on the basis of **gender**. This means that the fact that someone is married or has children cannot be used as a reason to treat them unfairly. Under the Sex Discrimination Act interviewers must not ask about childcare or other caring responsibilities during employment interviews. Good practice would also ensure that there is a balance in terms of gender of those sitting on interviewing panels. The view that jobs such as dinner lady or nurse are 'women's jobs' has had to be radically re-thought in the light of the legislation.

The Sex Discrimination Act 1986 widened the areas covered by legislation. Employment by small firms, employment in private households and collective agreements by employers were also included under the law as required by the European Community.

Employment Equality (Sexual Orientation) Regulations 2003

These regulations came into force in December 2003 and now cover direct and indirect discrimination, victimisation and harassment on the grounds of sexual orientation. Until these regulations came into force there had been a major gap in the legislation. Harassment is defined in the regulations as unwanted conduct that violates people's dignity or causes an intimidating, hostile, degrading, offensive or humiliating environment. These regulations cover heterosexual relationships as well as same-sex and bi-sexual relationships. If an individual is harassed or discriminated against on the grounds of who he or she associates with, this is also covered by these regulations. However, these regulations only cover areas relating to employment.

Race Relations Act 1976 and Amendment Act 2000

The Race Relations Act 1976 made discrimination unlawful on the grounds of colour, race, ethnic or national origin or nationality. The legislation applies as much to discrimination towards a white person on the above grounds as to any other nationality or race. In 2001, case law identified that Scottish, Irish, English and Welsh are recognised as national origins and are, therefore, covered by this area of legislation. In certain situations the Race Relations Act 1976 allows 'permitted discrimination'. This covers the issues outlined in Figure 3.28.

The Act also established the Commission for Racial Equality, which not only assists individuals but has a key role in publishing codes of practice to identify good practice. Of particular importance in the area of health and social care, section 71 of the Race Relations Act requires all public bodies to eliminate unlawful discrimination, and to promote equality of opportunity and good relationships between people of different racial groups. These duties have been extended to all public authorities

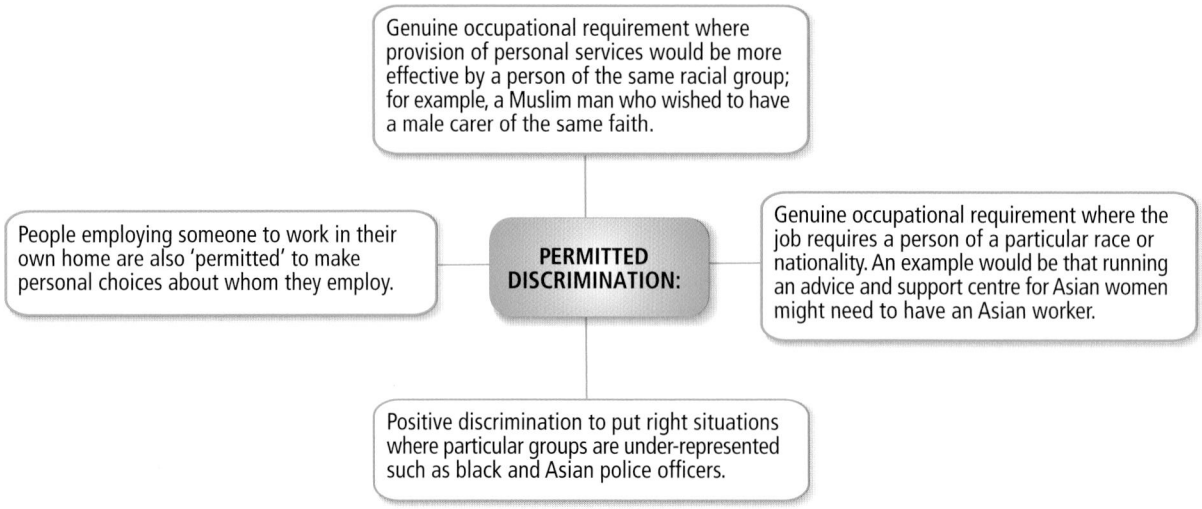

FIGURE 3.28 *Areas of permitted discrimination under the Race Relations Act 1976*

(including the police force) by the Race Relations Amendment Act 2000. All functions carried out by public authorities are now covered, whereas previously the areas covered only included employment, provision of facilities, goods and services, employment and housing.

These two Acts now make clear requirements on all public bodies to:

* review policies and functions every 3 years to ensure they are compliant
* monitor ethnic background of staff and in applications for employment
* ensure minority groups have access to information about the services provided
* identify and publish a race equality scheme
* identify arrangements to consult on the impact of new policies.

Employment does not just cover recruitment but also includes promotion, training opportunities and access to facilities

Employment Equality Religion and Belief Regulations 2003

These are similar to the regulations regarding sexual orientation; people are now protected from harassment, prejudice, victimisation and harassment on the grounds of religious belief. Both sexual orientation and religion/belief regulations bring the UK into line with European law and also protect people from discrimination on the grounds of perceived, as well as actual, religion or belief (this means assuming correctly or incorrectly that someone has a belief or religion). The government aims to bring consistency to the field of **anti-discriminatory** practice. At tribunals the employer must show that any difference in treatment is justified rather than the claimant having to prove that he or she has been discriminated against.

Disability Discrimination Act 1995

This Act is different to the Race Relations Acts and the Sex Discrimination legislation in that there is not a clear category of indirect discrimination. The requirement on employers to 'make reasonable adjustment' is seen as the equivalent. Under this Act, discrimination in employment, buying or renting land and property, and the provision of goods and services is illegal. Transport services were not covered directly by the Act although 'right of access' provisions are included in Part III of the Act together with a separate code of practice, which came into force in October 2004. In terms of education, the Special Educational Needs and Disability Act amended the Disability Discrimination Act by making it unlawful for the bodies responsible for schools to discriminate against existing or prospective disabled pupils. A Special Educational Needs Tribunal has also been established to make judgments in this area of education. In 1999 the Disability Rights Commission was set up by an Act of Parliament.

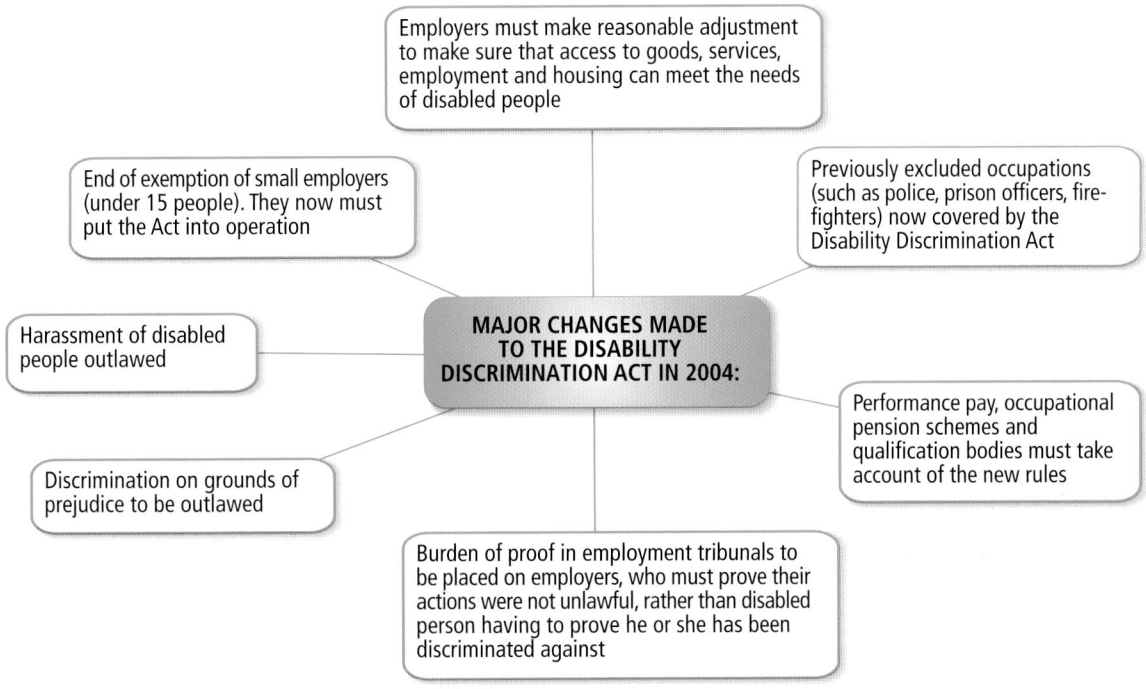

FIGURE 2.29 *Changes introduced by Part 111 of the Disability Discrimination Act in 2004*

Like other commissions it can issue a 'non-discrimination notice'. Individuals can seek redress through the county court in relation to goods and services.

The third part of the Disability Discrimination Act came into force in October 2004. The main points that have changed are shown in Figure 3.29.

Data Protection Act 1998 and Freedom of Information Act 2000

The Data Protection Acts of 1984 and 1998, Access to Personal Files Act 1987 and Access to Health Records Act 1990 made it a legal requirement to keep service user information confidential.

The 1998 Data Protection Act establishes rights to confidentiality covering both paper and electronic records. This Act provides people with a range of rights including those shown in Figure 3.30.

*** DID YOU KNOW?**

All services now have to have policies and procedures on the confidentiality of recorded information. The Data Protection Act 1998 has implications for confidentiality and the disclosure of records to friends and family; it also covers a person's right to see his or her own records.

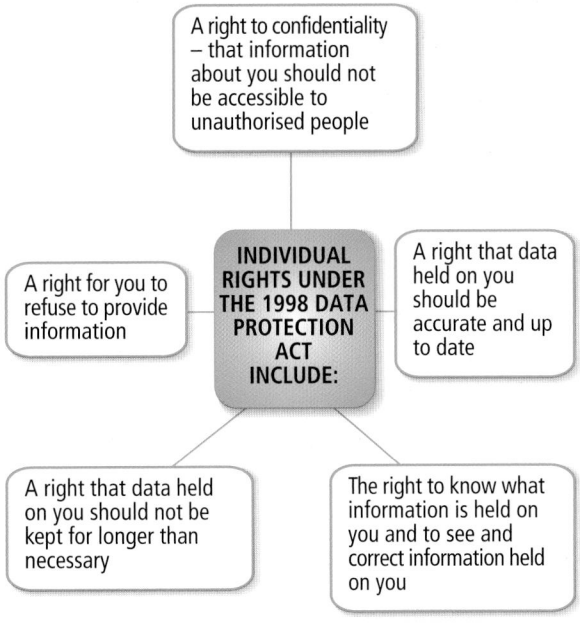

FIGURE 3.30 *Rights introduced by the 1998 Data Protection Act*

The Data Protection Act was passed by Parliament to protect people's rights in relation to the way information could be stored about them. The Data Protection Act 1998 replaced an earlier law from 1984. All information about people now has to be kept in accordance with the following principles:

* information or data must be fairly and legally obtained. People must not be misled about the purposes for which information is gathered
* data must be gathered with the permission of the people involved and processed for limited purposes
* data gathered has to be adequate, relevant and not excessive
* data must be accurate and kept up to date
* data must not be kept for longer than is necessary for the purpose it was originally gathered for
* people have the right to find out or access personal data being kept about them and certain other rights about the way in which data can be used
* data must be kept secure. Organisations must make sure that data is not lost or made available to unauthorised persons. The security principle means that data must be kept confidential
* data must not be transferred to a country out side of the European Union unless there are guarantees of data protection.

The Freedom of Information Act 2001

This was implemented in three stages and came into force in January 2005. It is part of government policy to increase openness and to reduce unnecessary secrecy. The Data Protection Act 1998 covers access to information by individuals, whereas the Freedom of Information Act covers information about public bodies. The principle underlying this Act is that information should be readily released unless there is evidence that harm would be caused. The Act identified rights to access information and also set up an Information Commissioner and Information Tribunal hear cases of complaints. All public authorities need to have schemes for publication of information. The format for these schemes has to be approved by the Information Commissioner.

Specific laws in social care

Within health and social care there are important Acts of Parliament that cover particular areas of practice. Three of the main acts – the Children Act, the National Health Service and Community Care Act, and the Mental Health Act – are considered below. The White Paper 'Valuing People,' for people with learning difficulties, is also included.

The Children Act 1989

The Act defined the duties and responsibilities of local authorities and established clear principles to follow. The Act established **rights and responsibilities** of parents and tried to set a framework for balancing the rights of children and parents against the responsibilities of the local authority to protect children from harm. The Children Act applies to all statutory and voluntary organisations providing care to children.

Key principles for working with children were established. They include:

* that children are better brought up within their own families
* the welfare of the child is always the highest priority (known as the paramountcy principle)
* no court order should be made unless it is essential to do so (no order principle)
* the views of the child must be sought and taken into account if of a suitable age or mature enough to express his or her wishes
* the child's race and cultural needs must be taken into account in order to maintain his or her identity
* no delay in working with children
* a welfare checklist must be followed by the court in any decision involving children.

The Children Act 1989 also emphasised that local authorities *must* work in partnership with families. A new Children Bill is going through Parliament in 2004/5 and this will make partnership a duty in law that local authorities must carry out.

EQUITY LAW	
Gender Equality Equal Pay Act Northern Ireland (1970)	Broadly similar legislation to the equivalent Acts within other UK countries
Sex Discrimination, Northern Ireland Order (1976)	Broadly similar legislation to the equivalent Acts within other UK countries
Race Equality Race Relations Northern Ireland Order (1997)	Legislation that introduced similar provision to the 1976 Race Relations Act in other UK countries
Disability Disability Discrimination Act (1995)	Legislation that applies across the UK
Equality, Northern Ireland Order (2000)	Legislation that expanded the duties and powers of the Equality Commission for Northern Ireland in relation to disability matter
Sexuality Employment Equality (Sexual Orientation) Regulations Northern Ireland (2003)	Similar legislation to other UK provision to prevent discrimination on the basis of a person's sexuality
Religion and Political Beliefs Fair Employment and Treatment, Northern Ireland Order (1998)	Legislation that makes it unlawful to discriminate against someone on the grounds of religious belief or political opinion. All UK countries now have legislation to prevent discrimination within employment on the basis of religion. Citizens of Northern Ireland currently have some additional rights preventing discrimination on the basis of religion or politics, as compared with other UK countries

The Children Act also sets out the responsibilities of local authorities towards children in need. The Act defines a child in need as one whose health and welfare would suffer without support from social services. Any child with a disability is automatically considered to be a child in need. There are also clear duties under the Act for local authorities to provide support services such as nurseries and family centres.

Social services also have duties to protect children from harm. Significant harm was a term adopted by the Act and is defined as ill treatment, impairment of health or impairment of development. The Adoption and Children Act 2002 has added an extra category of children witnessing violence as another important area to be taken into account when deciding if a child is in danger of being harmed. Social services must take into account not only the harm a child may have already experienced, but also the future possibilities of significant harm.

Parental responsibility was established by the Children Act and sets down the idea that parents have fundamental responsibilities as well as rights towards their children. Parents cannot lose their rights (except trough adoption) but their responsibilities can sometimes be shared with the local authority. Even if a child is living away from his or her parents as a result of a Care Order, the parents still keep their responsibilities. Clear guidelines were set down by the Children Act defining who automatically has parental responsibility and how it can be acquired through the courts.

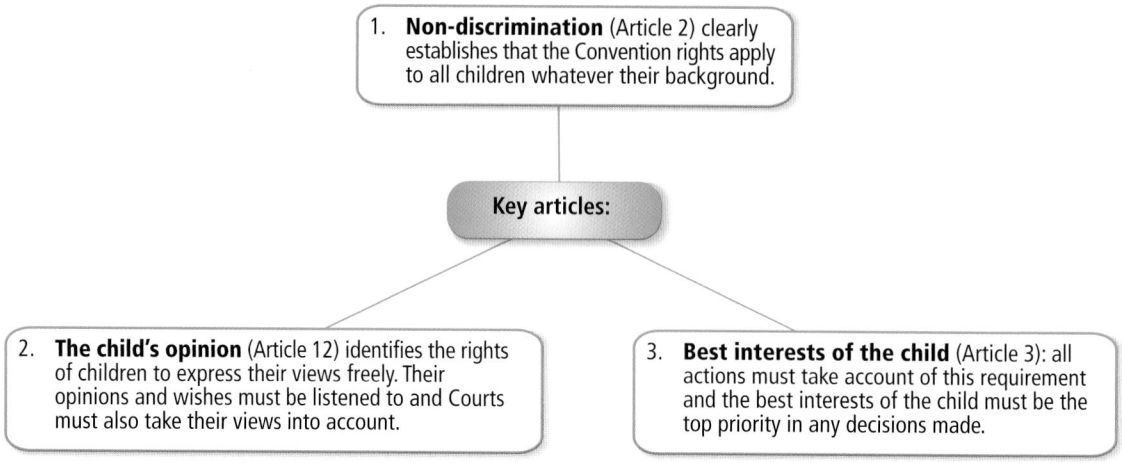

FIGURE 3.31 *Key articles of the United Nations Convention on the Rights of the Child*

In addition to the principles laid down in the Children Act, social services must also ensure that work with children follows the key requirements of the United Nations Convention on the Rights of the Child. These rights were agreed to in the UK in 1991 and set important standards and rights for children. The principles must be taken into account by English Courts. There are three key principles:

* participation in expression of views, protection of privacy
* protection from abuse and exploitation
* provision of education, and an adequate standard of living.

There are three Key articles that must also be followed. These are shown in Figure 3.31.

The United Nations Convention on the Rights of the Child, together with the Children Act 1989, sets out a clear framework that the welfare of all children must be taken very seriously. Social services must look at all aspects of a child's welfare as well as his or her physical safety. A child's need for identity, education and healthy development must always be taken into account.

Figure 3.32 shows how the different laws work together in the field of childcare.

As can be seen from the pyramid, the principles and important parts of the Act are underpinned by law which covers the rights of all people in terms of discrimination, information and their Human Rights. These laws must be followed as well as the particular instructions that laws specific to children impose.

In addition to the law around the welfare of children there are clear duties and responsibilities towards children who commit offences. Like the Children Act 1989, there are clear principles that

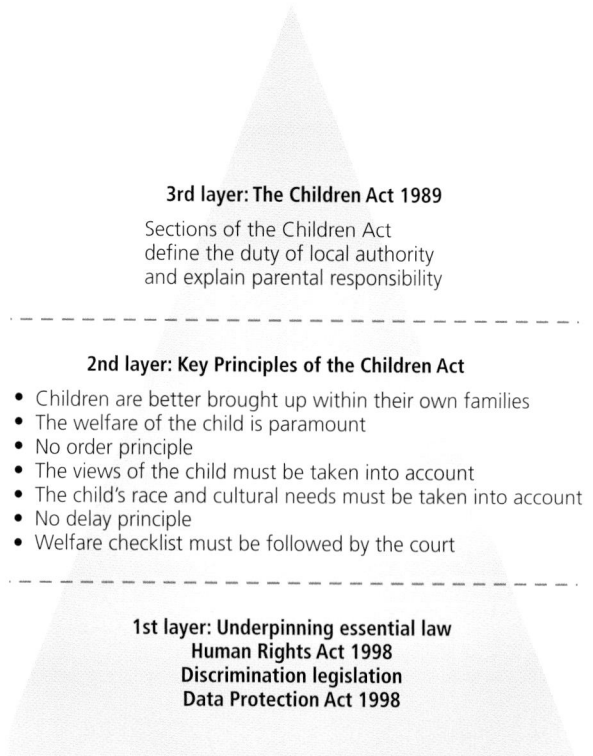

FIGURE 3.32 *Different laws working together in childcare*

youth justice workers, the courts and the police have to follow. They are shown in Figure 3.33.

In addition, the local authority has responsibilities to reduce the need to bring criminal proceedings and must also encourage children not to commit offences. Current laws in the youth justice area provide a variety of measures to deal with juvenile crime. Under the Crime and Disorder Act 1998 local child care curfews can be used for children and young people under 16 years of age. These give the police powers to take children home if they are in a particular area or out after a particular time at night. Another order under the same Act is an Anti-Social Behaviour Order (ASBO) whereby young people who are causing a continued nuisance or damage can be banned by a youth court from being in one or a number of particular places. The conditions of the ASBO can be very detailed even to the extent of specifying what someone is allowed to wear. The strong connection between truanting and crime has led to the police having the power under the Crime and Disorder Act 1998 to pick up children who they believe are truanting from school.

NHS and Community Care Act 1990

The aim of the NHS and Community Care Act was to enable people to stay at home for as long as possible. Admission to residential or nursing care was seen as the last resort under the Act. Prior to this, people did not receive an assessment of need before going into long-term care. The Act also introduced business ideas into social care services. Eighty-five per cent of a local authority's budget has to be spent in buying care services from private, voluntary and independent providers of care.

Before this Act, the local authority was a major provider of services, whereas under the NHS and Community Care Act the key roles for local authorities are now:

* assessment of need – this means identifying what help a person needs
* commissioning/purchasing of services such as residential care and home care
* monitoring of services in terms of quality and value for money
* hospital discharges – key role in arranging quick hospital discharges Community Care (Delayed discharges) Act 2004
* protection of vulnerable adults from abuse.

Assessment of need of a disabled person

The NHS and Community Care Act gave people with a disability much clearer rights in terms of automatic entitlement to an assessment. The NHS and Community Care Act 1990 makes it clear that there are two situations when someone is eligible for an assessment. These are:

DUTIES AND RESPONSIBILITIES TOWARDS CHILDREN WHO COMMIT OFFENCES	
Restorative justice: (covers 3 areas)	**Restoration:** where the young offender acknowledges and makes amends for their crime, including apologising to the victim **Re-integration:** an offender moving away from offending behaviour **Responsibility:** offenders and parents taking responsibility for their actions and preventing further behaviour occurring
Welfare principle	The youth justice system must take into account the welfare of the child in terms of removing him or her from undesirable surroundings and ensuring a proper education
Prevention of re-offending	This is the primary responsibility of Youth Courts

FIGURE 3.33 *Principles that youth justice workers, the courts and the police have to follow in dealing with child offenders*

* when they need or appear to need community care services
* when someone is disabled they now have an automatic right to an assessment and should be informed of this.

The Act makes it clear that it should not be difficult for an assessment to be made. Sometimes this goes wrong, as is shown in the following situation.

SCENARIO

Individual needs

In one case, a woman whose husband was due to have an operation on his brain phoned social services, asking for help with her mother who had Alzheimer's disease (memory problems) and was living with her. Clearly, looking at the above Act the woman's mother and husband should have been offered an assessment. The woman herself should have been offered a Carer's Assessment, as she was looking after both of them. Instead, social services asked how much money her mother had saved, as the worker was muddled between the rules about offering an assessment and charging for services offered. No assessment was made and the only help the woman received was a booklet containing a list of private care homes. The situation came to a crisis point some months later after the woman had struggled alone to cope and had placed her mother in a residential home that was unsympathetic to her mother's needs and wanted her moved within 24 hours. An assessment was then made and a suitable place eventually found for her mother; but this example shows how important it is for a social care worker to understand what the law says.

The purposes of the NHS and Community Care Act have been set down as key objectives. These are shown in Figure 3.34.

KEY OBJECTIVES OF THE NHS AND COMMUNITY CARE ACT:	
Home	Keeping people within their own home wherever possible
Carers	Support and help for carers is a high priority
Assessment	This is the cornerstone of good quality care
Mixed economy of care	85 per cent of the local authorities' budgets are to be spent in the private, independent and voluntary sector to buy in the services people need
Responsibility	Clear statement of who is responsible for assessing need and arranging services
Better value for taxpayers money	The money given to local authorities must be spent wisely

FIGURE 3.34 *Purposes of the NHS and Community Care Act*

The Mental Health Act 1983

The Mental Health Act defines who is regarded as mentally disordered and sets out rules detailing when someone can be admitted to a hospital against their wishes.

The principles covering the Mental Health Act 1983 are defined by the Mental Health Act Code of Practice 1983, revised in 1999. They include:

* recognition of human rights
* respect for individuals and anti-discriminatory practice
* needs to be assessed
* treatment must be the least controlling possible, taking into account risks to others
* care should promote self-determination and personal responsibility
* to discharge a person from compulsory sections as soon as possible and safely.

The Act is due to be changed within the next two years, as parts of it do not meet the requirements of the Human Rights Act.

✱ DID YOU KNOW?

Before someone can be compulsorily detained in hospital they have to be diagnosed as suffering from a mental disorder. This is defined under section 1 of the Mental Health Act 1983 as:

'Mental illness, arrested or incomplete development of mind, psychopathic disorder and any other disorder or disability of mind.'

White Paper 'Valuing People'

In 2001 the government published a White Paper for people with learning difficulties. A White Paper is a statement of the government's policy or plans. Although no Act of Parliament has followed this, 'Valuing People' is now the driving force directing service provision for people with learning difficulties in England.

There are four key principles in the White Paper:

- legal and civil rights
- choice
- inclusion
- independence.

Up to £50 million has been made available to change the services available for people with learning difficulties. People are to move out of long-stay hospitals; day services are to become more personal and meaningful; everyone will have a health plan and those with a learning difficulty will have a personal plan for their lives including housing, employment and leisure services. The process for this is called **person-centred planning**.

Redress for service users

Within current legislation there has been growing awareness that service users need mechanisms to make their voice heard. This can be linked to the consumer movement, which began in the 1970s to ensure that organisations were more accountable for their actions and to provide ways in which injustices could be addressed and put right. Within social care and discrimination law there are clearly defined procedures for service users. These operate at two levels:

- local complaints procedures
- formal and legal avenues of challenge.

Local complaints procedures

Complaints within social and health care organisations

Agencies must have their own complaints procedures as required by the Care Standards Act 2000, but they are also accountable to the complaints procedures in the local authority. As purchasers of the service, the local authority is also accountable for the standards and quality of care provided.

In a local authority, complaints follow a 3-stage procedure as shown in Figure 3.35. There are clearly defined time limits that each stage has to follow as required by government regulations.

There are also conditions about who can make a complaint. Technically, complaints must relate to a 'qualifying individual.' A qualifying individual is someone for whom the local authority has a **power** or a duty to provide social services; and the person is known to the social services. Financial compensation can be offered where complaints are upheld, but this is by no means commonplace. If policies and procedures are changed as a result of a complaint it is good practice for the person who has complained to be advised of this.

Formal and legal avenues of challenge

If the local complaints procedures have not resulted in the problem being resolved there are other legal options for the service user. These include:

- the Commissioner for local administration (Ombudsman)

3-STAGE PROCEDURE FOR LOCAL AUTHORITY COMPLAINTS:		
1	Informal	Attempts are made to resolve concerns at a local level with the social worker or team manager. The complaint does not have to be written; it may be made by a phone call
2	Formal	The complaint must be written and is dealt with by the local authority's designated complaints officer. Senior managers in social services may be involved
3	Review	An independent person leads and chairs a panel, which may require people involved in the complaint to attend a hearing. Their conclusions are made as a recommendation to the Director of Social Services. Although the Director is not legally bound to follow these recommendations, he/she has to show good cause why they are not followed if the matter is contested in court

FIGURE 3.35 *Procedure in local authorities for complaints*

* default powers
* judicial review
* civil action for damages/negligence
* whistle-blowing procedures.

Ombudsman

A person with a complaint can approach the Commissioner for Local Administration (also known as the Ombudsman). The Ombudsman looks at the actions of the local authority to see whether there has been maladministration. Maladministration is where the local authority has handled a situation dishonestly or inefficiently and this has caused an injustice to the service user. The Ombudsman can make recommendations about compensation but often it takes a long period for an investigation to be carried out. The process is free and the Ombudsman has powers to access information from local authorities (but is not able to look at general policies). The recommendations made by the Ombudsman are not legally binding on local authorities, although in practice most accept them as such.

Default powers

The Secretary of State has powers under the Local Authority Social Services Act to hold an inquiry where a local authority fails to carry out any of its statutory duties for adults. However, this power has never been used in practice, although the Secretary of State can require a local authority to comply with the requirements of the law.

Judicial review

A decision can be challenged in court but the courts are limited in that they look at the process followed rather than the content of the decision. The courts identify if the process followed was legal, rational and reasonable. As from October 2000 the courts also have to check if the local authority has followed the requirements of the Human Rights Act.

Negligence and damages

A service user has to prove that he or she has suffered a 'wrong' as a result of the actions of a local authority. Proving negligence can be very difficult as three separate conditions have to be evidenced. Although the civil courts work in terms of 'balance of probabilities' rather than 'beyond reasonable doubt' (as for criminal cases) it is still by no means easy and straightforward for negligence to be proved in law.

Whistle blowing

The Public Interest Disclosure Act 1998 now gives protection to workers who 'blow the whistle' on bad practice, to protect them from being penalised or losing their job as a result. It is a sad fact that in many scandals in health and social care the person who is brave enough to speak out is victimised. Disclosures must be made 'in good faith' to prevent malicious allegations from being made. All local authorities have to have whistle-blowing procedures and social and health care providers would also be covered by these.

Implementing redress involving discrimination

Tribunals

Tribunals are special courts put in place to administer specific areas of civil law.

Currently there are over 2,000 different tribunals administering legislation such as that relating to appeals against compulsory detention in a psychiatric hospital (Mental Health Tribunal). Other examples are rent tribunals and employment tribunals, which hear cases where either a tenant or an employee feels they have been treated unfairly. People are encouraged to state their own case for themselves. There are appeal mechanisms for some but not all tribunals. There are advantages to this system as it does not take as long for a tribunal to hear a case as it would do for a court case to be heard. The proceedings are not as formal as in a court. However, it is not always clear why a tribunal has made a particular decision. Some tribunals have the power to award compensation and in the field of employment some very big pay outs have been awarded.

FIGURE 3.36 *Tribunals are not as formal as courts*

Commissions

Commissions are government-appointed agencies that implement and monitor key areas of legislation. Examples include the Commission for Racial Equality. In April 2004 the **Commission for Social Care Inspection (CSCI)** was created, the role of which is to inspect social care services. The Commission also has responsibilities for inspecting the standards for some health services.

The work of each Commission will focus around specific legislation. Common tasks for Commissions involve investigating complaints or concerns such as standards of care in the case of CSCI. The Commissions also have a role in providing information and support about good quality practice. The codes of practice are valuable for measuring whether good standards are being achieved. The Equal Opportunities Commission and the Commission for Racial Equality both have published codes of practice to guide employers and workers on how to eliminate discrimination.

Codes of practice for social care workers have been published by the General Social Care Council (See Unit 2). These define the standards of professional behaviour that must be upheld.

Ofsted

The Care Standards Act 2000 modified the Children Act 1989. The modified Children Act now places the responsibility for quality inspection of childcare services with the Office for Standards in Education (Ofsted). Since 2001 Ofsted has been responsible for the registration and inspection of day-care and child minding. Ofsted is responsible for the:

* registration of all day-care providers
* inspection of all day-care provision
* investigation of complaints or concerns about day-care provision

* enforcement of quality standards
* provision of advice to central and local government on childcare issues.

Ofsted uses National Standards published by the Department for Education and Skills to guide its inspection work.

FIGURE 3.37 *National standards have to be met for all types of childcare*

There are national standards for each type of childcare provision including:

* full day-care
* sessional day-care
* crèches
* out-of-school care
* child minders.

The relationship between law and rights for service users

There are different ways that service user rights can be understood. These range from generalised human rights and protection from discrimination to the belief commonly held that individuals have an automatic right to services. Each approach has limitations and many of these approaches are the subject of misunderstanding by the general public. The ability to know the problems in the area of rights is essential in understanding how to promote a positive care environment.

Clear rights in law

One of the clearest lists of rights in law has been made by Brammer (2002).

The list includes the right:

* to an assessment for services under the NHSCCA 90
* of a carer to an assessment of their needs under Carer and Disabled Children Act 2000
* not to be discriminated against in specified circumstances, e.g. provision of goods and services on specified grounds, race, sex, disability, sexual orientation, religion or belief
* of a child (of sufficient understanding) to make an informed choice to refuse a medical and/or psychiatric examination under the CA 89 (Gillick Competence)
* of access to information held about you under the Data Protection Act 1998.

Right to protection from discrimination

Another major area of development in terms of service users' rights has been the development of anti-discriminatory legislation. The enforcement of these rights is through Commissions such as the Commission for Racial Equality, which can provide advice and support for individuals. However, the codes of practice published by the different Commissions do not have the same force of law as an Act of Parliament. Law on its own does not always change people's behaviour or attitudes.

Rights as an automatic entitlement to a service

This is the biggest area of misunderstanding in the area of service user rights. There is a widespread belief that people are automatically entitled to services and provisions from the local authority. In reality, this is not the case as successive governments since the 1970s have been concerned about local authorities' increasing expenditure. When the Welfare State was set up in the 1940s the key principle was that the State would provide for all its citizens' needs 'from cradle to grave'; this is the foundation of many people's belief that they are entitled to services. The reality is that people may be entitled to an assessment and it is only if, as a result of that assessment, it is agreed that the conditions set by the local authority have been met that services will be provided. However, charges are also made for those services.

Rights to information and consultation

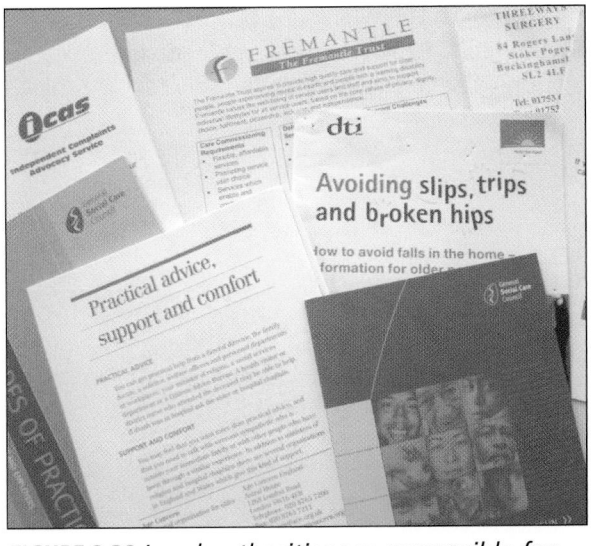

FIGURE 3.38 *Local authorities are responsible for up-to-date information on services*

The law is very clear that local authorities must provide information about the services it provides. This dates back to the National Assistance Act 1948. Three other Acts also emphasise what local authorities must do. These include the 1970 Chronically Sick and Disabled Persons Act, and the Disabled Persons Act 1986. The NHS and Community Care Act 1990 requires each local authority to publish a plan of its current services. The Children Act 1989 also makes it very clear that an essential part of working in partnership is to provide accurate and up-to-date information to parents and children.

There are also clear duties for each local authority to consult with service users about service provision. Providing information about people's rights is crucial to good practice in health and social care. For example, many carers do not know they are legally entitled to an assessment of their needs. People with a disability also have an automatic right to an assessment.

However, many people still do not receive up-to-date information, as this is expensive for local authorities to produce and there are concerns about creating more demand when local authorities cannot cope with the present level of demand.

Summary of Section 3.4

Consider this

Kai has a learning difficulty and has worked out a number of life goals that he would like to achieve through a process of person-centred planning with his key worker. Kai would like support to enable him to attend religious meetings now that he has become a Muslim. Kai would also like help to identify appropriate food, and to advise him of what he should not eat. Kai's key worker has since left and no progress has been made on meeting his needs. Kai has an advocate who intends to try and get social services to do something for him.

Using concepts can you identify?

1. What actions could an advocate consider in order to achieve an improvement of services?
2. What moral rights might Kai have in relationship to the value base of care?

Go further – can you analyse issues using theory?

What legal rights does Kai have in relation to his religious and ethnic group identity. As a person with a learning difficulty, what legal rights does Kai have for services to meet his needs?

Go further – can you evaluate using a range of theory?

Can you explain why many people believe they are entitled to services, and yet legislation does not provide a legal right to the services that they might expect?

UNIT 3 ASSESSMENT

How you will be assessed

In order to achieve this unit you must produce a report that explains how a service user group accesses services. Your report must focus on either people who are ill, young children, older people or individuals with special needs.

You will be given instructions regarding the structure of the report, but your report will need to include evidence for each of the following:

ASSESSMENT OBJECTIVE	DETAILS
AO1 Rights of service users	You must explain the rights of service users when accessing services.
AO2 Barriers to accessing services	You must explain the potential barriers experienced by that service user group when accessing services and the effect of these barriers.
AO3 Policies and practices	You must explain the policies and practices designed to create a positive care environment.
AO4 Legislation	You must evaluate how legislation safeguards and promotes the rights of service users, together with an evaluation of organisations' responsibilities under relevant legislation and an explanation of methods of redress open to service users.

Assessment preparation

The best way to write report might be to focus on a real local service, and to research the way that service works. Ideally, you may be able to listen to talks, and go and visit work settings where you can explore what senior staff say about the importance of: care values, how to overcome barriers to accessing services and how policies and legal requirements enable staff to promote positive care environments. Again, if the opportunities exist, it would be ideal if you could actually interview a care worker after you have collected some ideas about care values, potential barriers, and what it takes to create a positive environment. If you can interview someone you may be able to get detailed guidance on legal issues as well as examples of how barriers to access can be overcome. The material you get from talking to care workers can be used in conjunction with the theory in this chapter to help write a report.

In order to undertake a successful interview you will need to plan the questions you would like to ask and perhaps discuss your plans with a tutor. It will be important to discuss the issue of confidentiality before starting any interview.

AO1 Rights of service users

To achieve the highest marks you need to show that you have in-depth knowledge and understanding of service users' rights. You must be able to clearly explain the importance of a value base in relation to the support of these rights. Overall, you must demonstrate that you have excellent understanding of the issues by providing full and accurate explanations in you work.

AO2 Barriers to accessing services

To achieve the highest marks you need to show that you can thoroughly apply your knowledge and understanding of potential barriers to access. You must be able to Identify the different barriers, provide a full explanation and discussion of each and their effects. The application of your knowledge to the promotion of positive care environments must be appropriate and accurate.

AO3 Policies and practices

To achieve the highest marks your research and analysis of the factors that influence the creation of a positive care environment must be of a high level. You need to analyse and explain at least three ways in which positive environments can be promoted in organisations through the development and implementation of positive policy and practice.

AO4 Legislation

To achieve the highest marks your evaluation of how legislation safeguards and promotes the rights of service users must be excellent. You need to be able to analyse and explain the responsibilities of organisations under relevant legislation. You must also show detailed knowledge of the methods of redress open to service users by providing clear explanations and analysis of at least three methods.

Unit test

1. What are care values and why are care values important when working with vulnerable service users?
2. Explain the concept of empowerment and provide an example of empowerment relevant to working with young children and an example relevant to working with older people
3. List three different types of consequence that could result from care workers failing to maintain confidentiality
4. Identify at least three different types of barrier to access to services

5. Explain some of the consequences of discrimination
6. What is the difference between anti-discriminatory practice and non-discrimination?
7. If you were researching the degree to which a particular care environment could be considered to be positive list at least four areas that you might focus on.
8. What laws protect people from discrimination on the basis of their religion?
9. What methods of redress are open to a service user who is dissatisfied with the quality of service that they receive?
10. Discuss the effectiveness of legislation in ensuring that service users' rights are maintained and that service users receive a high quality of service.

The answers to these questions are provided on page 157 of this book.

References and further reading

Adams, R. Dominelli. L., and Payne. M. (1998) *Social Work: Themes, Issues and Critical Debates* (Palgrave, Basingstoke)

Biestek , F. P. (1961) *The casework relationship* (London, Allen and Unwin)

Brammer, A. (2002) *Social Work Law*, (Harlow: Pearson)

Braye, S. (2003) *Social Work Law* (Harlow: Pearson)

Collins (1995) Dictionary of Social Work (Collins)

Cull, L. A. (2001) *The Law and Social Work* (Palgrave, Basingstoke)

Giddens, A. (1997) *Sociology*, 3rd ed. (Cambridge: Polity Press)

Katz, J . (1978) *White Awareness: Handbook for AntiRacism Training* (Massachuseths, USA:Greenfield)

Mandelstam, M. (1999) *Community Care Practice and the Law* (Jessica Kingsley, London)

Payne, M. (1991) *Modern Social Work Theory* (Macmillan, Basingstoke)

Roche, J. (eds) *Hunter Kane* (1996) Hunter Kane Management

Seligman, M. (1975) *Helplessness* (San Francisco: W. H. Freeman & Co.)

Shardlow, S. (1998) quoted in *Social Work: Themes, Issues and Critical Debates* (ed. Adams. R., Dominelli. L. & Payne. M.) (Palgrave, Basingstoke)

Thompson, N. (1997) *Anti-discriminatory Practice* (Macmillan, Basingstoke)

Thompson, N. (2000) *Understanding Social Work* (Palgrave, Basingstoke)

Thompson, N . (1993) *Anti-discriminatory Practice*, (Basingstoke and London: Macmillan)

Tuckman, B. (1965) *Development sequence in small groups* in Psycological Bulletin, vol. 63, No. 6

Relevant websites

Please see www.heinemann.co.uk/hotlinks (express code 370XP) for links to the following websites which may provide a source of updated information:

* Government legislation
* Learning matters
* Commission for Racial Equality
* General Social Care Council
* Equal Opportunities Commission
* British Association of Social Workers
* Council of Europe consultation paper on mental health and human rights
* Department of Health summary of human rights cases
* European Convention on Human Rights
* Disability Rights Commission
* Mobility and Inclusion
* Nursing & Midwifery Council
* Surestart

UNIT 4

Social Aspects and Lifestyle Choices

This unit contains the following sections:

4.1 Lifestyle choices and life course events

4.2 Social factors affecting health and well-being

4.3 Care professional/service user relationships

Introduction

This unit explores how social factors including life course events and lifestyle choices influence people's health and well-being. The first section explores some of the processes involved in coping with change and the interaction of lifestyle choices with life course events. The role of social support and self-efficacy in enabling people to cope with change are also discussed. The second section explains some key social factors that influence health and well-being. The third section of this unit explores some of the consequences of social factors for relationships in care.

How you will be assessed

This unit is externally assessed through a written examination.

4.1 Lifestyle choices and life course events

Predictable life course events

Figure 4.1 lists some of the predictable changes that can be associated with human development.

Infancy	Forming a first attachment
Childhood	Starting school – making friends
Puberty	Being accepted by peer group Adapting to own sexuality Making close friendships
Early adulthood	Choosing a marriage/partnership formation Starting work
Adulthood	Choosing to start a family, maintaining employment, caring for parents Retirement from full-time work
Late adulthood	Coping with reduced physical stamina

FIGURE 4.1 *Some predictable changes in human development*

Many of the events listed are regarded as positive and desirable changes in life. Even so, they may involve the need to change our assumptions about life and adjust to a changed lifestyle. Making a major change in the way we live is likely to involve:

* a sense of *loss* for the way things used to be
* a feeling of *uncertainty* about what the future will be like
* a need to *spend time* and/or money and/or emotional energy sorting things out
* a need to *learn* new things.

For example, starting school can involve a sense of loss. This might be the first morning a parent leaves a child to cope with lots of other people on his or her own. The child might cry because he or she misses the parent. Starting school usually gives children a sense of uncertainty about what to expect from all the strange new people they meet. Starting school involves spending time and energy learning lots of new things – how to find your way round the building, how to get on with other people, what you have to do and so on. Starting school involves learning to become increasingly independent and grown-up. A child's view of him or herself may change as he or she gets used to school.

SCENARIO

Starting school

Samuel is a black 4-year-old, who is starting nursery school. Until now he has always been at home with his mother. He has played with other children many times in his home and also when his mother visited friends. Samuel is an only child. He has a close, loving relationship with his mother.

Samuel's first reaction to school was one of shock – there were so many other children and it was noisy. He had always looked to his mother for guidance, but she wasn't there and he was on his own. Samuel had been told all about school, but he couldn't really understand or imagine what it would be like. Another adult who looked very different from his mother was trying to encourage him to join in a game. Samuel felt frightened and lost. Samuel cried for his mother and told staff that he wanted her. A kind adult, who looked a little like his aunt, spent time with him and he felt better.

Later in the day, Samuel enjoyed some food and joined in making music with the other children. When his mother came to collect him, he was relieved. He didn't really feel safe until she appeared. Now he felt tired, but important. He had been to school, he had learned about music, and his mother made him feel that everything was all right and safe again. This was a real adventure!

The next few days at school were easier for Samuel. He stopped worrying about not being with his mother and he started to like school.

Think it over...

Using the scenario above, identify how Samuel may have experienced a sense of loss, a sense of uncertainty, how he may have used 'emotional energy' trying to cope, and how new learning is involved in coping with this life course event.

Employment

Getting and starting a job can involve a feeling of loss; it might be stressful to change routines. It also involves lots of uncertainty: 'Will I like the people there?' 'Will they like me?' 'Can I do the job?' Getting a job and getting started takes up a lot of time and energy. Starting a new job involves lots of new learning: who is who, where things are, what you have to do, and so on.

Think it over...

How does the idea of loss apply in the story below?

Why might Jai have experienced some stress?

What have uncertainty and emotional energy got to do with stress?

What new learning is involved?

Can you see any similarity between the issues involved in starting a new job and the issues that may be involved in coping with a serious illness?

Retirement

Retirement can represent a major change for people who have worked in a demanding full-time job and then suddenly stop working. In the future, retirement may become very flexible with some people retiring in their 40s and others continuing to take on work in their late 60s and 70s. Many people might continue to work as self-employed or temporary workers after leaving full-time employment.

People who experience a sudden break from full-time work might experience loss. A person might lose his or her self-concept and self-esteem as a worker following retirement. A person may lose his or her routine and perhaps work friends when they retire. Some people may experience uncertainty and not be sure how to use the leisure time they have. Some people might feel a loss or an uncertainty about their purpose in life and might say that they are no use to anyone. People who have to live on the State pension alone may experience a loss of income.

Most people who retire will have to work out how to use their time and how to budget for things they would like to do. Retirement provides great opportunities to learn new leisure activities and to learn to lead a new lifestyle.

SCENARIO

Starting work

Jai is 18 and has successfully completed an information technology course at college. Jai wrote over 30 applications to companies in his area asking for work. Eventually he was successful in gaining a temporary job, helping to design spreadsheets and doing data entry for a local company.

Jai felt very anxious on the first day. He wanted to do well and prove he was 'smart'. Jai did not know what to expect. He didn't know what he would be asked to do or how other people would treat him. Jai was worried about the older workers in the company. Some might see him as a threat; others might be prejudiced against him.

On his first day he was warmly welcomed by a senior member of the company, who suggested that he work closely with a 38-year-old manager. Jai was nervous at first but soon found that his new boss was easy to get on with. During his first day, Jai began to feel that the job would be interesting and that the people were all right to work with. At the end of the day, Jai felt exhausted but looked forward to the weeks ahead.

Because the staff understood how difficult it is to start a new job, they helped him and gave him a guide or 'mentor' to teach him all the new things he needed to know. Anxiety turned into excitement. Jai felt he could cope. Jai felt that the effort to learn a new way of working would be worthwhile.

City of Westminster College
Learning Services / Queens Park Centre

SCENARIO

Retirement

Nathan has worked in the store room of a light engineering company for the past 18 years; he is 62 years old. The company needs to reduce the number of people it employs and has offered Nathan an early retirement deal. Nathan will receive a small company pension. Although Nathan will have a lot less to live on each week, he will not have the expense of travelling to work. In addition, he can use some of his retirement settlement to pay off his mortgage, so he will save money as a result.

Retirement will mean that Nathan and his partner can now buy a small boat and go sailing during the week. Nathan has only had limited time to do this before. The freedom of retirement will mean that Nathan can spend more time with friends and relatives. He is not worried about money, so he sees retirement as a very positive life event.

Think it over...

How does receiving support from colleagues help a person to undertake the new learning that coping with change involves?

Marriage

Many heterosexual couples live together without marrying; some go on to marry after living together for some years, but about half of all couples who live together do not marry. Current trends suggest that perhaps about one in five people will never be married during their lives.

Marriage involves a commitment to live with a partner permanently. It ties financial resources and networks of family relationships together. Marriage is a big change in life. It can involve moving house and leaving your family. This may cause a sense of loss. Many people feel some anxiety about getting married. Are they marrying the right person? Will they both get on together? What will living together for ever be like? Marriage and coping with married life involves a lot of time, money and energy. Living with a partner may involve a new lifestyle and new learning about negotiating with a partner.

Unpredictable life events

Some life events are unpredicted and unwelcome. Events such as accidents or serious illness, breakdown of relationships, the loss of a job, financial difficulties, having to move to a new area, or a change of status at work might create physical and emotional stress. Coping with stressful change will involve new learning in a similar way to coping with predictable change. Coping with stressful change is also likely to involve a great deal of the emotional work associated with going through a 'transition'.

Key concept

Transitions: A transition is a life event that involves changing assumptions about life and moving from one way of life to a new way of living.

Barrie Hopson (1986) identified a seven-stage process, which, he argued, could be used to understand how people react to major life changes. The seven phases that he identified are explained in Figure 4.2.

Think it over...

Analyse the scenario above using Hopson's seven stages for understanding personal change. What evidence can you identify in the story for each of the seven phases?

Bereavement

People can lose their partners at any stage of life. As couples grow older the chances that one person will die increase. Bereavement causes a major change in people's lives. You might lose the main person that you talked to, the main person who helped you; you may lose your sexual partner, a person who you shared life with and a person who made you feel good. Living without a partner can involve great uncertainty. Your partner may have helped with sorting out household bills or with shopping or housework, and now you have to do it all yourself. Bereavement can mean you have to learn to live a new life as a single person again. Coping on your

STAGE	PEOPLE'S REACTIONS
Immobilisation	This first phase involves being unable to cope and perhaps a denial that anything will need to change. A person might feel frozen and unable to respond to the situation
Minimisation	This phase involves denying the extent of any change and instead pretending that nothing much needs to be done. Hopson explains that 'denial provides time for a temporary retreat from reality' (1986: 146). Retreating from reality gives us time to come to terms with change
Depression	When a person becomes aware of the full need for change, he or she may experience depression. Major change may threaten a person's self-esteem and such a person may feel he or she does not have the emotional energy to cope. A person may attempt to withdraw into depression as a response to the need for change
Letting go	This involves accepting the need for change and letting go of attempts to deny or minimise the need for change
Testing	This phase involves trying out new behaviours and experimenting with new lifestyles
Search for meaning	During this phase a person attempts to make sense of what has happened
Internalisation	An individual finally internalises a new lifestyle and perhaps a new self-concept. That person can now feel secure and safe again, having gone through a process of adapting to change

FIGURE 4.2 *Hopson's seven-stage process (1986)*

SCENARIO

Serious illness

Jasminder ('Jas') is 33 years old. Until a year ago, she was enjoying a well-paid career, working long hours as a manager within a large company. Six months ago Jas began to feel unwell. At first, she thought she had flu, and took a couple of weeks off work.

Jas felt exhausted and unable to return to work. Even simple tasks such as washing up felt too difficult, and Jas spent much of the day sleeping. Her doctor diagnosed M.E., an illness that can result in a person being unable to work for a considerable period of time. Jas was told that she needed total rest and that perhaps she would be unable to return to her previous career.

At first Jas could not believe what she was told. 'They must have got this wrong – this can't happen to me.' Jas then thought, 'Oh, this won't take too long – all I need is a couple of weeks off and I'll be back to normal.' But after a few weeks Jas still had no energy and was not able to go back to work. At this point, She started to say that her life was not really worth living and she would always be ill.

After six months Jas accepted that she would not return to work as a manager. She accepted that she would need to learn to manage her own health, and perhaps spend a maximum of two hours a day reading and writing. Jas spent time searching the Internet for ideas that would help her to achieve a better quality of life.

One year later Jas has become involved with a support group for people with M.E. She has accepted that she will not be able to follow a career as a manager, but she feels that her life has purpose in providing support to others.

own can take a lot of time and energy.

Hopson's seven phases represent one way to describe the process involved in coping with stressful change. Colin Murray Parkes (1975) identified a slightly different process in his study of grieving individuals. Initially, many people experience shock and numbness when confronted with a loss, and there is a tendency to block out or deny the loss. This phase may be followed by a reaction of searching for the lost person – a 'refusing to let go' phase. A third phase involves trying to come to terms with the loss. Some people may experience emotions of self-blame or anger towards others as part of the emotional work that they need to go through. Parkes referred to this phase as 'mitigation'. Finally, people develop a new sense of self separate from the lost relationship and this phase might be called a phase of reconstruction.

As we grow and develop, we learn to build a concept of self. This concept of self might be likened to building a house of cards. We develop an idea of who we are – bit by bit – like building level after level in a house of cards. A major upset – such as the death of a partner – can destroy the sense of self that we have built, in much the same way that a breeze can destroy a card structure.

FIGURE 4.3 *A sense of self can be destroyed by a stressful incident*

SCENARIO

Bereavement

Jack had been married for 22 years when his partner unexpectedly died of a heart attack. They had been very close. When Jack was first told about the death he displayed little reaction. Friends had to persuade Jack not to go into work the next day. Jack had said that it would give him something to do, and would take his mind off things. Later, at the funeral, Jack said that he felt frozen inside and that he did not want to eat. It was some weeks later that Jack said he felt better because he could talk to his partner, sitting in a chair late at night. Jack became angry and bitter about how badly everything had gone, saying that perhaps he was to blame for the illness and he should have noticed things earlier. Months later, Jack explained that he had sorted his life out a bit and would learn to cope alone.

After a year and half, Jack still misses his partner but he now says that the experience has made him stronger: 'It's as if I understand more about life now. I feel that if I could cope with this – well, there isn't much I can't cope with.' Jack has now become involved with the local voluntary support group for people who are bereaved. He says that helping others has helped him. 'It has given me new meaning and purpose in life. I had a good life before and now I've got a new life to lead.'

Jack has come through the experience in a positive way, even though he will always wish that his partner had never died. Bereavement can lead people to start what might feel like 'a new life'.

Think it over...

Can you identify a phase of shock, a phase of search, a phase of coming to terms with loss (mitigation) and a phase of reconstruction in Jack's story?

Using a more general overview of the process of change, can you reinterpret Jack's story in terms of denial, struggle and rebuilding a strong sense of self?

Theories of transition and grief identify a process of having to rebuild a sense of who you are. In general, this process may often involve a reaction of denial followed by a period of struggle to come to terms with the need to change, and then a period of rebuilding.

How stressful are different life events?

Holmes and Rahe (1967) produced a catalogue of life events that people have to cope with. Hopson (1986) stated that this general index was found to be consistent across European countries and with the cultures of Japan, Hawaii, Central America and Peru. Naturally, each person experiences change in his or her individual way. Each person has particular vulnerabilities, strengths and weaknesses. The Holmes-Rahe scale is no more than a general overview, originally researched in the USA in the 1960s. The 10 most stressful and least stressful of life events as detailed in the Holmes-Rahe scale are listed in Figure 4.4.

The Holmes-Rahe scale suggests that on average the death of a partner involves nearly 10 times the change, and perhaps the threat, that being caught for speeding does. The scale represents a useful list of some changes and transitions that might happen to adults. But it is important to remember that few people are 'average'. In your personal life, you may rate some issues as far more, or less, stressful than the scale suggests.

How many people have experienced particularly stressful life events? Social Trends (2002) reported the percentage of males and females aged 16–75 who stated that they had

	LIFE EVENTS	VALUE
10 most stressful	Death of partner	100
	Divorce	73
	Marital separation	65
	Going to prison	63
	Death of a close family member	63
	Personal injury or illness	53
	Marriage	50
	Being dismissed at work	47
	Marital reconciliation	45
	Retirement	45
10 least stressful	Change in recreation	19
	Change in religious activities	19
	Change in social activities	18
	Mortgage or loan less than one year's net salary	17
	Change in sleeping habits	16
	Change in number of family get-togethers	15
	Change in eating habits	15
	Holiday	13
	Major festival, e.g. Christmas	12
	Minor violations of the law	11

FIGURE 4.4 *The 10 most stressful and 10 least stressful events in the Holmes-Rahe life-event scale*

LIFETIME EXPERIENCE OF STRESSFUL LIFE EVENTS BY TYPE OF EVENT AND GENDER, 2000

EVENT	MALES (PER CENT)	FEMALES (PER CENT)
Death of a close friend or other relative	68	73
Death of a close relative, i.e. parent, partner, child or sibling	51	55
Being sacked or made redundant	40	19
Serious or life-threatening illness/injury	30	22
Separation due to marital difficulties or breakdown of steady relationship	25	29
Bullying	19	17
Serious money problems	14	8
Violence at work	6	2
Running away from home	5	5
Violence at home	4	10
Being homeless	4	3
Being expelled from school	2	1
Sexual abuse	2	5

FIGURE 4.5 *Reports of stressful events by males and females aged 16–75*

Source: Social Trends (2002)

experienced a number of stressful events during their lifetime. These events are listed in Figure 4.5.

Figure 4.5 shows that a majority of people experience the death of close friends or relatives. Only a minority experience homelessness or expulsion from school.

LIFE COURSE EVENT	PHYSICAL ISSUES	INTELLECTUAL ISSUES	EMOTIONAL ISSUES	SOCIAL ISSUES
Starting school	Anxiety, tiredness, stress	New learning about people and places	Feeling unsure or unsafe in the new setting	Making new friends, being accepted
Marriage or partnership	Coping with strong emotions	Learning a new lifestyle	Loss of previous lifestyle Attachment to another person	New social roles
Starting work	Anxiety, stress	Learning new routines and skills	Developing the self-confidence to cope	Making new friends and being accepted
Retirement	Anxiety, stress	Learning a new lifestyle	Coping with loss of previous way of life	Developing new social activities
Bereavement	Anxiety, stress, depression, exhaustion	Letting go of an attachment Learning to cope alone	Coping with loss	Finding support and developing new social routines
Facing own death	Anxiety, stress, depression, exhaustion, possible pain	Summarising your own life and sense of meaning	Achieving an emotional acceptance of death	Preparing to leave close friends and relatives
Serious illness and accidents	Anxiety, stress, depression, exhaustion, possible pain	Understanding and learning about your illness	Coping with loss of previous lifestyle	Finding support and coping with the reactions of others
Relationship breakdown	Anxiety, stress, depression, exhaustion	Learning to cope with the consequences of separation	Coping with the loss of the previous attachment	Finding support, adapting to social change
Loss of job	Anxiety, stress, depression	Learning to find a new job or coping with a different lifestyle	Coping with loss	Losing a network of work colleagues
Financial difficulties	Anxiety, stress, depression	Adapting to a changed lifestyle	Coping with a loss of the previous lifestyle	Coping with the reaction of others
Moving to a new area	Stress	Learning to live in a new environment	Coping with loss of old setting	Meeting new people
Promotion or demotion at work	Anxiety, stress, excitement or depression	Learning a new work role	Coping with loss of previous work role	Coping with new social reactions

FIGURE 4.6 *Possible impact of life course events on people*

Think it over...

What differences in life experience can you see between males and females? What reasons might explain these differences?

The possible impact of life course events on people, using **'PIES' categories**, are shown in Figure 4.6 opposite. (Further discussion of PIES categories can be found on page 250.)

Relationships

Steve Duck (1988) argues that personal relationships and friendships make life meaningful. For many people, relationships are the most important aspect of life. Relationships with parents, children, partners and work colleagues will have a major impact on our quality of life and on our health and income. The social and emotional consequences associated with coping with change are often about changes in relationships. The importance of relationships starts at birth. Babies have an in-built reaction to bond with their caregiver, and mothers may have an in-built tendency to communicate with their child. Throughout the whole of our life, relationships will influence our learning, our lifestyle, our career opportunities, our self-esteem and even our physical health. Duck (1988) quotes evidence that good quality social relationships are

GOOD QUALITY SOCIAL RELATIONSHIPS MAY BE ASSOCIATED WITH:	POOR QUALITY SOCIAL RELATIONSHIPS MIGHT RESULT IN:
Infancy A secure attachment that provides a good basis for self-esteem and loving relationships later in life	Insecure or ineffective attachment. A poor foundation for forming later relationships or developing positive self-esteem
Early childhood An emotionally secure home (safe base) from which to learn about the world. A good basis for developing self-esteem. Social support with learning	A stressful environment, neglect and abuse. Inconsistent /ineffective primary socialisation, negative self-esteem
Later childhood Increasing independence within an emotionally supportive environment. A growing sense of self as a confident and capable person	Unmet emotional needs 'to belong'. Inconsistent /ineffective primary socialisation, a growing sense of self as a person who is not confident and capable
Adolescence The development of a friendship network, a sense of belonging within a social and cultural context. The development of a clear identity/ self-concept and associated confidence and self-esteem	Inconsistent /ineffective secondary socialisation, no clear sense of self. A lack of self-confidence and negative self-esteem
Adulthood A partner and a network of friends and family to provide help and support. Emotional safety, a sense of meaning and purpose in life. An effective sense of self, self-confidence and self-esteem	A lack of social support, lack of protection from stress and depression, increased vulnerability to poor health. Low self-esteem and self-confidence
Late adulthood A partner and a network of friends and family to provide help and support. The ability to maintain an effective sense of self, self-confidence, and self-esteem	A lack of social support, a risk of social isolation, no social protection from stress. The risk of depression and despair. Loss of self-esteem

FIGURE 4.7 *Some important consequences of relationships*

associated with good health, freedom from depression, and satisfaction with life. The development of human relationships is discussed in Unit 1, but some important consequences of relationships are summarised in Figure 4.7.

Supporting people to cope with change

Change can be stressful. Loss, uncertainty, having to spend time and energy engaging in new learning can result in tension, anxiety and even physical and emotional exhaustion.

Buffering – the role of friends, family and colleagues

Close networks of friends, family and colleagues help to protect people from some of the stresses involved with change. Friends, family, partners and involvement with a local community all act as a 'buffer' against stress. Michael Argyle (1987) writes: 'Many studies have found that distress is caused by stress. This effect is, however, greatly reduced or minimised if there are supportive relationships. This is known as **buffering**.'

Key concept

Buffering: A buffer is something that absorbs shock and protects from damage. Friends and family can buffer us from stress; they can help to absorb shock and protect us from harm.

Argyle quotes a study of 7,000 people in California during the 1970s (Berkman and Syme, 1979). Those with supportive social networks had a much lower death rate even after initial health, health practices, obesity, smoking, drinking and social class had been taken into account. In terms of support, marriage produced the strongest protection, with friends and relatives then offering more protection than belonging to churches or other organisations.

Mildred Blaxter (1990) published the results of a national survey into health and lifestyles. She reported that 'self-perceived stress was strongly associated with poorer health of every kind.' She notes: 'Social loss or social isolation are particular forms of stress which have been shown to be particularly dangerous to health. Life event such as widowhood or other bereavement, divorce, job changes, unemployment, migration, even moving from one home to another, are all associated with increased risk of morbidity (disease) or mortality (death).'

Blaxter (1990) reported that 'Family relationships and close bonds have been shown to be strongly protective, perhaps through effects on self-esteem and feelings of control. Certainly, the relationship between social networks and health has been found to be so strong that it can be used predictively in relation to mortality.'

Blaxter's study (1990) provides evidence that there is a positive relationship between marriage, or living with a partner, as compared to being single. This relationship was particularly significant for men and, indeed, older men. For men especially, living alone was associated with more illness and poorer psychological and social well-being. The number of social roles a person had (such as parent, worker, regular worshipper) also related to measures of good health. Although these general findings from a survey cannot be used to make predictions for individual health and happiness, it does appear that partners, friends, family and community social links help protect people from stress. People with close supportive relationships may have useful resources to fall back on when they encounter life-event threats. Socially isolated people may lack a buffer to protect themselves against the anxiety, strain and threat that change may cause.

So Argyle's and Blaxter's work suggests that people with poor social support may be at more risk of dying from an illness than those with close relationships. But how do relationships make a difference to a person's physical health? Argyle (1987) writes: 'One way in which stress is bad for health is that it impairs the immune system, the natural defence against disease. Social support could restore the immune system, by its power to replace negative emotions like anxiety and depression, and their accompanying bodily states, by positive emotions. A second way in which relationships may affect health is through the adoption of better health practices. Those who have good relationships are able to cope with stress by seeking help and social support. Those without are more likely to use other means of coping, like smoking and drinking.'

More recently Seligman (2002) published a study of happiness and how to achieve happiness in life. Among the general conclusions were the observations that being married and also having a 'rich social network' were associated with a high level of happiness. Interestingly, having lots of money and believing you are healthy are not particularly associated with being happy, and yet so many people's lifestyles are focused on money and health!

Good relationships with friends, family and colleagues may result in the types of support illustrated in Figure 4.8.

Lifestyle choices

Think it over...

Thinking of yourself in 15 years time, what do you hope your life will be like? What kind of work will you do? What kind of partnership or family do you hope to have? What kind of house or flat do you hope to live in? What dreams might actually work out for you? Get together in a group and share your thoughts with others.

Did you all come up with the same hopes? People have quite varied ambitions and often choose different lifestyles.

What is a lifestyle?

Chaney (1996) explains that lifestyles 'are patterns of action that differentiate people' they are 'a style, a manner, a way of using certain goods,

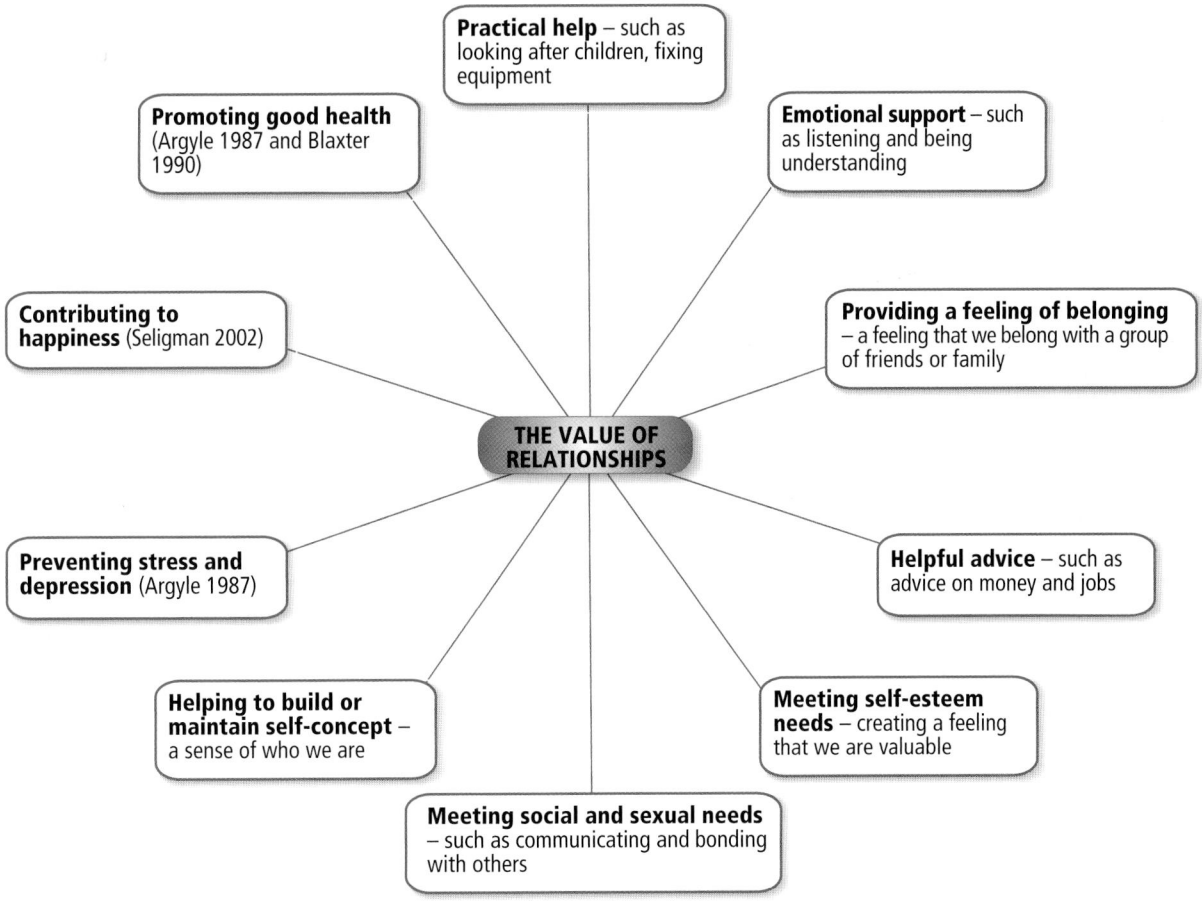

FIGURE 4.8 *The effects of good relationships*

places and times that is characteristic of the group but is not the totality of their social experience.' People use lifestyles in everyday life to identify and explain wider complexes of identity and affiliation.' So lifestyles are ways of working and living that help people to develop a sense of belonging. Lifestyles contribute to a person's understanding of who he or she is. Lifestyles help to provide a sense of identity for people.

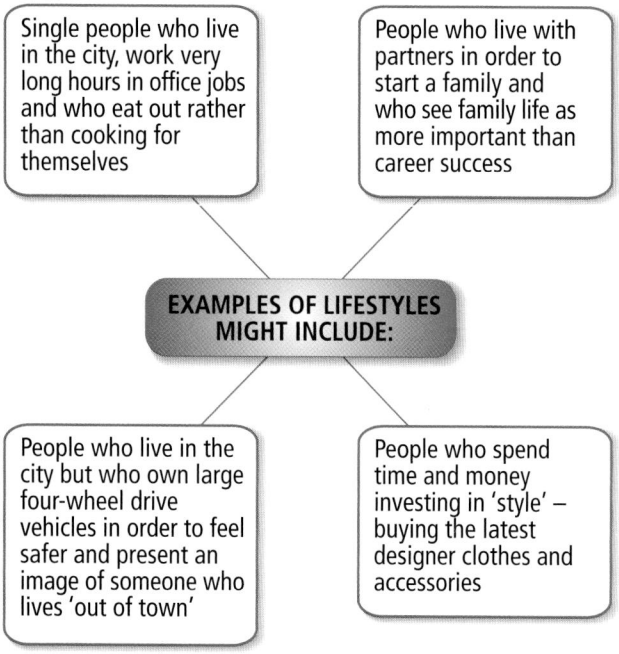

FIGURE 4.9 *Some examples of lifestyles*

People who choose a particular lifestyle are likely to identify with other people who make the same choices.

Lifestyles are based on the way you choose to spend your money and time. Chaney (1996) states that 'lifestyles are therefore usually assumed to be based on the social organisation of consumption rather than the social organisation of production which has classically been taken to be the basis of class structures'.

Key concept

Lifestyle: How a person spends time and money to create a style of living.

Social class: The type of occupation (work) that a person does in order to get money.

Lifestyle choices and life opportunities

The time and money resources that a person has will influence the range of lifestyle choices available to them. You cannot, for example, choose a lifestyle of continually going on world cruises if you have little money and you have to work long hours, leaving you little time for such activity. A person's social class and the income and wealth that they have (see Section 4.2) will have a major influence on the lifestyle choices open to him or her. Lifestyles are always chosen from the range of options that a person perceives to be possible for him or her. Some people – perhaps as many as 22 per cent of the population – have very limited lifestyle choices, because they have a low income. The government uses the term 'social exclusion' – i.e. people who are excluded from the opportunities open to the majority – to identify people with restricted lifestyle options (see Section 4.2).

People's lifestyles are not simply influenced by the work they do and the money they have. People's lifestyles are influenced by the culture they grow up in and by the expectations of friends, relatives, work colleagues and other people that they mix with. You will develop a self-concept – a view of yourself will guide your lifestyle 'choices'. Your view of yourself will be influenced by the people you mix with – as in Figure 4.10.

Most people will develop lifestyle habits as a result of the influences that surround them. Very few people choose healthy or unhealthy lifestyles as result of assessing research data. We find ourselves drifting into a way of living; we do not choose how to behave after reading a catalogue of alternative lifestyles! The word 'choice' can therefore be misleading, as few people actively choose an unhealthy lifestyle.

Many people in the UK do not follow a healthy lifestyle. Some evidence of lifestyle behaviour is presented below.

FIGURE 4.10 *Circles of influence*

Health behaviour

An individual's health is influenced by diet, exercise and lifestyle factors, such as choosing to smoke cigarettes, drink alcohol and use drugs. For further information on the importance of exercise in maintaining good health, see Unit 1.

A healthy diet

Government guidelines recommend that a healthy diet should include at least five portions of fruit and vegetables a day. A national diet and nutrition survey carried out between 2000 and 2001 found

FIGURE 4.11 *Seeing every lifestyle as consciously chosen can lead to the judgmental attitude that 'people only have themselves to blame'*

that only 13 per cent of men and 15 per cent of women follow this advice. No young men between 19 and 24 were following this advice. The survey found that there was a substantial variation between age groups in the number of people who were following this advice.

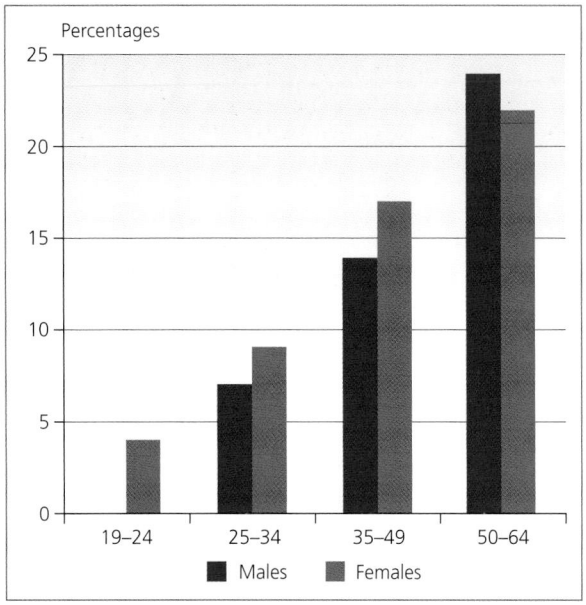

FIGURE 4.12 *Population following advice on 'five portions of fruit and vegetables a day'*

Source: National Statistics (2004)

Think it over...

Why, on average, do more older people eat a healthy diet than younger people? Why do so few people follow government health guidelines?

Smoking

Smoking is associated with heart and lung disease among other serious risks to health. Smoking is statistically associated with socio-economic class. See figure 4.13.

Think it over...

What influences might cause more unskilled workers to smoke than professional workers? What influences might cause more men to smoke than women?

CIGARETTE SMOKING IN 2000		
	MALES (IN %)	FEMALES (IN %)
Professional	17	14
Employers and managers	23	20
Intermediate/junior non-manual	27	26
Skilled manual	33	26
Semi-skilled manual	36	32
Unskilled manual	39	35
All adults	29	25

FIGURE 4.13 *Cigarette smoking in the UK in 2000*

Source: Adapted from Social Trends (2003)

Alcohol

A large number of people use alcohol in a way that may put their health at risk. The Department of Health recommends that men should not drink more than four units of alcohol in a day and that women should not drink more than three units of alcohol in a day.

Figure 4.14 shows the proportions of men and women who exceeded these guidelines on at least one day during the previous week according to the Household Survey 2001/02.

ADULTS WHO EXCEEDED RECOMMENDED LEVELS OF ALCOHOL INTAKE ON AT LEAST ONE DAY OF THE WEEK		
	MALES (IN %)	FEMALES (IN %)
16–24	49	39
25–44	46	30
45–64	36	19
65 and over	18	5
All age groups	39	22

FIGURE 4.14 *Percentage of adults who exceeded DoH guidelines for recommended maximum levels of alcohol in 2001/02*

Source: Adapted from Social Trends (2004)

Think it over...

What influences might cause so many people to consume alcohol in a way that is unsafe for their health?

Drug misuse

Young people between the ages of 16 and 24 years are more likely to take drugs than older people (Social Trends, 2004). Figure 4.15 lists the prevalence of drug misuse by people aged 16 to 24 years in the year 2000–01 according to the British crime survey.

DRUG MISUSE		
	MALES (IN %)	FEMALES (IN %)
Cannabis	33	21
Amphetamines	7	3
Ecstasy	9	4
Magic mushrooms or LSD	3	1
Cocaine	7	2
All class 'A' drugs	12	5
Any drug	35	24

FIGURE 4.15 *Drug misuse by 16–24 year-olds in the year 2000–01*

Source: Adapted from Social Trends (2004)

Think it over...

What influences result in a third of young males and a fifth of young women using cannabis?

The role of self-concept in enabling choice

Unit 1 provides an introduction to self-concept, self-image and self-esteem.

General or global self-concept may also include our assessment of how good we are at things such as sport, at academic learning and controlling our own habits. Our assessment of how good we are at something can be referred to as 'self-efficacy'. The psychologist Albert Bandura (1989) uses the term self-efficacy to include a person's ability to understand his or her capabilities, motivation, thought patterns and emotional reactions. Self-efficacy is how you estimate your abilities or what you believe about yourself. Self-efficacy is learned from past experiences, watching and thinking about what happens to others, copying others and from the feedback we get from other people. High self-efficacy means believing you will succeed at a task. Low self-efficacy means believing you will fail.

Once a person believes he or she is good at something, this belief will provide motivation to keep building on success. Of course, the opposite is also true. If you believe you are no good, then you will probably withdraw from the activity and avoid it.

Some people may learn to think of themselves as being able to control habits such as over-eating or taking drugs; other individuals may develop a low sense of self-efficacy and feel that they are unable to control their own lifestyle. People with low self-efficacy may experience their lives as a series of events that just 'happen to them'. Taking control of your own lifestyle may require a sense of confidence in your own emotional abilities. This sense of self-confidence might be learned in the company of family friends and work colleagues.

Key concept

Self-concept: The understanding that we have of ourselves. It is a learned idea of how we are distinct from other people. Self-concept may be understood as including an image of self and also the degree to which we value what we are – self-esteem.

Self-esteem: The degree to which we value ourselves. Self-esteem is likely to influence how we relate to other people and how confident we are.

Summary of Section 4.1

The following key areas of theory have been covered in this section:

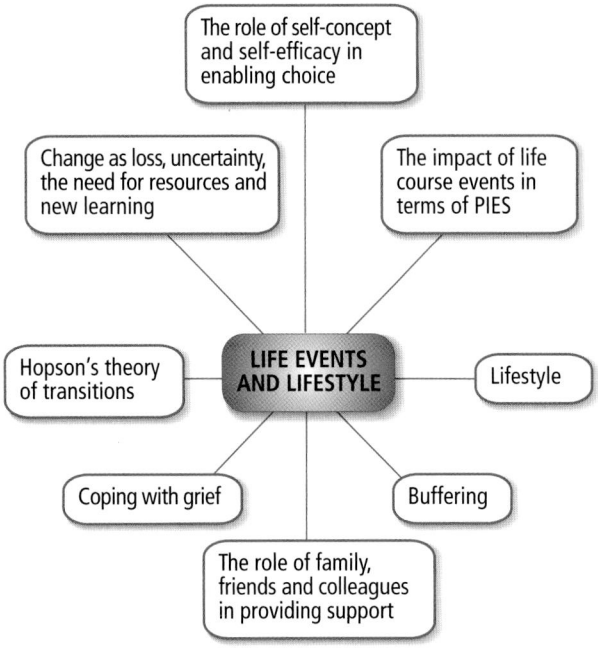

Consider this

Dahlia is a lone parent living in a rented flat with her young son. Dahlia used to work only part-time, but she now works full time following her stressful divorce. Dahlia says that she always feels tired and that it is difficult for her to prepare fresh food. She mainly eats ready-made meals and snacks on chocolate. She knows she is putting on weight but says that the chocolate makes her feel better. Many of Dahlia's friends smoke, and she has now gone back to smoking since the divorce.

Dahlia was recently visited by her mother. Her mother was shocked to find out that she was smoking again. Dahlia's mother told her that she needed to eat more fresh fruit and vegetables and stop living on chocolate and processed food. Dahlia said, 'You just don't understand' in response to her mother.

Using concepts, can you identify?

1 What are the possible consequences of Dahlia's lifestyle choices with respect to diet and smoking?

2 What 'life course events' might Dahlia have to come to terms with?

Go further – can you analyse issues using the theory?

Can you analyse how time and money pressures, loss, and the need for new learning might be affecting Dahlia following the divorce and a return to full-time work? Can you analyse how Dahlia's story might involve Hopson's seven-stage theory of transition? Can you explain why Dahlia does not take her mother's good advice and change her lifestyle?

Go further – can you evaluate using a range of theory?

What connections can you see between Dahlia's current circumstances and her diet and smoking habits? Can you explain how 'life course events' might have an influence on lifestyle behaviours associated with consequences for health?

4.2 Social factors affecting health and well-being

Social class and income distribution

Since the 2001 Census, a new system for classifying social class has been used in all official statistics and surveys. This system uses eight classes to classify occupations and is called the National Statistics Socio-economic Classification. The whole system is very complex and can be viewed through the website www.heinemann.co.uk/hotlinks (express code 370XP). The eight 'analytic classes' used in the system are set out in Figure 4.16. (See also page 267).

1	Higher managerial and professional occupations. This class is split into:
	1.1 Large employers and higher managerial occupations
	1.2 Higher professional occupations
2	Lower managerial and professional occupations
3	Intermediate occupations
4	Small employers and own account workers
5	Lower supervisory and technical occupations
6	Semi-routine occupations
7	Routine occupations
8	Never worked and long-term unemployed

FIGURE 4.16 *The National Statistics Socio-economic Classification – analytic classes*

A person's occupation may have a major impact on the expectations and assumptions that he or she may make about him or herself and individual lifestyle choices. Self-employed people may make different demands on themselves compared with individuals who report to a 'boss'. There is evidence (Michael Argyle, 1994) that people in professional roles often experience their work as more enjoyable and more productive of self-esteem than people who work in routine occupations.

While the analytic classes of the socio-economic classification system shown in Figure 4.16 do not simply reflect income levels, people who work in routine occupations are generally less well paid than people in the higher classes. General income level is likely to be a major factor in influencing a person's expectations and assumptions about life.

Wealth and income

The economic resources that an individual or family has can make a major difference to the quality of life a person leads. Economic resources include wealth and income. Wealth includes:

* savings, in banks or building societies
* the value of your home, if you own it
* shares, life assurance and pension rights
* any other property that belongs to you.

Wealth is not shared out evenly in the UK. Figures for 2001 reported in Social Trends (2004) show that the poorest half of the population only own 5 per cent of the country's wealth and property.

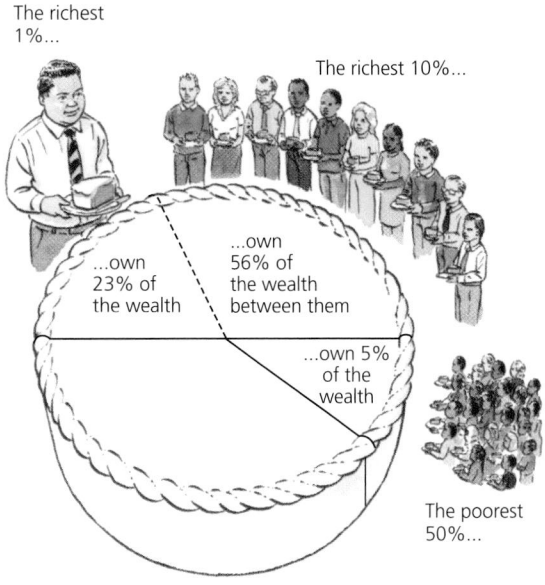

FIGURE 4.17 *The UK wealth cake (based on 2001 figures)*

The top 1 per cent of the richest people own 23 per cent of the UK's wealth. The richest 10 per cent of the population own 56 per cent of the wealth. If wealth was a cake, Figure 4.17 shows how it would be shared out.

Income is what really impacts on the daily lives of the majority of people; your weekly income enables you to pay for your house or flat, and feed and clothe yourself. Income mainly comes from:

* wages you are paid
* profits from your business if you are self-employed
* benefits paid by the government
* money from invested wealth, such as interest on bank accounts or bonds
* money raised through the sale of property you own.

Wealth can be converted to income. For example, some older people might have a low income but own their own house. If necessary, a home owner might raise money on their home through special re-mortgage schemes, or sell up and move to a cheaper house, or move into leased or rented accommodation.

As with wealth, income is not distributed equally in the UK. The top 20 per cent of households receive around 15 times more money each year than the poorest 20 per cent of households. Income is subject to redistribution, however: this means that the highest paid have to pay tax on their income, while many poorer households receive benefits that increase income. After tax and benefits have been paid out, the richest 20 per cent are only four times better off than the poorest 20 per cent of households (National Statistics, 2004).

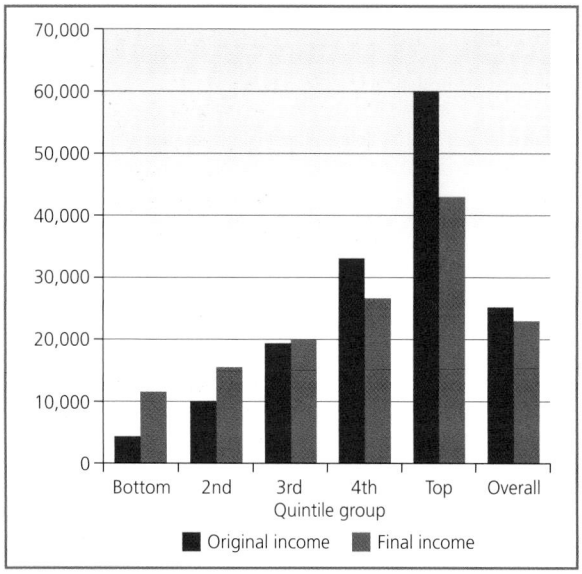

FIGURE 4.18 *The richest 20 per cent are four times better off than the poorest 20 per cent*

Source: National Statistics (2004)

*** DID YOU KNOW?**

Approximately 10 per cent of the United Kingdom population have no savings or investments at all. Among the 20–34 age group, 20 per cent of people have no savings or investments and among young people aged 16–24, 56 per cent have no savings. (The Institute for Public Policy Research, 2004).

Poverty

A century ago the term poverty was associated with families who did not have sufficient money to provide food, shelter and warm clothing for themselves. The term **absolute poverty** is now used to describe a level of deprivation where the basic physical necessities for survival are not available. Homeless children living in London during the 1880s would have been at risk of dying of hypothermia during the winter because of a lack of food and warm clothing. Today, benefit systems are available to prevent UK citizens from experiencing absolute poverty and the risk of dying from hunger or cold.

Peter Townsend (1974) distinguished between absolute poverty and **relative poverty**. Relative poverty means that a family group is deprived in comparison to the standard of living enjoyed by the majority of people. A person living in a household that is suffering from relative poverty may have warm clothing, shelter and food. A household in relative poverty may not be able to afford to own a computer, or pay for access to the Internet or to buy the latest style of clothing. Relative poverty involves being excluded from the lifestyle choices available to the majority of UK citizens.

Key concepts

Absolute poverty: Not having sufficient resources (money/social support) to ensure that you can survive. Your life is at risk from problems such as starvation, exhaustion or hypothermia.

Relative poverty: Not having sufficient resources to live to the same standard that the majority of people do in this country; having an income that is less than 60 per cent of the income that an average person might expect.

Today, poverty is usually measured in terms of households with an income that is less than 60 per cent of 'median' income in the UK. A median is the middle value in a range of numbers – like an average, but not mathematically the same as an average. Low income means having an income that is only worth 60 per cent of the average **income level**. This low-income measure of poverty, which is a measure of relative poverty, is used by the government's Social Exclusion Unit and also by the European Union for making comparisons between member countries. People with a very low level of income are poor relative to the expectations of most people.

Key skills

Work out the difference between an average income and a median income using some figures from Internet research. This work could contribute to Key Skills Number and Information Technology work.

Just over one-sixth of Britain's population (17 per cent) were estimated by the Institute for Fiscal Studies to be living in relative poverty (low income) in the period 2001/2002 (Social Trends, 2004). If a measure of income after housing costs is used, then 22 per cent of households live in income poverty (Paxton and Dixon, 2004). People who receive less than 60 per cent of the income that an average person expects may be considered to be at risk of 'social exclusion'.

Key groups of people who have to live on very little money include: one-parent families, people who are unemployed, elderly people, people who are sick or disabled, single earners, unskilled couples (where only one person works, in an unskilled job).

It is estimated that around 30 per cent of children (3.8 million children) live in low-income households (after housing costs). Furthermore, it is stated that 'children living in workless families or households have a much higher risk of low income than those in families with one or more adults in full-time work'. Around three-quarters of children living in 'workless' or lone-parent families live in low-income households (Social Trends, 2004).

The impact of poverty

Paxton and Dixon (2004) quote research conclusions which show that: 'Children who grew up in poverty during the 1970s did worse at school, were six times less likely to enter higher education, and one-and-a-half times more likely to be unemployed – and earned 10 per cent less during their lifetimes than those who did not experience poverty as children.' The

POVERTY IN THE UK TODAY	
Poverty is associated with being a victim of crime	*'4.8 per cent of people who earned under £5,000 a year were burgled in 2003/4 compared to only 2.7 per cent of people who earned over £30,000'*
Poorer communities are more likely to live in polluted areas	*'In 2003 there were five times as many industrial sites in the wards containing the most deprived 10 per cent of the population and seven times as many emission sources than in wards with the least deprived 10 per cent'*
Low social class is associated with an increased risk of dying young	*'In 2003 children of fathers in the lower social class were twice as likely to die within one year of birth, five times more likely to die in a traffic accident and 15 times more likely to die in a house fire than those in the highest social class'*

FIGURE 4.19 *The disadvantages of poverty (Paxton and Dixon 2004)*

Source: Paxton and Dixon (2004)

disadvantages of poverty, as quoted by Paxton and Dixon (2004), are shown in Figure 4.19.

Social class and health

In 1998, Donald Acheson published an 'Independent Inquiry into Inequalities in Health', a report that had been commissioned by the Government. This report provides evidence of differences between the health of people in different class groups, and also evidence that these differences have become more extreme since the 1970s.

People in the lower social classes are more likely to die before the age of 65 than are people in the higher social classes (Acheson, 1998).

Argyle (1987) offered an explanation as to why social class influences health. He stated, 'The lower social classes are affected by most illnesses more often, take more days off from work, and die a little sooner because of them [the illnesses]. This is partly due to inequalities in the conditions of life – smaller homes, less heating, larger families, less good food, and so on.'

A study by Blaxter (1990) found a very strong relationship between low income and disease, disability, illness and poor psychological and social (psycho-social) health. But it seems that it is poverty that is associated with ill-health, rather than that health gets better the richer you are! Blaxter's studies show that there might be slightly more illness and disease for the very rich than for the more moderately well off. Money itself doesn't seem to create health; but a lack of money may be strongly associated with disease and illness. Blaxter wrote, 'The apparently strong association of social class and health is primarily an association of income and health.' Blaxter's study found that self-perceived stress was strongly associated with poorer health of every kind, but, 'It is notable that the relationship was particularly strong for men in manual classes, at all ages.'

Current research such as 'The Health of Children and Young People' published by the Office of National Statistics in March 2004 continues to report an association between social class and health. This report found that the average birth weight of children born to fathers in manual occupations was lower than the birth weight of children born into non-manual families. The study also reports slightly more long-standing illness amongst children of manual working parents than among children of non-manual parents. Social Trends (2002) states: 'inequality in life expectancy between social classes has widened over the last 20 years'.

Poverty and diet

The Acheson report (1998) refers to 'food poverty' and notes that people in low socio-economic groups 'spend more on foods richer in energy and high in fat and sugar, which are cheaper per unit of energy than foods rich in protective nutrients, such as fruit and vegetables'.

'People on low incomes eat less healthily partly because of cost, rather than lack of concern or information. Therefore, increased availability of affordable 'healthy' food should lead to improved nutrition in the least well off'. The Acheson report notes the following evidence among people in low socio-economic groups:

* eat more processed foods containing high levels of salt, thus increasing the risk of cardiovascular disease
* there is more obesity in low socio-economic groups than in higher groups – increasing the risk of ill-health for low socio-economic groups
* babies born to mothers in low socio-economic groups are more likely to have reduced birth weights than higher groups. Low birth weight is linked with the risk of cardiovascular disease in later life
* women in lower socio-economic groups are less likely to breast-feed their babies. Breast-feeding helps to protect infants from infection.

People who are poor will find it harder to travel to supermarkets and stock-up on cheaper food. The Acheson report notes that 'healthy food' often costs more than processed food, which contains higher amounts of sugar and salt. Poverty may push people to choose an unhealthy diet, because it can be harder and more expensive to choose a healthy one.

Smoking

The Acheson report points out that there are major class differences in smoking behaviour. The report stated that only 2 per cent of men and 16 per cent of women in professional occupations smoked, whereas 41 per cent of men and 36 per cent of women in unskilled occupations smoked. The report notes that people in the lower socio-economic groups find it harder to give up smoking.

Poverty may remove many of the small daily satisfactions of life, such as buying small presents for friends, going out and 'treating yourself'. Poverty or low income may also threaten self-esteem and create stress for individuals. If you cannot afford what other people can, you might evaluate yourself as a loser. This alone could create stress.

When a person feels stressed, anything which promotes an easing of tension will be very desirable. Oakley (1989) quoted in Nettleton (1995) 'found that smoking was significantly inversely related to income, housing tenure, access to a car, telephone ownership and central heating.' In other words, the poorer people were, the more likely they were to smoke. Nettleton theorises that poor health 'choices' like smoking may enable people to cope with poverty. 'Thus whilst affecting people's physical health, smoking may facilitate their mental well-being.' People who are poor and/or stressed may find it harder to trade a long-term future for tempting and stress-relieving treats that can be enjoyed in the present.

Think it over...

Make a list of health risks that might be associated with low income. How might older people on a low income be at risk? If you were a care worker working in the community, how might you expect poverty to influence the people you were working with?

Poverty and housing

People in the professional classes often feel confident about their future and their ability to take out a mortgage to buy their own home. People in the higher social classes can choose where and how they would like to live.

People in the unskilled social categories tend to have less choice, which sometimes forces them to rent property in more densely populated housing areas. Wealthier people will often live in more spacious surroundings and less stressful conditions than people on low incomes.

According to the Acheson report, 'Poor quality housing is associated with poor health. Dampness is associated with increased prevalence of allergic and inflammatory lung diseases, such as asthma.' The Acheson report also noted that '40 per cent of all fatal accidents happen in the home. Almost half of all accidents to children are associated with architectural features in and around the home. Households in disadvantaged circumstances are likely to be the worst affected by such accidents.'

FIGURE 4.20 *Housing in spacious surroundings*

FIGURE 4.21 *Densely populated housing area*

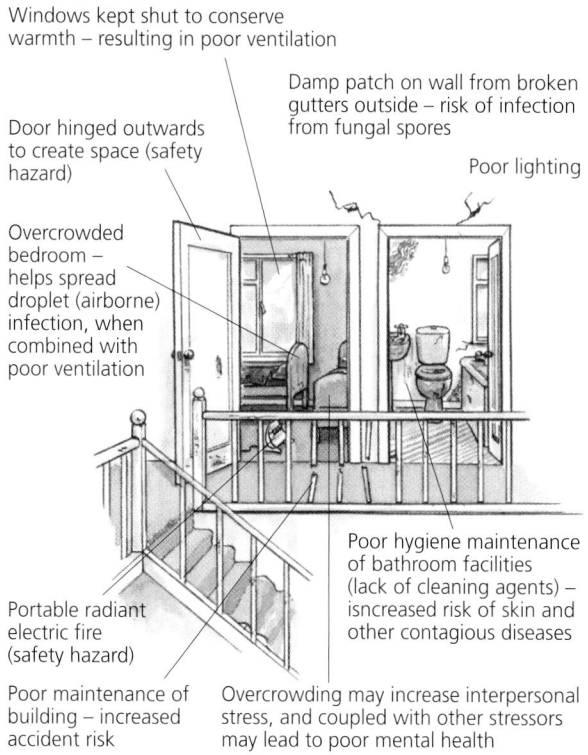

FIGURE 4.22 *Poor housing may create a range of risks*

Older properties are often less insulated than modern properties. Many older people on low incomes worry about the cost of heating in their homes. Older, poorly maintained homes are likely to cost more to heat than recently built properties. For some people who live on a low income in high-density housing, the following problems may create stress:

* noise from neighbours
* more chance of being woken up at night
* stress from neighbours' behaviour
* nearby busy roads where traffic fumes create pollution
* overcrowded rooms and facilities (waiting to get in the bathroom etc.)
* higher risk of becoming a victim of crime
* poor car parking and travel facilities.

The Social Exclusion Unit Paper 'Opportunity for All' (1999) explains that some communities are 'trapped outside mainstream society'. The

FIGURE 4.23 *Problems faced by deprived communities*

problems deprived communities face include those illustrated in Figure 4.23.

Poverty can create a vicious circle

Growing up and living in the most deprived neighbourhoods may greatly restrict an individual's chance of developing his or her full intellectual, social or emotional potential. The problems of poor facilities and crime may prevent employers from starting businesses. Poor facilities and crime may help to cause unemployment. Unemployment may contribute to poor facilities because people have little money to spend. Growing up in a neighbourhood with widespread unemployment, crime and poor facilities may do little to motivate children to achieve a good education. If people do not achieve a good standard of education they may find it harder to find jobs. The problems 'feed off' each other, creating housing estates and areas which are stressful to live in. Neighbourhoods may have a major impact on a person's life chances of growing up to lead a fulfilled life.

Unemployment

'Opportunity for All' (1999) noted that 'unemployment rates are twice as high in the 44 most deprived local authority districts compared with the rest of England.' Inner cities often have 'extreme concentrations of joblessness, perhaps because inner city residents do not have the education and skills needed for the jobs that are available.' The report also notes that race discrimination is likely to be a factor in creating unemployment in many communities.

Crime

'Opportunity for All' (1999) explained that 40 per cent of all crime may happen in just 10 per cent of areas in England. 'The most deprived local authority districts in England experience poor housing, vandalism and dereliction two or three times higher than the rest of England.'

Paxton and Dixon (2004) note that 'for many categories of crime it is those on low incomes and those who live in disadvantaged areas, who are more likely to be victims'. Quoting Home Office statistics, Paxton and Dixon state 'overall, 4.8 per cent of individuals earning under £5,000 were burgled in 2003–4, compared with 2.7 per cent of those are earning over £30,000'. With respect to fear of crime, the percentage of people from the lowest income group who had a 'high fear' of burglary, and of having their car stolen, was approximately double that for people with the highest incomes.

FIGURE 4.24 *Crime is more common in disadvantaged areas*

Poor services

The 'Opportunity for All' paper notes that 'Of 20 unpopular local authority estates in England surveyed in 1994, none had a supermarket or a range of shops, and no more than five had a post office, a GP/clinic, a launderette or a chemist.' Poor communities tend to have:

* a poor range of shops
* above average cost for food and essentials (one study found that food in small shops can cost 60 per cent more than in supermarkets)
* poor public transport
* poor access to information technology and even telephones
* poor access to financial services.

Source: Adapted from 'Opportunity for All' (1999)

The disadvantages found in some housing estates and communities mean that life is both more stressful and shorter than for people in wealthier areas. The 'Opportunity for All' paper quotes a study that suggests that mortality (death) rates are 30 per cent higher in the most deprived local authority districts in England, as compared with the rest of the country.

Think it over...

What stresses might a person with restricted mobility experience if he or she had a low income and lived in a deprived area – compared to if he or she was well off and lived in an affluent area?

Education

Education levels in the poorest communities are lower than for the country generally. The government regards the improvement of primary and secondary school achievements as a major priority, in order to equip people with the skills needed to achieve jobs and careers.

The Acheson Report (1998) notes that schools in deprived neighbourhoods are likely to suffer more problems than schools in more affluent areas. 'Schools in disadvantaged areas are likely to be restricted in space and have the environment degraded by litter, graffiti, and acts of vandalism. This contributes to more stressful working conditions for staff and pupils. Children arriving at school hungry or stressed as a result of their social and economic environment will be

FIGURE 4.25 *A private school and an inner city one*

unable to take full advantage of learning opportunities. Stress, depression and social exclusion may reduce parents' capacity to participate in their children's education.'

Education has a link with health, in that low levels of educational achievement are associated with poor health in adult life (Acheson 1998.) This link may be caused by the fact that poverty causes both poor educational achievement and poor health.

Paxton and Dixon (2004) discuss the links between low income and educational achievement. At primary school level they note 'between 1999 and 2002 pupils in schools where a lower proportion of the intake is eligible for free school meals made more progress at both Key Stage 2 (age 7–11) and Key Stage 3 (age 11–14) than those in schools where more were eligible for free school meals'.

At secondary education level Paxton and Dixon (2004) note '74 per cent of children from the highest social classes achieved five or more GCSEs at grades A to C in 2002, more than twice the proportion of children in the lowest social classes, and 86 per cent were participating in education post 16, 26 per cent more than the lowest social classes'.

It is likely that the combined effects of poor resources, low expectations and the need to earn money often influence young people from low income families to give education a low priority.

In the past there were strong environmental influences that tended to exclude people from a working class background from the higher levels of educational achievement.

Think it over...

Imagine you were working with young children. How would you expect social class and family income level to influence a child's educational development? Make a list of some of the issues that might be different for children from well-off backgrounds as compared with children from low-income families.

Poverty and lifestyle

Growing up in a low-income household is likely to influence the opportunities open to a child. A low-income family may have enough money for food, for some clothes and for heating, but poverty means that there is little money for the interesting purchases that buy into exciting lifestyles. People who depend on benefits have limited life choices.

FIGURE 4.26 *Income will influence what you can choose*

The latest clothes, nice reliable cars, latest electronic equipment, digital TV and so on may not be choices for people on low income. People with little money have to restrict what they can buy when they visit a supermarket or shopping centre.

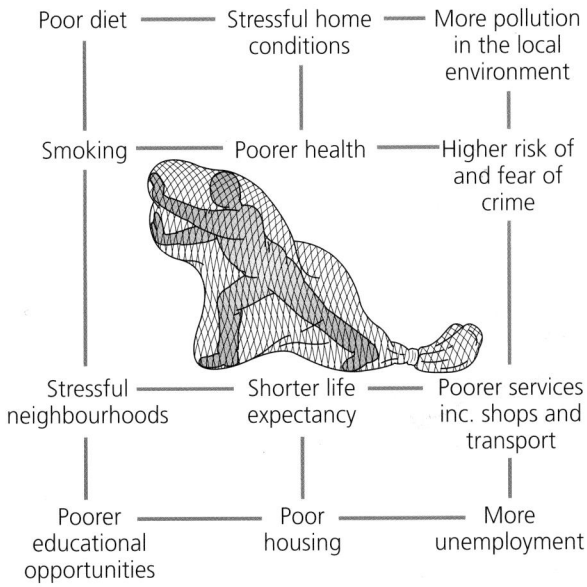

FIGURE 4.27 *Low income is associated with a range of disadvantages*

Many lifestyles are not possible for people in poverty. Belonging to a sports club is not possible if you cannot afford the membership fees, the equipment and so on. Even an activity such as jogging may not be possible if you think your neighbourhood isn't safe to go out in.

People in low-income households will simply not have the same opportunities open to them as people in better off households might have. All the factors listed in Figure 4.27 interact to influence the lifestyle of people who experience relative poverty. It would be wrong to assume that people in low-income households somehow choose a lifestyle that involves smoking, poor diet, poor health and so on. People in low-income households have less opportunity to avoid these disadvantages.

Think it over...

In the following scenario, how far do you think that Thomas has actively chosen his lifestyle? How far has Thomas simply copied the behaviour of other people? What opportunities for different lifestyles has Thomas really had? Thomas knows that his lifestyle is unhealthy. Evaluate why Thomas is not able to change his

SCENARIO

The impact of deprivation

Thomas grew up in a low-income family. His father had difficulty finding regular employment and his mother was treated for depression on many occasions. Thomas often felt anxious and tense because of the 'atmosphere' in the house where he lived.

Thomas's school friends did not enjoy school and used to say that it was a waste of time, as 'there was no chance of a good job anyway'. Many of his friends smoked, drank alcohol and experimented with drugs in the evenings after school.

Now that Thomas is 18 years old, he has a lifestyle that involves a poor diet, smoking, excessive alcohol most days of the week, and taking drugs. Thomas's lifestyle is likely to cause him health problems and to shorten his life.

Gender

It was only in 1928 that women were granted equal rights with men to vote in elections. Eighty years ago women were considered to have a lower social status than men. UK society largely assumed that women should look after children, do housework, cook and generally tidy and do 'light' jobs. Women were often perceived as having the social role of supporting a male 'bread-winner'. Men did the more valuable administrative, management and labouring jobs.

Key concept

Gender roles: Historically there were different expectations as to how men and women were expected to live their lives. There were different expectations about social behaviour, dress, the kind of work that men and women did, and different expectations about behaviour within the family. These expectations create different acts or roles for each gender. These different expectations still exist, to some degree, today.

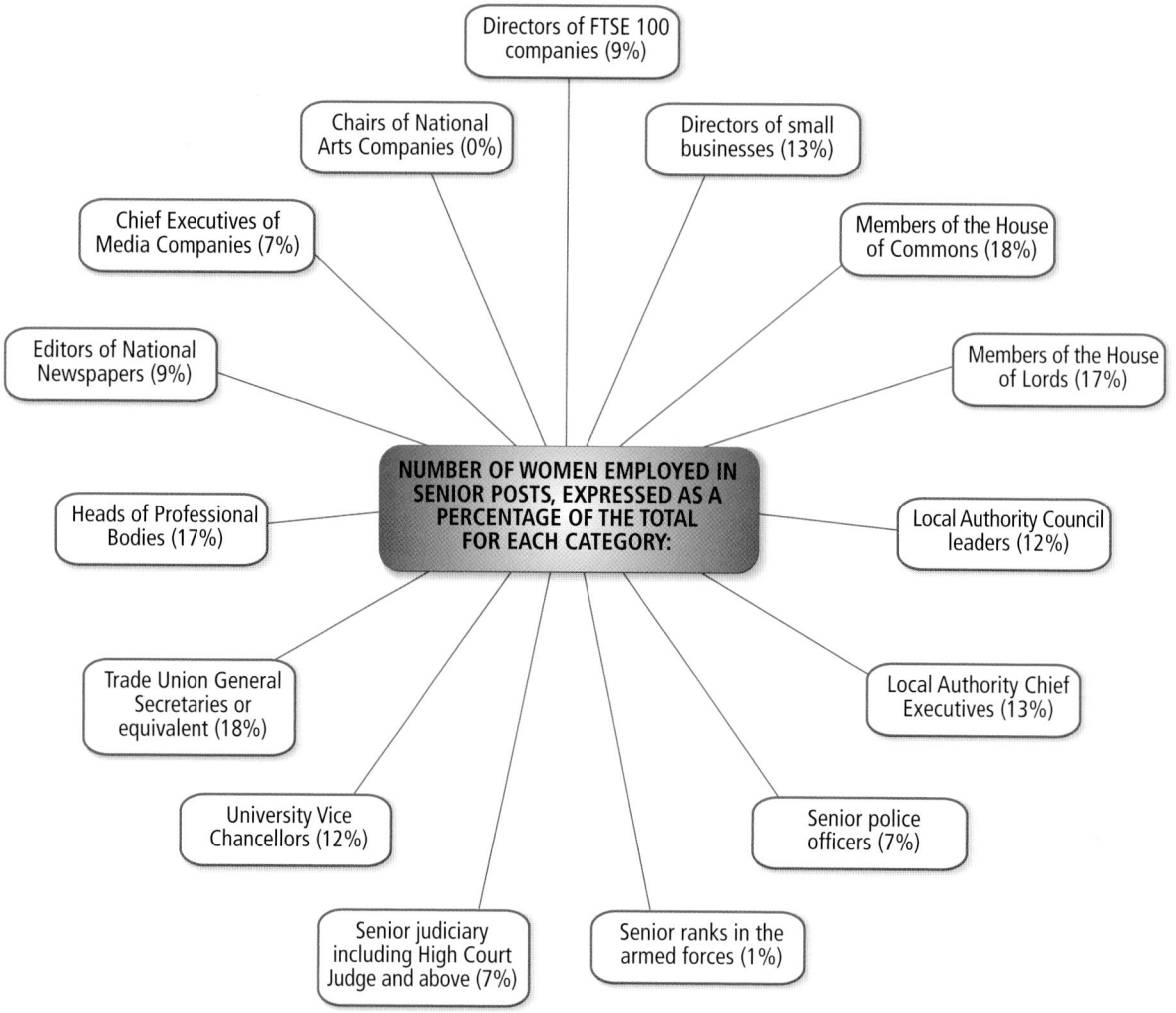

FIGURE 4.28 *Numbers of women holding senior appointments across a range of occupational areas*

Great changes have come about in the nature of work and family life since 1928. Women are now generally seen as having equal opportunities in education and employment. The Sex Discrimination Act of 1975 made it illegal to discriminate against women in education and employment.

However, National Statistics (2004) report that women who work full-time are paid on average just 82 per cent of men's earnings. This is the smallest gender pay gap on record. In 1986, for example, women earned just 74 per cent of average male pay. In London, however, National Statistics reported that average women's pay was just 76.4 per cent of average men's pay.

In January 2004 the Equal Opportunities Commission published a paper entitled 'Sex and Power: Who Runs Britain?' This paper contains a range of statistics with respect to senior appointments. The paper quotes studies that shows women's representation in various sectors of the economy. These are shown in Figure 4.28.

In a press release on the paper Julie Mellor the chair of the Equal Opportunities Commission stated: 'Almost 30 years since the Sex Discrimination Act was passed, women are still massively under-represented in positions of influence in Britain. No one can argue anymore that it's just a matter of time until more women make it to the top (. . .) Women are still often prevented from getting to the top because they take on more caring responsibilities than men. Until every organisation accepts that they can't

THE DIVISION OF HOUSEHOLD TASKS				
TASKS	MALES (IN %)		FEMALES (IN %)	
	ALWAYS ME	USUALLY ME	ALWAYS ME	USUALLY ME
Does the laundry	3	5	52	29
Makes small repairs around the home	36	44	3	7
Looks after sick family members	2	4	29	33
Shops for groceries	3	6	22	27
Does the household cleaning	2	5	31	33
Prepares the meals	3	11	29	33

FIGURE 4.29 *Household tasks*

Source: Adapted from Social Trends (2004)

capitalise on the talent available without taking account of people's caring roles, the profile of the people who run Britain will not change.'

There is compelling evidence of inequality that results in disadvantage for women. Women still hold fewer top jobs and seem to profit less from promotion. Women far outnumber men in jobs like nursing and primary school teaching. Often these jobs are not highly paid. Men usually get the more highly paid jobs such as head teachers, even within areas of work mainly dominated by women. When it comes to domestic work, men still seem generally to do less child care, washing and cooking duties, although they may do more gardening and maintenance jobs.

Figure 4.29 above is adapted from Social Trends (2004). The responses are from male/female couples married, or living together, in response to the question 'In your household who does the following things?' In general, it would appear that men and women still make gender role assumptions about who should do what jobs within the household.

Think it over...

How are household tasks shared in your home or the homes of other people that you know? Are some tasks seen as male tasks and other tasks as female? Why is this so?

Ethnicity

The National Census in 2001 used the system set out in Figure 4.30 in order to identify ethnic group membership.

National statistics suggest that there are significant differences in the experience of economic activity, low income and risk of becoming a victim of crime between different ethnic groups.

The 2001 National Census reports that people from minority ethnic groups were more likely than white people to live in low-income households in 2000/2001. Sixty-eight per cent of Pakistani and Bangladeshi respondents are reported as living in low-income households. Forty-nine per cent of black non-Caribbean households were reported as living on a low income as compared with 21 per cent of white people.

The 2001 National Census reported that 20 per cent of Bangladeshi men were unemployed compared with 5 per cent of white men. Social Trends (2003) reports that more black and Asian families are likely to have a low income as compared to white families. Figure 4.32 shows the proportion of people from different ethnic groups who were in the bottom 20 per cent of the population for the amount of disposable income that they had.

ETHNIC GROUP	CATEGORIES
White	* White * White British * White Irish * Other white background (Statistics can be totalled for all white groups – 92.1 per cent of the United Kingdom population)
Mixed	* Mixed white and black Caribbean * Mixed white and black African * Mixed white and Asian * Other mixed background (statistics can be totalled for all mixed groups – 1.2 per cent of the United Kingdom population)
Asian or Asian British	* Asian or Asian British * Indian * Pakistani * Bangladeshi * Other Asian background (statistics can be totalled for all Asian groups – 4 per cent of the United Kingdom population)
Black or black British	* Caribbean * African * Other black background (statistics can be totalled for all black groups – 2 per cent of the United Kingdom population)
Chinese or other ethnic group	* Chinese * Other ethnic group (statistics can be totalled for all Chinese and other groups – 0.8 of the United Kingdom population)
Ethnicity not stated	(statistics cannot be gathered for all ethnic groups and also for people who choose not to state their ethnicity)

FIGURE 4.30 *Ethnic group membership*

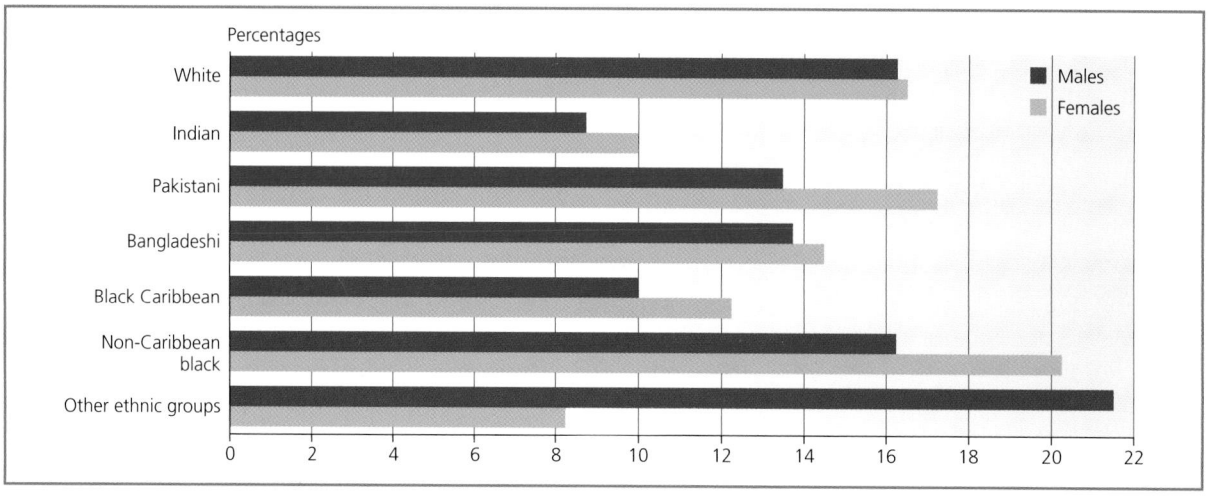

FIGURE 4.31 *Unemployment rates*

ETHNIC GROUP	
White	19 %
Black Caribbean	24 %
Black non-Caribbean	34 %
Indian	29 %
Pakistani / Bangladeshi	64 %

FIGURE 4.32 *The percentage of families with the lowest 20 per cent of disposable income*

Source: Social Trends (2003)

National Statistics (2004) states that almost 60 per cent of Pakistani and Bangladeshi people were living in low-income households, and this figure rises to 68 per cent after housing costs are taken into consideration. Similarly, 49 per cent of black non-Caribbean households also live in low income households after housing costs are deducted. National Statistics (2004) states that 'minority ethnic groups have lower levels of household income than the white population'. Only 21 per cent of the white population were estimated to be living in a low-income household after housing costs.

Both black and Asian people are more likely to be victims of crime than are white people. The British crime survey in 2000 showed that black and Asian adults in England and Wales were roughly twice as worried about becoming victims of crime as white people. Figure 4.33 displays the percentage of people in different ethnic groups who were worried about crime.

	WHITE (IN %)	BLACK (IN %)	ASIAN (IN %)
Theft of car	20	37	37
Theft from car	15	33	30
Burglary	18	37	41
Mugging	16	32	38
Physical attack	17	35	38
Rape	18	34	34

FIGURE 4.33 *The percentage of people who were worried about various crimes*

Source: Home Office (2000

With respect to racial crime, the 2001 census reports the risk of being a victim of a racially motivated crime as 4.2 per cent for Pakistani and Bangladeshi people, 3.6 per cent for Indian people, 2.2 per cent for black people and just 0.3 per cent for white people.

The brief range of statistics presented here might be interpreted as providing evidence of inequality in the experience of different ethnic groups within the UK.

Key concept

The importance of ethnicity: Within a care context it will be important to recognise that ethnic group membership may be central to a persons self-concept. Service users may also be at risk of discrimination if services do not take account of different ethnic identity needs. If a service 'treated everybody the same' and ignored dietary requirements, the need to celebrate different religious festivals, different styles of dress and so on, then various ethnic groups might be discriminated against. The term 'colour-blindness' is sometimes used to describe the tendency to ignore ethnic diversity.

Socialisation

Socialisation means 'to become social'. Children learn to fit in with and be part of a social group. When children grow up within a family group, they will usually learn a wide range of ideas (or norms) about how to behave. For instance, at mealtimes, some families will have strict rules that everyone must sit down at the table and it is considered 'rude' if one person starts to eat before the others.

Other families may not even have set mealtimes – people may just prepare food for themselves when they feel like it. In the evenings, some families might sit round the TV as a social group, while other families might all sit in different rooms doing different activities. Some families are very concerned that people take their outdoor shoes off before coming into the house, and others have no rules about shoes.

Families and similar social groups develop attitudes about what is 'normal' or right to do.

Think it over...

Are, or were, any of the following 'norms' important in your family?

* to say 'thank you' or 'thank you for having me' to the head of a household you visited
* to give thanks in prayer before a meal
* to eat hot food with your fingers
* to go to bed at a fixed time – unless there is a special event or festival
* never to interrupt when an older member of the family is speaking
* that children have set tasks to help adults with the housework
* that male members of the household are responsible for decorating and repairing the house
* that female members of the household are responsible for all the washing and ironing.

You could compare your list with others in your group.

Sociologists call these beliefs 'norms'. Each family will have 'norms' that cover how people should behave.

During childhood, children learn ideas about what is right or wrong. They learn the customs of their culture and family, they learn to play gender and adult roles, and they learn what is expected of them and what they should expect from others. Socialisation teaches children ways of thinking, and these ways of thinking may stay with a person for life.

Key concept

Socialisation: Giddens (1997) explains socialisation thus: 'socialisation is the process whereby the helpless infant gradually becomes a self-aware, knowledgeable person, skilled in the ways of the culture into which he or she is born'. Socialisation involves learning the social norms of your culture.

Primary socialisation

Not everything that a child learns during first (or primary) socialisation within the family group is learned by copying adults. Children also spend time watching TV, listening to the radio and playing computer games. Children will be influenced by the things they see and hear over the media as well as their experiences within the home.

Think it over...

Look at the picture of a breakfast scene in Figure 4.34. Think carefully – how many influences on the children can you spot?

FIGURE 4.34 *Breakfast time*

Did you notice the media influence in this home? The radio sends messages about love and relationships in the songs that are playing. The TV sends messages about news and opinions. The newspaper invites the reader to share its views on current events. Even the cereal packet has an advert encouraging the family to adopt a lifestyle!

Did you notice the gender roles in this home? Who is preparing the children's breakfast, and who is being waited on? What differences are there in the way the two children are playing? What toys have they chosen?

Note the ethnicity of the family. How far might social norms be different for other ethnic groups? Note the norms about length of hair for males and females. Why are there different norms for boys and girls in this setting?

Thinking about this scene, what do you think the children might be learning? Will the daughter tend to copy her mother's behaviour as she grows up? Will she see her role as 'looking after people'? Will the son copy the father's role and expect to be waited on at mealtimes? What expectations might people develop just from being with each other? How far does the media influence people's expectations of their life?

Friendships

Young children enjoy playing with others and will often see children that they play with as being their friends. Children aged 3 and 4 years will often show a need, or even a preference, for being with parents rather than with friends. This is sometimes called 'safe base behaviour' where the child seeks affection and reassurance from parents. By 7 years of age most children will express a preference for playing with others, rather than needing the security of being in close contact with carers.

Friendships become increasingly important as children develop. Older children will see friendships as based on trust. Friends are special people who are trusted – not just people that are available to play with. As children grow older they become increasingly independent. Friendship groups now exert a major influence on behaviour. For a few individuals, the norms and beliefs of friends may conflict with the values and norms learned during primary socialisation.

Secondary socialisation

During adolescence the importance of the family group begins to change. Between 11 and 15 years of age adolescents become very involved with their own group of friends. Most adolescents have a group of friends who influence what they think and believe, usually people of the same age. This is the second influential group to which people belong, and it creates a second type of socialisation, which sociologists call secondary socialisation.

After the age of 12 or 13, a person's sense of self-worth is likely to depend more on the reactions of others of the same age than on what parents say. During adolescence it is important to be accepted and to belong with friends. Adolescents may tend to copy the way other adolescents behave, although adolescents usually retain the values and cultural norms they learned during primary socialisation.

Think it over...

Try to remember when you were 14 or 15 years old. Can you recall what you and others in your class at school thought about the following topics? What sort of beliefs and values did your parents have at that time? Which beliefs are closest to your beliefs now?

1. It is important to get a good job.
2. It is bad and dangerous to use drugs.
3. It is important to go out and have a good time.
4. Wearing the right clothes to look good is a priority.
5. Saving money is a priority.

Key concepts

Primary socialisation: First socialisation within a family or care group.

Secondary socialisation: Later socialisation with friends and peer groups.

The importance of relationships

Socialisation within a family and then later with friendship groups provides an example of how relationships will influence our attitudes, beliefs and lifestyle choices. Throughout our life the people that we mix with and work with will influence us.

A person's culture, beliefs, and lifestyle will be strongly influenced by his or her life experience. Influences on lifestyle work at a number of different levels. Figure 4.35 below presents a summary of these influences.

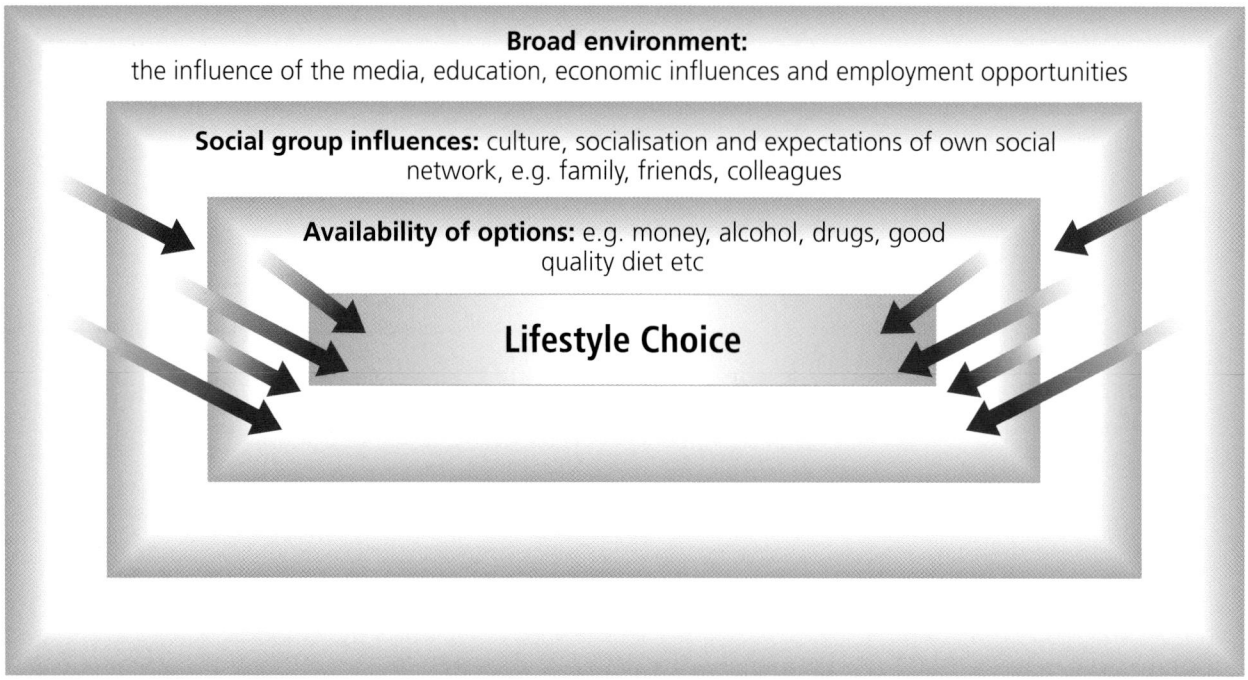

FIGURE 4.35 *A summary of influences on lifestyle choice*

Each person is unique

The influences in Figure 4.35 all interact in order to influence the lifestyle choices that a person might make. But social class, ethnicity, gender, socialisation and income level are simply influences: they do not fix a person into a specific lifestyle. Each individual person will have experienced different relationships and life events. These experiences are interpreted in the context of a person's culture and socialisation. Each individual person is expected to develop his or her own self-concept. The way a person understands him or herself will be unique.

It is very important to understand how a service user's life experience might be different from your experience. It is very important not to judge people because you would have made different choices. It is therefore important for you to be able to identify some of the influences that affect the way people live their lives.

Knowledge of issues such as relative poverty, ethnicity, socialisation and so on can never be enough to enable you to fully understand a person. Each person has his or her own special story to tell. In care work, it is important to be able to understand people as individuals as well as some of the general influences that effect the choices that they make. The third section of this unit explores this individual aspect of care practice.

Consider this

Peter is 28 years old. He grew up in a low-income household in an area with high unemployment. Peter has a large group of male friends who drink heavily. One night Peter was involved in a road accident that left his legs paralysed. Since the accident Peter has become depressed and is now dependent on alcohol.

Kamal is also 28 years old. He also grew up in a low-income household and experienced a wide range of disadvantages. Kamal uses a wheelchair, following an industrial accident. Kamal is very focused on following a career and states that disability should not be an obstacle to leading a full life.

Peter and Kamal meet and exchange their thoughts about their own personal life events. Kamal says, 'Well, I believe that God gave me this life and that I have to do the best I can to be happy and cope with whatever life throws at me. There are always possibilities – things you can achieve. When one door shuts another one opens. You must never give in to negative thoughts'. Peter says, 'Well, it ain't like that in my life – I don't see anything to look forward to. You can't have had the tough life that I have had.'

Using concepts, can you identify:

1. Possible ways that social relationships may have influenced the differences in the way that Peter and Kamal think?
2. Possible differences in the socialisation processes that Kamal and Peter may have experienced?

Go further – can you analyse issues using theory?

How can you explain how, while Peter and Kamal both grew up in low-income families, they have very different attitudes to coping with disability? What are the key factors that may be influencing the different lifestyles of these two people?

Go further – can you evaluate using a range of theory?

Using the story of Peter and Kamal, can you evaluate how a wide range of different influences might interact to create different attitudes to life and lifestyle choices?

4.3 Care professional/ service-user relationships

Absolute poverty existed in the UK during the 19th century. At this time some charitable care services focused on providing food, shelter and warmth in order to help people to survive. For example, Dr Barnardo saved the lives of children who did not have food or shelter.

Fifty years ago absolute poverty had largely ceased to exist. Caring approaches no longer needed to focus on pure physical survival, but a focus on physical care and safety still dominated service provision. Some care services for young children focused on 'minding them,' protecting them and ensuring that they did not come to harm. Some services for people with a learning difficulty catered for them in special institutions such as hospitals and centres where they were separated from the rest of society in order to 'protect them'. Care of older people focused on homes where older people could be depandent and 'be looked after'. 'Patients' were 'treated' as dependant people that could benefit from expert medical intervention without needing to understand what was happening.

Today, care services in the United Kingdom are becoming increasingly focused on service users as people with social, emotional and intellectual needs as well as being people who may have physical and safety needs. See Figure 4.36.

MEETING THE NEEDS OF SERVICE USERS	
Health care	Service users are being encouraged to become more active in the management of chronic illnesses and in making healthy lifestyle choices
Learning difficulty	People with learning difficulty are being encouraged to take control of their lives through initiatives such as Person Centred Planning
Older people	The importance of 'the person' and personal choice is stressed in person-centred approaches to care
Early years	The central importance of meeting educational needs is now emphasised in care services. National Curriculum standards emphasise the importance of enabling children to develop a sense of emotional well-being, a sense of belonging and a sense of self-assurance. Services must meet social, emotional and intellectual needs; services can no longer just be about 'looking after' or minding children

FIGURE 4.36 *The changing focus of care services*

Service-user centred relationships

People who receive health care are referred to as 'patients'; this is because, in the past, individuals had to wait patiently while doctors and nurses did things to them. Today, the government is concerned that service users should have more choice over the services they receive, and that they should have a say in the way that they are cared for. An example of this new approach is the 'Expert Patient' initiative referred to in Unit 2.

It is easy to imagine that health care is just about having things done to you – for example, having the right operation or receiving the right drugs.

Think it over...

When you go to the dentist for a tooth filling, perhaps all you want is to have the filling and get it over with. You might not expect much conversation – you might only have a 15-minute appointment, and you find that you cannot talk with a drill in your mouth!

Compare this to being told that you have a serious illness. You would probably want to talk this through with a health professional as much as possible. The way you were treated would probably have a big impact on the level of distress you experienced. You would probably want to talk to a health-care worker who understood the technical nature of your illness, but who could also provide a 'caring presence'.

Engebretson (2004) explains the importance of being open to the experience of other people. Health and care work cannot simply be about 'doing things' to people. Creating a caring presence is about sharing an understanding of the feelings that service users have. Engebretson explains how nurses can work on an emotional level in order to make a real difference to what people experience when they receive health care.

Person-centred care

Government policy and associated national standards are recognising the importance of service users' intellectual, social and emotional needs.

For example, services for very young children now emphasise the importance of educational development. Care environments must encourage the development of human potential. Proposed occupational standards for 2005 NVQ awards stress the value of placing 'children and young people's preferences and best interest at the centre of everything you do'. A second values statement requires workers 'to work in partnership with children and young people, parents, families, carers and those within and outside your organisation to enable the children and young people's needs, wishes and preferences to be met'.

Key concept

Person-centred care: Care that places 'the person' at the centre of decision-making and activities; care that seeks to value the individual 'personhood' of service users.

In services for people with learning difficulties, the government White Paper 'Valuing People' (2001) argues that services should use person-centred approaches when planning care. Person-centred means that care must be focused on the specific needs and wishes of the service user. Service users plan their own lives and make their own choices using help from family, friends and professionals. Service users are empowered to have control of their own lives; they are not controlled by the wishes of other people.

Personhood

Some of the most vulnerable people who receive care services are older people with Alzheimer's disease or dementia. Kitwood (1997) explains how, in the past, people with dementia often experienced very poor-quality care. Dementia is an illness that includes problems with thinking and making sense of what is happening around you. If care is seen as just about 'looking after people', 'making people better' or 'meeting physical needs', then working with people who have dementia can feel hopeless. People with dementia have often in the past been understood in terms of 'no cure, no help, no hope' or 'the death that leaves the body behind'. Kitwood argues that there is an alternative approach to caring for people, based on the principle of 'personhood'. Carers need to establish a relationship involving recognition, respect and trust. The first task of care is to maintain a service user's sense of being a person – not to find a cure for the dementia.

Key concept

Personhood: Recognition and respect for the self-concept and self-esteem needs of service users.

Kitwood (1997) argues that: 'The prime task of dementia care is to maintain personhood in the face of failing mental powers. Now it is possible to go further and suggest that this will occur through the sensitive meeting of this cluster of needs.' Kitwood's approach to maintaining personhood is summarised in Figure 4.37.

NEED	EXPLANATION
Comfort	'... *the soothing of pain and sorrow, the calming of anxiety, the feeling of security which comes from being close to another. To comfort another person is to provide a kind of warmth and strength which might enable them to remain in one piece*'
Attachment	'... *without the reassurance that attachments provide it is difficult for any person, of whatever age, to function well*'
Inclusion	Kitwood argues that all people need a distinct place in the *'shared life of a group'*. Individual care plans may overlook the social needs of individuals
Occupation	People need a sense of purpose and need to be involved in personally significant activities that draw on their abilities
Identity	*'To have an identity is to know who one is. (...) it means having a sense of continuity with the past, and hence a 'narrative, a story to present to others'*

FIGURE 4.37 *The needs of people with dementia, based on Kitwood (1997)*

Kitwood's approach might be seen as arguing for person-centred relationships. A person-centred approach involves more than simply providing choice. Person-centred approaches place great value on the social, emotional and identity needs of each unique individual person.

The risk of stereotyping

It is very hard to really understand people. Sometimes people try to make life easy by using fixed ideas to explain 'what people are like'. When a person has fixed ideas that he or she uses to see people as 'all being the same', this is called

SCENARIO

Two care settings

What evidence can you find of a person-centred approach in either of the two care settings below?

The Meadows is a modern purpose-built care home that accepts service users with dementia. The home is often short-staffed but residents are always well fed, and the home is clean and well equipped. Residents always have a choice of food, although communication difficulties often result in service users not understanding what they are being offered. A 'service user plan' for each service user is kept in the office, but some care workers say they do not have time to use these plans.

'12 Springfield Road' has a specialist unit caring for people with dementia. There is a good ratio of care workers to service users, and staff try to build a supportive relationship. All care workers understand the personal history and interests of the service users. Carers spend time listening to and reminiscing with service users, despite the fact that service users often repeat statements and say things that are not easy to follow. Care staff understand that people with dementia often have important emotional needs that may not be clearly expressed in verbal communication. Carers explain that 'you need to listen for the message behind the words – and not just for the words themselves'. Some care workers have learned basic aromatherapy and foot-massage techniques, which are offered to service users. Carers explain that these approaches can help anxious people to relax and feel safe.

Although The Meadows offers choice, and a clean, well-equipped setting, there is little evidence of a person centred approach there. Springfield Road offers:

Comfort	Foot massage and aromatherapy
Attachment	Staff try to build supportive relationships
Inclusion	Staff listen – despite the difficulties
Occupation	Some reminiscence activity and foot massage and aromatherapy
Identity	Concern for service user's identity (staff learn their history)

'stereotyping'. Making generalised assumptions about people is, in many ways, the opposite of person-centred working.

Key concept

Stereotyping: Stereotyping is a fixed way of thinking, involving generalisations and expectations about an issue or a group of people.

Some adults might even have a stereotyped view of children. Every child is an individual person with his or her own personality, but some adults might think of children as problems that have to be managed. Thinking of a child as a problem might be caused by stereotyped assumptions such as those listed in Figure 4.38.

People make assumptions based on stereotyped thinking. For example, an adult might say to an early years worker: 'I don't know how you do your job – working with noisy children all day, they would drive me nuts!' This person might be making assumptions based on the stereotype that young children are all 'difficult, naughty and noisy'.

Stereotypes of people with disability are common. Disabled people are often understood as being damaged versions of 'normal' people. When disabled people are negatively stereotyped in this way, they may be pitied and ignored. The classic example iswhen someone asks a disabled person's carer 'Does he take sugar?' The person using a stereotype assumes that the disabled person is 'too damaged' or 'too in need of care' to answer a question by him or herself.

Older people are often negatively stereotyped. Old age is sometimes thought of as a time of decline and decay. The individual potential of a person is ignored and they become just 'another problem old person.'

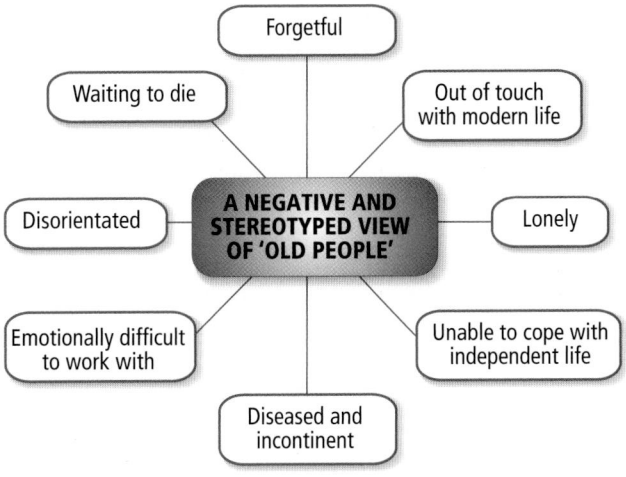

FIGURE 4.39 *Examples of negative stereotypes of older people*

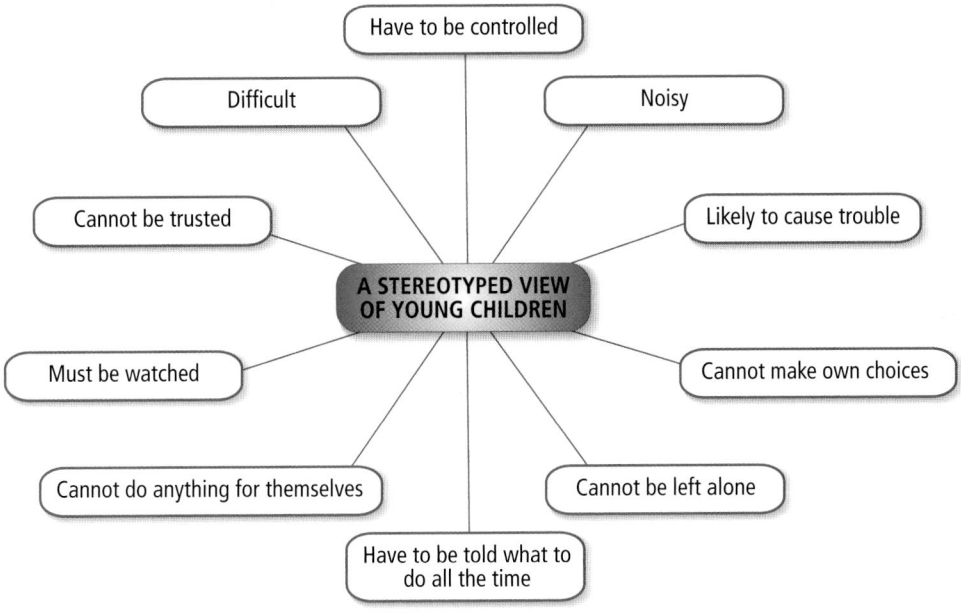

FIGURE 4.38 *Examples of stereotyped assumptions about children*

A negative stereotype of older people might include concepts such as those illustrated in Figure 4.39.

All stereotypes involve making assumptions; the assumptions in Figure 4.39 may have negative, discriminatory and damaging outcomes for older service users.

Not all stereotypes are 'put-downs': some are 'put ups'! Some people get 'put-up' as having unrealistic abilities. An example might be the stereotype that some patients have traditionally held about doctors. This is the stereotype that doctors are 'all knowing' and 'all seeing'; the patient simply needs to 'be patient' and obey doctor's orders. Such a stereotype could be referred to as a positive stereotype insofar as it creates an unrealistic 'positive' set of assumptions about medical practitioners. Any stereotyped thinking – whether positive or negative – may result in problems. Patients with unrealistic assumptions about the power of their GP may become angry and dissatisfied with a less than superhuman performance. 'But why didn't my GP notice that I had a rare medical condition?' The answer is that the GP does not know everything – but such an answer will not please

MORAL RIGHTS OF SERVICE USERS	THE DANGERS OF STEREOTYPED THINKING
Respect for diversity and difference and the equal value of different people	Stereotyped thinking makes fixed assumptions about different groups. These fixed assumptions may result in a lack of respect for diversity. Fixed assumptions may also result in some groups being valued more highly than others. A carer might think 'these people are different from me – therefore there is something wrong with them or bad about them'
Treating people as individuals	Stereotyped thinking ignores individuality and sees all members of a group as being the same
To be free from discrimination	Because stereotyped thinking involves assumptions, stereotyping may result in discrimination. 'These people are lucky to be cared for – I can treat them however I want to'
Confidentiality	Stereotyped thinking might result in this right not being seen as important. 'Oh, they won't understand or know what I'm saying so it doesn't matter if we break confidentiality!'
Control over own life – independence	Stereotyped thinking might result in not seeing people as having individual needs. 'I won't bother getting to know them; they are all the same anyway'
Choice	Seeing people as similar might result in not bothering with choice. 'I won't bother asking their opinion – I'll treat them all the same; it's quicker that way'
Dignity and privacy	Fixed assumptions might result in a lack of dignity and privacy. 'Oh, this person is old/disabled/has a learning difficulty/is very young – so they won't understand or remember what is going on'
Effective communication	Fixed assumptions could result in some workers deciding that communication doesn't matter. 'Just tell them what to do – there is no point in talking with them'
Safety and security	Stereotyping might result in some risks not being spotted. 'I can see a trip hazard; surely they can see it as well!'
The right to take some risks	Fixed thinking might result in overprotective behaviour. 'You've all got to stay in because it is cold outside and you might catch a cold if you go out'

FIGURE 4.40 *Some service-user rights associated with care values found in the GSCC Code of Practice*

people who like to live in a simple world of assumptions.

Stereotyped thinking might result in a care worker ignoring a service user's rights. For example, a worker might think 'I won't offer this person a choice because she's old – old people don't remember, so it doesn't matter what I do'. Stereotyped thinking might result in carers failing to follow the code of practice (see Unit 2).

Skilled caring starts from being interested in people's individual differences. Stereotyping is likely to 'clump' people together as 'all the same'.

The impact of stereotyping

Acting on generalised assumptions about people might result in behaviours that infringe the rights of service users. Figurer 4.40 lists some examples of service-user rights and the dangers of stereotyped thinking.

Key concept

Care value base: A series of principles that guide care practice. These principles were originally identified in National Vocational Qualifications but can also be identified in codes of care practice.

The care value base

The importance of person-centred and empowering care approaches is that they enable service users to achieve a 'quality life'. Just meeting physical needs for food, shelter and warmth cannot in itself result in a quality life. Using Abraham Maslow's theory of human needs (1970), a quality life involves feeling safe, feeling that you belong and feeling that you are worth something. Modern, empowering care approaches will result in service users developing their potential, and building or maintaining a sense of self-esteem. Values specified in national occupational standards, and values specified in the GSCC (General Social Care Council) Code of Practice will contribute to meeting a broad range of human needs, so improving the quality of life experienced by service users. See Figure 4.41.

HUMAN NEEDS	HOW VALUES MAY CONTRIBUTE TO A QUALITY LIFE
The development of potential	Meeting intellectual and educational development needs will help a child to develop his or her full potential
Self-esteem	Individuality and choice will help to promote self-esteem. Respect for dignity and privacy will help to promote self-esteem
Belonging	Respect for diversity may help to promote a feeling of inclusiveness and belonging. Effective communication may be necessary to meet belonging needs
Safety	Freedom from discrimination and maintenance of confidentiality will help to create emotional safety. Risk assessments and arrangements for security may help to promote physical safety
Physical needs	A safe and secure environment will include facilities to meet physical needs

FIGURE 4.41 *The importance of values in meeting human needs*

Empowerment

Person-centred approaches aim to put the individual person at the centre of the way care services work. The individual person will have power over how he or she lives his or her life. The theory of empowerment involves service users having the power to choose how care services work for them.

Key concept

Empowerment: Empowerment enables service users to make choices and take control of their own life. The opposite of empowerment is dependency, where service users are expected to accept whatever services the State or their carer chooses to provide for them.

SCENARIO
Learning difficulty

Drew is a 22-year-old man with learning difficulty. Drew is currently working on his own life map, together with Alex (a care worker), in order to map out his life story. This life story will include Drew's likes and dislikes, his hopes and fears for the future and his dream of what he would really like in life. Drew's life map will help him to work out what kind of living arrangements and services he wants. Direct payments (cash payments made to people who have been assessed as needing social service provisions) might enable Drew to choose the services that are right for him.

Andrew lived in a large 'Hospital for the Mentally Handicapped' in the 1960s. His daily routine followed a strict pattern of getting up and going to bed at the same time every day. Andrew received three meals a day, but was never offered a choice of food. Staff would say, 'Oh it would be unkind to offer them a choice, they would only get confused – we make all the decisions for them so that their life is easy.' There was strict security in the hospital and Andrew was not allowed to go outside 'for his own good – in case he got lost.' Andrew was only allowed to mix with friends in supervised settings so that staff could 'keep an eye on him.'

Think it over...

Who had power in Andrew's story? Can you see any evidence of stereotyped assumptions about people with learning difficulty in Andrew's story?

What has changed between Drew's experience and Andrew's experience? Who has power in Drew's story?

Some aspects of empowering care are illustrated in Figure 4.42. A fuller explanation of this is offered in Figure 4.43.

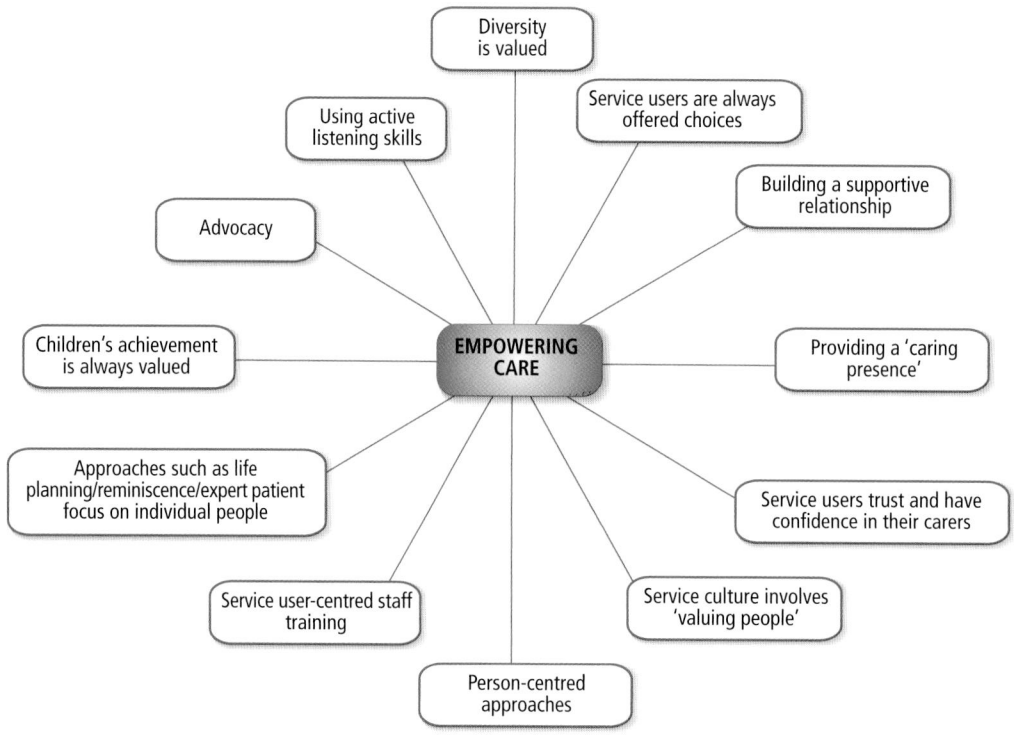

FIGURE 4.42 *Aspects of empowering care*

ISSUE	EXPLANATION
Diversity is valued	Services do not discriminate against, stereotype or judge people who are different. Different lifestyles, different cultures and different life experiences are valued. Difference is not seen as a threat to carers
Using active listening skills	An important practical skill for showing respect and value towards others is to prove that you listen to what people have to say
Building a supportive relationship	Active listening can enable a carer to build an understanding of an individual service user. Empowering, individual care depends on building understanding. An understanding, warm and friendly approach together with honest, genuine behaviour may help to achieve a supportive relationship (see Unit 2 for further details)
Providing a 'caring presence'	In some situations service users may not want to talk. A person who understands this might support a service user 'just by being there'. Emotional support can be conveyed without words. A service user might feel respected, valued and empowered just by the way in which staff responds to him or her
Person-centred approaches	Person-centred work focuses on the needs and wishes of the individual person. A person's needs are not assessed in terms of what experts think. Each individual person's way of thinking has to be understood and respected
Staff training that is centred on service users	The GSCC Code of Practice emphasises the importance of staff training. The Nursing and Midwifery Council also emphasises the importance of maintaining professional knowledge in its code of practice. An empowering service might be expected to evidence specific training or staff development approaches that will support carers to empower others
Service users always offered choices	Empowerment involves offering service users choices such as diet and approaches to personal care. Service users can always be offered a choice of how, where and when services are offered
Adopting a non-judgmental approach	Because people have different life experiences it is important not to judge people on the basis of your expectations and assumptions about life
Advocacy	When a service user cannot understand the possible choices open to them or cannot express his or her choice, an advocate may be able to speak for him or her. Group work can help people to understand the choices open to them. This approach may involve self-advocacy
Service users trust and have confidence in their carers	When people feel respected, valued and supported to make their own decisions, they may respond by trusting and valuing the people that work with them. Empowering approaches should result in staff being trusted
Service culture involves 'valuing people'	Carers will feel that their work is important and valuable if they are successful at empowering service users. For staff to work effectively they will need to feel that they are respected and valued as individuals by the service they work for
Children's achievement is always valued	Healthy emotional development during our early years may be influenced by the positive feedback we receive from others. Praise and acknowledgement of a child's achievements – such as putting his or her work on the wall – may help to boost the child's self-confidence

Continued overleaf

ISSUE	EXPLANATION
Approaches such as life planning/ reminiscence/expert patient focus on individual people	Adult services may develop specific approaches that focus on maintaining or developing individual service user's self-confidence and self-esteem. Life planning work may help people with learning difficulty to make lifestyle choices. Reminiscence work may help older people to maintain a sense of identity in self-esteem. The expert patient initiative may help people with chronic illnesses to feel in control of the management of their condition
Building and maintaining personal identity	If empowering approaches are effective they will result in service users developing and keeping a sense of who they are and a sense of self-esteem

FIGURE 4.43 *Explanations of some of the issues raised by 'empowering care'*

Empowerment involves the opposite of stereotyping. In order to empower, carers need to build a relationship that involves understanding the unique story of each person. An empowering approach can never involve seeing a group of people as 'all being the same'.

Empowerment involves the opposite of making judgments about people. An empowering approach involves understanding that our life experiences and socialisation are likely to be different from other people's experiences. It is not appropriate to interpret other people's lives in terms of our assumptions.

Empowerment involves the opposite of the service user being dependent on his or her carers. Empowerment means that the service user takes control of important decisions.

Empowerment involves the opposite of inequality and discrimination. Empowerment involves service users and carers enjoying an equal status. The care worker is not a person of higher status than the service user.

Think it over...

In the scenario below, Zoë's behaviour does not fit with the values expected of care workers. What is the central problem with her behaviour? Zana's behaviour is much more positive and could be seen as fitting with person-centred and empowering philosophies. Evaluate what it is about her behaviour that is so positive.

The importance of self-concept and self-esteem

One way of understanding how our self-concept develops is that we are strongly influenced by the

SCENARIO
Meeting needs in an early years setting

Zoë does some babysitting with 10-month-old Mark during the day, in order to earn a bit of extra pocket money. Zoë has never had any professional training. She likes children, but she is 'addicted' to day-time TV soaps. Zoë will play with Mark for a little while, but as soon as her favourite programme appears on TV, she straps Mark into his pushchair in the hope that he will go to sleep if she ignores him.

Zana is a professional early years worker. Zana is focused on the need to respond to Mark's behaviour. When Mark makes sounds, Zana will respond by speaking in a high-pitched tone designed to attract Mark's interest. Zana spends time smiling at Mark and talking to him in order to build a relationship with him. Zana sees the purpose of her work as meeting Mark's needs, which include emotional and intellectual development needs.

way other people treat us. Cooley (1902) believed that a person's idea of him or herself was created by seeing what was reflected in the opinions and reactions of others. This theory of self is called the 'Looking Glass' (or Mirror) theory of self. If other people appear to like you, listen to you, enjoy your company and treat you with respect then you will come to see yourself as a worthwhile person and begin to develop self-confidence and self-esteem. If other people appear to treat you as a nuisance, a burden, someone who is not worth talking to, or someone to avoid then you are likely to develop a low opinion of your own value and low self-esteem.

Today, most social scientists would explain self-concept as being created by a person's imagination as well as by the impact of other people's behaviour. But perhaps there is some truth in the idea that our self-esteem can be strongly influenced by the people around us – even if the role of other people does not explain everything.

Care values, theories of empowerment and person-centred working all emphasise the value of each individual service user. All the little things that carers do – whether or not they acknowledge you, whether they smile at you, whether they have time to talk to you, whether they can remember things you've told them – will influence how you see yourself reflected in their 'mirror of value'.

Figure 4.44 *Our self-esteem can be influenced by those around us, in the so-called 'mirror of value'*

Activities such as reminiscence work with older people, life-story and person-centred planning work all involve helping a person to maintain or develop a strong sense of who they are and what they want from life. Empowering approaches enable people to develop and maintain self-esteem. Effective and supportive interaction with young children will enable a child to develop an idea of him or herself as valuable. Ultimately, the importance of care values is that service-user rights should result in service users developing and maintaining a strong sense of self-worth and self-esteem.

Summary of Section 4.3

The following key areas of theory have been covered in this section:

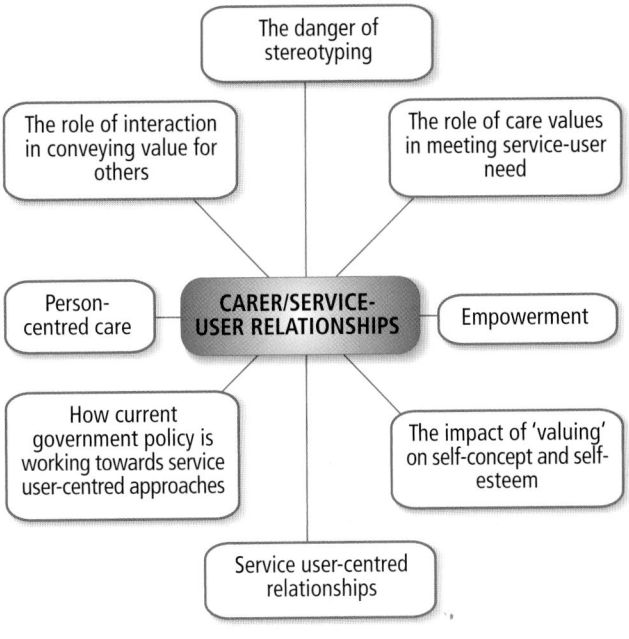

Consider this

Gloria grew up on the island of St Kitts in the Caribbean. She has lived in the UK for the last 40 years. One year ago Gloria was diagnosed as having Alzheimer's disease (a type of dementia) and she now lives in a care home. She appears restless and makes statements about needing to go out to the market in order to buy yams for the children.

Some care workers respond to her statements in a routine, stereotyped way, saying things like 'Never mind all that, you live here now', and they talk to each other and say 'It's the dementia, she doesn't know what she is saying'. Olara is also a care worker, but Olara spends time sitting with Gloria and listening to her. Olara will sometimes remind Gloria to look at a photograph of her daughter and grandchildren. Gloria will then discuss her early life in St Kitts. Gloria recognises Olara and appears happier in Olara's company.

Using concepts, can you identify:

1. What kind of stereotyped assumptions are being made about Gloria?
2. What aspects of Olara's behaviour might contribute to an empowering approach?

Go further – can you analyse issues using theory?

How might carers who make stereotyped assumptions influence Gloria's self-concept and self-esteem? How might Olara's approach influence Gloria's self-concept and self-esteem? Is there any evidence that Olara's behaviour is having a positive influence?

Go further – can you evaluate using a range of theory?

Evaluate how far Olara's approach might be described as person-centred and empowering. Evaluate how far the other care worker's behaviour (as described above) might be contrary to the care values referred to as a 'value base'.

UNIT 4 ASSESSMENT PREPARATION

How you will be assessed

This unit will be assessed through a 1½ hour test. You will receive further guidance and help to prepare you for this test, but some outline questions are set out below in order to review the content of this section of the book.

Test questions

Scenario 1

Nicola and Richard are a couple in their late 30s, with a 6-year-old daughter called Cyan. Nicola works part-time and cares for her mother, who lives on her own and has a heart problem. Nicola helps her mother with housework, shopping and by keeping her company.

Both Nicola and Richard are going to move to a different town 40 miles away because the company they work for is relocating. Nicola still intends to visit her mother twice a week, but she will have to give up her gym membership, as she will have less time in future. Cyan will have to join a new school and make new friends. Although the move is exciting, both Nicola and Richard feel stressed. Nicola has started smoking again, despite having previously given up smoking.

1 In relation to the story above, describe examples of one physical, one intellectual, one social and one emotional consequence of moving home. (4)

2 Describe the possible consequences of a lifestyle that involves a lack of exercise and smoking. (3)

3 Explain some of the possible experiences that Cyan may have when she moves to a different school. (3)

4 Explain some of the possible benefits that Nicola's mother may receive from her relationship with her daughter Nicola. (4)

5 Starting a new job, in a new location, could involve a sense of loss and even grief; explain some of the processes people might go through in order to adjust to loss and grief. (4)

6 Nicola and Richard have chosen to move house in order to keep their jobs. For Nicola this choice will result in a lifestyle with less exercise. Thinking about the content of this unit:

a) evaluate the possible consequences for Nicola and Richard if they had chosen to stay where they are and live on a low income.

b) Nicola's decision to give up exercise might be described as a lifestyle choice but what social factors will be influencing this choice? (A: 5, B: 4)

7 Explain the difference between absolute poverty and relative poverty. (3)

Scenario 2

Jake is six years old. He is extremely excited by football. Not only does he play football a lot with his friends, but he also knows a great deal about current football players, football clubs and who is likely to win the Cup. Jake's father is a very keen football supporter who spends a lot of his time at home watching football on TV and reading about football in the papers. Jake often sees his father talking to friends about football.

1 Describe what is meant by the term 'primary socialisation'. (2)

2 Describe any evidence you can see of a 'norm' to be interested in football in Jake's household. (2)

3 Jake may have copied some of his father's behaviour, but can you explain some of the influences that might have resulted in his father being interested in football? (3)

4 If Jake went to a new school and made new friends at the age of 12–16 and these friends were not interested in football, how might mixing with these new friends influence his behaviour? (2)

5 Explain a range of social influences that can affect the lifestyle choices people make. (5)

Scenario 3

You are talking to a care worker who works with adults. The worker says 'The work is very interesting and challenging. You see, I have to get to know the small group of people that I work with very closely. In the past, many of these people were put down as being too limited to live independently or choose what they wanted.

My job is to help these people to make choices, and yet they don't know what they can choose between. So I have to find ways to help them to choose what they like and don't like. Sometimes it's easy – like food. You can provide different things and they tell you whether they like it or not. Then we make a plan together and this plan records their choices. They keep the plan and it's theirs. But other times we get into discussing big things, like where to live, and then there are all sorts of resource problems. We can't always give everyone what they would like, but we can try to work towards their dream.'

1 With reference to the story above, describe a way in which service users may have experienced stereotyping. (2)

2 Describe what is meant by a stereotype. (2)

3 Using examples of values, describe what the 'care value base' means. (5)

4 Identify two care values that the care worker in the story is using to guide his work. (4)

5 Explain how far the approach described above might be an empowering approach to care work. (5)

6 Explain some possible consequences of the approach above for the self-concept and the self-esteem of service users. (3)

7 The relationship between carers and service users in the conversation above might be described as part of a 'service user-centred approach'. Explain what is meant by 'service user-centred'. (7)

References and further reading

Acheson, D. (1998) *Independent Inquiry into Inequalities in Health* (London, HMSO)

Argyle, M. (1987) *The Psychology of Happiness* (London and New York, Methuen)

Argyle, M. (1994) *The Psychology of Social Class* (London and New York, Routledge)

Bandura, A. (1989) *Perceived self-efficacy in the exercise of personal agency,* 'The Psychologist' 2 (10) 411–24.

Berkman,? and Syme,? (1979)

Blaxter, M. (1990) *Health and Lifestyles* (London and New York, Routledge)

Chaney, D. (1996) *Lifestyles* (London and New York, Routledge)

Cooley, C. H. (1902) *Human Nature and the Social Order* (New York, Charles Scribner)

Duck, S. (1988) *Relating to Others* (Milton Keynes, Open University Press)

Engebretson, J. (2004) 'Caring presence: A case study' in *Communication, Relationships and Care,* Robb, M., Barrett, S., Komaromy, C. and

Giddens, A. (1997) *Sociology* (3rd edition) (Cambridge, Polity Press)

Holmes, T. H. and Rahe, R. H. (1967) 'The social readjustment rating scale', *Journal of Psychosomatic Research* 11, 213–18

Hopson, B. (1986) 'Transition: Understanding and managing personal change' in Herbert, M. (ed.) *Psychology for Social Workers* (London, British Psychological Society and Macmillan)

Kitwood, T. (1997) *Dementia Reconsidered* (Buckingham UK and Bristol USA, Open University Press)

Maslow, A. H. (1970) *Motivation and Personality* (2nd edition) (New York, Harper & Rowe)

Murray Parkes, C. (1975)

Rogers, A. (eds) (London & New York, OU & Routledge)

Nettleton, S. (1995) *The Sociology of Health and Illness* (Cambridge, Polity Press)

Paxton, W. and Dixon, M. (2004) *The State of the Nation – an Audit of Injustice in the UK* (London, Institute for Public Policy Research)

Seligman, M. (2002) *Authentic Happiness* (London, Nicholas Brealey Publishing)

Social Exclusion Unit (1999) *Opportunity for All* (London, HMSO)

Social Trends, Vol. 32 (2002) London: HMSO

Social Trends, Vol. 33 (2003) London: HMSO

Social Trends, Vol. 34 (2004) London: HMSO

Townsend, P. (1974) 'The concept of poverty' in Wedderburn, D. (ed.) *Poverty, Inequality and Class Structure* (Cambridge, Cambridge University Press)

Useful websites

Please see www.heinemann.co.uk/hotlinks (express code 370XP) for links to the following websites, which may provide a source of updated information:

Commission for Racial Equality

Equal Opportunities Commission

General Social Care Council

Institute of Fiscal Studies

Institute for Public Policy Research

National Statistics (2004)

UNIT 5

Activities for Health and Well-being

This unit covers the following sections:

5.1 Types and benefits of activities

5.2 The planning and implementation of activities

5.3 Evaluation of activities

Introduction

In this unit you will learn about how activities may be included in care settings that satisfy service users' physical, intellectual, emotional and social needs and that sometimes any one activity can satisfy more than one need. An overview of the many types of activities is included, together with an outline of the benefits of each to a range of service users. There is also a discussion of the factors that you need to consider when planning and implementing an activity. Finally, you will learn about the importance of evaluation and how to carry out an evaluation of your activity.

How you will be assessed

This unit is internally assessed. You must produce a written report.

5.1 Types and benefits of activities

This section explains how the different needs of service users can be met by a range of activities. The different types of activities are categorised according to the four broad human needs:

* physical
* intellectual
* emotional
* social.

We will also see how closely these four areas of need are interrelated.

Meeting different kinds of need

Everyone has to have several needs satisfied in order to live a happy and fulfilled life. As each person is also unique, it follows that such needs will vary tremendously between individuals. An artistic person, for example, might have a very strong need for self-expression (perhaps by painting pictures or making music). Someone else may not be happy unless he or she spends a lot of time with friends, or in activities involving groups of people such as drama. However, the immediate needs of a homeless person are likely to be more physical, such as finding food and a warm, safe place to sleep at night.

Think it over...

What kinds of needs do you have? What kinds of things make you happy? Is there anything you don't have that you need right now?

Put your list in order of priority.

Is there anything that has to happen first, before the other needs can be satisfied?

By putting your list in priority order, you may have discovered that some of the things you want cannot happen unless something else happens first. It's the same for everyone.

A person who uses a wheelchair and wants to learn to play basketball will have to have certain physical needs addressed (perhaps getting hold of an adapted or custom-built wheelchair) before he or she can move on to satisfy the ultimate goal of joining in with training sessions. The homeless person may really want to write poetry (perhaps for the *Big Issue*), but until he or she has found a regular safe place to sleep, exhaustion (and financial constraints) may prevent this from happening.

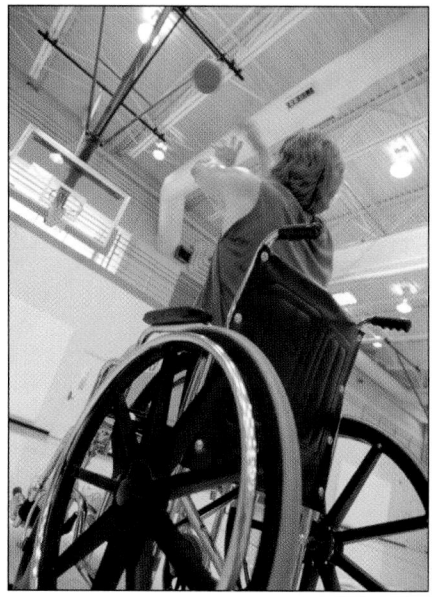

Figure 5.1 *Before a person with a physical disability can achieve his or her ultimate goal, certain physical needs will have to be addressed*

Maslow's Pyramid

Abraham Maslow (1908–1970) was a psychologist who worked out a theory of human needs. He said that the ultimate goal of human life is to achieve personal growth, i.e. to develop personal ability and potential. However, before this can happen there are a number of other needs (which he called deficiency needs) that have to be met. He set out this theory in a pyramid – see Figure 5.2.

In the bottom two layers of Maslow's Pyramid are the immediate physical, safety and emotional needs of the human being. The homeless person, for example, needs to be fed, warm and safe before he or she can think about anything else. Similarly, the person who uses a wheelchair has to work through a number of technical issues relating to using a sports-adapted chair before moving on to satisfying the 'higher' needs of

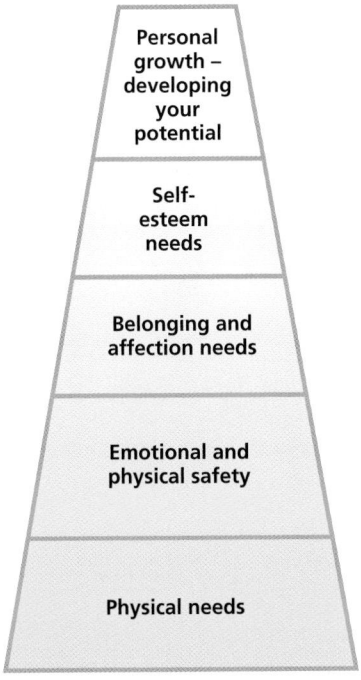

Figure 5.2 *Maslow's Pyramid*

belonging (to a team), enhancing self-esteem and personal growth that membership of a basketball team will give.

SCENARIO

Bereavement

Esther lost her husband 2 years ago. She misses him very much. Before he died, they both used to be active members of a local choir, but she lost confidence after his death and stopped going to choir practice. She has become very depressed.

In the last 12 months, she has also developed visual problems, and is reluctant to go out alone in the evenings. However, Esther still loves her choral music. She has a large collection of recordings which she plays regularly, and always listens to concerts on the radio or TV.

1. **What kinds of need does Esther appear to have?**
2. **What kinds of question would you like to ask her to find out more about her situation?**

Physical, intellectual, social and emotional needs (P-I-E-S)

Esther appears to have a range of needs. Since she has developed visual problems, she has at least one area of physical difficulty that requires attention before she can do anything else. She has become depressed and may be missing the intellectual stimulation and social warmth that belonging to the choir gave her. She is certainly missing the emotional support and love that she got from her husband. The self-esteem and sense of personal creativity that she used to get from singing regularly with the choir (including public performances) is also lacking. Esther therefore has requirements relating to the four broad areas of human need, which can be categorised as physical, intellectual, emotional and social.

You can remember these four areas of need by the acronym P-I-E-S.

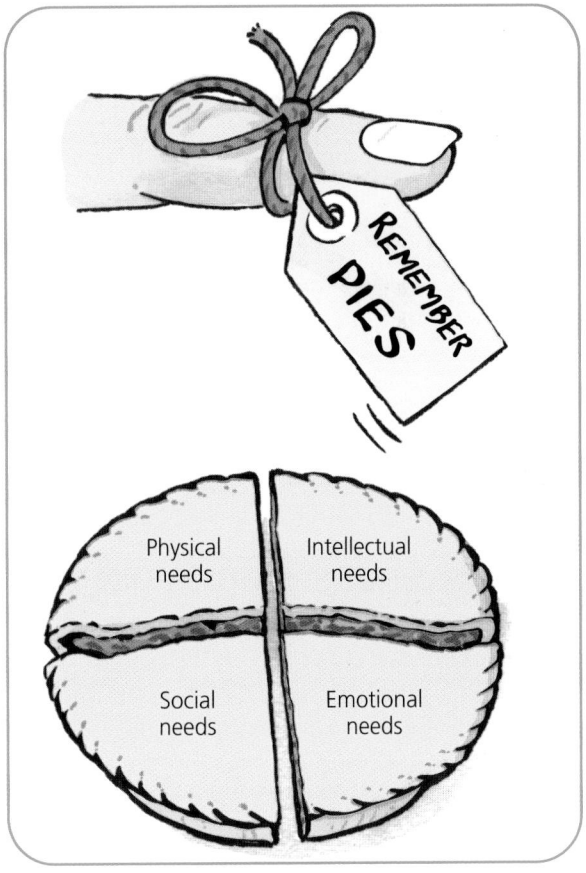

Figure 5.3 *Human need can be categorised as physical, intellectual, emotional and social*

In this unit, you will be asked to distinguish between the physical, intellectual, emotional and social needs of people who use health and social care services, and the kinds of activity that can satisfy these needs. One activity can satisfy several different kinds of need. When a person plays basketball in a wheelchair, they satisfy the physical developmental needs of the body (for example, cardiovascular and muscular exercise), the intellectual development of concentration, memory (rules of the game) and communication skills, the expression of emotion through the desire to compete, and the social needs for friendship and belonging to a group. The person's self-esteem is thus enhanced, together with the expression of one aspect of his or her personal identity.

Carers have needs too

Sometimes, a person with significant needs may rely heavily on one other person for his or her physical care. This person is often known as the carer, and may also play a significant role in fulfilling that person's emotional and social needs. Even when carers are devoted to their relatives or friends, the stress put onto them can be very great. People with dementia, for example, may forget where they are, or the names of people close to them. They may ask the same questions repeatedly, or get lost when they go out.

In the last 10 years, carers from all over the UK have been working together to gain recognition and support for the work they do. In 1999, the Government published a National Strategy for Carers, acknowledging their value and recognising their needs (DoH, 1999). Many authorities now have a Carers' Charter, setting out the rights that carers have. These rights include being consulted and involved at every stage of service delivery, and also having their own needs addressed.

By working to help service users with their health or well-being, you may also be taking some of the pressure off their carers. Taking the carer into consideration is something that needs to be done when choosing and planning an activity for a service user.

Figure 5.4 *Carers have needs too*

Meeting needs: people first

Imagine that you're attending college, and one day you're in the coffee bar with your friends talking about what you're all going to do that weekend. Suddenly, someone sees a poster that's just been put on the notice board that morning. There is to be a line-dancing class on Thursday night, and everyone is required to attend. It has been decided that line-dancing would be good because the college Principal feels that not everyone is getting enough exercise; he also feels that this activity would give shy students the chance to make friends and mix with other people.

How would you react? Would you think that this seems like a good idea, so you don't mind going along? Or would you be appalled at the idea because you don't like Country and Western music? You might have some kind of physical disability, and therefore be worried about your ability to take part in this event; or you might simply have other plans for Thursday evening. Whatever you feel about the event, it's very likely that you would feel indignant about not having been consulted: the college Principal has made a global decision about what is 'good' for the students, and has imposed it on everybody.

Think it over...

Have you ever been in a situation where someone else has made a decision that directly affects you, but hasn't consulted you first?

How did this make you feel?

The chances are you felt angry and compromised by this. You might even have felt disempowered and devalued, as if your individuality had been threatened.

If professionals don't give full respect and consideration to the feelings of people who come to them for help, then people can feel devalued. Consider the experience of Kim, set out in following scenario.

SCENARIO

A 'patient' not a person

Kim has multiple sclerosis. She has had a series of MRI scans to confirm the diagnosis and to monitor the progress of her condition.

She had her last scan in May, and it is now September. When she finally sees her consultant, she discovers that he wrote to her GP about the findings of that scan (in May), but didn't write to her.

The scan showed that her condition has not deteriorated, something that is reassuring for her. However, the fact that the consultant cut her out of the correspondence has not only delayed this piece of good news, but also makes her feel as if she has little importance in the diagnostic process.

It appears that she is a 'patient' rather than a person.

Of course, the term 'patient' is one that is widely used and recognised. The important point to be made here is that the consultant seems to have forgotten that patients are people too. It is only courteous to give someone personal information that rightly belongs to him or her. In this case, this was very important information that Kim was anxious to receive. Writing to the GP without including Kim was thoughtless as well as discourteous.

When you are choosing an activity for someone who uses health or social services, it is vital to remember that he or she is a person before all else. An individual service user is just that – an individual – with physical, intellectual, emotional and social needs like everyone else. People do not give up their individuality and personhood just because they need the services of doctors or social workers. You will need to work *with* them as well as *for* them, in order to plan and help deliver an activity that will be of value. In no sense do any of the activities in this unit require that you do something 'to' a service user.

In the following scenario, the care worker encourages a group of older people to take part in an art class.

SCENARIO

Small steps lead to bigger things

In a residential unit for older people Sarah, one of the care workers, feels that she would like to offer something more creative for the residents to do.

She is not sure what the reaction will be, however, so she decides to try things out slowly and carefully. On the first day, she sets out a table in the day room, which has some art materials on it. Rather than circulating among the residents and trying to make them sit at the table, she just sits there herself and starts playing around with the paint.

After a little while, one man sits by her and asks what she's doing. She shows him and suggests he might like to try. This man doesn't, but a few minutes later two ladies come up and want to try out some drawing.

Sarah repeats the event the following week, and gradually a small art group of five people develops. New friendships are formed, and the unit eventually hosts a small exhibition of the residents' work. The local paper does a feature about it, which makes everyone feel very proud – even residents who are not part of the art group.

Contrast Sarah's way of going about things with the following scenario.

SCENARIO

Voting with their feet

In Great Gables care home, the manager has decided that regular music and movement sessions would be a good idea.

Someone has been engaged to run weekly sessions, but the residents find her a bit aggressive, and not very empathetic with their personal circumstances.

Every Friday, just before the teacher is due to arrive, the day room mysteriously empties. Finally, there are only two people left in there when the teacher arrives, and the classes have to be cancelled.

This example constitutes a classic case of someone making decisions for other people, without checking what they would like. Perhaps it's simply the teacher that the residents don't like; another more empathetic person might have proved more popular. The manager has compounded her original mistake (to impose music and movement sessions) by not asking the residents what they thought of it.

Consider this

Rita has recently lost her sight as a result of having diabetes. She needs to work and wants to develop her ICT skills so she can get a job. The local college is offering courses through the Learn Direct scheme, and she is keen to attend and get a qualification.

She has a computer at home, but this hasn't been adapted for use by a non-sighted person.

1. Which of Rita's needs will have to be addressed first?
2. How might this be done?
3. Who is responsible for doing this?
4. When Rita gets to college, what other types of need might be met by attending the course?

Activities to meet physical needs

Everyone has basic physical needs relating to the effective functioning of the human body. We all need food, warmth, air and so on in order to continue to function effectively. Everyone needs to make sure that these bodily functions are well-maintained by eating properly, taking regular exercise and not imposing too much strain on the body (for example, by excessive drinking).

There are many activities designed to meet a person's physical needs, and these will vary tremendously in the demands that they make on the body. If you decide to choose an activity that meets a service user's physical needs, you will need to consider his or her condition very carefully, in consultation with a key worker or health professional, in order to make sure that the activity is appropriate for that person.

Physical activities for older people

After the age of 65, people tend to experience a number of physical and mental changes.

Elastic tissue, which is found in many organs, degenerates with age, and this is most readily seen in wrinkled skin. Blood capillaries are more fragile, so bruising occurs from relatively small injuries. Because nerve cells in the central nervous system decrease, older people may experience poorer memory, difficulty in learning new skills quickly and slower reaction times.

Taste, smell and hearing can become less acute. The focusing power of the eye weakens, which may mean that people require a much larger print, or need to hold smaller print at arm's length. Almost everyone over the age of 65 has some degree of cataract, where the lens in the eye has started to become opaque. The condition tends to progress with advancing years and most people have some loss of vision due to cataract formation at around 75 years.

The body also gradually loses its sensitivity to cold, so that older people are more likely to develop hypothermia in cold weather.

Heart, breathing and circulation all become less efficient, causing difficulty with climbing stairs and with strenuous exercise. Muscle thins and weakens, while joints become less mobile and total height shrinks.

For all these reasons, it is important for older people to have the opportunity to engage in regular gentle exercise, in order to alleviate some of the associated problems such as joint or muscle stiffness. Physical activities particularly suited to older people include Tai Chi, keep fit to music, and armchair aerobics, although there are many forms of exercise that can be adapted to suit people with limited movement. (It should be remembered though, that many older people are perfectly fit, and remain very active.) Figure 5.4 gives a few examples of types of physical activities for adults and includes notes on special considerations that might apply in certain cases. Many of these activities meet emotional and social needs as well. It is important not to make assumptions about what a person will want to do, or what he or she is capable of (see the section on 'Stereotyping and labelling', page 229). For example, it would be misleading to suggest a definitive list of activities that are suitable for older people, simply because it is clearly not the case that all older people are interested in the same things.

Physical activities for individuals with special needs

Similarly, people with certain learning difficulties also tend to experience a number of associated physical (or psychological) problems. People with Downs Syndrome, for example, can experience heart problems or early dementia. If you choose to plan an activity for a person with a learning difficulty, you must be responsive to that person's physical needs, and take advice on this from the person's care worker.

Physical activities for children

Children aged 0–3 years

The physical, intellectual, emotional and social developmental needs of very young children are

PHYSICAL ACTIVITIES FOR ADULTS		
ACTIVITY TYPE	POTENTIAL BENEFITS	NOTES
Dance (ballroom, line-dancing, disco-dancing) Music and movement	Promotes cardiovascular health, fitness, stamina Social and emotional benefits	RM
Games of all kinds: ball-throwing, quoits, bowls etc.	Cardiovascular health, fitness, stamina; muscle development; hand-eye coordination	
Gymnastics	Cardiovascular health, fitness, stamina; muscle development	
Armchair aerobics	Cardiovascular health, fitness, stamina; muscle development	Aerobics adapted for older people
Tai Chi Yoga	Oxygenation of blood; muscle toning, improved posture, greater flexibility; improved blood and lymph circulation; stress relief, relaxation	
Walking	Cardiovascular health, fitness, stamina	
Swimming	Cardiovascular health, fitness, stamina	RegM
Physiotherapy/targeted exercise	Physical improvements as specified by physiotherapist	RegM
Note: RM = can be adapted for people with restricted movement RegM = often useful for people regaining movement after illness or injury		

FIGURE 5.4 *Suggestions of some physical activities for adults*

clearly set out in Government guidance. These needs are described in *Birth to Three Matters: A Framework to Support Children in Their Earliest Years* (DfES/Sure Start, 2002). This guidance identifies four 'Aspects' of development, which are set out in Figure 5.5.

ASPECTS OF DEVELOPMENT IN CHILDREN AGED 0–3 YEARS	
A Strong Child	Relates to developing a sense of identity and belonging
A Skilful Communicator	Relates to the child's growing ability to communicate and make meaning
A Competent Learner	Relates to the child's intellectual and creative development
A Healthy Child	Relates to the child's physical and health needs

FIGURE 5.5 *Children aged 0–3 years: aspects of development*

Source: DfES/Sure Start (2002)

The physical development needs of very young children are thus catered for by the *Healthy Child* aspect of this framework for effective practice (although there are also emotional elements to this aspect of the framework). The framework describes four stages of physical development for children aged 0–3 years, as shown in Figure 5.6.

PHYSICAL DEVELOPMENT IN CHILDREN AGED 0–3 YEARS	
STAGE	AGE (IN MONTHS)
Heads up, Lookers and Communicators	0–8
Sitters, Standers and Explorers	8–18
Movers, Shakers and Players	18–24
Walkers, Talkers and Pretenders	24–36

FIGURE 5.6 *Four stages of physical development in children aged 0–3 years*

Source: DfES/Sure Start (2002)

The framework also defines the key physical needs of very young children. These are set out in Figure 5.7.

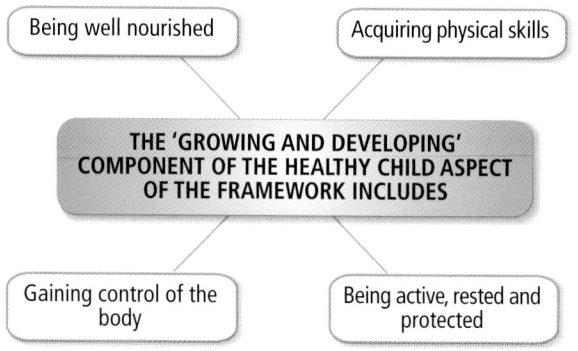

FIGURE 5.7 *Children aged 0–3 years: physical development needs*

Source: DfES/Sure Start (2002)

Activities designed to address the physical needs of children aged 0–3 years will encourage age-appropriate development. For example, crawling, hiding and peeping can be encouraged by the careful arrangement of toys and materials.

Children aged 3–7 years

Between the ages of 3 and 7 years, the developmental needs of children are described in two key Government documents. The first is the 'Curriculum Guidance for the Foundation Stage' (DfEE/QCA 2000), which describes the development needs of children aged between 3 and 5 years; the second is the Key Stage 1 (5–7 years) section of the National Curriculum (DfEE 1999).

Between these years, the child's body develops, together with key physical abilities. **Gross motor skills** (e.g. jumping, standing on one leg) are acquired, as are **fine motor skills** (e.g. holding a pencil between the thumb and first two fingers). By the time children have reached the age of 7 or 8, they can usually ride two-wheeled bicycles, swim, write and draw and start to play a musical instrument.

In the same way as the framework for working with very young children describes all four areas of developmental need, so the 'Curriculum

Guidance for the Foundation Stage' sets out six areas of learning (for children aged 3–5 years) that encompass all types of need (i.e. physical, intellectual, emotional and social). These are illustrated in Figure 5.8.

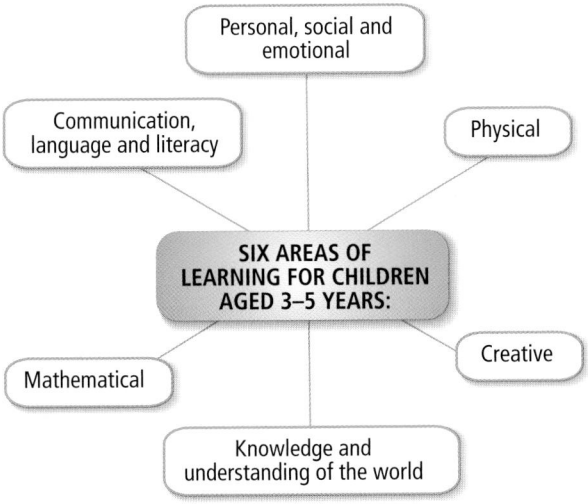

FIGURE 5.8 *Children aged 3–5 years: six areas of learning*

Source: DfEE/QCA (2000)

The physical developmental needs of children between 3 and 5 years are thus an integral part of the Foundation Stage curriculum. This is also

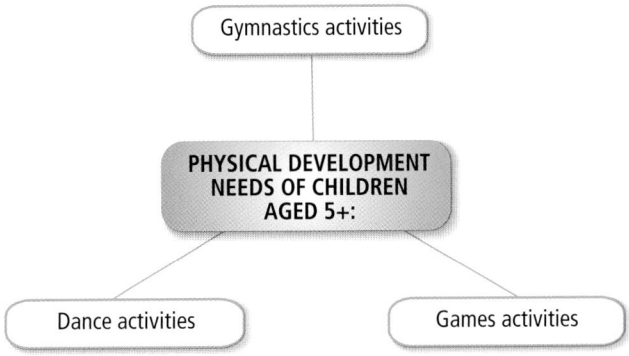

FIGURE 5.10 *The physical development needs of children aged 5 years and upwards*

Source: Riley (2003)

reflected in the National Curriculum for older children, which states that from 5 years upwards, children should have the opportunity to be involved in a wide range of movement experiences.

Care settings for children will have plenty of equipment and space to cater for their physical development needs. Many early years centres regard the use of an outdoor play area as essential, often seeing it as an extension of the indoor space (Lewisham, 2002). Equipment might include A-frames, planks, wooden slides and ladders. Wheeled toys can be used, and these can

PHYSICAL ACTIVITIES FOR CHILDREN		
ACTIVITY TYPE	**POTENTIAL BENEFITS**	**NOTES**
Climbing (A-frames, wooden slides, ladders) Obstacle course Using wheeled toys	These activities satisfy physical developmental needs, especially gross motor skills. They help a child to gain control of the body and acquire physical skills	*Knowledge and understanding of the world* can be incorporated (e.g. use of toy fire-engine or ambulance)
Bat and ball Quoits	Physical development plus hand–eye coordination	Social skills are also enhanced through cooperation with other children
Tactile experiences (e.g. bath foam, string painting) Digging	Hand–eye coordination and fine motor skills	*Knowledge and understanding of the world* can be incorporated into such activities
Note: Remember that activities for children are often linked to the National Curriculum guidance		

FIGURE 5.9 *Physical activities for children*

also be combined with role-plays. Small equipment can include bats and balls, quoits, hoops, skittles and beanbags. Such outdoor areas are often designed to allow for all six of the learning areas (for example, the provision of an alphabet and number line attached to the fence and pots for children to grow their own plants in).

Some ideas for physical activities for children are given in Figure 5.9. Many of these activities meet emotional and social needs as well.

Activities to meet intellectual needs

Intellectual needs are related to the working of the human brain and the mental processes that people engage in. We often refer to this simply as 'thinking' (something that human beings are continuously doing). The process of thinking is also referred to as **cognition**, and the development of thinking skills is known as **cognitive development**.

Thinking skills are used to interpret and make sense of the world. Specific thinking skills include the ability to concentrate, the recall of facts or events via the memory, solving problems and creative work using the imagination. The development of spoken language belongs in this category of skills ,together with reading and writing (literacy) and using figures (numeracy).

SCENARIO
The Bridge School

A group of friends who all live in sheltered flats for older people have agreed to play Bridge together every Friday.

As Bridge is a card game that requires players to use their memories, as well as to anticipate the cards held by the others, it is a game that develops and maintains several cognitive skills.

Members of the group take it in turns to host the Bridge game, providing tea and biscuits and a place to play. After the game, people usually stay around to chat about what's been happening during the week, and sometimes to discuss problems that individuals may have.

As well as being essential to survival in the world, intellectual skills can also be a source of fun and pleasure. For example, some people get a great deal of enjoyment from reading books – combining literacy skills with the power of the imagination to enter into different and absorbing fictional worlds.

Exercising intellectual skills can give a great deal of pleasure, as the scenario below demonstrates.

This Bridge School thus provides its members with social and emotional support, as well as the intellectual stimulation involved in the game. As with many of the scenarios given in this unit, one activity can simultaneously satisfy a number of different needs.

In this section of Unit 5, intellectual needs will be considered firstly in terms of the development of cognitive skills, and then with respect to the need for fun, stimulation and interest. The two are not rigidly distinct, however, as it is quite possible to enjoy yourself at the same time as learning a skill. Developing or maintaining cognitive skills can also be a source of emotional and social satisfaction, as the story of the Bridge School illustrates.

We all have cognitive developmental needs, and there is a sense in which we never stop learning. You may even know of someone who has suddenly decided to go to an evening class to learn French at the age of 50, or of someone else who has decided to train to be a plumber after 20 years of being an accountant.

FIGURE 5.11 *Intellectual skills can be a source of fun and pleasure*

However, there are two groups of people for whom cognitive developmental needs are particularly critical. These are children and people with learning disabilities.

Activities to meet cognitive developmental needs

Children aged 0–3 years

The cognitive development of small children is complex. The growing infant (from birth to 18 months or 2 years) firstly moves through a **sensorimotor stage**, in which he or she applies sensory experience to understand new experiences. For example, the sucking behaviour used to get milk from its mother is used to explore other objects such as toys, fingers and so on. The application of existing knowledge to a new situation in this way is also called **assimilation**. Later on, the child learns to adapt to new ways of doing things – for example, using a cup to drink (rather than sucking). The development of new, internal knowledge such as this is known as **accommodation**.

Everyone learns to adapt to the changing demands of life using a mixture of assimilation and accommodation. In the first year of life a child learns to deal with its environment by developing its own motor actions: firstly coordinating tongue and lip in order to feed (up to 3 months), then reaching out to grasp hold of things to suck (up to 9 months), then crawling towards things. Children also begin to develop **spatial awareness** in the very early years.

At the end of the sensorimotor stage (about 18 months), children will have arrived at a point where they can understand that objects have a permanent existence (**object permanence**), and will be starting to use one- and two-word utterances. At this time, children enter into a pre-operational stage, in which they have not yet developed logical thinking, and find it hard to imagine other people's perceptions.

The Government guidance document *'Birth to Three Matters: Framework to Support Children in Their Earliest Years'* (DfES/Sure Start 2001) identifies *The Competent Learner* as a key aspect of development at this very early stage. Elements of this key aspect are set out in Figure 5.12.

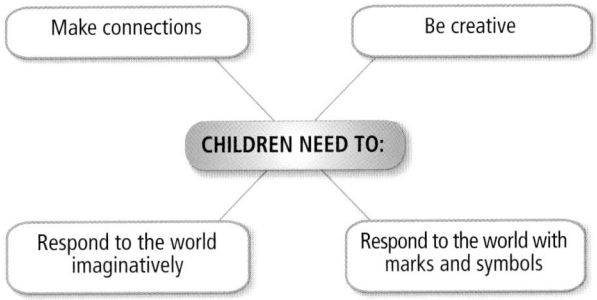

FIGURE 5.12 *The intellectual needs of children aged 0–3 years: the competent learner*

Source: DfES/Sure Start (2002)

Children aged 3–7 years

Children continue to develop their cognitive abilities during this period. They learn to create meaning through language, to solve puzzles and to realise gradually that other people may see things differently from themselves.

The development of cognitive skills is very closely linked with that of social and emotional skills. During this period, the need for children to cling to their parents gradually lessens; they start to make relationships with other children and to become more independent. They still need close emotional bonds (i.e. with their parents), but this usually forms a secure base from which to explore relationships with others.

In the Foundation Stage curriculum guidance for children aged between 3 and 5 years, four of the six categories relate to a child's intellectual development. These are:

* communication, language and literacy: learning through speaking and listening, reading and writing
* mathematical development and education
* knowledge and understanding of the world
* creative development: learning and the arts.

These aspects of development are picked up by Key Stage 1 of the National Curriculum.

Early years care settings are designed to provide stimulating learning environments.

Activities will be carefully planned, monitored and evaluated against the learning requirements of the Foundation Stage guidance. It is likely that there will be workshop areas, toys and equipment to allow construction-type activities, sand, water, books, plenty of graphics, musical instruments and ICT facilities. Different textures will be available for the children to explore, displays will be interactive and resources will be presented in ways that will excite and interest the children.

In the scenario opposite, string painting thus satisfies some of Adnan's physical, intellectual and emotional needs.

Activities designed for children are very likely to encompass several areas of need, as well as a number of elements or aspects from the appropriate curriculum guidance. Consider the activities designed for Joe in the second scenario.

This very simple but short activity has helped Joe in developing his fine motor skills (placing the pieces on the peg-board), his mathematical knowledge (matching shapes), concentration (the activity is a bit longer each time) and also his self-esteem (he has finished a puzzle and enjoyed praise).

Joe's story shows how working to develop his cognitive skills has also enhanced his self-esteem and made him feel good about what he has achieved. As Joe also has autism, the way the staff have adapted the task to suit his needs shows that having such a disability in no way prevents a child from enjoying the same activities as the others.

SCENARIO

Adnan

Adnan is three years old and has cerebral palsy.

He loves to do string painting. This involves dipping string in paint, placing it on a piece of paper, folding the paper over the string then opening it again to see the shapes that have been made.

String painting develops Adnan's fine motor skills and also his awareness of colour. Putting his picture on the wall afterwards gives him a sense of achievement. He also enjoys getting messy and feeling the string between his fingers.

SCENARIO

Joe

Joe is three and a half years old. He has autism, and is experiencing a global delay in all developmental areas – physical, intellectual, emotional and social.

He attends an Early Years Development Centre, and the staff are careful to make sure that Joe can take part in as many activities as possible with the other children. However, his concentration span is very short, so activities have been adapted to make sure he can gain a sense of achievement from the things he does.

Today he is doing a peg-board puzzle, matching up coloured shapes. The whole activity will take just three minutes, including the starting up time; last time it lasted for two minutes. A key worker guides his hand as he matches up the shapes.

At the end of the activity, the key worker claps and praises Joe for what he has achieved. Joe is given a sticker, and the completed puzzle goes in the 'Finish Box', together with the work of all the other children.

People with learning disabilities

Adults with learning disabilities tend to need help in developing their cognitive skills. Those who use social services regularly are likely to have a Person Centred Plan that sets out all their needs, including their need for cognitive development.

People with learning disabilities often need help in making decisions, particularly when it comes to learning about the choices that are available. Consider the following scenario, in which John is helped to learn more about certain kinds of foods, as well as to decide what he actually likes.

If you decide to work with a service user who has a learning disability, you will have to pay particular attention to making sure that he or she fully understands the options that are available

SCENARIO

Learning about what's available

John has a learning disability and regularly uses day services provided by his local social services department. Like many people with a learning disability, he is not used to being asked to say what he wants, and usually gives answers that he thinks the staff want to hear. He also has a limited knowledge of what kinds of things are available to him.

The day unit staff have devised a way of finding out what each service user wants, and they invite John to attend a regular group meeting, in which people are helped to decide what they like.

This week, the subject is 'fruit'. Staff have brought in a very wide range of fruits for everyone to try. As each fruit is tasted, service users explain how they liked it by pointing to a face-symbol: a smiley face for 'love it', a grumpy face for 'don't like it' and so on.

John discovers that he loves fresh pineapple, something he's never tasted before, but he's not very keen on kiwi fruit.

John keeps this information in his own box, which will eventually include details of the people who are important to him, music he likes, where he would like to live, who he'd like to live with, and where he wants to go on holiday. Everyone attending the meetings has one of these boxes, which can be used for future decision-making.

when choosing an activity. You may have to spend a considerable amount of time on the explanation and discussion stage of planning. There may be some cognitive developmental needs to be taken into account before you can actually move forward to implementing the activity.

The need for fun, stimulation and interest

Most people feel the need to exercise their minds, even if this is as simple as going to see a film or reading a book. Others like to do crossword puzzles or to play card games, as we saw in the scenario about the Bridge School on page 212.

Sometimes these kinds of activity can help a person to retain or maintain one or more of their cognitive functions. For example, older people often enjoy reminiscence sessions. During such sessions, a therapist will encourage a group of people to talk about their memories of their early lives. Objects may be used to start off these discussions, such as old kitchen utensils or photographs.

Music is often used to provide enjoyable recreational sessions that can also be of value with respect to cognitive and other areas of need. The following scenario describes how music is used in one setting for young people who have learning disabilities.

SCENARIO

The Music Man

A group of young people at a day facility for people with learning difficulties look forward to their weekly sessions with Asif, who is a music therapist. The young people call him the 'Music Man'.

Asif encourages the young people to learn to sing and to use various musical instruments. Songs are often memorised, which is a good intellectual exercise; using the instruments helps one or two of the group with their fine motor movements, while moving to the music is good for physical coordination.

There are young people from different cultures attending the facility, so Asif is careful to use different kinds of music, including Asian, British and black British sources.

Asif's music sessions cater for a range of needs, physical and intellectual, while at the same time providing an important emotional outlet for the young people who attend the sessions. Friendships have been made at this group, and Asif's concern to include music from different cultural groups has given the young people the chance to see if they like music from a wide range of cultures.

INTELLECTUAL ACTIVITIES FOR ADULTS		
ACTIVITY TYPE	**POTENTIAL BENEFITS**	**NOTES**
Art: Drawing, painting, pottery and sculpture Crafts: Sewing, woodwork, macramé, making soft toys etc.	Improvement of memory and concentration; development of the imagination	Artistic activities can improve hand–eye coordination Emotional needs are satisfied by artistic expression and creativity Working in a group can satisfy social needs
Memory Sessions: Discussion groups Reading Poetry Drama Going to the theatre	Improving memory and concentration	Emotional and social needs can be satisfied by this kind of activity
Music: Singing Listening to music Music Therapy	Concentration and memory	Singing has physiological benefits (increased oxygenation of the blood, elimination of carbon dioxide, massage of some internal organs/muscles) Music therapy can also relieve depression, insomnia, anxiety and chronic pain (in some cases)
Life skills activities: Cookery Using money Shopping Self-advocacy training	Problem-solving, learning basic processes, following instructions, decision-making	LD Such activities can also satisfy some emotional and social needs
Note: LD = often suitable for people with learning difficulties		

FIGURE 5.13 *Suggestions for intellectual activities for adults*

Source: Lewisham (2002)

If you decide to develop a fun activity with a service user, remember that you may also be satisfying a number of others needs as well.

Figures 5.13 and 5.14 list a few examples of types of intellectual activity for adults and children, with some notes on special considerations. As with physical activities, it is essential that you do not make assumptions about people's preferences when it comes to intellectual activities.

Activities to meet emotional needs

All human beings have a strong need to express their emotions, whether positive (for example, happiness or enthusiasm) or negative (for example, anger or jealousy). Expression of emotion can bring relief from stress, and, indeed, problems can occur when people are unable to work through their feelings. Stress can build up, and in turn can lead to physical or psychological problems. In contrast, positive emotions such as feeling secure, being contented or happy, or simply the 'high' that people get from having fun, can enhance physical health and well-being.

Activities to meet the emotional needs of adults

In one sense, it can be said that any activities that bring pleasure, or that help people to express

INTELLECTUAL ACTIVITIES FOR CHILDREN		
ACTIVITY TYPE	**POTENTIAL BENEFITS**	**NOTES**
Chalking on blackboard Large floor puzzles Reading Using puppets to retell stories Clapping and rhyming games Making displays Hopping along alphabet line on floor (calling out letter names)	Satisfy *Communication, Language and Literacy* needs of Foundation Stage curriculum guidance	May also meet social needs, and can be used to enhance *Knowledge and Understanding of the World* aspects of curriculum guidance
Hopping along number line on floor (calling out numbers) Giant dice Numbered beanbags Measuring things Sorting/counting objects (e.g. pebbles, shells) Singing number rhymes/songs	Satisfy *Mathematical Development* needs of Foundation Stage curriculum guidance	May also meet social needs, and can be adapted to enhance Knowledge and Understanding of the World aspects of curriculum guidance
Growing plants (outdoors and in) Keeping a small pet Drawing maps Making displays of photographs of self as a baby (time) Using computer Taking things to bits, then reassembling (lock and key, nuts and bolts) Cooking Tactile experiences	Satisfy *Knowledge and Understanding of the World* aspects of Foundation Stage curriculum guidance	Can be linked to other aspects of Foundation Stage curriculum guidance
Note: Remember that activities for children in an early years setting will form part of a complex and ongoing programme		

FIGURE 5.14 *Some ideas for intellectual activities for children*

Source: Lewisham (2002)

themselves and find fulfilment, are activities that satisfy emotional needs. For one person, painting and drawing will satisfy these needs; for another, hill-walking will result in the same benefits. Similarly, any activities that bring relief from stress (such as yoga) or that help people to relax and feel secure and happy (perhaps listening to music) also satisfy emotional needs. Finally, activities that help people to redirect or rechannel destructive or negative behaviour patterns (such as art or music therapies) can also be said to be meeting emotional needs.

The list contained in Figure 5.15 should, therefore, be taken as suggestive. In reality (as with physical and intellectual activities) each person is unique, and consequently any activities must be individually chosen.

Stressful life events can bring emotional upheaval. For example, suffering from a long-

Think it over...

Make a list of all the things you like to do when you need to cheer yourself up.

ACTIVITIES FOR ADULTS: MEETING EMOTIONAL NEEDS		
ACTIVITY TYPE	POTENTIAL BENEFITS	NOTES
Dancing	Stress relief; personal expression; pleasure; diversion of thoughts from problems and anxieties	Physical benefits; social needs also met
Art/ Art therapy	Relief of stress and anxiety; sense of being in control; self-expression; expressing difficult feelings; turning negative behaviours into positive ones; relief of depression	Improves memory and concentration Group work brings social benefits
Music/ Music therapy	Relief of stress and anxiety; relief from depression; self-expression; pleasure and fun	Group work brings social benefits
Drama	Self-expression and confidence; diversion from problems and anxieties	Group membership and teamwork brings social benefits
Note: Any activity that brings pleasure satisfies emotional needs		

FIGURE 5.15 *Activities to meet emotional needs: some suggestions for adults*

term illness, developing a disabling condition or moving into residential care can bring a number of undesirable effects. A person who has lost a limb in a road accident may experience an altered sense of body image that makes them feel 'unlovely' or undesirable. Someone else who might have developed severe arthritis and become house-bound may lose contact with others simply because he or she is unable to get out and about. Such a person may no longer be able to enjoy the self-expression that comes from meeting and chatting with others on a regular basis. An older person giving up his or her own home to go into care might experience a drastic loss of self-esteem as a result of being treated as a 'resident' rather than as an independent person.

Even if a person is experiencing some kind of intellectual impairment such as **dementia**, this does not mean that he or she no longer has emotional (or social) needs. Kitwood (1997) has shown that people with dementia have the need to feel loved, which requires that a person experiences comfort, attachment, inclusion, occupation and a feeling of identity.

In fact, we could say that all of us have these needs. Figure 5.16 (an adaptation of Kitwood's diagram) shows us that intellectual, emotional and social needs are very closely interconnected. Comfort here means the experience of warmth and strength that you get from another person. Attachment refers to the bonds or closeness that one person can experience with another (for example, with a spouse, a parent or a close friend). Inclusion relates to the human need to belong to a group of people. Occupation here

*** DID YOU KNOW?**

Laughing is very good for you. When a person laughs, chemicals called 'endorphins' are released, which give a feeling of happiness.

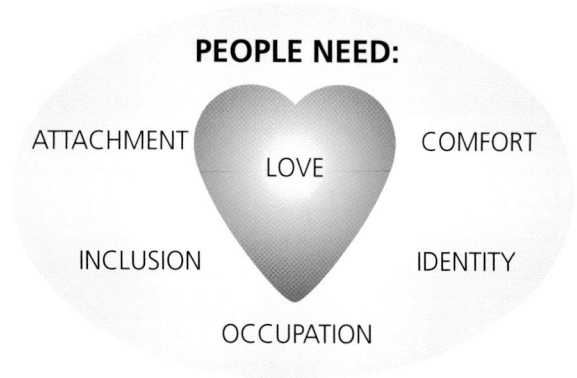

FIGURE 5.16 *People's needs*

Adapted from Kitwood (1997)

doesn't mean 'going to work'. Rather, it means doing things that have personal significance and that use your own unique abilities. The people who set up their own Bridge Club (Scenario, page 212) had found meaningful occupation in playing cards. Being meaningfully occupied is a form of intellectual activity. Finally, everyone has a need for a sense of identity. This means knowing who you are, where you came from, how you see yourself and an awareness of how you like to be perceived by others. We'll talk more about the issue of identity and self below. For now, it is important to note that everyone has an emotional need to have a strong sense of self.

Think it over...

Think about yourself. What kind of person are you? How would you describe who you are to another person?

(Note: This doesn't mean how tall you are, or what colour your hair is. It refers to who and what you consider yourself to be. For example: a trainee social worker who likes to work with other people, and who is also very involved in local charity work.)

It follows from what Kitwood says that many kinds of activity can satisfy a person's emotional needs. Activities can also be very simple, as the following scenario demonstrates.

Children in the early years

Government guidance on the developmental needs of young children has already been referred to with particular reference to their physical and intellectual needs (above, pages 209–217). This guidance also takes into account their emotional and social needs and, as with adults, these two areas of need are often closely related.

The guidance framework for working with very young children *Birth to Three Matters* DfES/Sure Start, 2002), identifies four 'aspects' of development. One of these is *A Strong Child*. This aspect includes the social and emotional needs identified in Figure 5.17.

SCENARIO

Doris and Ruth

Doris is 79 and has been in hospital for several months after being knocked down by a car. She has metal pins in her right leg, and the injury is taking a long time to heal. Although she can walk about with help, it has been decided that she is too frail to go home.

Every day she goes to the day room and sits next to Ruth, with whom she feels comfortable. Ruth is hard of hearing, so they don't talk much. However, Doris likes to knit and Ruth likes to read, and that's how they spend most of their time together.

The companionship that Ruth and Doris experience in sitting together each day satisfies their need for attachment, while the knitting and reading provide meaningful occupation. They get comfort just from sitting together, and also a feeling of inclusion (as they both belong to a special friendship).

Through activities that respect and foster these aspects of personhood, a child develops an awareness of self, realises that he or she can be valued and important, becomes more confident in his or her own abilities and also develops a sense of belonging. These elements can be encouraged by very simple means, such as putting Adnan's string painting on the wall to be admired and praised by others (see above, page 214).

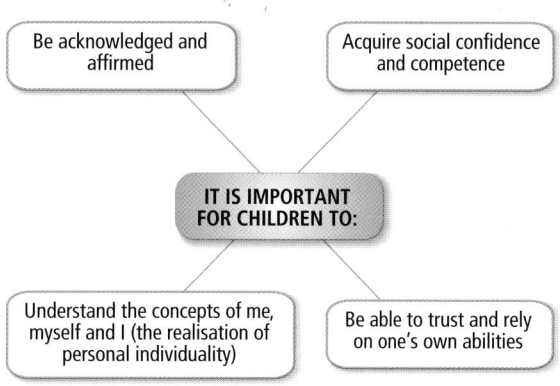

FIGURE 5.17 *The social and emotional needs of children 0–3: a strong child*

Another key aspect of the framework is *A Skilful Communicator*. This aspect covers the social and emotional needs identified in Figure 5.18.

FIGURE 5.18 *The social and emotional needs of children 0–3: a skilful communicator*

Finally, the aspect *A Healthy Child* includes emotional well-being as an important developmental area for children.

Group activities such as singing or role-plays give children the opportunity to develop as communicators, and to learn the give and take that forms part of living in society. Staff working with children will make sure that everyone is included, and activities may be adapted so that, for example, children with disabilities can take part equally with the others. Praise and recognition for achievement, however small, are important elements in fostering a child's emotional well-being.

FIGURE 5.19 *Group activities give children the opportunity to develop as communicators and to learn to give and take*

Many activities designed for early years children will include addressing aspects of social and emotional need. Teachers working with children at Key Stage 1 will also be careful to ensure that these important elements are not overlooked, as it is vital not to damage children's confidence in themselves as learners (Riley, 2003). Children who feel emotionally secure will be better able to learn. Developing the communication skills necessary to build and maintain social relationships is essential if young children are to develop self-esteem and a sense of personal identity, both as individuals and as group members.

Care staff and teachers working with early years children will be careful to design activities that relate closely to all aspects of national guidance. If you choose to work with young children, you will have to be clear how the activity you choose relates both to the relevant government guidance and to the planned programme taking place within your chosen care setting (and see below, Figure 5.20, page 221 for working within existing programmes).

As with all of these attempts to categorise activities, in reality one activity can satisfy several types of need.

Activities to meet social needs

Many emotional needs are satisfied by belonging to a group, or by having a significant attachment to one or more people. We have an inbuilt need to be with other people, and in fact many different kinds of need can be satisfied through the relationships we make and maintain.

Group membership can sometimes meet our daily living needs. For example, we might receive practical help in the form of someone doing our shopping for us, giving advice, or even lending money if the relationship is close enough. Being a member of a family group or having a close circle of friends can satisfy the need we have to feel safe. Friends or family can help us through problems and anxieties simply by being there to listen. Through social group membership we develop a sense of self-concept. By interacting with friends and relatives, we learn that we are significant as

ACTIVITIES FOR CHILDREN: MEETING EMOTIONAL NEEDS		
ACTIVITY TYPE	**POTENTIAL BENEFITS**	**NOTES**
Role-plays and dressing up Cookery	Satisfy the need for personal expression which is part of the *Personal, Social and Emotional Development* aspect of the Foundation Stage curriculum guidance	Also enhance communication skills
Painting Drawing Making music Puppet theatre Making collages (including natural and reclaimed materials) Weaving with paper strips Wax-resist paintings	Satisfy needs within the *Creative* aspect of the Foundation Stage curriculum guidance	Can help cognitive development in children, including hand–eye coordination and communication skills Can also be linked to other aspects of the Foundation Stage curriculum, e.g. *Knowledge and Understanding of the World*

FIGURE 5.20 *Activities to meet emotional needs: some suggestions for children*

Source: Lewisham (2002)

FIGURE 5.21 *We have an inbuilt need to be with other people*

individuals, which in turn gives us a feeling of self-worth.

Social relationships

Through these relationships we have a 'social life'. By this we mean doing all the things that are important to us and that give us pleasure (for example, going bowling, singing in a choir, playing team sports or simply meeting up with people to chat and enjoy each other's company). In talking to friends and family about the things that are important to us we can develop a sense of purpose in life – planning what we want to do after leaving college, or working out the steps that need to be taken to get where we want to be. Being with people who share the same interests is also intellectually stimulating – two friends who are passionate about downloading music from the Internet, for example, can talk for hours about the technicalities of downloading and storage, as well as about the music itself.

Any one person is likely to be a member of several social groups, depending on his or her interests.

Think it over...

Make a list of all the groups you belong to (e.g. close family, football team, college society and so on).

Put them in order of importance for you. How would it make you feel to lose the support or pleasure that you get from each of these groups?

Unfortunately, some people may find that they lose the benefits of social group membership either gradually or suddenly. For example, the onset of illness, the development of a disability or the advancement of the ageing process may result in physical problems such as loss of mobility or difficulties with hearing or vision. Such problems may restrict what people are capable of doing. This in turn means that they may no longer be able to take part in activities they used to enjoy, may have less energy to engage in these activities, and may even have less money to spend on doing the things they like. The provision of activities that meet the need for social group membership may thus be very welcome to people experiencing isolation through illness, physical disability or simply getting older.

When group membership is a problem

For some people, group membership may be problematic. People with **Asperger's Syndrome**, for example, find it very hard to relate to others, as they cannot read non-verbal 'signals' such as body language or tone of voice. Consequently, they find it hard to work out what someone else is really feeling, and what sort of response or reaction would be appropriate in any given situation. (If you are interested in finding out more about this condition, a very good novel to read is *The Curious Incident of the Dog in the Night Time*, by Mark Haddon (Vintage, 2004). Nevertheless, despite these difficulties, people with Asperger's Syndrome still have the same emotional needs for attachment and comfort as everyone else. They simply need some help and consideration from the people around them. Similarly, someone who has developed the condition known as **dementia** (in which memory and recognition are seriously impaired) still retains the same emotional needs as everyone else, even though he or she may have lost many of the social skills necessary to develop and maintain relationships. A skilled care worker will devise ways to include anyone who has difficulties in being part of a group.

The following scenario describes a situation in which a group of people are failing to socialise with each other. Read it through, and then decide what could be done to improve things.

Sometimes, people from different cultural groups find themselves together in the same service setting. Care workers need to make sure that the importance of these groups to their members is recognised and respected, and that a sense of mutual understanding and respect is cultivated. This is certainly the case at the Early Years Development Centre described in the scenario on page 223.

SCENARIO
Life at The Elms

The Elms Care Home is typical of many older residential units in that it has one very large day room for people to use when they are not in their own rooms. It is supposed to provide a place where the residents can socialise with each other.

The day room is quite large, and the chairs are arranged around the walls facing into the centre of the room.

One problem is that many of the residents are hard of hearing or have visual problems. As a result, it's very hard for a person sitting on one side of the room to see or hear someone sitting on the other side.

The residents tend to sit in the same chairs every day, and talk only to the people sitting close by, if at all. The staff want to encourage more people to get to know each other, but are not having much success.

1. **What changes might you make to the day room to encourage more friendships to develop amongst the residents?**
2. **How else could people be encouraged to socialise with each other at The Elms?**

SCENARIO
Celebrating diversity

At an early years development centre, the major festivals of all the children currently attending are celebrated.

Activities this year have included baking salt dough bread for the Christian Harvest Festival, making clay lamps and painting hands for Diwali, and creating dragons, junks and animal masks for the Chinese New Year.

Next year, the centre will be celebrating Black History Month.

Such activities enable the children to recognise and value the existence of different groups and cultures.

FIGURE 5.22 *It is important to celebrate diversity and to develop mutual understanding and respect*

Key concept

Diversity: The term diversity refers to the variation that exists within and between people's cultures and ways of living.

Belonging and identity

People often get a very strong sense of who they are from the social groups they belong to. Doing things you like with people you like can give a reassuring awareness of your personal **identity**. Being aware of your own identity or individuality is very important. We also refer to this awareness as a **sense of self**. This sense of being a person can also give you a feeling of having value within society.

Group membership can reinforce this sense of self. For example, people who go abroad to live and work often associate very closely with other people from their own country. Similarly, within a diverse society like the one we have in the UK, many people derive a strong sense of identity from their membership of a cultural or ethnic group. This identity is often expressed through using the same language or languages, and having the same religious or cultural practices. Consider the situation of Vikram, a multilingual social worker from London, in the scenario below.

SCENARIO
Expressing yourself

Vikram comes from a Panjabi Hindu family and lives in Southall. He works in North London as a social worker. He speaks English at work, but at home several languages are used including Panjabi, Hindi, Urdu and English. He attends the Hindu temple where he is also a member of the executive committee. He was born and educated in Southall where he has friends both within and outside the Panjabi Hindu community.

It is quite possible for a person to consider him or herself to be a member of several different groups. Vikram, for example, certainly has a strong sense of himself as being a member of the Panjabi community, but he is also a social worker and part of his identity comes from this. He uses the same jargon and terminology as his colleagues in the Youth Outreach Team where he works, and he speaks English with a London accent. When he goes to court to speak on behalf of a service user, he expresses himself as a professional worker using legal jargon, and he also dresses differently for court appearances. In a sense, Vikram has at least four different aspects to his identity: at home with his family, in the temple where he has a position of responsibility, at work with service users and colleagues, and in court.

If Vikram were asked to think about it, he might come up with some more groups from which he gets a sense of self. In fact, you don't have to speak several languages to experience different aspects of your own personality.

For example, you might have a close friendship with some people you have known from schooldays. Perhaps you were a bit more reserved then than you are now, so with these friends you are still fairly quiet, as they expect you to behave in this way. However, at the drama society you may be a leading light, taking key roles in stage productions and enjoying being the centre of attention. Both ways of behaving are aspects of yourself and both give you satisfaction (because you still love to be with your old schoolfriends, even though you are fairly quiet with them). You value both social groups for different reasons.

Consider Nina's story in the scenario below. We can see from just these few scenarios that belonging to a group is extremely important to having a sense of identity, and to building up healthy feelings of self-esteem and personal worth.

When choosing and planning an activity for and with a service user, you must make sure that this activity (together with the way you go about the task) enhances self-esteem. Anything that devalues the service user as a person is not acceptable.

As with physical, intellectual and social needs, individual preferences and wishes must take priority in any selection of activities. Some suggestions for activities for adults and children that meet social needs are given in Figures 5.23 and 5.24.

In the next section we will look more closely at the factors involved in choosing an activity, and the way in which you should undertake this task. First, however, it would be helpful for you to do the following exercise on page 221 and to identify how important group membership is to you.

Think it over...

Take the list of groups you identified in the exercise on page 221. These should be all the groups that you belong to.

For each one of these groups, decide which of your needs (physical, intellectual, emotional and social) are met.

An example is given in Figure 5.25 to start you off.

SCENARIO
A sense of identity

Nina has **Tourette's Syndrome**, a disturbing condition that can prevent a person from controlling his or her social behaviour.

As a result, Nina is very shy and has found it hard to make friends. However, she is a superb pianist and has found that when she plays, she never shows any signs of Tourette's. She has been asked to join a small band, and they have begun to play gigs in local pubs and clubs. Her friends in the band value the cohesion that she gives to their performances – her keyboard skills keep the group together – and she is also able to coach them on aspects of their performance.

If she does have a Tourette's-related outburst while they are not playing, they either ignore it or help her to see the funny side of it.

Nina has found a sense of self as a musician. The value that her friends place on her contribution to their music has enhanced her self-esteem. At last she feels she can do something that gives pleasure both to other people and to herself. Although she is still troubled by Tourette's when she is not at the keyboard, the sense of personal worth she gets from playing with the band is strong enough for her to be able to deal with any difficult situations she may get into as a result of not being able to control her verbal behaviour fully.

ACTIVITIES FOR ADULTS: MEETING SOCIAL NEEDS		
ACTIVITY TYPE	**POTENTIAL BENEFITS**	**NOTES**
Music: * Choral singing * Singing in a small group * Playing an instrument in a band or orchestra	All the social benefits of group membership: company of like-minded people, sense of purpose etc.	Emotional needs also satisfied, e.g. stress relief, pleasure etc. (see above, Figure 5.15)
Art: Workshop activities	As for music, above	Emotional needs also satisfied, e.g. self-expression etc. (see above, Figure 5.15)
Memory sessions	As for music, above	Cognitive skills and memory developed; emotional needs (e.g. recall of happy memories), reinforcement of personal identity

FIGURE 5.23 *Activities to meet social needs: some suggestions for adults*

ACTIVITIES FOR CHILDREN: MEETING SOCIAL NEEDS		
ACTIVITY TYPE	**POTENTIAL BENEFITS**	**NOTES**
Role-plays and dressing up Walks around local area Playing with multicultural dolls and toys All-group work Singing as a group	Satisfy *Personal, Social and Emotional* aspect of Foundation Stage of curriculum guidance	Can be linked to *Knowledge and Understanding of the World* aspect of curriculum guidance

FIGURE 5.24 *Activities to meet social needs: some suggestions for children*

Source: Lewisham (2002)

In the example given below, 'Bowling Club' is given as a social group. Going bowling will arguably satisfy some of a person's physical needs because of the exercise involved in playing the game. Social group membership needs are met (assuming that nobody falls out!) and having fun meets the emotional need to feel good. You might also argue that chatting with friends meets an intellectual need for stimulation and interest.

GROUP	PHYSICAL NEEDS	INTELLECTUAL NEEDS	EMOTIONAL NEEDS	SOCIAL NEEDS
Bowling Club	Practising hand–eye coordination	Chatting with friends	De-stressing through enjoyment of leisure activity	Feeling part of a group and catching up with friends

FIGURE 5.25 *The needs met from belonging to listed social groups*

Think it over...

Take another look at the social groups you belong to that you identified in the last task.

1. How important are these groups and activities to you?
2. How far does belonging to these groups help you express your own identity?
3. How far does membership of these groups help to enhance your own feeling of self-esteem?

Summary of Section 5.1

The following key areas of theory have been covered in this section:

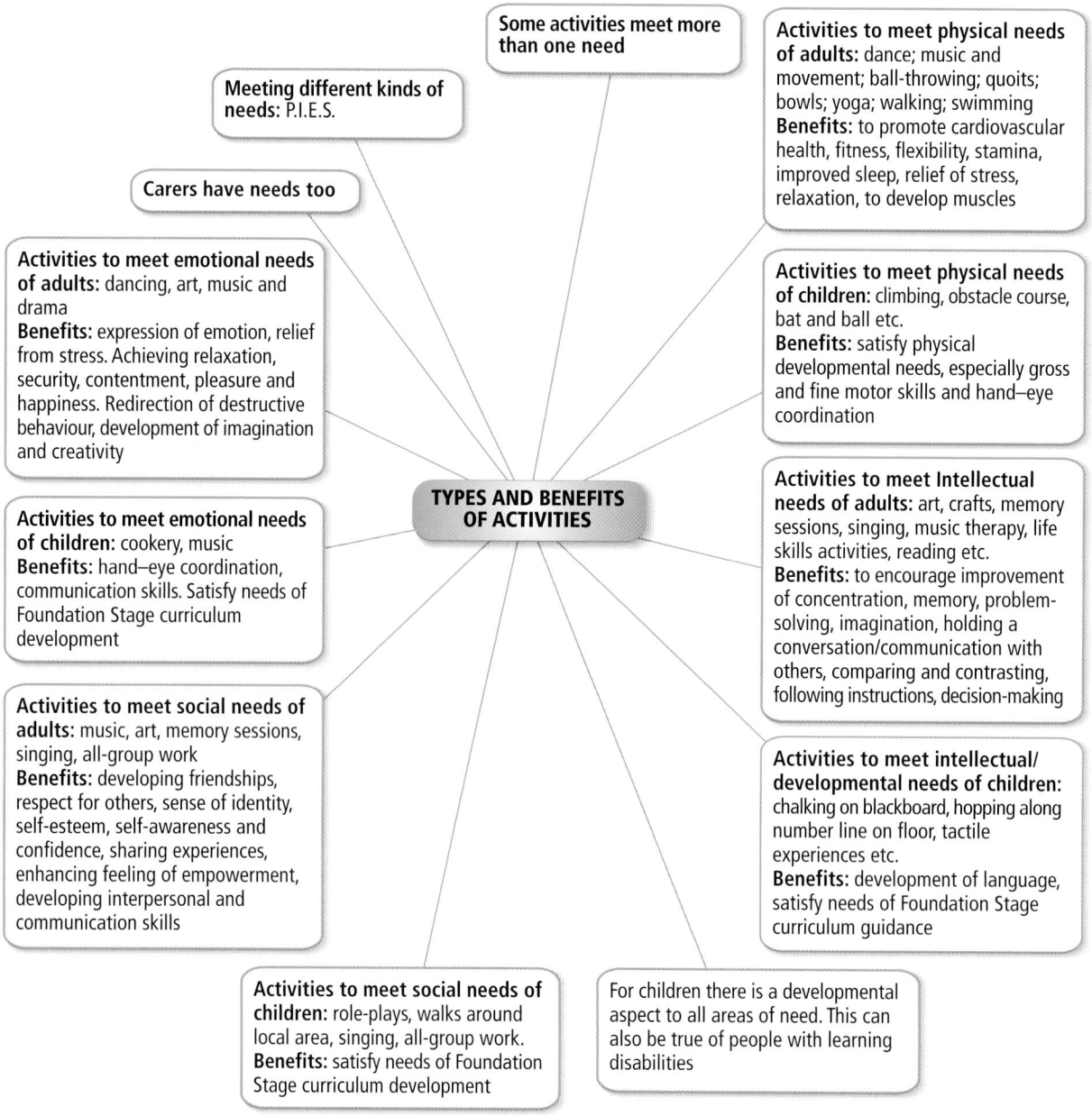

Consider this

Jan has just come out of hospital after suffering serious facial disfigurement in a car accident.

She now feels ugly and unlovely, and has totally lost confidence socially.

Before her accident, she used to play ten-pin bowling for a local team. This meant a lot to her, and she had been the life and soul of the regular weekly bowling sessions. Now she cannot bear seeing everybody.

Her friends have been very concerned for her, and several of them have visited her regularly while she has been in hospital. Her parents have also been very supportive, but are now very anxious about what will happen when she comes home and has to rebuild her life.

Using concepts, can you identify:

1. What types of need does Jan have?
2. How could she be helped to move forward? What kinds of activity might help this along?
3. Who might need to be involved in this process?
4. Do you think her parents need support? How might they get this?

Go further – can you analyse the issues using theory?

How far are issues of self-esteem important when working with Jan? What would help her to build a positive level of self-esteem?

Go further – can you evaluate using a range of theory?

If you had to assess the value of an activity for Jan, what key factors would you need to consider?

5.2 The planning and implementation of activities

In Section 5.1 it was emphasised that it is vital for you to remember that a service user is, above all else, a person – an individual with physical, intellectual, emotional and social needs just like everyone else in society. It was stressed that activities cannot be imposed on people (even children should be encouraged to do things rather than being forced), and that a care worker works 'with' a service user rather than doing things 'to' him or her.

When you start to work with a service user to complete the task for this unit, you will need to keep the principles outlined in Figure 5.26 firmly in mind.

FIGURE 5.26 *Choosing an appropriate activity: key principles*

Think it over...

1. What do you think it means to respect diversity?
2. What things might you have to take into consideration in order to do this?

Getting to know your service user

By now you should have decided which group of service users you would like to study: people who are ill or injured, children in the early years, older people or people with specific needs. You should also have confirmed whether or not you will be able to have a placement in a health or social care setting.

Key concept

Care setting: A care setting is any place where care is given to one or more service users. This can be in a person's own home. It can also be in any of the places where health and social care services are delivered, such as hospitals, outpatient units, day care units, residential establishments, Early Years Development Centres and so on.

Before you choose a service user or an activity, you should make at least one visit to your chosen care setting (if you are successful in getting a placement). This will enable you to get to know the care worker who is going to help you with your assignment, and to begin to understand the kinds of activities that service users regularly do or take part in. The care worker can help you to identify a service user who is willing to work with you.

If you are not able to get a placement, it may be possible to arrange visits to your school or college from professionals in the health and social care fields. If so, you can take the opportunity to ask questions about care settings.

The *Framework for the 'Assessment of Children in Need and Their Families'* (DoH, 2000) identifies five key steps that social workers should take when assessing the needs of children. It is such good advice that it is relevant to anyone who is planning to work with a service user, whatever their age or the nature of their needs. This guidance is set out in Figure 5.27 below.

COMMUNICATING WITH CHILDREN/SERVICE USERS: CRITICAL COMPONENTS	
Seeing	You cannot make an assessment of a person's need without actually seeing him or her
Observing	You need to observe someone's responses to different events and activities
Engaging	It is important to develop a relationship with the person, in order to help him or her express thoughts, concerns and opinions as part of the process of making choices
Talking to children/ service users	This requires time, skill, confidence and careful preparation
Activities with children/ service users	Doing things with the service user can help you to develop mutual trust

FIGURE 5.27 *Communicating with children/service users*

Source: Adapted from Department of Health (2000: 43–44)

If you have a placement in an actual care setting, you will need to meet the person you are going to work with, and to observe how he or she behaves and what he or she likes doing, and how he or she relates to other people in the care setting. To engage with someone means to develop a relationship with that person, giving him or her the chance to tell you first hand about what is important. Getting a good relationship going will be important when you come to suggest an activity to your service user – he or she must feel that there is a choice, and be allowed to express that choice clearly and freely.

The *Framework for Assessment* also describes what children have said they value in social workers. Once again, this is so helpful that it could apply to service users and care workers in many care settings, to all ages and to all types of need. See Figure 5.28.

Hopefully, you can see that all service users would value someone who listens carefully and who is easy to approach. The care worker needs to be non-judgmental in his or her work. Although it is quite acceptable to suggest a number of options to a service user, it's not appropriate to be critical of his or her likes and dislikes, or to try to impose an activity that is not acceptable, for whatever reason.

As well as talking to the service user, you might also like to take part in an activity with him or her, to get a good sense of that person's needs and preferences.

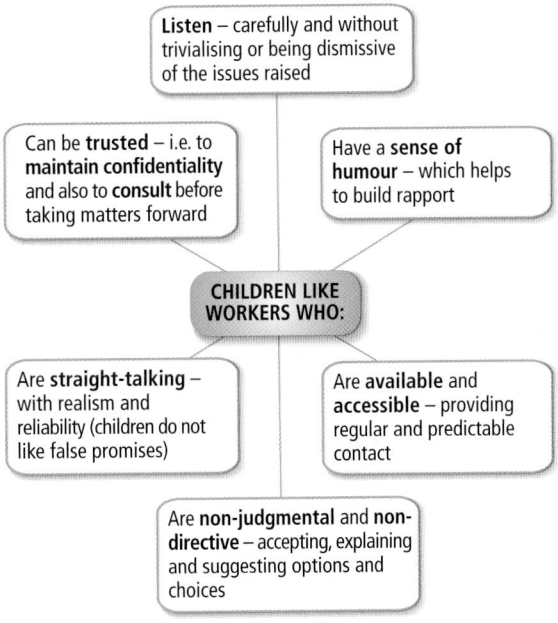

FIGURE 5.28 *What children value in social workers (could apply to all service users)*

Source: Adapted from Department of Health (2000)

Stereotyping and labelling

It is very easy to make assumptions about people based on their appearance, the way they speak and the things they do. Often, these assumptions can be negative. People sometimes assume, for example, that a person who is deaf is also unintelligent, or that a person who uses a wheelchair is incapable of making decisions. To see only the condition, rather than a person who has a condition, is known as **labelling**. This is a rigid way of thinking about people that prevents you from seeing them as individuals.

Key concept

Labelling: Classifying someone in a fixed way that refers only to one aspect of that person – for example, his or her physical appearance, nationality, disability and so on. Such a label would refer to someone as 'a wheelchair' rather than as a person who uses a wheelchair (see Scenario on page 231), or as 'a Down's Syndrome', rather than as a person who has Down's Syndrome.

People also sometimes assume that those who share the same disabling condition must also have the same outlook on life and will behave in the same way. Similar assumptions are sometimes made about people from the same ethnic group. Making these types of assumptions is known as **stereotyping**. This also puts people into a rigid 'mould'.

Key concept

Stereotyping: Assuming that people who share one characteristic (for example, having a disability, using the same language, having the same religious or cultural background) will automatically be the same in every respect.

Of course, it is not wrong to use terms such as 'wheelchair user', or 'a person with Down's Syndrome'. But it is wrong to assume that all such people are the same in every respect. When helping a service user to choose an activity, you will need to avoid making the kind of assumptions involved in labelling and/or stereotyping. For example, just because a person attends a day unit for older people, it doesn't automatically follow that that person will want to do music and movement, simply because there is a session there every Wednesday.

FIGURE 5.29 *Don't make assumptions about what the service user will want to do*

WHAT PEOPLE WITH LEARNING DISABILITIES SAY

People with learning disabilities have been consulted on a number of issues that are important to them.

Those consulted said this about the ways they like to spend their time:

- people with learning disabilities want to do lots of different things
- they want to do things in ordinary places, where anyone can go to

They said the following things about getting out and making friends:

- young people with learning disabilities like to do the same things as other young people
- they like to spend time with their friends, even though they have some problems with making friends
- they like to go to places where they make new friends
- they like to have young and energetic support workers.

FIGURE 5.30 *Thoughts of people with learning difficulties*

Source: Plain Facts, Issues 22, 23 and 29

Every person who attends day unit is unique, and has his or her personal history, likes and dislikes, aptitudes and preferences. In fact, it's likely that the only thing they all have in common is that they are all over a certain age.

Similarly, it would be wrong to assume that all people with learning difficulties like trips to the seaside or making clay models, or that all blind people want to listen to talking books.

Some people with learning disabilities have expressed this very well in the magazine *Plain Facts*, which makes research findings understandable to people with learning difficulties. Each person, they say, has his or her own needs and should be consulted about what they want, although many people may need help to express their views and make a choice. This may be true for any service user who may be at a disadvantage when it comes to asking for things whether through illness, disability, language differences or lack of self-esteem.

Watch your language!

Language can sometimes reveal what we are really thinking deep down. Consider the following scenario.

The store manager is guilty of labelling Jo – he has seen only the wheelchair and not the person in it. He was right to help Jo with her access problem: the situation could have been dangerous both for Jo and the people around her if no one had taken control of managing the crowd. However, the manager's choice of language reveals that deep down he sees her as a wheelchair case who is also a 'problem'.

Think it over...

Write down all the words you have heard to refer to:

* disabled people
* people from different ethnic groups.

How many of these words are positive, and how many have negative connotations?

This exercise may have revealed many negative words that are used about people who are in the minority within society. This is because many people just don't try to see things from other people's point of view. However, the good news is that by making a conscious effort to change our language, we can eventually bring about a change in our own thinking, and may also influence other people's views.

Sometimes people think that they have to say the right thing (for example, using the term 'disabled people' rather than 'spastics') just to be 'politically correct'. It is certainly true that

SCENARIO

'Let the wheelchair through!'

Jo is an avid reader of science-fiction novels. A new book has just been published by her favourite author, and there is to be a book signing at the local bookstore.

As Jo uses an electric wheelchair and is very independent, she is able to go into town by herself, and is looking forward to meeting this famous writer.

When she gets there, the book signing has already started and there is a big crowd in the shop. There doesn't seem to be a queue, and everyone is 'pushing and shoving'. As Jo is deciding what to do, the store manager rushes forward and shouts: 'Stand back please! Let the wheelchair through!'

Jo has mixed feelings. She's glad to be allowed straight through, but she's also offended. She is not a 'wheelchair', but a person who happens to use a wheelchair.

What would you have said if you were the store manager?

support workers must display anti-discriminatory practice (ADP) when working with service users, and using offensive language would certainly fall short of the standards required by current guidance.

However, there is a more positive reason to watch your language, especially when you are working with a service user. If you are truly to value the service user as a person with unique needs and the same rights as everyone else, then your language (and the attitudes that lie behind that language) must reflect this. You cannot value a person as an individual if you speak of him or her as a 'spastic' or an 'Alzheimer's'. If you do this you are showing that you label that person and are treating him or her merely as a 'case' rather than as an individual.

WATCH YOUR LANGUAGE! WHEN SPEAKING ABOUT PEOPLE WITH DISABILITIES:	
DO SAY	**AVOID**
People with disabilities People with special needs Disabled people	The disabled Handicapped Afflicted Helpless Incapacitated Cripples Unfortunates Victims Sufferers
People with cerebral palsy	Spastics CPs The cerebral palsied Cerebral palsied people
Disabling condition Impairment	Affliction Handicap
Learning difficulties/ disabilities	Mentally handicapped Sub-normal Retarded
People who use wheelchairs Wheelchair users	Confined to a wheelchair Wheelchair bound
Able bodied Non-disabled	Normal

FIGURE 5.31 *Advice on how to avoid offensive language*

Source: Reproduced with permission from SCOPE

Advice from the organisation SCOPE explains that the word 'handicap' originally referred to someone begging with cap in hand. As such, it creates an extremely negative image of someone with a disability as being helpless – a victim of circumstances who must rely totally on others. It is better to refer to someone as a person with a disability or as a disabled person – a person rather than a condition. Similarly, it does not help to talk about 'the disabled', which also ignores the fact that these are people before all else. Expressions that refer to disabled people as victims or sufferers are also extremely negative. Many disabled people live very active and fulfilled lives, and have no time for such attitudes. In some respects, other people's attitudes are more disabling than the disability itself.

Choosing an activity

Once you have studied the advice and information given so far in this unit, and done a little more research into the issues that may be important to the people in the service user group that you have chosen to work with, you will then be in a position to go forward and start to work with and for an individual service user or for a group of service users.

If you decide to work with an individual service user, then you should work alone. If you choose a group activity, then you can work with a partner or group of other learners. If you do this, however, your own role must be made clear in your report, and the evidence you present must be your own and presented in your own words.

Figure 5.32 sets out the steps you will need to take when choosing an activity with the service user or group.

Having visited one or more care settings and decided on the service user (or group) you would like to work with (and who would also like to work with you), you will need to choose an activity and make arrangements to do the tasks outlined in Figure 5.32.

STEPS TO TAKE WHEN CHOOSING AN ACTIVITY		
1.	Get to know the service user (see page 229)	You will need to have explained what you are doing and why If you are working with a child, you may want to observe him or her as a first step
2.	Discuss with the service user what activity he or she would like you to help to plan	You should also involve the care or key worker in this discussion
3.	Identify whether the chosen activity will form part of a wider programme of development or scheme of activities within the care setting	For example, a child at an Early Years Development Centre will already have a plan linked to the Foundation Stage curriculum guidance
4.	Identify the needs that will be met by the chosen activity: physical, intellectual, emotional or social	Remember that one activity can satisfy a range of needs
5.	Keep a record of what you have decided	Show this to the service user and to the key/care worker
Note: Checklist 5.1 will help you to establish the range of needs that will be met by any given activity.		

FIGURE 5.32 *Choosing an activity*

Remember that one activity can satisfy more than one area of need, whether physical, intellectual, emotional or social. In using Checklist 5.1 on page 239, you may be surprised at the range of needs that an activity can meet. It is important to be as imaginative as you can in choosing and planning an activity, as there may be benefits you didn't think of in the first place.

SCENARIO

Jasminder

Jasminder was born without legs from just below her knees. She is now four and a half years old, and has been attending an Early Years Development Centre for the past 2 years.

She has artificial legs that cannot be jointed until she gets older. This means that her legs splay out, especially when she sits down. The legs are attached to her by a harness, which can make undressing difficult. The other children have had to learn not to be rough with her, as she can overbalance easily.

Group activities have been adapted so that Jas can take part. The foam bath for providing messy play has been put on the floor rather than on a table, so that Jas can get her hands into the foam and play with the objects with her friends.

When Jas needed a Life Story Book as a preparation for going into mainstream school, the other children also did Life Story Books so that she would not be made to feel 'different'. However, her book contained greater detail, as it was necessary to explain to the other children in her new school why she has artificial legs, and how they could best help her integrate into her new class.

During her time at the centre, every effort was made to ensure that Jas could achieve just as much as the other children. Great attention was paid to the development of her self-esteem and identity as a person; having to show consideration to Jas also helped the other children to develop social awareness and communication skills.

There may also be benefits to others who are indirectly involved in the activity, as the scenario above demonstrates.

The service user in context

No activity takes place in complete isolation. When making plans, several contextual factors must be taken into consideration, including the type of care setting and the facilities available, existing development programmes or curriculum guidance, health and safety issues (including the size of the group that will be involved in the activity) and any barriers to access for the service user in taking part in the activity.

Type of care setting and available facilities

Activities may be limited by the facilities available within the location. Clearly, if an activity takes place within a service user's own home, facilities such as large workrooms or physical education equipment may not be available.

Conversely, a large, purpose-built establishment such as a local authority day unit may offer a range of options such as large and small meeting rooms, communication equipment such as overhead projectors or microphones, rooms for pottery or art work (with sinks and large work surfaces), and/or facilities for drama work such as a stage. Large units will often have plenty of furniture (for example, both soft and hard chairs and tables), and other resources such as art materials, TV, video and DVD players and exercise equipment (for example, quoits, balls, mats, etc.).

The location of the activity may limit or enhance what it is possible to achieve. You should take these factors into consideration at this stage.

Development programmes or curricula

Any activity you devise with your service user will be taking place in the context of a wider agenda.

Residential or day care facilities for older people, for example, often have a programme of activities with regular timetables. Activities such as reminiscence sessions or music and movement are often scheduled on a weekly basis, and you might like to consider doing something within the context of such an existing programme. You will need to work closely with the person who delivers such sessions in order to make sure that your proposed activity forms a natural component within the larger scheme of activity that the therapist or trainer has in mind.

People with learning disabilities may have Person Centred Plans, setting out their developmental needs. You might like to do something with a service user that moves him or her along the developmental pathway that has already been agreed. Once again, you will have to work very closely with the service user together with the key worker or support worker to make sure that anything you do is in line with the existing plan.

Consider this

John has a mild learning disability. He is 45, and has lived with his parents all his life. His parents are now quite elderly, and are getting worried about what will happen to John when they are no longer able to care for him.

Plans are being made for John to have a home of his own. He has been assessed as being capable of learning how to cook, shop and look after himself with a bit of help from a carer, and he has been learning how to do these things at his day centre.

However, John has said that he doesn't want to live on his own – he says he would be lonely. At the day centre he has lots of friends – in particular Eric, with whom he goes every week to watch their favourite football team.

Through using the Person Centred Planning process, a solution has been found that everyone is happy with. John and Eric are going to share a flat, and a care worker will go in every day to make sure they are managing.

Both John and Eric are very excited, and although John says he'll be a bit sad to leave his mum and dad, he is really looking forward to his new life.

By taking everyone's wishes into account, a solution has been found that will satisfy John's and Eric's physical, social and emotional needs.

What kind of activities might need to be planned to make sure that John and Eric can move successfully into their new home?

Children in early years settings will certainly have very structured programmes of activity in line with the National Curriculum guidance. An Early Years Development Centre has very tightly planned schedules for each week, and centre workers have to make sure that every aspect of that week's plan has been covered. Such centres are subject to regular checks by Ofsted, the government's inspection unit for educational services. If you have opted to work with a child, or a group of children, you'll need to make sure you have information about the topics that are already planned, and the ways in which they will relate to the National Curriculum. In the following Scenario, the manager at an Early Years Development Centre has integrated the Foundation Stage Curriculum Guidance into a well thought-through programme of activities for all the children.

If you are working with a service user in a care setting that is different from his or her own home, there is a strong possibility that you will have to take into account an existing programme of scheduled activities. These could be either personal to the service user (in terms of a Personal Development Plan), or apply to the care setting as a whole. The checklist 5.2 on page 240 will help you to work through the various considerations involved with respect to the service user's care setting. If you are role-playing planning an activity, or using a family member, it will still be important to show in your report that you are aware that contextual issues can be significant.

The timing of activities

The timing of an activity is critical to its success.

Good weather will be essential for an outdoor activity, and therefore certain times of year may be less suitable for country walks. Similarly, during winter it may be necessary to make sure that room temperatures are not allowed to fall below a certain level.

If it is a time of fasting or of a particular religious festival, some service users may be precluded from taking part in certain kinds of activity. It is vital that you check out whether your service user observes a particular festival, what this involves (for example, fasting or abstinence from certain foods), and whether or not this festival falls at about the time your activity is due to take place.

The time of day may also be an issue. You may want to consider whether or not your service user

SCENARIO

The Early Years Centre – meeting national guidance requirements

The Centre's theme for this month is 'People Who Help Us' (at home and in the community). Some of the children are taken out for a walk around the shops, and to get there they have to cross the road. The worker points out people who help us: in this case the lollipop lady and a policewoman.

This forms part of the curriculum area *Knowledge and Understanding of the World*, but has also provided some physical development activity. On the walk, the importance of holding hands and listening carefully is stressed, as is helping each other to cross the road. This is an aspect of the *Personal, Social and Emotional* area of the curriculum.

Back at the centre, the children dress up (as policemen/women and a lollipop person) and role-play helping each other to cross the road. This addresses the *Creative* area of the curriculum.

Later, they use a Children's Traffic Club storybook and tape to reinforce the message of listening carefully to traffic. This helps with the *Communication/Language and Literacy* curriculum area. They also count the beeps they hear on the tape, and the wheels they see on pictures of cars and other vehicles. This satisfies an aspect of the *Mathematics* curriculum area.

Everything that is done at the Early Years Development Centre has been very carefully planned to meet curriculum requirements.

needs to rest at certain times as a result of an illness or disability. Some religions – for example – Islam, observe regular prayer-times throughout the day, and you may need to make sure that your activity is not timed to clash with such observances.

If the activity is taking place in a large facility, there may be other things that your service user wants to do that are already in the schedule (for example, have his or her feet done by the chiropodist). Regular daily events in the setting may also include meal times or the drugs round.

Before you go too far into the plan for the activity, check out all these basic things in order to enhance success.

Health and safety issues

When planning and implementing an activity it is absolutely essential to consider issues of health and safety, not only for the service user but also for yourself and for staff working in the care setting. It is not a good idea, for example, to let children play with sharp implements or near very hot radiators. Similarly, to organise a dancing session for older people in a room with trailing cables or loose carpeting would be very ill-advised.

The management of health and safety is regulated by law, and your chosen care setting will almost certainly also have its own Health and Safety Policy and associated guidance. These documents will explain the law, and will also set out the rules that must be observed by staff (and service users) while on the premises.

The Health and Safety at Work Act 1974 (HASAWA) provides the foundation for the way in which health and safety issues at work are managed. Since 1974, there have been numerous Acts of Parliament and guidance documents dealing with all aspects of safety, including manual handling (which covers the lifting and moving of people as well as of heavy objects), hazardous substances, provision in case of fire and the use of fire-fighting equipment, to name but a few. These laws and guidelines cover all the things that might go wrong in the workplace including accidents, injuries caused by lifting someone in the wrong way, exposure to dangerous substances and so on.

It is not necessary for you to be familiar with the details of all this legislation, but it is vital that you are aware of potential hazards, and that you follow the rules for your care setting at all times. Of course, the employer must take a great deal of responsibility for making the workplace safe, but the HASAW Act makes it clear that each employee must also take a personal responsibility for health and safety issues. These responsibilities are set out in the below.

HEALTH & SAFETY AT WORK ACT 1974: STAFF RESPONSIBILITIES

Section 7 of this Act says that employees must:

* take reasonable care for their own health and safety and that of others affected by their acts or omissions at work
* cooperate with the employer
* report any situation thought to be unsafe or unhealthy.

While you are on the premises of your chosen care setting, you must behave in the same way as any staff member with respect to health and safety issues. It is essential that you follow the law and the rules in the same way as other staff, and you must be prepared to take the responsibility (and the initiative) for making the environment (and the activity) safe for the service user.

FIGURE 5.33 *A carer must be aware of potential hazards*

Barriers to access

You will need to take into account the additional needs of your service user, in particular those that may impede them from enjoying an activity to the full.

A person with mobility problems may need a ramp or a lift to access a particular room, particularly if he or she uses a wheelchair or has to walk with a stick. Some people may need a handrail in order to tackle stairs, and for people who use wheelchairs, wide doorways are essential to allow access to a room. Some people with physical needs may also require a personal helper.

Deaf people may need a signer or communicator if the activity is to include people who can hear. There is now equipment that allows a typist to transcribe what is being said, and the text appears immediately on a large overhead screen. Such equipment is a great help when deaf people are taking part with a large group of hearing people. Blind people may need written materials to be reproduced in Braille.

Someone for whom English is not a first language may benefit from the presence of a translator.

People with learning disabilities may require additional help to understand the choices available to them. Provision of a mentor, or facilitated sessions to help in making choices, will make sure that whatever is planned is acceptable to the service user with a learning disability, and not just something that seemed like a good idea to someone else.

Setting clear aims

When planning an activity with and for a service user, it is essential to have clear aims and benefits in mind. If aims are not clearly stated at the outset, then the activity itself may not have any meaningful benefits for that person.

These aims will have to be written with the expressed needs of the service user in mind.

For example, someone who has expressed the need for more company may not necessarily appreciate taking part in old-time dancing if he or she dislikes dancing, or has a mobility problem that prevents him or her taking part. This person is more likely to feel socially excluded by being asked to take part in a dance session. The activity must be tailored to individual needs, and this is done by the setting of clear aims and goals.

An example of such goal-setting is given in Figure 5.34, using Checklist 5.1 on page 239 as a framework.

By setting out these very clear expectations right at the start, you are more likely to achieve some benefits to the service user. This goal-setting also gives you something to measure when evaluating the impact of the activity (see Section 5.3).

SERVICE USER:	Mr Smith Day centre user Centre for older people
PROPOSED ACTIVITY:	Tai Chi at regular weekly session
TYPE OF NEED	**EXPECTED BENEFIT**
Physical need	Tai Chi should help with promoting Mr Smith's fitness and flexibility. It should help relaxation and improve sleep.
Intellectual need	The need to memorise a long sequence of movements should help Mr Smith maintain his concentration and improve his memory.
Emotional need	Tai Chi often promotes relaxation and relief from stress, together with pleasure and a sense of happiness.
Social need	Belonging to the Tai Chi group should give Mr Smith a new circle of friends, and enhance his sense of belonging.

FIGURE 5.34 *An example of goal setting*

Working out the details

Checklists 5.3 and 5.4, on pages 240 and 241, give you some ideas to consider when planning your activity.

You will need to take into account the size of the room you will need, together with the facilities that will have to be laid on for you (for example, running water for art work, or an accessible power-point to plug in equipment such as a CD player). It is advisable to make a list of the furniture you will require, together with any equipment. For example, you may need comfortable chairs (rather than straight-backed ones), or you may want to have an overhead projector.

It is essential to consider the access needs of your service user. Does he or she use a wheelchair, for example? If so, the room you book must be fully accessible, and provision may also have to be made for a personal helper to accompany him or her. If your service user is deaf, you may need to book a signer or communicator. This may also be the case with someone whose first language is not English.

Finally, think about health and safety issues in advance. You will need to make sure that the venue is safe and can accommodate the number of people who will be present during the activity. You should also consult the care setting's health and safety policy and guidance to make sure of the specific rules that apply. Use Checklist 5.3 as a guide when making practical plans.

Checklist 5.4 sets out the stages to go through when planning an activity. Consultation with both the service user and his or her care team (or key staff member) is absolutely vital. You will need to write a plan that sets out the aims of the planned activity (see the plan for Mr Smith above). The plan will also need to set out how the activity will be accomplished, step by step. This might include approximate timings for each stage. It is best to consult the key worker or other professional for advice on doing this.

A simple plan for delivering an activity might look like the one shown in Figure 5.35. The student's name is Mac, and the activity involves a memory session with older people.

Mac's memory session will be the subject of further discussion below (Implementing Activites, page 244, and Evaluating the activity, page 248).

Implementing activities

Once you have planned your activity carefully, you can then go forward to implement it with everyone's understanding and agreement.

Explaining the activity

It will be extremely important for everyone involved or affected by the activity to understand what is going on. For example, you may have booked a room especially for an afternoon, but this room would normally be used by someone else at that time, say, for a regular meeting. You'll need to make sure that the people concerned are given plenty of notice, and also an alternative venue for their meeting. Most people are extremely understanding when arrangements have to be altered, as long as this is not at the last minute.

As well as making sure that everyone else knows what's going on, it is really important that the service user understands clearly the nature of the activity, especially if it is something new. If your service user has a sensory problem, then you may need to consider carefully how best to explain things – perhaps you may need to have a set of instructions prepared in Braille, or in the service user's language; or you might need to have a signer present to make your instructions clear. A person with a learning disability may need extra support to understand what is going to happen. Always be receptive to questions, and

(continued on page 243)

FIGURE 5.36 ***Misunderstandings happen!***

ACTIVITY PLAN: MEMORY SESSION		
TIME	ACTION/ACTIVITY	NOTES
2.00 pm	Welcome the group and explain what will happen	Therapist to introduce
2.10 pm	Show slides of town centre in 1900s, 1930s etc.	Mac to present
2.30 pm	Discussion: pairs	Therapist to encourage people to talk Mac to observe and get involved as appropriate
2.50 pm	Discussion: whole group	Therapist to lead, and then to bring session to a close
3.00 pm	Close and tea	Mac to help serve, and also to chat to people as appropriate

FIGURE 5.35 *Example of a plan for delivering an activity*

CHECKLIST 5.1
CHOOSING AN APPROPRIATE ACTIVITY

Use this checklist to make sure you have considered fully your service user's needs.

Proposed activity.....

TYPE OF NEED	EXPECTED BENEFIT(S)	TICK IF NEED IS MET BY ACTIVITY
Physical need	Activity to promote cardiovascular health, fitness, flexibility, stamina, improved sleep, relief of stress, relaxation Activity to develop muscles, improve hand–eye coordination Activity to reduce weight or stimulate appetite	
Intellectual need	Activity to encourage cognitive skills (concentration, memory, problem-solving, imagination, development of language, holding a conversation/communication with others, comparing and contrasting, following instructions, decision-making) Development of literacy and/or numeracy skills	
Emotional need	Expression of emotion, relief from stress, diverting thoughts from problems and anxieties. Achieving relaxation, security, contentment, pleasure and happiness Redirection of destructive behaviour Development of imagination and creativity	
Social need	Developing friendships, sharing experiences, developing respect for others Development of sense of identity, self-esteem, self-awareness and confidence Enhancing feeling of empowerment Developing interpersonal communication skills	

You may want to make a few copies of this so that you can test out several options before you finally decide on an activity that you would like to work on. This checklist may also help you in completing your assignment. You may decide to include it in your final report.

CHECKLIST 5.2
PLANNING AN ACTIVITY: THE SETTING

Use this checklist to review the context for your planned activity.

Is the activity part of a longer developmental or education programme? Examples: * National Curriculum (Foundation Stage) * Person Centred Plan	If 'yes', you'll need to be very clear how your activity fits in Your report will have to explain how the planned activity forms part of this programme
Is the activity part of a programme of scheduled activities in that care setting? Example: * Music and movement class	See notes above
What time of day would be best for this activity? Of course, the time may be fixed already if it is part of a longer programme (above)	Is your service user likely to be tired? Are there any religious or cultural considerations (e.g. prayer-time)?
What time of year would be best for this activity?	Is the weather likely to be an issue (e.g. for an outdoor activity)? Is this a time of fasting or of a religious festival? Will you need to control the room temperature?
What else might be going on in the care setting at this time? Examples: * meal-time * drugs round * chiropody sessions etc.	Make sure that what you are planning doesn't clash with something else that your service user wants to do; or that the room you need hasn't been booked for something else

CHECKLIST 5.3
PLANNING AN ACTIVITY: THE VENUE

Use this checklist to make sure that you have put in place everything you need to make the activity a success.

	NOTES
Is the room the right size for the planned activity? * How many people will be involved? * Will you need space for them to move about? * Will you need to move furniture about? * Is there good ventilation and heating?	
What facilities will you need? * Power-point for CD player, TV or video? * Water for art work? * Loop system for deaf or hard-of-hearing people? * Is the lighting good enough for what you need to do? * Are the acoustics good enough for what you plan to do?	

What furniture and/or equipment will you need? * Tables (large, small, moveable)? * Types of chair (e.g. comfortable or upright)? * TV, video, CD/cassette player? * Art materials? * Exercise equipment?	
Is there easy access to the room/building? * Are there ramps or a lift? * Are there handrails? * Are the doors wide enough to allow people in wheelchairs to get through?	
What additional help will you need? * A signer/communicator for deaf or hard-of-hearing people? * Personal helper for anyone with a mobility problem? * A communicator/translator for someone who doesn't have English as a first language?	
What other aids or equipment will you need? * Braille translation of written materials?	
What health and safety issues do you need to consider? * The condition of all furniture and equipment (including electrical equipment) * Safe access and exit (all emergency exits to be easily accessible) * Trip hazards to be eliminated * Adequate heating and ventilation	
Note: There will be guidance on health and safety in the care setting where you are working. Be sure to check this out with the manager	

CHECKLIST 5.4
PLANNING AN ACTIVITY

IN PLANNING ACTIVITIES YOU WILL NEED TO:	NOTES
Consult with and get permission from the care team	
Consult with and get the agreement of the service user	
Establish clear aims/benefits to the service user (see Checklist 5.1)	
Develop the different steps or stages of an activity, including timing of these steps or stages	

Continued overleaf

Checklist 5.4 continued

Know when you (and the service user) will need assistance or supervision	
Identify the resources needed and how you will obtain them	
Organise and prepare for the activity (including space, resources)	
Prepare everyone who will be involved (the service user, other service users, staff, carers etc.)	

Consider this

Mac is an A Level student who has chosen to work with an older person for Unit 5. He wants to work alongside the therapist who delivers regular reminiscence sessions at a day unit, and he plans to lead part of the discussion. He is doing this with and for Mrs Harris, who has been suffering from depression since her husband died two years ago.

This group has been getting bigger, so the therapist cancels the original room booking, and asks Mac to book the main hall for the next session. Mac goes to do this straight away, but the day unit secretary is off sick, so he leaves a message with a care worker who happens to be in the office at the time.

On the day, Mac and the therapist arrive early to set out the room. To his dismay, Mac finds that a very important meeting is taking place in the main hall. People start turning up for the reminiscence session, and the room that they normally use is now being used by the visiting hairdresser, so they cannot go there.

The day unit manager steps in and they find space in a smaller room, but it's very cramped and the session gets off to a bad start.

1. Where did Mac go wrong?
2. What could have been done to prevent this from happening?

Think it over...

Ideally, how should the room have been set out for Mac's activity? There are now 10 people in the group, plus Mac and the therapist. Remember they have an OHP on a trolley (with castors) and an extension lead for the power.

The activity will involve a big group discussion, and then some smaller group or pair work. Mac and the therapist plan to move around the group to make sure everyone is involved.

The main hall would have been a great venue for the memory session, with plenty of room to arrange 12 chairs in a circle. The OHP and its trolley could have been kept to one side until required, but with any extra cable taped to the floor so that no one could trip over it. Mac and the therapist would have needed plenty of space to move around both behind and within the circle. The main hall is well-ventilated but warm, and the blinds can be drawn if the sun is in anyone's eyes. Either Mac or the therapist should have put a notice on the door to the hall explaining that the session was taking place. This would have kept interruptions to a minimum.

The care setting you work in will have a policy and guidance on health and safety. You should be sure to see copies of any relevant information on this, and to observe the house rules for your particular setting.

remember that what seems clear to you may not necessarily be clear to other people.

Mac knows that Mrs Harris is quite shy, so he has explained what happens at a memory session, and also that she doesn't have to say anything if she doesn't want to. He knows that she is interested in the history of their town, so he has prepared some transparencies showing photographs of the town centre 50 years ago. He plans to use these at the next session.

Maintain safety

As part of the planning for your activity, you will have anticipated potential health and safety requirements to be observed during the actual event itself (see above, page 241). If we stay with Mac's memory session, for example, the enforced use of the smaller room compromised the health and safety of the group. After 30 minutes the therapist decided to call a halt to the session, as the room was very stuffy and there was insufficient space to move around. Mac had planned to use an OHP to show his photographs of the town centre, but the projector and stand would have taken up too much space. If there had been a fire drill (or a real emergency), the situation could have been very dangerous.

Delivering the activity

Imagine now that Mac has reorganised the event, having reflected on what happened and learned from the experience. The group is settled in the main hall, and Mrs Harris (Mac's chosen service user) is taking part for the first time. Mac has carefully explained to her what is going to happen, and he and the therapist have a carefully timed plan for the whole session, which will last one hour.

Mac hopes that his pictures of the town centre from 50 years ago will trigger some memories and get everybody talking. As he shows his transparencies, he is careful to observe how Mrs Harris responds to the pictures and to what he is saying. He is careful to make regular eye-contact with her, and is relieved when she nods to him to show that she understands and appreciates what he is saying. The therapist supports Mac by encouraging everyone to comment on each picture, and Mac notices that some people are much more talkative than others. Mrs Harris doesn't say very much at this point. By the time they have got to the last photograph, several smaller conversations have begun and the therapist lets these continue. At this point, Mac goes to sit in between Mrs Harris and Mr Brannigan, her neighbour, and encourages a conversation between them. He succeeds, and they begin to exchange stories about their war-time experiences. The conversation is eventually going so well that he withdraws, and simply observes Mrs Harris as she begins to relax and enjoy the conversation.

After about 30 more minutes, the therapist senses that some of the group are beginning to get tired, so she decides not to introduce any new topics. She brings everyone back into one large group (as opposed to four or five small ones) and makes some closing remarks. The session ends with tea and biscuits, which Mac helps to serve. Mrs Harris's care worker comes in to have tea, and to see how she has enjoyed the session.

After tea, Mac helps to pack up the OHP, and puts away all his transparencies. He helps the care worker to move all the dirty cups into the kitchen; she says that Mrs Harris seems quite animated and was actually smiling at one point. She hasn't seen Mrs Harris smile during all the time she has been coming to the unit.

Mac then finds a quiet space to write up his own account of what has happened during the session, and what he has observed. In fact, he's

FIGURE 5.37 *A memory session can act as a catalyst for sharing experiences*

CHECKLIST 5.5
IMPLEMENTING AN ACTIVITY

WHEN IMPLEMENTING AN ACTIVITY, MAKE SURE THAT YOU:

- Explain the activity fully and clearly
- Maintain safety
- Observe service users' behaviour
- Interact and communicate with service users and care workers
- Monitor and observe the service user's reactions and abilities
- Know when to intervene to give guidance or help
- Maintain detachment when involved in an activity
- Be aware of when it is appropriate to finish an activity
- Tidy and clear up, as relevant, after an activity
- Observe the instructions and guidance of the professional with whom you are working.

done everything right, and has included all the things in the checklist above.

Under the supervision of the therapist, Mac was careful to watch what was going on, in particular Mrs Harris's reactions. He interacted with the group during the big discussion, and later chose to intervene to help Mrs Harris, who couldn't get a conversation going easily. When he felt that she was getting on well with Mr Brannigan, he didn't get too involved, but left them to enjoy their conversation. It was the therapist who decided to close the activity, but Mac was sensitive to the signals she gave him, and he supported her by moving back to his seat and giving her his full attention. Later, he didn't have to be asked to tidy up. He also took the opportunity to speak to Mrs Harris's key worker. He then wrote up his notes while it was all fresh in his mind. He was then ready to evaluate the activity.

Summary of Section 5.2

The following key areas have been covered in this section:

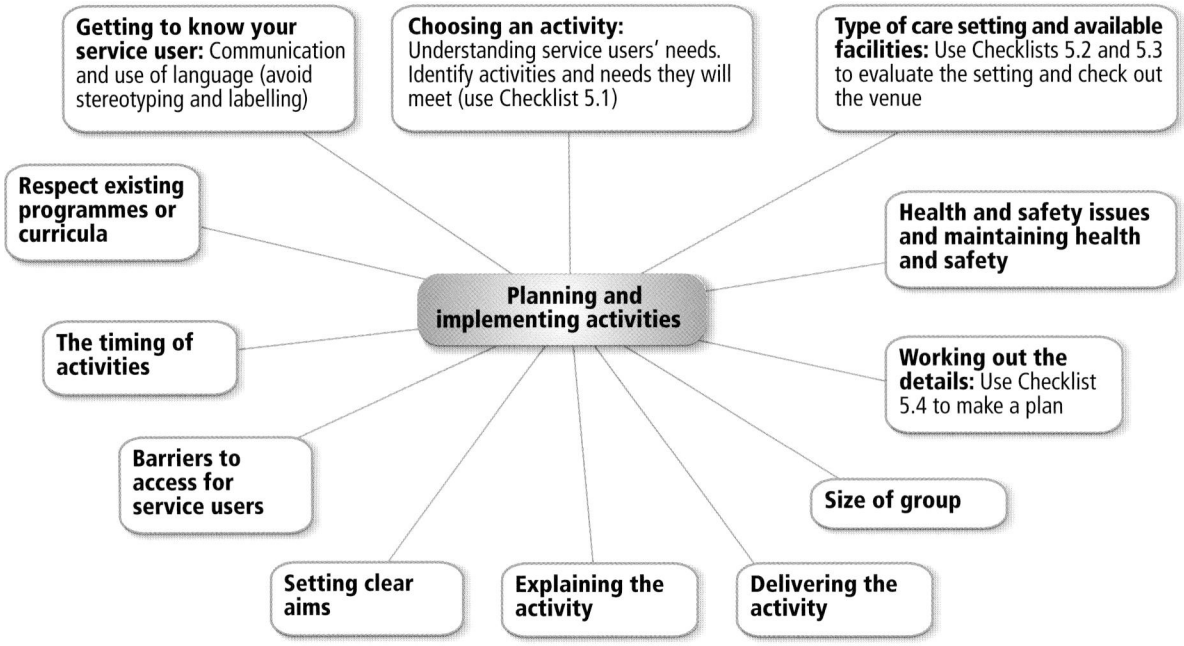

Consider this

Peter has a learning disability, and regularly attends a local centre provided by social services.

He loves music, and is desperate to learn to sing the latest song by his favourite artist.

Make a plan for this activity using Checklist 5.4 (in conjunction with the other three checklists, as appropriate).

Go further – can you analyse the issues using theory?
How would you be able to tell if you had observed key principles when working with Peter?

Go further – can you evaluate using a range of theory?
In what ways are people with learning disabilities stereotyped?

Consider this

Peter's music session is about to take place at the day centre. What health and safety issues would you have to consider before, during and after the session?

Go further – can you analyse the issues using theory?
Why is it essential to work with a supervisor? What are the benefits of taking advice and supervision from a professional or other member of staff?

Go further – can you evaluate using a range of theory?
How many different types of need would be met by Peter's music session?

5.3 Evaluation of activities

It is not enough simply to devise a plan and to deliver activities. The success or failure of any planned programme or activity must be assessed, to see whether or not the objectives were met. **Evaluation** is an essential part of work with service users, and forms part of a constant cycle of planning, implementation and review.

Key concept

Evaluation: To evaluate something is to assess it, in particular its worth, value or importance.

At the end of the memory session, Mac went home feeling pretty good about the way things had gone. The whole group seemed to have enjoyed themselves, Mrs Harris had been able to chat to Mr Brannigan; Mrs Harris's care worker seemed pleased, and there was a 'feel-good factor' about the whole session. However, Mac cannot leave it here. He has to do a thorough evaluation of the whole event, from start to finish. This means he has to review how he went about choosing and planning the activity, exactly what happened on the day and (most importantly) what benefits resulted from the activity, both to Mrs Harris and the other people involved.

When evaluating something, it's important to give a balanced view. After thinking it over and discussing it with other people, Mac may want to identify things that could have been done better, as well as pointing to things that went well. This process of critical thinking about something is also known as **reflection**. It's impossible to evaluate something fully without spending some time reflecting on it.

Key concept

Reflection: Reflection is the act of thinking about something critically and calmly.

Evaluation methods

It is a good idea to think about how you will evaluate quite early in the planning process. Some of the ways in which an activity may be evaluated are outlined in Figure 5.38. When Mac was helping to choose an activity for Mrs Harris, the care worker said that she would like to see her begin to socialise a little more and to enjoy herself. The memory session was planned with the aim of bringing both emotional and social benefits to Mrs Harris, with the added intellectual stimulation of recalling old memories. These aims were written into the plan. The care worker challenged Mac to say how he would know if the activity had met these aims. Mac realised that he would be able to observe how Mrs Harris responded to the activity, to see if she was enjoying herself. The care worker then pointed out that Mac could also ask Mrs Harris herself how she felt about the memory session.

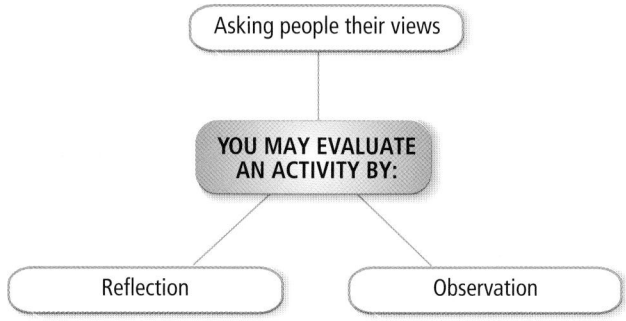

FIGURE 5.38 *How to evaluate an activity*

The care worker also said that she would give Mac her views on how the session went, together with her observations of any changes in Mrs Harris. They decided to make a note of these evaluation methods in the plan.

When to evaluate

Mac thus had identified a number of different ways of evaluating the benefits of the memory session to Mrs Harris. However, it is important to bear in mind that the benefits of an activity are not always felt immediately. Mrs Harris might enjoy the session, and then go on to feel even better in herself in the following days. Mac and the care worker decided that not only would they evaluate the impact of the session during and immediately after it had taken place, but also that they would do a follow-up review one week later. The care worker agreed to observe and talk to Mrs Harris during that week to see if there were any longer-lasting effects.

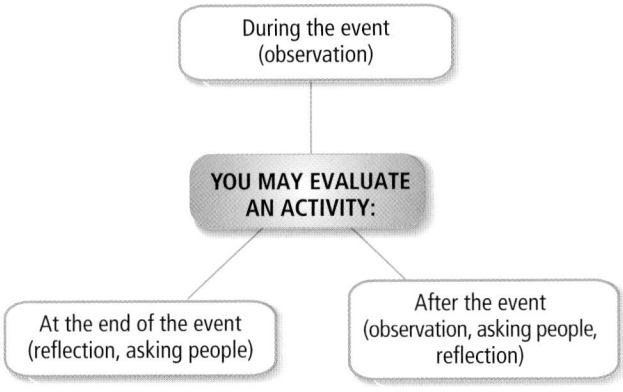

FIGURE 5.39 *When to evaluate an activity*

In fact, Mrs Harris had been quite deeply affected by Mac's session. She actually turned up at the day unit a couple of days later for morning coffee, and the care worker saw her sitting with Mr Brannigan and Mrs Singh, who was also at the memory session. Mrs Singh came to the UK some 30 years ago, and she was very interested to see how the town centre had changed from when Mrs Harris was young. She was also able to share her own memories of growing up in her own country.

The care worker had arranged for Mac to come back and talk to Mrs Harris himself. Mac spoke to her just before the next memory session. By this time she needed no encouragement to attend, and was really keen to take part.

Figure 5.39 sets out the various times at which you may evaluate an activity.

Who to involve

Mac spent about half an hour with Mrs Harris. He had prepared a list of questions to ask her, but was also careful to let her express herself in her own words. The care worker sat with them while they talked. Figure 5.40 illustrates effective methods that may be used when evaluating an activity by asking people for their opinions.

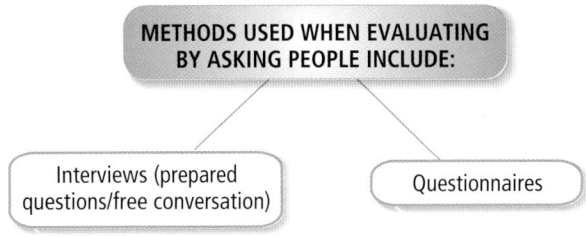

FIGURE 5.40 *Evaluation: asking people*

The therapist was also interested in Mac's work. She pointed out that Mrs Harris was not the only person to enjoy the picture session, so she prepared a feedback sheet (a very simple questionnaire) for the other group members. She wanted to evaluate the impact of the memory session on the group as a whole, in addition to what they thought of Mac's photo session, and also to find out what other topics the group would like to explore. She had also prepared a longer questionnaire for the day unit staff. The memory sessions had been taking place for six months, and the therapist wanted to find out if staff had observed any differences amonge service users as a result of having attended her sessions.

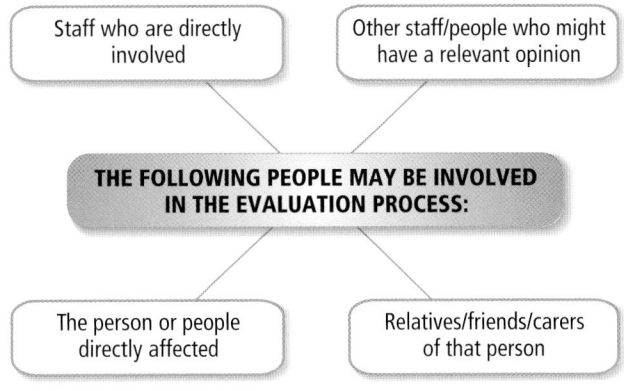

FIGURE 5.41 *Evaluation: who to involve*

Figure 5.41 lists those people you may choose to take part in your evaluation of an activity. Evaluation can thus be a very wide-ranging activity, giving everyone a chance to reflect on what has happened and its worth both to individual service users and to the care setting as a whole.

Evaluating the benefits to service users

It was noted above that Mac and the care worker had set out some very clear anticipated benefits to Mrs Harris as a result of attending the memory session. These had been set out in the plan. Mac used something similar to Checklist 5.1 to set out these planned benefits (see page 239).

SERVICE USER: Mrs Harris

ACTIVITY: Memory session: photographs of Town Centre to trigger discussion

NEEDS	ANTICIPATED BENEFITS
Intellectual	Stimulation of cognitive skills by recall of personal memories of town's history.
Emotional	Diverting thoughts from problems and anxieties, achieving relaxation and pleasure.
Social	Developing friendships. Sharing experiences, developing confidence.

FIGURE 5.42. *Example of a plan drawn up for a service user*

Because the desired benefits had been set out so clearly, Mac and the care worker had something to measure their success by. It was quite clear from observing Mrs Harris that the pictures triggered her interest during Mac's talk. She didn't speak up in the big group, but with Mac's help she had spoken to Mr Brannigan. She appeared relaxed at the end of the memory session.

She had surprised the care worker by attending the coffee morning quite unexpectedly, where she was seen to socialise with Mr Brannigan and Mrs Singh. When Mac interviewed her a week after the event, she told him that it had meant a lot to her, and that she planned to carry on going to the memory session on a regular basis. The care worker told Mac that she was very pleased at the outcome of this activity, as for the first time in two years Mrs Harris was showing signs of returning to a happier state of mind. There was still a long way to go, but staff at the day unit hoped to build on what Mac had started.

Later, Mac discussed it all with his tutor. They agreed that it would be a good idea for Mac to make another visit in two months, to see how Mrs Harris was getting on. Checking someone's progress over time is also known as **monitoring** them. Mrs Harris was happy to agree to this, and it was arranged that Mac would actually attend another memory session so that he could talk to Mrs Harris, the therapist and the care worker.

Evaluating the activity

There had been a positive outcome for Mrs Harris in terms of the hoped-for and planned-for benefits. However, it is also important to review the planning and delivery of any activity (including the cost of doing it) to determine whether it could have been done differently, or better, or both.

Mac and his tutor looked back at how the plan had been made for Mrs Harris, including the initial conversations with everyone concerned. Identifying the anticipated benefits had been a critical part of this stage of the process (see above, Figure 5.42). Mac realised he had spent quite some time in preparing his part of the memory session, not just in making up the transparencies but also in timing how long each bit of the session would last. After the mistake with the room booking (see page 242), he had made checklists (similar to 5.2, 5.3 and 5.4) to make sure he had considered everything that would be necessary. These checklists had stood him in good stead, and he felt that this had been an essential and valuable part of the planning process.

Looking back on the event itself, Mac felt that perhaps he had talked too quickly when he was presenting the slides, and that he should have paused more to let group members speak. The therapist agreed with this in her feedback to him, but said that it is quite normal to be nervous and to talk too much when speaking to a group for the first time. Mac had enjoyed it, however, and decided that he would like to do something similar on another occasion.

Evaluation of the event thus confirmed a good standard of planning (after a rocky start), some possible improvements in implementation and a potential development of the activity.

It remained for Mac to evaluate the costs of the activity, both in terms of resources and time. Since he was also doing A Level Photography, he was able to prepare the slides himself (and also to use them as part of his Photography coursework). If this hadn't been the case, he would have been able to borrow some material that the therapist already had in reserve. The weekly memory session was part of the day unit's ongoing programme, so there was no additional cost to the budget. The care worker had spent quite some time with Mac before, during and after the memory session. She did this as part of her usual shift, so this activity did involve an extra time-commitment on the part of the day unit, whose manager allowed her to spend time on Mac's project and away from her usual duties. However, when measured against the progress made by Mrs Harris, this was felt by the manager to be time well-spent.

Reflection on experience: making links

For Mac, the experience of completing Unit 5 had triggered an interest in mental health. He did some further reading on depression, and also on the impact of bereavement. When writing up his evaluation, he was able to make links from this reading to his analysis of how Mrs Harris had benefited from the memory session.

He also recognised that in his conversations with Mrs Harris, and with professionals, he had been applying several theories of communication that he had studied in Unit 2. Again, he was careful to make these connections in his final evaluation.

Building on the activity

Mac planned to do some more reminiscence work at the day unit, which would form part of his own personal development.

However, conversations with both the therapist and the care worker had given everyone ideas for how the reminiscence work could be developed. It was now planned to make and publish a book of recollections, combining Mac's photographs and the comments of the people attending the group. There was great excitement about this, and several more people at the unit (both staff and users) wanted to be involved.

The therapist had been asked to do a similar piece of work with people with learning disabilities, but it was felt that old photographs would not be suitable as the focus. Instead, it was decided to use present-day photographs, some taken by people with learning disabilities themselves. A book would be made combining these images with the views of these service users about their town. The therapist will have to redesign her sessions, and to use different techniques to make sure that all the people with learning disabilities would express themselves fully.

Mac added this information to his assessment evidence.

Summary of Section 5.3

The following key areas have been covered in this section:

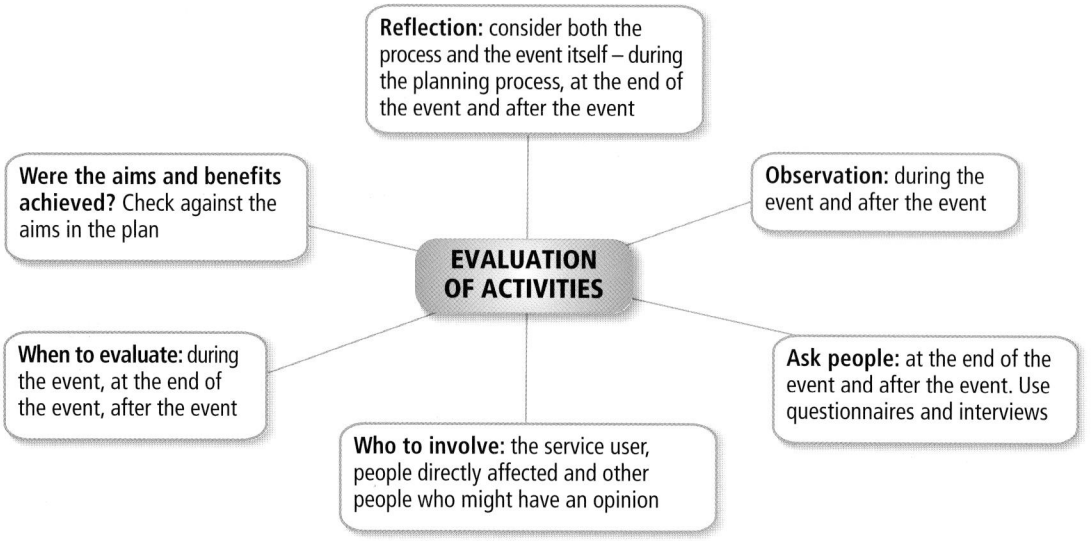

Consider this

For Unit 5, Amir has been working with Susan, who has a learning disability. He has helped her prepare for a small part in a play put on by a local theatre company. This company integrates people with learning disabilities into productions with non-learning-disabled young people.

1. Who should Amir talk to in order to evaluate the success of the activity?
2. When and how should he talk to these people?

Go further – can you analyse the issues using theory?
What do you think the aims of this activity might have been?

Go further – can you evaluate using a range of theory?
How could Amir help Susan to move forward and build on all that has been achieved with this activity?

UNIT 5 ASSESSMENT

How you will be assessed

Evidence

In order to achieve this unit you must produce a report of an activity carried out in your chosen context with people who are ill, older people, people with special needs or children.

If you are working with an individual service user, then you should work individually. If undertaking an activity with a group you should work with a partner or a group.

Make sure you make clear notes at all stages of your work for this unit. If you make notes about real people ensure that you anonymise the material, and also store the information securely.

Key skills Your report may contribute towards your Key Skills Communication and IT evidence.

Your report needs to include evidence for each of the following:

a **Types of activity considered and reasons for your final choice**

You should demonstrate clearly which areas of need (physical, intellectual, emotional and social) are being addressed by the chosen activity. Remember that one activity often satisfies a number of different areas of need at the same time.

You will need to show that you have an understanding of types of activities included in your report.

b **The benefits for the health and well-being of the service user**

You will need to show that you can apply your knowledge of benefits for the service user with reference to the benefits of the activity.

c **Planning for and implementing the activity**

You will need to show that you have skills in planning, implementing and analysing the activity.

A good plan will have clear aims (in this case in the form of clearly stated anticipated benefits to the service user) and will show how you intend to go about achieving these aims.

d **Evaluating the activity**

You will need to show that you have evaluated the activity and indicated the benefits for the service user.

Assessment guidance: Area (A)

Types of activity considered and reasons for your final choice

You may want to use the notes made during interviews and conversations with everyone concerned, including the service user, the main carer or carers of the service user, care workers and other professionals. Use Checklist 5.1 when considering options for activities. If you are role-playing the unit activity, you can still indicate who you would have consulted when choosing an activity.

If you are able to relate the choice of activity to factors such as the service user's health, mental health or stage of development, this will get a higher mark as it shows a deeper level of analysis of the person's need.

It would be good to link your choice to medical information (for people who are ill), Person Centred Plans (for people with learning disabilities) or to the relevant professional guidance for working with children in the early years.

Assessment guidance: Area (B)

The benefits for the health and well-being of the service user

Once again, Checklist 5.1 should allow you to work through the potential benefits to the service user. Benefits can also be anticipated by reference to other documents such as Person Centred Plans and professional guidance for working with children.

If you are role-playing the activity, you can still show an awareness of the possible existence of such documents.

Assessment guidance: Area (C)

Planning for and implementing the activity

Checklists 5.2, 5.3 and 5.4 could be used when you are working through the planning stages for the activity. These checklists will provide evidence for you to draw on when compiling your final report.

Reference to the health and safety regulations and policy of the care setting will be essential.

It will be important to show that you have maintained good communication with everyone involved, not least the service user.

Assessment guidance: Area (D)

Evaluating the activity

You will need to be prepared to receive feedback, both positive and negative, to take this on board and to learn from it. You will also need to be able to reflect on and analyse your own actions, and to be willing to accept when there is room for improvement.

Checklist 5.1 could be used to set out the perceived benefits to the service user, assuming that you had clearly stated aims in the plan.

Your mark

In order to achieve a 'pass' level, your report will need to give a clear description of the service user's situation and his or her perceived needs. You will need to explain how key principles have been applied when planning and delivering the activity: this should include factors such as valuing diversity, avoiding labelling and stereotyping, recognising service-user choice, working with the service user (rather than doing something 'to' him or her), valuing the service user as a person, promoting dignity and enhancing self-esteem.

Your plan for the activity should have clear aims and be well laid-out. In your report you should describe the activity and give an account of reactions to it (including those of the service user, care workers and other relevant people). Finally, the report should include your evaluation of the effectiveness of the activity.

A 'good report' will contain all of the elements needed to achieve a pass level. In addition, you should also provide evidence that a wider range of activities was considered, with reasons for the final choice. You should show good use of specialist vocabulary, such as diversity, cognitive development, reflection on experience and so on. There should also be an analysis of some of the issues, with reference to additional information and theory: for example, the Foundation Stage of the National Curriculum, information about a specific condition such as Asperger's Syndrome, and so on. Your report should illustrate conclusions that have resulted from reflections on experience.

An 'excellent report' will contain all of the foregoing. It will also include detailed use of specialist vocabulary that makes links between some of the key concepts. It will provide full explanations for decisions made and demonstrate an imaginative approach to research and planning. Your discussion about the evaluation of the outcome of an activity will use a range of theories: for example, theories about child development; theories of communication (Unit 2); ideas about the implications of the activity; and what it means for the service user in terms of future development.

Unit test

1. What are the four broad areas of human need?
2. When working with a service user to satisfy needs, what principles should you keep in mind?
3. What kinds of need might be met by the following types of activity:
   - a group visit to a theatre (by coach)
   - a line-dancing session
   - singing songs from the 1940s?

4 What is the difference between labelling and stereotyping?

5 Why is it important not to label or stereotype someone?

6 How can you ensure that an activity will enhance a person's self-esteem?

7 How can you ensure that confidentiality is maintained?

8 List five things that you can do to ensure the health and safety of people attending a group session in a room in a day or residential unit.

9 Why is it important to set clear aims by stating the anticipated benefits of any planned activity?

10 List three ways of evaluating the effectiveness of an activity for a service user.

References

DfEE (1999) *National Curriculum for England and Wales* (London, DfEE)

DfEE/QCA (2000) *Curriculum Guidance for the Foundation Stage* (London, QCA)

DfES/Sure Start (2002) *Birth to Three Matters: A Framework to Support Children in Their Earliest years* (Pack of materials) (London, DfES)

DoH (1999) *Caring About Carers: A National Strategy for Carers* (London, Department of Health)

DoH (2000) *Framework for the Assessment of Children in Need and Their Families* (London, Department of Health)

Haddon, M. (2004) *The Curious Incident of the Dog in the Night-Time* (London, Vintage)

Kitwood, T. (1997) *Dementia Reconsidered: The Person Comes First* (Maidenhead, the Open University Press)

Lewisham, London Borough of (2002) *A Place to Learn: Developing a Stimulating Learning Environment* (London, Lewisham Early Years Advice and Resource Network)

Plain Facts (Bristol, Norah Fry Research Centre)

Riley, J. (ed.) (2003) *Learning in the Early Years. A Guide for Teachers of Children 3–7* (London, Paul Chapman Publishing)

Useful websites

Please see www.heinemann.co.uk/hotlinks (express code 370XP) for links to the following websites which may provide a source of updated information:

Carers' website: lots of information about research.

Home page for Department of Education and Skills

Main website for Department of Health website

Needs of carers

Norah Fry Research Centre

OMNI: Searchable catalogue of Internet resources in health and medicine.

People first: for what people with learning disabilities are saying

Qualification and Curriculum Authority website

SCOPE: Organisation for people with cerebral palsy

Sure Start programme: brings together early years education, childcare, health and family support

Valuing people: for lots of information about work for and with people with learning disabilities

UNIT 6 Public health

This unit contains the following sections:

6.1 Public health: origins, aims and data

6.2 Current issues in public health

6.3 Promoting and protecting public health in the UK

Introduction

Public health is concerned with protecting and improving the health and welfare of whole populations, rather than with individual health. Addressing the health issues of populations as a whole involves looking at a wide range of different factors that can affect health and well-being, including environmental pollution, poverty and inequality, as well as diseases and infections. Public health therefore operates within a broad, **holistic** definition of health that includes social welfare.

How you will be assessed

This unit is internally assessed. You must produce a written report.

6.1 Public health: origins, aims and data

Key concept

Health: The World Health Organisation (WHO) has defined health as:

'the state of complete physical, mental and social well-being and not merely the absence of disease or infirmity.'

In 1984, WHO considered the outcomes of health to be:

'the extent to which an individual or group is able, on the one hand, to realise aspirations and satisfy needs and on the other hand, to change or cope with the environment.'

These definitions are still relevant and encompass the broad scope of public health.

The main characteristics of public health

Aspects of public health and the relationship between them are illustrated in Figure 6.1.

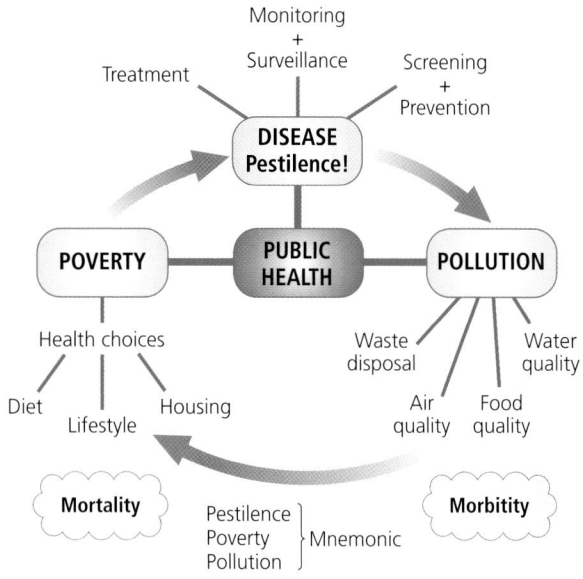

FIGURE 6.1 *Why public health is everybody's business*

Key concept

Morbidity: Morbidity refers to having ill health. It includes disability and chronic ill health, as well as episodes of illness. Like mortality rates, it is usually shown statistically, as the number of cases that occur each year per thousand of the population.

Key concept

Mortality: Mortality refers to death. The mortality rate is the number of deaths from a given cause in a year.

People in Britain today are generally healthier than ever before, but this has been a gradual process and is due to a combination of factors such as most people having access to clean water and effective waste disposal facilities, the availability of better food and improved nutrition, together with advances in science and medical technology. However, not everyone enjoys good health and there are still marked differences in health between different population groups and in different parts of the country. This is known as **health inequality** and the government has stated its commitment to reducing these differences across the population as a whole, and for families with children in particular.

Key concept

Public Health: The **Wanless Report** of 2004: *Securing Good Health for the Whole Population,* defines public health as:

'the science and art of preventing disease, prolonging life, and promoting health through the organised efforts and informed choices of society, public and private organisations, communities and individuals.'

The Wanless Report was commissioned by the government to identify cost-effective action that would improve the health of the whole population and reduce health inequalities.

Because human beings are individuals, there are natural biological and genetic differences that affect health, and cause health variations in populations. There are also social differences, both within and between societies and communities that can affect health, particularly mental health. For example, the different ways in which social and parental roles are allocated, or the way that groups and communities are structured and the extent to which these structures are effective in providing support for individuals and families.

Social justice

The concept of health inequalities refers to the extent of what are generally agreed to be unfair or unacceptable differences in health between different individuals and groups; this idea is underpinned by belief in **social justice**, i.e. that in a developed and civilised society all people should be treated equally and none discriminated against. Social justice in health care, for example, means: equal access to available care, equal treatment for equal cases and equal quality of care' (WHO, 1985). Social justice, in terms of health and well-being, means: 'ideally, everyone should have the same opportunity to attain the highest level of health and none should be unduly disadvantaged' (WHO, 1985). Many of the issues affecting health and well-being are beyond the control of individual citizens, and therefore public health issues require government action in many instances.

Government involvement in public health issues

The extent to which governments become involved in public health issues tends to be influenced by political beliefs concerning the degree to which governments have the right to interfere in the lives of individuals for the good of the population as a whole; one example of this would be whether it is right for governments to insist on compulsory immunisation.

There is also an economic argument for governments to be concerned with the health of their populations; people who are ill are not only unable to contribute to the economy through work, affecting productivity, but also cost money to treat. This is evident in the Wanless Report, which was concerned with the implications of predicted ill health to the future cost of the NHS. Health inequalities are linked to income inequalities in complex ways, and therefore political beliefs concerning how government should manage the economy to benefit all those who contribute to it are important.

For example, in the mid-19th century, the established political philosophy was one of individualism: that is, the belief in an individual's freedom to act primarily in their own interests. The government held the belief that it was not its responsibility to regulate the economy beyond the minimum to allow a free enterprise system to operate. This 'hands-off' philosophy also applied to individuals, so that health provision – for sickness and old age – were considered to be the responsibility of the individual. By the mid-20th century, health had been redefined as the responsibility of government, and the **Welfare State** was developed in recognition that some individuals were unable to make such provisions for themselves. These ideas became popular once more in the 1980s, when the government of the day restructured the Welfare State.

Think it over...

The government is considering a ban on smoking in public. Is it right that the government should do this, acting in the interests of everyone, or is the government unnecessarily restricting the individual's freedom of choice?

In your group, debate these issues. Carry out research into the issues and prepare arguments for and against a ban on smoking in public. Elect one member of your class to speak for a ban and another to speak against. At the end of the debate, take a poll to identify the majority view.

Origins of public health

Public health is part of the **Welfare State**, and shares the same origins in the conditions created by the Industrial Revolution of the late 18th and 19th centuries. Prior to this, in pre-industrial England, most people lived in the countryside, usually on farms or smallholdings in villages and towns as part of the traditional manorial system of organising agricultural labour. In the 1700s the population was small, and had grown only slowly over the preceding centuries as a result of periodic epidemics of bubonic plague, and famine caused by poor harvests.

By the early part of the 18th century, the Industrial Revolution began to take hold and manufacturing industry began to emerge. At the same time, the population began to increase rapidly, partly due to new innovations and advances in agricultural methods, such as the seed drill and crop rotation, which increased food production; the need for agricultural labourers was alsso reduced. People began to move away from the countryside to the towns in search of work.

The population continued to increase into the 19th century, doubling between 1801 and 1851, and in 1890 the birth rate exceeded the death rate in London for the first time. The first census in 1801 and subsequent census of 1811 revealed the population had increased from 9,168,000 to 10,488,000 in the 10 years between. London had the fastest increase, having over one million inhabitants by 1811 compared to Manchester's 137,000, and Glasgow and Edinburgh which both had over 100,000 inhabitants. By 1901 the total population stood at approximately 30 million.

However, the huge growth in population and rapid urbanisation generated problems, as the towns and cities were ill equipped to cope with the large numbers of people they now contained.

Conditions in towns

Urbanisation placed great strain on the physical environment. There was not enough accommodation to meet the needs of the growing number of workers and their families, so many houses were overcrowded, often with more than one family sharing premises and whole families occupying one bedroom. For example, the population of Glasgow grew by 37 per cent between 1831 and 1841, while the housing stock increased only by 18.5 per cent. The situation was even worse in parts of London: Blackfriars grew by 40 per cent, but there was no additional housing built. There was no public transport, so housing for the factory workers was usually located close to the factories – which were often built by the factory owners themselves, who were then able to charge rent and deduct it from the wages of the factory workers. The type of housing for industrial workers varied in different parts of the country; for example, terraced back-to-back houses were typical in the North West, whereas Glasgow inhabitants were housed in tall tenements. Although the standards of building and materials used were better than might be expected – many of the buildings are still standing – there were no building regulations in place and the majority lacked basic amenities such as natural light, air, running water and sanitation. In some places only one toilet existed for every three houses; in London in 1857, 250 tons of faeces were deposited into the River Thames every day. In Edinburgh in 1847 water consumption was limited to 1 gallon (8 pints or about 4 litres) per person per day.

At that time there were no formal administrative organisations to take responsibility for the condition of towns, and most communities lacked basic facilities such as drainage, sewerage and a constant water supply. It was common to use any readily available water supplies such as natural springs and wells, with waste being conveniently disposed of in the local river, which then became an open sewer as a result.

*** DID YOU KNOW?**

In the long, hot summer of 1858, the smell from the Thames was so bad that it overwhelmed all of those nearby, including the occupants of Parliament, which had to be adjourned. This event became known as ' The Great Stink of London'.

FIGURE 6.2 *'The Great Stink of London'*

Infectious diseases were common

As a result of these conditions infectious diseases were common. There were regular epidemics of cholera – notably in 1831, 1848 and 1866, together with typhus, a disease associated with cramped, insanitary conditions, and tuberculosis (TB), which may have caused up to a third of all deaths. The causes of these diseases were unknown at the time, as medical science was in the very early stages of development. The mortality rate (the number of annual deaths per 1000 of the population) was very high and life expectancy was short. Prior to 1831, the average mortality rate was estimated at 19 per 1000; by 1838 it was 22.4 per 1000, rising to over 25 per 1000 in 1849 as a result of the cholera epidemic of 1848. There was also a discrepancy between the urban and rural mortality rates; for example, in 1830 the death rate was 18.2 per 1000 in rural areas but 26.2 per 1000 in urban areas. In some cities, the mortality rate was over 30 per 1000. The present-day mortality rate is around 10.2 per 1000. The mortality rate was much higher in the areas of towns occupied by poor people, mainly as a result of the overcrowding and lack of facilities, but also because they did not have the financial resources to guard against unemployment. Sickness and ill health occurred more frequently when people were malnourished due to lack of food: no work meant no money, and no money meant no food. Elderly people, women and children, and men disabled as a result of industrial accidents, suffered most.

The higher social classes of people became increasingly concerned, since infectious diseases were no respecters of class boundaries, and this was highlighted by the death of Prince Albert as a result of typhoid in 1861. There were also concerns that servants, especially those who did not 'live in', would bring infections from their homes. 'England paid for the economic benefits of increased production with the social costs of rapid urbanisation' (Fraser, 1986). The conditions created by the Industrial Revolution highlighted the link between economic progress and public health.

Consider this

Using local and national sources of information, find out what industries were operating in your local area in the 1800s.

Give a presentation to your group about a typical day's work for a working person (man, woman or child) in one industry. Your presentation should include:

* hours of work
* holiday entitlement
* levels of pay, if possible, compared to the national average
* conditions at work.

Health reforms

During the late 18th century and throughout the 19th there were several significant discoveries and developments that increased understanding of health and disease. These developments influenced government action, culminating – in the 20th century – in what we now describe as the Welfare State.

From the later part of the 18th century, doctors began to notice the impact of the environment on health and mortality, and some began to carry out statistical surveys of the incidence of disease in their local populations, known today as **epidemiology**. For example, John Haygarth of Chester began in 1764, to carry out statistical surveys of the town's population and the incidence of disease. Others, such as Charles

Turner Thackeray of Leeds, looked at the impact of different occupations on illness and life expectancy. By 1830, information had been collected on the impact of cholera in Leeds by Robert Baker, who also provided maps charting the spread of the disease, and the incidence of typhus in Glasgow, which was analysed by Richard Miller, James Kay's survey of Manchester, 'The Moral and Physical Condition of the Working Classes', was published in 1832.

John Snow

Little was known about the origin of diseases, and although it was recognised that some diseases such as smallpox, measles and syphilis were infectious, those that caused epidemics, such as typhoid and cholera, were thought to be due to miasma – air that was polluted by the terrible smells from decaying matter. This also seemed to explain why the poor, who lived in overcrowded areas without water, sanitation or drainage, suffered more from these diseases than the better off. However, others were beginning to believe in germ theory – that infection was caused by some sort of living organism. This was finally recognised thanks to the work of the anaesthetist John Snow, who in 1854 mapped an epidemic of cholera in London and traced it to a water pump in Broad Street that had been used by all the people who died – while a brewery, also on Broad Street, was unaffected because it had a separate water supply. John Snow is credited with being the pioneer of epidemiology, due to his painstaking detective work, which identified cholera as a water-borne disease.

Edward Jenner and Louis Pasteur

Another milestone that contributed to disease prevention was that of immunisation. The first experiments were carried out as early as 1796 by Edward Jenner, who inoculated a young boy against smallpox by using the milder form of cowpox bacteria. However, it was not until the French chemist, Louis Pasteur, teamed up with Jenner in 1822 that the process of vaccination was developed. Pasteur had proved that there were bacteria in the air, which caused liquids to ferment and turn sour. He developed a process known as pasteurisation, in which liquids are boiled to kill bacteria and then allowed to cool before use. This process is still used today, and most dairy products are pasteurised.

The eradication and the control of infectious diseases, together with the invention of antibiotics, such as penicillin, in 1928 led to the use of medical science.

Key issue

The understanding of **germ theory** paved the way for the introduction and development of antibiotics and advances in surgery.

Environmental reforms

Edwin Chadwick

Edwin Chadwick was the secretary and administrator of the Poor Law Commission. The **Poor Law** was the mechanism by which vulnerable and needy people were supported financially through taxing the better off; this was commonly known as Poor Law relief, and people who received assistance from the Poor Law Commission were said to be 'relieved' of their suffering. Chadwick understood that poverty and illness were often caused as a result of illness from infectious diseases linked to the environment. He was concerned about the **economic costs** of administering the Poor Law, which had increased enormously as a result of epidemics, and he realised that preventing ill health and disease would be more cost-effective; spending on Poor Law relief could be reduced by environmental action to prevent disease. A systematic effort was made to generate statistical evidence to prove the need for environmental reforms. Under Chadwick's administration, the Poor Law Commission asked for an investigation into the connection between the environment and disease in some areas of London. This was undertaken by three doctors, James Kay, James Arnott and Southwood Smith. The study proved conclusively the link between environment and disease, persuading the government of the economic arguments for environmental reforms ultimately resulting in legislation. Chadwick's conclusions included recommendations on the disposal of sewage: he advocated water-borne disposal via glazed pipes – a system that is still in use today.

The Metropolitan Board of Works was established in London in 1856, with Joseph Bazalgette as Chief Engineer with the responsibility for building the London sewers and treatment works, completed in 1866.

Despite these environmental reforms, however, the mortality rate remained static.

Key issue

The 'environmental reform' highlighted that preventive health measures, financed by government, had economic and cost benefits.

Social reforms

Attitudes to poverty were shaped by the assumption that illness, unemployment and old-age were predictable, and that individuals who had not made provision for these expected life events were 'morally deficient'. Although the first national **census** was carried out in 1801, the real extent of poverty was unknown; it was assumed that the charitable and friendly societies, which sprang up in the latter part of the 1800s, were able to provide help to most people, and for everyone else there was the Poor Law.

Charles Booth

Charles Booth was a wealthy merchant originally from Liverpool. He was concerned with the sensational reports of working-class life, and began to investigate this. He was a pioneer of social inquiry who invented the concept of the 'poverty line' and set out to try and identify the causes of poverty. Booth investigated all aspects of working-class life, including employment and places of work, leisure activities, religion and living conditions. His work, the *Life and Labour of the People in London*, was published in three parts between 1889 and 1903, coming to the conclusion that 30 per cent of London's population was living in poverty – which was much more than previously thought, and more than the charities and friendly societies could hope to cope with.

Seebhom Rowntree

Seebhom Rowntree was from a prominent Quaker family, who owned the Rowntree's Cocoa works in York. The family devoted considerable time to public work, and the legacy continues today in the form of the Rowntree Trust, which continues to investigate social issues and provide charity in various forms. Rowntree was inspired by Booth's survey and decided to study the town of York to see if there were any comparisons. He too found that **poverty** was almost 30 per cent, suggesting a third of urban populations in the whole country were living in poverty. Rowntree's work was significant for distinguishing between **primary poverty**, where earnings were insufficient to live on, and **secondary poverty**, where earnings were above subsistence but spent unwisely.

These concepts have similarities with the concepts of **absolute** and **relative poverty** explained in Unit 4.

Rowntree also identified the **cycle of poverty** – stages in the life of the working classes during which poverty was likely to occur, namely in childhood, in the early years of marriage and childrearing, and in old age.

These studies demonstrated that poverty was the consequence of economic and social factors that were beyond the control of the individual and paved the way for government intervention.

Boer War

The Boer War (1899–1902) provided another milestone in the development of public health, when it was discovered that up to one third of the recruits were unfit to serve because they were so unhealthy. Government became concerned about 'national inefficiency' and the defence of Empire. Following the war, services for children were introduced in the form of the School Health Service, and screening programmes were introduced.

William Beveridge

By the beginning of the 20th century, the basic legislative framework was in place to improve the health of the population, and government had accepted some responsibility for this. This idea was further developed by the Liberal government of 1906 to 1914, when William Beveridge was an adviser to the government on old-age pensions and National Insurance. During World War II, when Beveridge was asked to report on how Britain should be rebuilt, he recommended in his report of 1942 that the government should find ways of fighting the five 'Giant Evils' of 'Want, Disease, Ignorance, Squalor and Idleness'.

Key issue

Consider factors leading to the emergence of the Welfare state and the significant features of the Welfare state in relation to public health.

Following a change of government in 1945, the Welfare State was introduced with the aims of free medical treatment for all and the provision of social security, so that people would be protected 'from the cradle to the grave'.

DATE	MAIN POINTS	COMMENT
1764	John Haygarth carried out a study into the incidence of disease in Chester 1764 to 1774	This pioneering study demonstrates that people were becoming aware of disease patterns
1795	In Manchester a Board of Health was set up by local men	Industrialisation was beginning to make its effects felt
1831–2	Cholera epidemic: causing 13,000 deaths	First epidemic of the 19th century; Boards of Health set up by some towns
1834	The Poor Law Amendment Act	Very important, as it appointed Poor Law medical officers
1838	4th report of the Poor Law Commission	Included the reports of Arnott, Kay and Smith into disease in London slums
1842	Report on the Sanitary Condition of the Labouring Population of Great Britain	Edwin Chadwick's famous report, demonstrating the social and economic cost of slums and the need for national action
1846	Nuisance Removals Act	The first of several Acts that aimed to identify unfit housing and the conditions that cause them, identified as 'nuisances'
1848	2nd cholera epidemic: 21,000 deaths Public Health Act	Burial grounds full First national measure to be passed, although quite restricted in scope. It permitted the creation of Local Health Boards, where 10 per cent of ratepayers requested them or where the death rate was over 23 per 1000. In London, the General Board of Health was set up
1854	John Snow linked cholera to polluted drinking water from a well in Broad Street, London	This was the beginning of germ theory, identifying the links between dirt, bacteria and disease
1858	'The Great Stink'	Parliament had to be adjourned because of the overpowering smell of the River Thames (a virtual open sewer) permeating Westminster

Continued

DATE	MAIN POINTS	COMMENT
1861	Prince Albert dies from typhoid	Typhoid was another major killer during the 19th century
1864	Octavia Hill began her work to provide decent housing for working people	This was the beginning of social housing
1866	4th cholera epidemic: 6000 deaths Sanitary Act	Sanitary Inspectors were made compulsory in urban areas and local authorities were made to provide fresh water. Overcrowding was classified as a nuisance
1869	The Peabody Trust builds cheap, good-quality flats in London	These buildings are still used today
1871	The Local Government Board was set up	This body supervised local authorities taking responsibility for public health
1872	Public Health Act	It became compulsory to appoint Medical Officers of Health in urban areas
1875	Public Health Act	Made provision for Health Inspectors, Sanitary Inspectors and slum clearance. Local authorities were able to make building by-laws
1886	Charles Booth begins his work 'Life and Labour of the People in London'	Booth documented in great detail the way working people lived their lives, and the conditions they lived in. He produced maps of London street by street, showing areas of poverty and affluence. One of the first studies to identify the extent of poverty in London
1890	Housing of the Working Classes Act	This gave local authorities, the power to build housing for working people – council housing
1902	London County Council takes over the water supply for London	Water was previously supplied by eight water companies, only five of which had filtered water
1909	Housing and Town Planning Act	Empowered the Local Government Board to fulfill its obligations under the 1890 Act. It required them to conduct housing surveys and banned back-to-back housing
1919	Ministry of Health	The government finally takes responsibility for public health

FIGURE 6.3 *Milestones in public health, and Public Health Act*

The NHS and the Welfare State

The development of the National Health Service (NHS) and the Welfare State demonstrated that government had now taken full responsibility for the nation's health and welfare. Between 1945 and 1970 advances in medical science and public health care continued. For example:

* antibiotics were prescribed for a wide range of infections
* a programme of mass immunisation was undertaken against major diseases such as polio, diphtheria and tuberculosis
* improvements in antenatal, neonatal and midwifery care reduced infant and maternal mortality
* welfare foods were introduced, with free milk and vitamins provided for infants.

Widening of health inequalities

The nation's health improved and the overall mortality rates dropped considerably, although this was not universal across all sections of the population; for example, the mortality rate for male workers in manual, partly skilled and unskilled ocupations remained static or increased, whilst the mortality rate for individuals in professional and managerial occupations dropped significantly. This led to a 'widening of health inequalities' between different groups by the beginning of the 1970s, and there were also regional variations in mortality rates.

The reasons for these health inequalities were generally believed to lie in the differences in lifestyle and health behaviour between different occupational groups. For example, male manual workers have traditionally been at much greater risk of dying from respiratory diseases than professional workers; the fact that they smoke more was seen to be the explanation for this. Other aspects of health, such as diet or access to health services, demonstrated different patterns between occupational groups. It became apparent that despite 40 years of achievements by the NHS in improving the health of the nation, there was a need for further work. Public health initiatives, particularly in the area of health education and health promotion, began to be targeted at individual behaviour as a way of achieving health equality.

The Black Report

The government was concerned that Britain had failed to match the improvements in health observed in other countries. Consequently a major report was commissioned in 1977 to examine these health differences, chaired by Douglas Black, whose terms of reference were:

* to assemble available information about the differences in health status among the social classes and about factors that might contribute to these, including relevant data from other industrial countries
* to analyse this material in order to identify possible causal relationships, to examine the hypotheses that have been formulated and the testing of them, and to assess the implications for policy
* to suggest what further research should be initiated.

The broad conclusions of the Black Report indicated that the poorer health experience of groups in manual occupations was apparent throughout their lifespan, and that much of the problem lay outside the scope of the NHS in social and economic factors such as income levels, environment, education, housing, transport and lifestyle. The Black Report calculated that by lowering the mortality rates of the manual occupations to those of professional and managerial workers then 74,000 lives would be saved, including nearly 10,000 children and 32,000 men aged 15–64.

The Black Report made 30 recommendations, and was followed by a further report in 1987, called *The Health Divide: Inequalities in Health in the 1980s*, which aimed to measure progress since the Black Report, particularly in relation to the World Health Organisation's (WHO) targets outlined in *Health for All by the Year 2000*. This document was endorsed by all member countries of the European Union, and aimed to reduce the differences in health status between groups and countries by 25 per cent through improving the level of health of disadvantaged groups. Many of the recommendations found in the Black Report form the basis of current government targets in relation to health and welfare – for example, a reduction in child poverty.

The importance of statistical data

All of the historical studies and investigations relied on statistical data to provide evidence in support of their arguments, and were influential in shaping the way that data is collected and used in the present day.

Practitioners of public health collect data about the social, economic, biological, environmental and lifestyle factors of the population as a whole, and examine this to identify the health status of individuals and groups. This helps to shape and inform government policy on health in its widest context, of which the NHS is only one small aspect.

The census

National information is collected every 10 years through the population **census.** Every household is required, by law, to complete a form giving details of their household on a particular day in the year.

The General Household Survey

In addition, the National Statistics Office carries out the General Household Survey, which provides a detailed picture of life in Britain by collecting information from individual households, including:

* family information, for example the names and ages of all members of the household
* marriage and cohabitation
* occupational and income details
* migration
* ethnicity
* health, including GP consultations, smoking and drinking
* education
* housing details, for example number of rooms, type of housing tenure (owner-occupier, tenant and so on)
* access to 'consumer durables' such as car ownership, central heating, refrigerators, TVs, Internet access.

The General Household Survey is carried out annually by taking a sample of approximately 13,000 addresses, based on postcode. Information is collected voluntarily.

Collection of information from health authorities and primary care trusts

Information is also collected quarterly from health authorities and primary care trusts and includes:

* numbers of inpatients, including age and gender
* number of outpatients treated, including accident and emergency episodes
* GP consultations
* communicable diseases
* immunisation rates
* conditions treated
* number of 'finished consultant episodes', that is the number of people having been discharged from hospital or outpatient treatment
* number of deaths and cause of death.

Registrar of Births, Marriages and Deaths

Another major source of information is that provided by the local Registrar of Births, Marriages and Deaths. Details of individuals are collected at registration. For example, parents are required to register the birth of a new baby within 6 weeks of delivery; the form they complete gives details of marital status, age, address and occupation. Similarly, deaths have to be registered and the death certificate signed by the doctor treating the patient, giving the cause of death and occupation; this has to be confirmed by another doctor. This information is sent to the General Register Office, which is part of the Office for National Statistics. Discussions are under way on the feasibility of developing a population register, to act as an index to existing records and databases. This would provide support for the public sector to deliver services more effectively, based on authoritative data. The General Register Office has a website that you can access through www.heinemann.co.uk/hotlinks (express code 370XP).

Socio-economic groups

The method of grouping people according to their occupation has been in use since 1913, and in the beginning, occupational categories were used to allocate individuals to a particular social class, derived from information collected by the Registrar General. There were a number of problems with this methodology. For example, women were assigned a social class on the basis of their husband's occupation, and retired people shared the same grouping as the unemployed, irrespective of their previous occupation. More recently it is thought to be appropriate to classify individuals based on economic status, which is clearly determined by hard data, rather than perceptions of 'skill' or 'social class'. The classifications are known as **socio-economic groups** (SEGs) and have recently been updated and modified to take into account economic and occupational changes over time – for example, the fact that many more women are now employed. The most recent version, reproduced below, has 14 occupational categories, which can be divided into 9, 8, 5 or 3 SEGs. See Figure 6.5.

Most government research uses the 8/9 class system and this is most frequently quoted structure for analysing socio-economic status.

Use of statistical data

Following the 'Inquiry into Inequalities in Health' (DoH, 1999), routine data has been used to develop measures that will indicate the relative affluence or deprivation at community level, to enable more effective service planning and responsive interventions to deprivation. Data is collected at regional level, and the NHS is divided into 11 regions covered by the Strategic Health Authorities, including 5 in London.

This information is further broken down at local level, based on local authority boundaries. Local authority areas of further subdivided into **electoral wards**, based on postcodes and covering a small well-defined area, each of which has a local councillor. English districts (metropolitan and non-metropolitan), London boroughs and unitary authorities average around 23 electoral wards/divisions each. Population counts can vary significantly, even within a single local authority, for example where there is a combination of rural and urban geography, but the national average is about 5,500. Electoral wards/divisions in large urban areas tend to have a more concentrated and larger population.

Deprivation is recognised as one of the most powerful determinants of health; in statistical terms there is a strong correlation between deprivation and health status. This is assessed and measured using socio-economic indicators such as the **Jarman Score.** Brian Jarman pioneered the use of socio-economic indicators of health status which are now used routinely to identify areas of deprivation at electoral ward level and, significantly, to influence planning and target resources in response to deprivation.

FIGURE 6.4 *The regional health authorities of the UK*

OPERATIONAL CATEGORIES	ANALYTICAL CLASSES			
	NINE-CLASS VERSION	EIGHT-CLASS VERSION	FIVE-CLASS VERSION	THREE-CLASS VERSION
1. Employers in large establishments	1.1 Large employers and higher managerial occupations	1. Higher managerial and professional occupations	1. Managerial and professional occupations	1. Managerial and professional occupations
2. Higher managerial occupations				
3. Higher professional occupations	1.2 Higher professional occupations			
4. Lower professional and higher technical occupations	2. Lower managerial and professional occupations	2. Lower managerial and professional occupations		
5. Lower managerial occupations				
6. Higher supervisory occupations				
7. Intermediate occupations	3. Intermediate occupations	3. Intermediate occupations	2. Intermediate occupations	2. Intermediate occupations
8. Employers in small establishments	4. Small employers and own-account workers	4. Small employers and own-account workers	3. Small employers and own-account workers	
9. Own-account workers				
10. Lower supervisory occupations	5. Lower supervisory and technical occupations	5. Lower supervisory and technical occupations	4. Lower supervisory and technical occupations	3. Routine and manual occupations
11. Lower technical occupations				
12. Semi-routine occupations	6. Semi-routine occupations and technical occupations	5. Lower supervisory and technical occupations	5. Semi-routine and routine occupations	
13. Routine occupations	7. Routine occupations	7. Routine occupations		
14. Never worked and the long-term unemployed	8. Never worked and the long-term unemployed	8. Never worked and the long-term unemployed	Never worked and the long-term unemployed	Never worked and the long-term unemployed

FIGURE 6.5 *Socio-economic groups*

It is possible to collect quite detailed information about the health and circumstances of individual neighbourhoods using information from the census. Using the Jarman or similar scales to analyse the information can demonstrate pockets of deprivation in what otherwise might be a relatively affluent area.

The Jarman Score

The Jarman Score uses eight socio-economic indicators, which are weighted (given different scores according to importance) and added together to calculate an overall score for an area. The higher the score, the greater the level of deprivation.

The indicators are:

1. Lone pensioners as a percentage of all residents in households
2. Children under 5 as a percentage of all residents in households
3. Persons in single-parent households as a percentage of all residents in household
4. Persons in households headed by a person in SEG 11 (unskilled) as a percentage of all residents in households
5. Unemployed persons as a percentage of all economically active residents aged 16 years and over
6. Persons in households with more than one person per room as a percentage of all residents in households
7. Persons changing address as a percentage of all residents
8. Persons in non-white ethnic groups as a percentage of all residents

An example of how the Jarman Score is used to monitor deprivation is given in Figure 6.6.

Indirect and direct indicators of deprivation

A criticism of the Jarman Score concerns the fact that it gives ***indirect*** indicators of deprivation; that is, it identifies the victims of the condition of deprivation – for example, single parents or elderly people – rather than the actual state of deprivation. However, not all single parents or retired older people in an area will be deprived; for example, they may be in full-time, well-paid work, or have significant savings and capital. Peter Townsend, co-author of 'Inequalities in Health: The Black Report', (1988) developed ***direct*** indicators of deprivation, intended to measure deprivation itself, rather than the victims, in order to find out how many individuals in a minority group were deprived: 'even if many among these minorities are deprived, some are not, and the point is to find out how many are deprived rather than operate as if all are in that condition. It is the form which their deprivation takes and not their status which has to be measured'. (Townsend, 1988)

Townsend's indicators are shown in Figure 6.7.

The Townsend Score is considered the best indicator of material deprivation currently available. Each indicator (variable) is given equal weight. Material deprivation is often accompanied by social deprivation – that is, isolation and non-participation in mainstream society due to lack of access to resources, amenities, goods and services.

Consider this

1. Examine the details given in Figure 6.6 and copy and complete the additional columns by placing a tick to indicate whether each ward has improved or deteriorated between 1981 and 1991.
2. Which ward was the most deprived in 1981?
3. Which ward was the most deprived in 1991?
4. Which ward has improved the most between 1981 and 1991?
5. Which is the ward with the least deprivation?
6. Consider reasons for the changes in levels of deprivation in this London borough. You may wish to find out more about Brent from the council's website by accessing www.heinemann.co.uk/hotlinks (express code 370XP) for a link.

Ward in Brent and Harrow	1981	1991	**Change 1981 to 1991**	Improved	Deteriorated
Alperton	16.9	24.7	**-7.83**		
Barnhill	-4.5	6.7	**-11.18**		
Brondesbury Park	30.9	28.1	**2.8**		
Carlton	-4.5	48.6	**18.43**		
Chamberlayne	20.1	21.9	**-1.82**		
Cricklewood	19.8	29.7	**-9.9**		
Fryent	5.4	15.9	**-10.5**		
Gladstone	6.1	14.3	**-8.2**		
Harlesden	33.3	30.5	**2.8**		
Kensal Rise	38.1	22.0	**16.1**		
Kilburn	35.0	33.5	**1.5**		
Kingsbury	-2.2	11.8	**-14.0**		
Mapesbury	31.3	28.1	**3.2**		
Preston	2.1	15.6	**-13.5**		
Queens Park	22.9	20.3	**2.6**		
Queensbury	5.5	14.5	**8.4**		
Roundwood	54.4	47.5	**6.9**		
St Andrew's	56.2	41.2	**15.0**		
St Raphael's	49.8	47.0	**2.8**		
Stonebridge	54.7	39.4	**15.3**		
Wembley Central	24.0	32.0	**-8.0**		
Willesden Green	37.7	30.2	**-7.5**		
Brent & Harrow		28.1			
England & Wales	0	0			
Note: Rank 1 = least deprived Rank 31 = most deprived					

FIGURE 6.6 *Jarman Score for 1981 and 1991*

Source: Brent and Harrow Health Authority

TOWNSEND'S DIRECT INDICATORS		
1	Unemployment	Percentage of economically active residents aged 16–59/64 who are unemployed
2	Car ownership	Percentage of private households who do not possess a car
3	Home ownership	Percentage of private households not owner-occupied
4	Overcrowding	Percentage of private households with more than one person per room

FIGURE 6.7 *Townsend's indicators of deprivation*

Other deprivation indices

There are a number of other deprivation indices such as those outlined below.

Department of the Environment's Index of Local Conditions (1991) which identifies 13 variables: seven of which are census variables and six of which are non-census variables.

Breadline Britain Score: two surveys carried out by MORI (Marketing and Opinion Research International) for London Weekend Television and the Joseph Rowntree Foundation in 1983 and 1990 pioneered the use of the 'consensual' or 'perceived' deprivation approach to measuring poverty – that is, below the minimum acceptable to society. The minimum standard of living was determined by interviewing a quota sample (based on age, sex and working status) of adults and covered a range of possessions and activities that relate to standards of living. For example, a television, a night out once a fortnight and a warm waterproof coat. There were two categories:

* those items that all adults should be able to afford and which they should not have to do without
* items that were considered to be desirable but not necessary.

The ONS (Office of National Statistics) Area Classification of Local and Health Authorities of Great Britain (1991): the ONS Area Classification is not actually an index of deprivation but an indicator of *'socio-economic similarity and difference between areas'*. However, the term 'deprivation' is used as a description of the values for a group of five variables, which form part of the classification, and which demonstrate poor socio-economic circumstances. To see this index and find statistics about your local area and electoral wards see www.heinemann.co.uk/hotlinks (express code 370XP). The statistics provide the following details and compare them with the national average:

* average age of the population (age profile)
* marital status
* ethnic group
* religion
* self-reported health status
* disability and long-term illness
* employment status
* educational qualifications
* type of housing
* levels of crime.

Consider this

With reference to the information on page 270 carry out an Internet search to find data about your neighbourhood by entering your postcode.

Compare the data with the national average and use your findings to draw conclusions about the relative affluence and health status of your local population.

For example, it is likely that if there are many people without educational qualifications, they are likely to be in low-paid jobs or unemployed. Similarly, if there are many older and retired people in your neighbourhood, you may also find that the self-reported health status is below the national average.

Walk round your local area and, if possible, take some photographs to illustrate your findings.

Prepare a short presentation for your group in which you describe your neighbourhood, and present your findings and conclusions. You may wish to do this activity with another student who has researched information about a different area, highlighting similarities and differences.

Rural areas and deprivation

Rural areas may suffer different problems, so indices of deprivation focus on amenities such as bus services and village amenities. The West Midlands Regional Forum of Local Authorities has identified six key services for rural areas:

* village shop
* post office
* pub
* school
* village hall
* daily bus
* weekly bus.

A valuable amount of data on rural issues is often available at a parish council level from the county councils and unitary authorities.

The variables and indices used to identify deprivation bear a striking resemblance to the **cycle of poverty** identified by Rowntree in the 19th century in that the individuals and groups at risk of deprivation are similar – for example, elderly people and families on low wages with young children. Although there are far fewer families with more than three children in the present day, there are other groups such as single parents and students who are now at risk.

There are other classifications, mainly used to target advertising and sales. The information for these is usually gathered from market research, including supermarket spending patterns. Much of this information is sold between companies as a commodity.

Aims of public health policy and practice in the UK today

The aims of public health policy and practice in the contemporary UK are concerned with identifying health needs of individuals and communities and developing programs to reduce current and future risks to health. The indicators are routinely used by government agencies, including the health services and local authorities to plan services and target those areas of need. However the agencies tend to have a preference for different indicators. For example, the Jarman Underprivileged Area Score is used by the Department of Health for making additional payments to general practitioners, whereas the Townsend Material Deprivation Score is favoured by health authorities. The ONS Area Classification is used extensively for resource allocation and performance management purposes by the NHS Executive, but local authorities tend to use the Department of the Environment, Transport and the Regions' Index of Local Deprivation. The Breadline Britain Score has been used by the media to estimate the percentage of poor households in a particular area. An example of how the information is used to develop programmes is in the Health Action Zones scheme.

Health Action Zones (HAZs)

These were introduced in April 1998 by the Department of Health and aim to reduce health inequalities by improving services and securing better value from the total resources valuable. HAZs bring together all those contributing to the health of the local population to develop and implement a locally agreed strategy for improving the health of local people. They involve local authorities, community groups, the voluntary sector and local businesses. HAZ status provides a framework for the NHS, local authorities and other partners to work together to achieve progress in addressing the causes of ill health and reducing health inequalities.

Health Improvement Programmes include screening for early disease in order to provide more effective treatments and avoid complications and **morbidity**. Treating diseases in the early stages is also cost-effective, reducing the need for expensive hospital beds and minimising time off work, which is beneficial for individual families and for the economy.

Monitoring the health status of the community

The purpose of monitoring the health status of communities is to identify patterns of disease and morbidity in order to plan local services and to target communities at risk of particular health problems; for example, some ethnic minority communities are more at risk from diseases such as diabetes or thalassaemia. Because disease is linked to environmental and social conditions, local information is very important and information is collected on a geographical basis. This highlights differences within a particular area, and can help to identify the causes of ill health. Information is collected on issues such as hospital admissions, vaccination rates, road traffic accidents and all diseases. Information is also available from a range of services such as school health services or dental services. Much of the work in monitoring health at a regional level is carried out by the Public Health Observatories (PHOs), set up as a result of the Government White Paper – 'Saving Lives: Our Healthier Nation'. The main task of PHOs is to support local bodies by:

* monitoring health and disease trends and highlighting areas for action
* identifying gaps in health information
* advising on methods for health and health inequality impact assessments
* drawing together information from different sources in new ways to improve health
* carrying out projects to highlight particular health issues
* evaluating progress by local agencies in improving health and cutting inequality
* looking ahead to give early warning of future public health problems.

There are nine Regional Public Health Observatories and the Welsh Centre for Health:

1. North East
2. North West
3. Yorkshire & Humber
4. East Midlands
5. West Midlands
6. Eastern Region
7. South West Region
8. South East Region
9. London.

The PHOs use a broad range of indicators which cover environmental issues, known as the 'Determinants of Health', in addition to deprivation indices. They include:

* levels of crime
* education
* unemployment
* environment – air quality, energy use, environmental health (the work activities of Environmental Health Officers employed by local authorities), noise pollution
* planning and health, radiation, waste management, water quality
* housing
* income
* transport.

For more information see www.heinemann.co.uk/hotlinks (express code 370XP).

Identifying the health needs of the population

In order to identify the health needs of the population as a whole, information has to be collected from a number of sources at regional and national level, including local health monitoring. However, assessing population profiles using information obtained from the Census is vital for planning services at a national level. For example, an ageing population, with an will have implications for the provision of services that deal with degenerative conditions and chronic health conditions that are more commonly found in older people. Local information is compared to identify trends in diseases – for example, whether the rates of heart disease are increasing or decreasing as a result of intervention and health education and promotion campaigns. The PHO in each NHS region monitors health to identify particular health issues so that resources can be targeted more effectively.

Consider this

In pairs, think of an affluent area and a poor area near to you. Answer the following questions about the health and opportunities of the population in each area.

1. Are you more likely to die prematurely in the affluent area?
2. Where are you more or less likely to change your job?
3. Where are you more likely to suffer long-term ill health (morbidity)?

The Department of Health is in the process of compiling a tool to show differences in health between different parts of the country. The tool can be seen on the Internet through www.heinemann.co.uk/hotlinks (express code 370XP).

Developing programmes to reduce risk and screening for early disease

Health screening takes place even before birth, with antenatal check-ups, and continues after birth, with routine screening for hearing defects and metabolic disorders. Screening services are provided through primary health-care services in the form of well-baby clinics, well-woman clinics and well man clinics, usually located at GP surgeries or health centres. School health services provide screening for school-age children, and may offer routine medical examinations.

Screening services developed fully in the 1960s, and are subject to strict criteria: conditions should have important health implications, usually affecting individuals throughout their lives, and possibly causing a degree of disability, and treatment should be available for those conditions. It is not considered ethical or desirable to screen for conditions that cannot be treated and there are also resource implications involved in the cost of screening for diseases affecting only a small proportion of the population. A National Screening Committee applies a scientifically based approach to proposals for new screening programmes. Adult screening services are usually voluntar – for example, breast screening services and cervical cancer services; however, take-up is monitored and individuals are encouraged to take responsibility for their own health by attending for screening.

Other screening services are becoming available more widely, for example through pharmacies, which may offer checks for blood pressure or cholesterol levels and, in some cases, allergies. However, these services are not universal, and have to be paid for; there is no automatic referral for treatment and they are not part of the national programme. Health screening may be carried out in the workplace, and some organisations have arrangements with private health-care providers to offer a health check for their employees as part of the package of pay and benefits. This is aimed at reducing sickness and absence levels among employees.

Child health surveillance and screening programmes are particularly important for long-term national health. Hall and Elliman (2003) document the screening programme and prevention services available for pre-school children.

Controlling communicable disease

Infectious diseases such as meningitis or measles are notifiable diseases, which mean they have to be reported to the local health authority by general practitioners. This information is collated by the Health Protection Agency. The information is used to monitor the spread and pattern of a particular disease, and may lead to a health education campaign to inform people on how to protect themselves. Recent examples include the MMR campaign, which encourages people to have their children vaccinated against measles, mumps and rubella in order to prevent outbreaks of these diseases and the morbidity associated with complications, such as deafness from rubella. Some infectious diseases have been eradicated in the UK as a result of immunisation – for example, polio. Others, such as TB, however, have increased due to a number of factors, including immigration and increases in some social problems such as homelessness. The increase in TB is also linked to the AIDS/HIV epidemic, because people with HIV have reduced levels of immunity. It is common to contract TB through close contact and prolonged exposure, and individuals who have reduced immunity are much more likely to contract TB than the general population. If there is a high enough level of immunity to a particular disease within the population to prevent infection spreading, then this is called '**herd immunity**'. In order to attain herd immunity, a high percentage of the population needs to be immune. For example, in the case of measles, it is estimated that between 90 and 95 per cent of the population needs to be immune for herd immunity to be attained. GPs are given immunisation targets for their local population in order to help achieve herd immunity, and are paid accordingly.

Key concept

Measles killed approximately 2 million Mexicans in the 1600s. They were invaded by the Spanish and had no natural immunity to the disease.

This has happened several times throughout the course of history; for example, Native Americans also suffered huge losses as a result of infectious diseases brought by settlers.

Measles still kills a considerable number of children in developing countries every year.

Health promotion policies

Health promotion is the aspect of public health that is concerned with encouraging individuals to lead healthier lives. It underpins the government health targets and often involves raising awareness of risks associated with a particular lifestyle or habit – for example, smoking – and encouraging people to change their behaviour. Health promotion campaigns can be targeted at specific groups who may be at greater risk of a particular disease, such as diabetes, or may be a more general health campaign aimed at the whole population – for example, to eat more fruit or less salt. Health promotion is not the responsibility of one specific agency, but is chanelled through various publicly funded agencies in order to reach particular target groups. For example, the government's Healthy School Standard initiative involves teachers and health professionals incorporating health promotion messages within the curriculum such as within Personal, Social and Health Education or Citizenship lessons.

Planning and evaluating national provision

One of the primary aims of planning for health care is to try and ensure equal access to health provision for the whole population. Available information demonstrates that there are differences in the way different groups use the health services, and that services are not distributed evenly throughout the country. Access to GPs, for example, will depend on different factors such as the number of GPs in a particular area; more affluent areas tend to have more GPs than deprived areas. For example, Liverpool has only half the number of GPs per 100,000 population than the rest of England. There are also historic differences in the allocation of resources across regions, and the Resource Allocation Working Party (RWAP) was set up in 1976 to try to address this; however, it mainly addressed acute service resources and was not designed to tackle inequality of access by different groups.

The incidence and spread of disease

Depending on the type of infective agent – for example, virus, bacteria, or anaerobic organisms such as tetanus – diseases can be transmitted either through direct contact from person to person or through **droplet infection**. Droplet infection involves organisms that are suspended in body fluids such as mucus. Many respiratory diseases are spread in this way, including the common cold. Diseases such as tetanus require an open wound in order to infect a person. In most cases, simple precautions such as hand-washing, covering the nose and mouth when sneezing and using disposable tissues can prevent infection from spreading. Immunisation is important to protect against many diseases that were previously extremely serious and often fatal. It is important that immunisation status is maintained, and in many cases, a booster dose of vaccine will be required after a certain time, such as 10 years in the case of tetanus.

Public health practitioners are concerned with the way in which infections and diseases spread through whole populations – in other words, how they are transmitted. For example, some diseases can spread from animals to humans; this is called **zoonosis**, and it first occurred when man domesticated wild animals. Examples of diseases

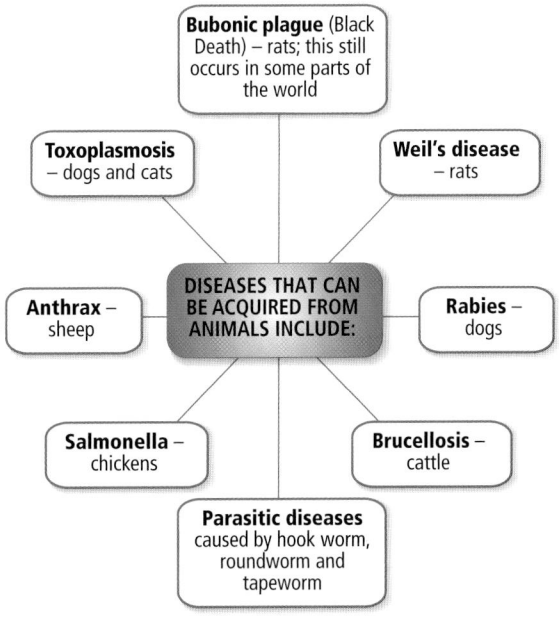

FIGURE 6.8 *Examples of diseases that can be acquired from animals*

that can be acquired from animals, even pets such as dogs and cats, are shown in Figure 6.8.

Many strains of influenza (flu) originated in birds. Public health has had a role in protecting the population from some of these diseases; for example, pasteurisation of milk prevented brucellosis, a disease of cattle, crossing into the population. Our laws relating to the importing of animals have prevented diseases such as rabies from becoming **endemic** in this country; however, it still exists in many other countries of the world.

Changing lifestyle patterns

One of the most significant changes to people's lifestyles is the frequency of air travel, especially to locations around the world that might have poorly developed public health systems and different hygiene standards. Infections and diseases to which the native population is immune are more likely to affect travellers. It is often necessary to have vaccinations and take other preventive measures, such as malaria tablets, in order to be protected against disease.

Effects of changes in work patterns

Changes in work patterns have affected many areas of life. In Britain, many women are in paid employment, and families in which both parents work are common. The cost of living in Britain is high relative to other countries. In particular, the cost of housing is high, partly because of the lack of subsidised housing and the culture of home ownership. In addition, Britain has a work culture in which long hours are considered normal, and those in full-time employment work the longest hours, on average, of any people in Europe. This leaves little time to carry out domestic responsibilities, particularly in food preparation and cooking. As a result, there has been an increase in the consumption of ready meals and fast food such as burgers and take-away meals, many of which are nutritionally unbalanced and contain a high proportion of fats and salt.

Unemployment

In households where there is unemployment or where both adults earn a low wage, access to good nutritional food is a problem because of cost as well as time. For example, the National Diet and Nutrition Survey of 2004 identified that only one in four people eat enough fruit and vegetables to protect against cancer and other serious diseases. The figure is even lower for those living in deprived areas.

'Sedentary occupations'

Changes in work patterns also include an increase in 'sedentary' occupations, i.e. those in which the worker is seated, often at a computer terminal, for much of the day. Physical activity has decreased as a result, and for many people the main leisure activity is watching TV. There has been a drive to encourage individuals to take responsibility for their own health in these areas, such as taking regular exercise. However, where leisure time is in short supply it is often difficult to manage the recommended 20 minutes of exercise three times a week, especially when domestic maintenance such as cleaning, shopping and clothes-washing must be fitted into a weekend.

Car ownership and use has increased markedly, partly because cars are seen as a symbol of affluence, but often because they are more convenient than unreliable public transport. The growth in out-of-town shopping areas, such as retail parks and supermarkets, has contributed to the increase in car use.

Reduction in children's physical activity

Fears for children's safety, whether real or perceived, mean that many children are driven to school instead of walking, and there has been an overall reduction in physical activities, such as playing sport at school. Many schools in inner-city areas do not have access to facilities such as playing fields or swimming pools. Access to soft drinks full of sugar (up to 6 teaspoonfuls per drink in some proprietary brands), crisps and chocolate full of fat is easy for most children, even at primary school, and the nutritional content and quality of school meals is not yet standardised across the country. Many children take packed lunches, which are often made up of high-fat and sugary foods that are easy to eat and which the child prefers.

All of these issues and cultural changes mean that much of the population is beginning to show signs of obesity, even in childhood, and this is leading to an increase in diseases such as diabetes in children. Heart attacks and strokes in the adult population, together with cancers, make up the primary causes of premature death in adults. Many of these diseases are preventable, or can be delayed into old age; however, current lifestyle patterns need to change significantly if this is to be achieved.

Mental health

Another significant and emerging problem concerns mental health. The incidence of mental illness, particularly depression, is increasing among all sections of the population but particularly among young people. People born since 1945 are 10 times more likely to suffer from depression, and it is now thought that most depression is due to non-biological causes triggered by changes in society, including:

* a breakdown in the extended family
* the dispersal of communities – family members now often live many miles from each other
* an increased focus on material wealth
* increased focus on individuals rather than communities or society as a whole
* a prevalence of global news, much of which contains negative content – for example, disasters, war and famine stories.

These changes leave individuals and families without effective support networks, while receiving a constant stream of negative news and information in a society where wealth is highly valued but unevenly distributed.

There are particular problems for young people and adolescents in a society in which what you have, or look like, means more than what you do, the sort of person you are, or what you achieve. This is one of the key factors in bullying. If young people feel personally inadequate or deprived, they can become depressed. Similarly, social rejection (by peers), family turmoil and failing exams can lead to depression in young people. Statistics provided by UNICEF (the United Nations Children's Fund) indicate that:

* suicide among teenagers and young adults is 3 times higher than in 1970
* 90 per cent of those who committed suicide had a diagnosable mental illness, of which depression was most common
* in 1996, suicide was the fourth biggest killer of children aged 10–14 and the third biggest killer of 15–24 year olds.

Attempts to identify government agenda for action

The government is increasingly concerned about the likely cost of these health problems to the economy and, in particular, to the NHS and other health resources, and commissioned the Wanless Report in 2004 to try and identify an agenda for action.

Predicting epidemics

Because there are endemic diseases in different countries, migration and immigration also contribute to the spread of disease, if not carefully monitored. The World Health Organisation monitors the spread of disease across different countries and alerts governments to potential threats, having a significant role in predicting and preventing **epidemics** and **pandemics**. For example, the WHO has predicted the likelihood of a flu pandemic originating in Asia: this is likely to be a form of avian flu (from birds) which has mutated in order to survive in humans.

Key concepts

Epidemic: A widespread outbreak of a disease within the population of a country or area.

Pandemic: A a global outbreak of a disease that affects many areas.

Preventive measures include monitoring the spread of the disease and modifying influenza vaccines to take account of changes (mutations) in the disease profile.

Government has a role to play in the preparation for treatment and containment by identifying suspected cases from the information collected from GPs and public health practitioners, providing information and advice to the public, and encouraging the uptake of influenza vaccination – especially in vulnerable people such as:

* individuals with depressed immune systems such as those undergoing chemotherapy
* people living in institutions
* health workers
* older people.

It is also the government's responsibility to ensure there is sufficient vaccine to support a preventive programme.

Global warming is likely to have an effect on public health as the climate changes, creating new opportunities for disease in areas previously unaffected. For example, as the temperature in Europe increases, disease-carrying creatures, especially insects, are able to spread from the African continent and the Middle East to European countries, where the population is vulnerable as there is no natural (herd) immunity. For example, the Department of Health is preparing contingency plans to protect the public's health from the threat posed by the West Nile Virus, a mosquito-borne disease that in 1999 spread across America, where it had previously not been seen. Although the Department has assessed the risk to the UK population as low, they have stated that management of the threat will require close cooperation between veterinary and health services at local, regional and national level.

Consider this

SARS (Severe Acute Respiratory Syndrome) first appeared in China in 1992 and spread rapidly around the world, causing death in about 10 per cent of infected people.

Carry out research into the SARS outbreak and identify:

1. Reasons why the epidemic spread rapidly
2. What steps were taken to contain the spread of the disease
3. Why there was no vaccine available
4. Why you think there were more infections and deaths in some countries than others.

Key issue

Consider how the use of data contributed to the emergence of theories of health, disease and disease prevention.

The determinants of health are illustrated in Figure 6.9.

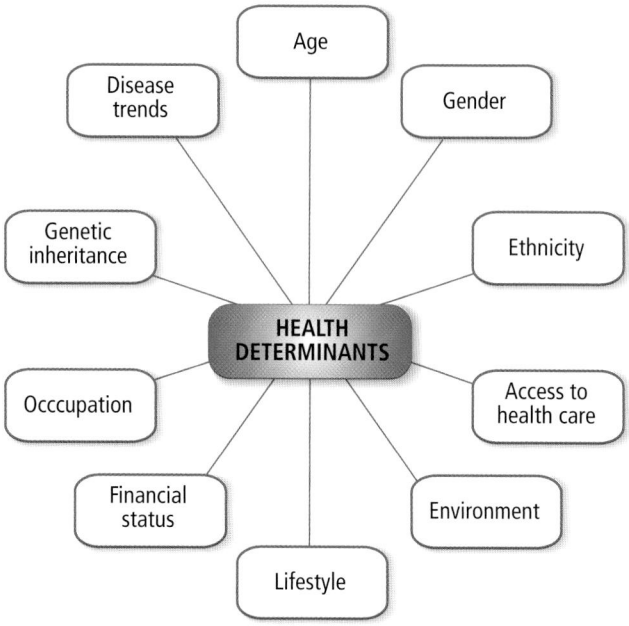

FIGURE 6.9 *The determinants of health*

Summary of Section 6.1

The following key areas have been covered in this section:

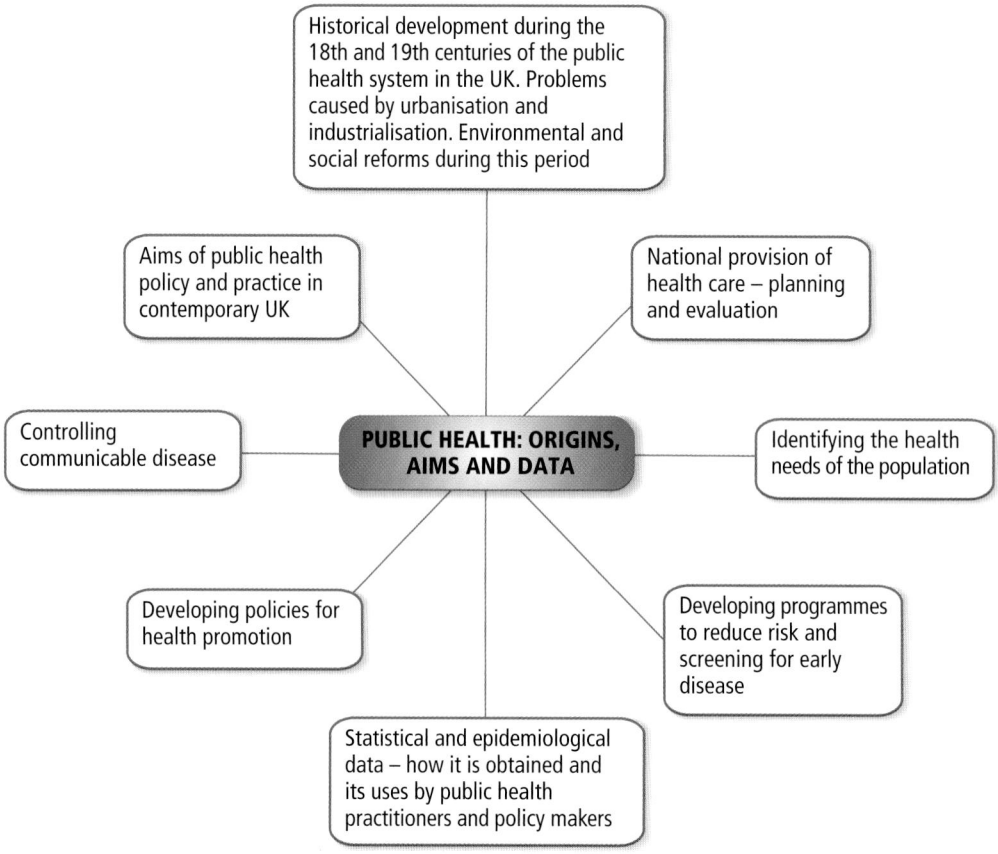

Consider this

The rates of childhood immunisations for measles, mumps and rubella (MMR) have been dropping nationally.

Investigate the levels and pattern of immunisation in your local area by gathering and analysing data, drawing conclusions and evaluating your findings. You will need to develop a questionnaire in order to ask a sample of local parents (this may be people you know) whether or not they intend to have their children immunised and their reasons for choosing whether or not to immunise.

Using public health concepts, can you identify:
Why it is important from a public health perspective to have children immunised.

Go further – can you analyse the issues using theory?
Analyse the data, including the results of your questionnaire, to identify patterns of immunisation take-up, and determine whether there are differences in behaviour and attitudes to immunisation among parents of different socio-economic status.

Go further – can you evaluate using a range of theory?
Evaluate the reasons parents give for non-immunisation and use this information to develop a health promotion campaign aimed at parents who do not currently intend to immunise their children.

Key issue

Consider how government policies can directly or indirectly influence public health.

6.2 Current issues in public health

Public health issues are important areas of concern to individuals working in the health-care professions. In 'Saving Lives: Our Healthier Nation' (DoH 1999), the government stated its intention to tackle poor health by:

* improving the health of everyone
* improving the health of the worst off in particular.

This document recognised that too many people are ill for much of their lives and too many die early from preventable illnesses.

Patterns of health and illness

In many areas, the health of the nation has improved over the last 40 years. Life expectancy has increased enormously: in 1901 the average life expectancy for men was 45 years and for women 49, whereas in 2002 it was 76 and 81 respectively. There has also been a significant drop in infant mortality, which is often used as a benchmark to gauge the relative health of a population in general. This has been brought about by improvements in maternity services, technological advances and better nutrition. There has been, on average, an annual decrease in infant mortality – for example, from 13.8 deaths per 1000 live births in 1978 to 5.6 in 2000. And the increase was especially significant in the case of neonatal mortality (death in the first week of life) as a result of better intensive neonatal care for very small babies who would otherwise have died.

However, there have been significant changes in the causes of death; some major causes of death have persisted and some have demonstrated increased rates. See Figure 6.10.

This demonstrates the huge success in overcoming infectious diseases following the wider use of antibiotics. Another significant contribution to the reduction in infant mortality has been the reduction in the number of cot

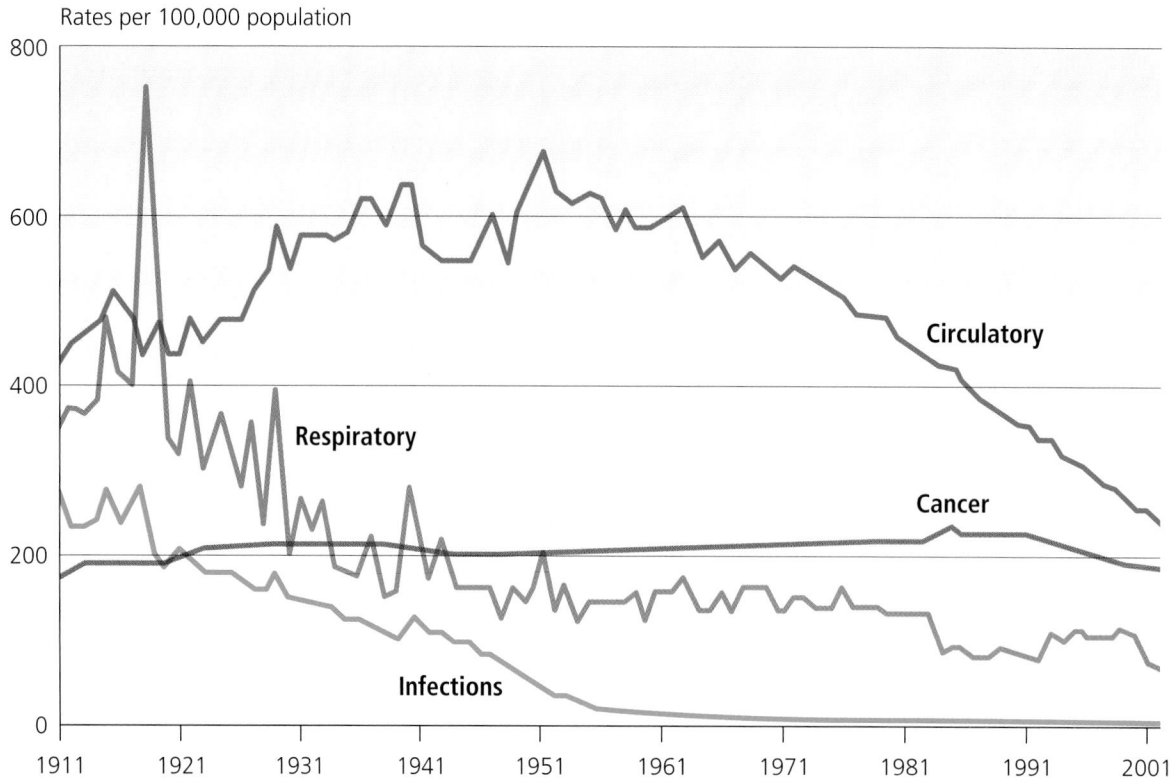

FIGURE 6.10 *The causes of death*

Source: National Statistics (2004)

deaths over the past few years. However, circulatory diseases, which include heart disease and stroke, have remained the leading cause of death overall in the last 90 years. Rates of cancer are increasing steadily and it is now the major cause of death in people over 65. There is great concern among health practitioners and government about the extent of obesity in the population, and childhood obesity in particular, which has increased significantly in recent years. Being overweight significantly increases the risks to health, particularly from diabetes, heart disease and stroke. It is estimated that by 2023, obesity will have contributed to an increase in Type 2 diabetes of 54 per cent, hypertension (high blood pressure) by 28 per cent, heart disease (heart attack and angina) by 30 per cent and stroke by 5 per cent.

New diseases and conditions have surfaced, or been discovered, some of which are responsible for life-limiting long-term illness. For example:

* HIV/AIDS; an estimated 53,000 people were HIV positive in 2003, up 7 per cent from 2002. The figure includes diagnosed and undiagnosed cases, and one quarter will be unaware of the condition
* CJD (Creutzfeldt-Jakob Disease)
* Hepatitis C, a blood-borne viral infection previously known as non A, non B hepatitis; it causes liver damage, in many cases years after initial infection.

Some diseases, previously almost eradicated, have resurfaced while others are increasing in prevalence, particularly in specific groups. For example:

* tuberculosis (TB)
* diabetes
* sexually transmitted infections such as chlamydia and gonorrhoea
* degenerative diseases such as Alzheimer's disease and Parkinson's disease
* autistic spectrum disorders.

It is important to recognise that it is not just current patterns of disease that are of concern to public health practitioners and the government, but that health behaviours are also of interest. Health behaviours are part of an individual's way of life, and risky health behaviour often has long term implications for health.

Inequalities in health experience

There are differences in the health experience at regional level, within local areas and between different groups of people.

Regional differences

In general people in the southern half of the country enjoy better overall health than those in the north, including Scotland. On average, 9.2 per cent of people in England and Wales said they suffered from poor health; however, certain parts of the country reported much poorer health than others. The regions reporting the worst health were:

* Durham, where 13.2 per cent said they had poor health
* Merseyside: 12.6 per cent
* Tyne and Wear: 12.3 per cent

Other regions that had more than 15 per cent of self-reported ill health were the North West, South Yorkshire and Derbyshire and coastal retirement areas. The areas with the best health were in the South East, excluding London, the Eastern region, the South East and Wiltshire. Many of the regions with poor health are industrial manufacturing areas that have declined as industries such as mining have decreased. This self-reported ill health is borne out by statistical evidence, for example:

* the life expectancy of men in Manchester is 8 years less than the national average
* the rate of death from circulatory disease is 25 per cent higher in the North West than in the South East.

There are also regional differences in **patterns of disease**. For example, a recent mapping exercise carried out on behalf of the Department of Health in order to plan services identified the Primary Care Trusts with the lowest and highest risk, using three indicators that would require specific service-targeted resources, namely:

* coronary heart disease
* diabetes
* winter hospital admissions.

The map identified areas with the lowest and highest risk and showed that some areas of the country were likely to have higher rates of diabetes than average, whereas other areas were likely to experience higher rates of coronary heart disease and winter admissions to hospital.

Local differences

These figures mask local differences; for example, in the district of Easington in County Durham, 17.3 per cent of the population reported poor health. Local area profiles obtained from neighbourhood statistics demonstrate that different electoral wards have different health profiles, with self-reported health varying according to the population profile of that ward. As noted in neighbourhood statistics, there are differences in the availability, use and access to services, those with fewer services or inacessible services tend to suffer from 'healthy poverty'.

Differences between groups

Ethnic minority groups have particular health problems; for example, high blood pressure and diabetes rates are higher in Asian and black communities, and genetic diseases such as thalassaemia and sickle-cell disorder affect black communities in particular. Other ethnic groups also have health problems; for example, children of parents from eastern European countries are more likely to be anaemic than the rest of the population.

In April 2001, Pakistani and Bangladeshi men and women reported the highest rates of both poor health and limiting long-term illness.

Older people

Older people tend to suffer worse health than the general population. As people get older their immune systems are less robust so they are at particular risk from respiratory infections. Similarly, they tend to be less active, which causes muscle tone to decrease, leaving them at risk of falls. It is very difficult for older people to maintain their independence if they become incapacitated as a consequence of fractures sustained during a fall.

Children

While childhood cancers are on the increase, the greatest threat to children's health is obesity. For example, in 1995, 18.6 per cent of boys and 23.5 per cent of girls aged 2–19 years were overweight; that is their **body mass index** was calculated at between 25 and 29. Of children who were obese – that is, they had a body mass index of more than

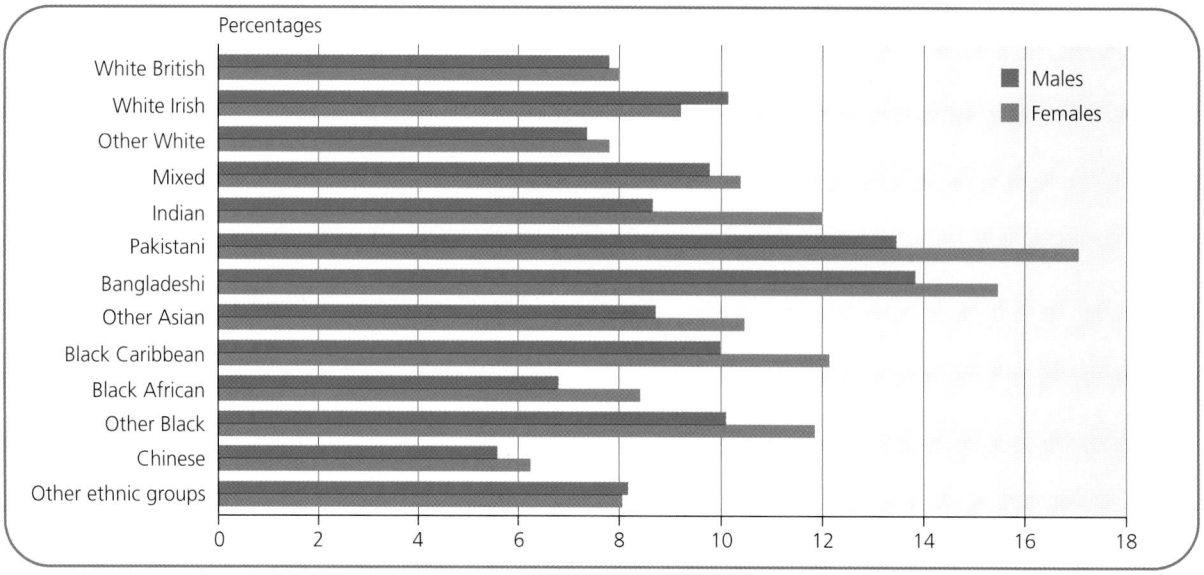

FIGURE 6.11 *Ethnicity and health*

Source: National Office of Statistics (2004)

30–3.7 were boys and 5.7 were girls. By 2000, the corresponding figures were 20.3 overweight boys and 26.6 overweight girls, 4.8 obese boys and 5.7 obese girls.

Socio-economic status

Differences in socio-economic status affect patterns of health and health experiences. Many studies show that people from lower income groups are generally less healthy than those who are more affluent, and this is true for all countries.

For example, in the early 1970s death rates of working men were twice as high for those in unskilled occupations compared to professional occupations. By the early 1990s they were almost three times higher. Some examples of health inequalities are shown in Figure 6.12.

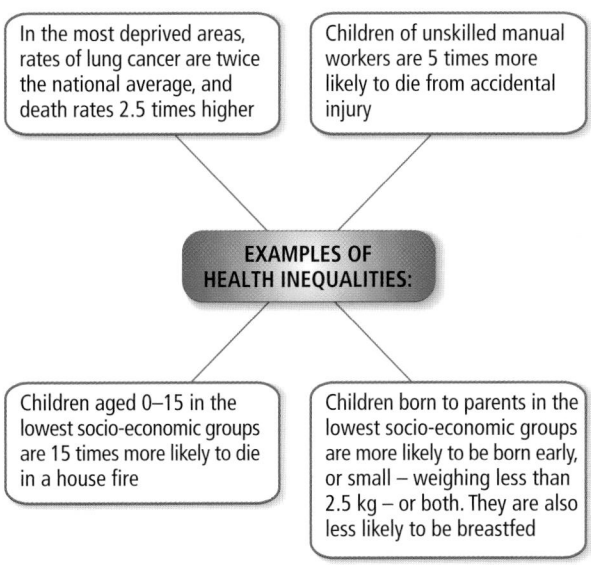

FIGURE 6.12 *Some examples of health inequalities derived from socio-economic status*

Use of services

There are differences in the patterns of use of health and preventive services; for example, Crombie (1984) identified that individuals from lower socio-economic groups did not access preventive service's for example immunisation and screening services, to the same extent as others, but had more consultations for acute episodes of illness and accidents. Lower socio-economic groups had more hospital admissions and higher attendance at accident and emergency departments than those from higher socio-economic groups, indicating that they were more ill when accessing services.

Think it over...

Can you think of the barriers different people might face when trying to access services? How would you improve access to services, taking a multi-agency approach? Can you think of the implications for the provision of health services in areas where there is:

* a high proportion of older people, for example retirement resorts
* a high proportion of adolescents and young couples
* a high proportion of people of African-Caribbean descent
* high levels of unemployment?

Emerging public health issues

The 2003 Health Survey, commissioned by the Department of Health, identified a number of factors that contribute to people's health and illness experience. These are **health behaviours** that increase the risk of disease and chronic ill health.

Smoking

Smoking has been identified as the single greatest cause of preventable illness and premature death in the UK, and one of the underlying determinants of health inequality. Of the population, 27 per cent of men and 24 per cent of women currently smoke, and this is higher among those under 45 years of age (30 per cent of men and just under 30 per cent of women). Levels of smoking vary according to socio-economic status, increasing as levels of income decrease: for example, 20 per cent of men in professional and managerial occupations, compared with 35 per cent of those in routine of semi-routine jobs. Smoking is associated with cardiovascular disease and respiratory infections, as well as lung cancer.

Alcohol consumption

The 2003 health survey found that 42 per cent of men and 26 per cent of women drink alcohol on at least three days a week, with 62 per cent of men and 49 per cent of women exceeding the recommended daily amount of 4 units for men and 3 for women on at least one of these days. Frequency of drinking varies by age, with 29 per cent of men aged 16–24 and 52 per cent of men aged 55–64 drinking three or more days a week. Younger people aged 16–24 are more likely to 'binge'-drink, defined as exceeding twice the recommended daily limits, with 36 per cent of men and 22 per cent of women binge-drinking. The average number of units drunk by young people was 11 for men and 6.1 for women (Health Survey, 2003). Binge-drinking is associated with age, socio-economic status and region, being more common among young people, those with routine or semi-routine jobs, and in the northern regions. Binge-drinking is particularly dangerous for pregnant women, since it can cause foetal alcohol syndrome, leading to permanent impairment of babies.

Diet

Only 26 per cent of women and 22 per cent of men consume the recommended daily amount of five or more portions of fruit and vegetables. Older people eat more than younger people – for example, where 3.6 portions are consumed among those aged 55 and over, only 2.4 portions are consumbed in young men aged 16–24 years. (Health Survey, 2003). Eating fruit and vegetables is thought to protect against certain types of cancer and is associated with income, with those in higher income groups consuming more.

In terms of overall diet, men's diet was higher in fat on average than women's, and over twice as high among young men aged 16–24 as any other age group. Men also used more salt than women, with 24 per cent adding salt to their food, compared to 15 per cent of women. Salt use in cooking was highest among the oldest age groups. Both the consumption of fat and salt increased as household income decreased. Fatty diets that are high in salt are associated with cardiovascular disease and high blood pressure.

Physical activity

Men participated in more physical activity than women (92 per cent), defined as any physical activity of moderate intensity for at least 30 continuous minutes. Physical activity was highest among those aged 16–24, and helps to protect against heart disease by strengthening the heart muscle.

Obesity and being overweight

The prevalence of obesity is increasing, and currently 65.4 per cent of men and 55.5 per cent of women are either overweight or obese. Obese people made up 22.2 per cent of men and 23 per cent of women, and in all age groups more men than women were overweight. Women were less likely to be obese in households of managerial, professional or intermediate workers than those in semi-routine or routine occupations. Obesity is strongly associated with an increased incidence of Type 2 diabetes, strokes and hypertension.

Physical and mental illness

In the same survey, 44 per cent of men and 46 per cent of women had one or more longstanding illnesses, 23 per cent of men and 26 per cent of women reported illness that limited their activities. Measures of psychological well-being indicated that 11 per cent of men and 15 per cent of women suffer from psychiatric ill health. Both physical and mental ill health were more prevalent as household income decreased, particularly for men. Mental illness and suicide rates are increasing, particularly among young people.

Teenage pregnancy

Teenage pregnancy rates are increasing or remaining high, particularly within disadvantaged communities. Babies born to teenage mothers are more likely to be stillborn, born prematurely and small, and are less likely to be breastfed; breastfeeding provides significant health advantages in many areas that are still being identified. They are at increased risk of dying in their first year of life, and are more likely to die of cot death than babies born to other mothers.

Sexually transmitted infections

Sexually transmitted infections (STIs) such as gonorrhoea, chlamydia, HIV/AIDS and syphilis are increasing, leading to higher levels of infertility.

Think it over...

Figures from the Health Survey (2003) suggest that many people lead unhealthy lifestyles, taking risks with their health. Can you identify some of the factors that might be causing this?

What health risks are linked to teenage pregnancy for mother and baby?

Why do you think sexually transmitted infections (STIs) are increasing?

Possible causes and explanations

The reasons for differences in health are complex and multi-factorial. Possible explanations include those of accessibility and use of services, lifestyle factors and material explanations for health inequalities.

Access to health services

The provision of health services will differ regionally and locally for historic reasons and as a result of the reorganisation of services. Access to health care depends on four main factors, which are shown in Figure 6.13.

Health services are not uniformly distributed across the country, partly because they have not always been allocated according to need. For example, the number of doctors needed by the NHS is predicted by the Department of Health in consultation with the General Medical Council and the academic institutions responsible for training them. Training places are accordingly made available at university medical schools, which usually have close links with local and regional Acute NHS Trusts (hospitals etc.) and Primary Care Trusts (GP services, health centres,

FACTORS THAT DETERMINE ACCESS TO HEALTH CARE:	
Availability of the required service	Some specialist services may only be provided regionally as they are often costly to deliver and fewer people need them Other services are not provided at times that make it easy for people to attend; for example, visiting the hospital or doctor may entail time off work Individuals may not know what services are available in their area, or may not be able to access information due to language difficulties
Physical locations	Some hospitals are located in the centre of towns and cities, but others, especially newly built and larger hospitals, may be located some distance away from the centre Primary care services, such as health centres and clinics, may not be aligned with local public transport services. They may be a long way from where people work
Accessibility	This depends on the availability of transport, either personal (car, etc.) or public, and on an individual's physical mobility (older people and those with disabilities can struggle to access suitable transport services) Buildings, especially older ones, may be difficult for some people to physically access – for example, where there are steps Access to sexual health services and free contraception can be difficult for young people due to the timing of clinics and embarrassing due to the perceived stigma attached to attending and worries about confidentiality
Cost	Some services, such as dentists, have a charging system for treatment (direct cost) If there is no suitable public transport available, individuals may have to pay for private taxis Mothers may have to pay for childcare in order to attend an appointment and people attending appointments in work time may not be paid or may be asked to take part of their annual leave entitlement (indirect cost)

FIGURE 6.13 *Factors that determine an individual's access to health care*

community care facilities etc.) to provide experience for medical students. Once a doctor has been trained, however, he or she is free to practice anywhere in the country, providing there are jobs available. In the case of GPs this means they can set up in practice anywhere because they are paid for general medical services depending on how many patients they treat. This may mean that a GP will set up a practice near to where they prefer to live, rather than on the basis of community need.

Lifestyle explanations

Lifestyle, as described in Unit 4, is a reflection of the choices that individuals make in how they live their lives. These can range from life-changing decisions such as getting married or starting a family, to choosing what to wear each day. Lifestyle is associated with patterns of spending: people spend according to the lifestyle they aspire to or can afford. However, lifestyle decisions depend on an individual's perception of the choices available, and take place in a social and cultural context, reflecting the values and cultural norms that a person has been socialised into (see Unit 4). We are constantly encouraged to live a 'healthy lifestyle' in terms of the food we eat, the leisure activities we indulge in and the choices we make. There is an assumption that individuals freely choose health-related behaviours – for example, smoking or eating certain types of food; however the Health Survey (2003) clearly indicates that health-related behaviour is strongly associated with socio-economic status and income. Individuals also have different perceptions of health risk, with younger people more likely to take risks, including health risks.

Values

While we live in a much more open and egalitarian society, it is still the case that a child will absorb the values of their family first and foremost – the parents are the child's first and most enduring educators. This is known as socialisation and is discussed in more detail in Unit 4. Values include the things families regard as important, such as getting a good education, learning a trade, marrying and having a family or following religious principles.

Patterns of behaviour are established in these early years and it is more difficult for a person to change patterns of behaviour that are embedded in the values they were socialised into; they may feel that they are going against their parent's wishes or feel that their parents do not understand them. Differences in values between family members can challenge the choices that a person may want to make if they do not conform, and family ties may have to be broken if someone is determined to change their behaviour.

Cultural 'norms'

These are the things that people from a similar background share and they often include social and leisure activities such as going for a drink after work on a Friday, or showing an interest in football or the arts. It also extends to the sort of food that is enjoyed and the clothes that people wear. Individuals who do not conform to these social and cultural 'norms' may be subjected to comment, ridicule or, especially in the case of children, bullying at school. Young people are particularly susceptible to these 'social sanctions' as they need to be accepted by their peer group and to separate from their parents as part of their social and emotional development. Bullying and social isolation can affect mental health and well-being.

Social mobility can change an individual's reference point for social 'norms'. Social mobility refers to a significant and permanent change in an individual's socio-economic status. Social mobility can be upward, as people improve their circumstances, – or downward, for example if people suffer from unfortunate life events. It is generally believed that education is the key to upward social mobility, due to increased earning power among graduates who may achieve higher socio-economic status than their parents.

SCENARIO

Adam

Adam was the son of a lorry driver and a cleaner at the local hospital. He was their only child and had shown interest and aptitude during his school years, culminating in a place at a highly regarded university to study law. His parents were incredibly proud of him and told all their friends about his success.

Adam threw himself wholeheartedly into university life, joining several societies and pursuing his interest in sport. He was popular with the other students and continued to do well in his studies, culminating in a first-class honours degree. This success was followed by the offer of a place with a prestigious law firm in London to continue his studies.

Adam's parents saw less and less of him and his visits home became awkward; Adam and his father began to argue about many issues such as politics, religion and money. Eventually Adam met Charlotte, a medical student, and they planned to marry. Charlotte's father was a company director and the couple spent many weekends with her family. Charlotte couldn't understand why Adam was so reluctant to take her to meet his parents.

1. **What do you think has happened to Adam?**
2. **Why has the relationship with his parents deteriorated?**
3. **Why do you think he is reluctant for Charlotte to meet his parents?**

Income

Having enough money increases the availability of lifestyle choices but does not necessarily determine them. Individuals who experience a sudden increase or decrease in their financial circumstances may find it difficult to adjust to the changes of culture. More money may simply enable people to indulge to excess in unhealthy habits, whereas a sudden decrease in finances may mean individuals getting into debt to try and maintain a lifestyle they can no longer afford.

Health information

Providing information about healthy lifestyles is unlikely in itself to change behaviour. Health information needs to be easily accessible, and to identify health risks to individuals and groups in a meaningful way. For example, information on health is often provided in the form of leaflets and posters in health centres and libraries. However, if individuals rarely go to the library, because they do not read books, or only go to the health centre when they are ill, they will not access the health information provided in this way. Even where health information is provided, individuals may choose not to follow it. For example, school children receive health information as part of Personal Social and Health Education, but they still make unhealthy food choices from the options available for school meals.

Individuals need to be motivated to change, and this involves providing information at the right time, when they are most likely to be receptive to changing their behaviour – for example, when someone becomes aware of the risk to health posed by their current lifestyle. An example would be someone who has recently been diagnosed with diabetes, or is suffering from frequent chest infections due to smoking.

Consider this

Identify local sources of health information.

Carry out a quiz in the classroom before doing any research to identify who knows where to get authoritative and reliable health information.

Identify a checklist. For example:

* Is the information in different languages?
* Could blind people access the information?
* Is it clearly written and easy to understand?

Add any criteria that you think are appropriate to enable everyone to access appropriate information. You should have about 6 criteria altogether.

Back in the classroom pool your resources and evaluate your findings.

Material explanations

The groups who experience the most inequality are those who are likely to be most disadvantaged materially. Deprivation is one of the most powerful guides to health status. Almost all health indicators are adversely affected by poverty, and the link between material and financial inequalities and poor health remains strong.

However, it is not just individual differences in wealth that are important, but rather the gap between the richest and the poorest in any given society. For example, Wilson (1996) states that: 'The healthiest societies in the world are not those that are the richest, but those in which income is distributed most evenly and levels of social integration are high. There is a strong correlation between mortality rates and income distribution, e.g. Sweden and Japan have better health than the USA.'

Although the population in the UK as a whole is affluent, it is the persistence of income inequalities, and the extent of these, that makes a difference to the health status of different groups.

'People who experience material disadvantage, lower educational attainment or insecure employment are likely to suffer poorer health outcomes and an earlier death compared to the rest of the population. There are striking health inequalities between groups and areas despite increased national prosperity, wider opportunity and improving health over the last twenty years. The gaps in life expectancy between different local authority areas, and infant mortality between different social groups, continues to widen.' (*Choosing Health, 2004*)

In 2002 to 2003, the average income of the top 20 per cent of households was approximately 15 times greater than the bottom 20 per cent at £60,300 per household per year, compared to £4,000, and after adjusting for taxes and benefits the ratio was 4 to 1, unchanged from previous years (National Office of Statistics, 2004). In households with limited incomes, spending must be prioritised if the serious consequences of non-payment are to be avoided. For example, non-payment of a mortgage or rent will lead eventually to repossession or eviction, non-payment of council tax will lead to fines and eventual imprisonment and non-payment of utility bills (gas, electric) will lead to supplies being cut off, fines and county court judgments being issued. One in five people are denied access to mainstream credit and have to borrow at very high rates of interest. Once a person has a court judgment against them they become a 'credit risk' and may be unable to borrow money or to obtain goods on credit.

Disadvantage affects some groups more than others; among the poorest households (Rowntree Foundation, 2000) in the UK are:

* lone parents
* people with a disability (adult or child)
* ethnic minorities
* people of pension age and older.

Adjusting taxes and benefits is one way that Government attempts to redistribute income to help those on low wages.

As can be seen from the table below, the extent of child poverty has reduced since its highest point in the early 1990s, indicating that some redistribution has taken place; however, it is still almost twice as high as it was in 1979.

Year	Before housing costs	After housing costs
1979	12	14
1981	18	20
1987	21	25
1988–1989	23	28
1990–1991	26	31
1991–1992	27	32
1992–1993	27	33
1993–1994	25	32
1994–1995	23	32
1995–1996	21	32
1996–1997	25	34
1997–1998	25	33
1998–1999	24	33
1999–2000	23	32
2000–2001	21	31
2001–2002	21	30

FIGURE 6.14 *The percentage of children living in households below 60 per cent of median income*

Source: National Statistics (2004)

Ethnic groups

Even within disadvantaged groups, some are more disadvantaged than others, for reasons that will be discussed later. This is particularly true of ethnic groups. For example:

* the unemployment rate for men of Pakistani or Bangladeshi origin in 2001/2 was 20 per cent – four times higher than that of white British men
* among young people under 25 years old, the rate was 40 per cent for Bangladeshi men and more than 20 per cent for young black African men, Pakistani men and women, black Caribbean men and women and those of mixed race
* this compares to a rate of 12 per cent for white British men and 9 per cent for white British women
* approximately 70 per cent of Bangladeshi and Pakistani children are living in poverty, a rate that is 2.5 times higher than children of white parents, and 41 per cent of black Caribbean children live in poverty.

While the rates of illness among ethnic minority groups could be down to lifestyle, the fact that many ethnic minority families are likely to have no worker to support them due to high unemployment rates suggests that material disadvantage is the most significant factor in their ill health. Unemployment has a high correlation with both physical and mental illness. Unsurprisingly, ethnic minority groups had the greatest rate of self-reported illness, with the highest in people of Bangladeshi and Pakistani origin (see Figure 6.11 on page 282).

The birth rate among ethnic minority populations tends to be higher, because they have a younger age profile, contributing to the number of children in poverty.

Similarly, some older people may not have had the opportunities to save or contribute to an occupational pension scheme during their lives. The value of the State pension has decreased in real terms since the link between earnings and pensions was broken – that is, pensions were up-rated in line with average earnings but are now up-rated in line with inflation, which the government has striven to keep low for the sake of the economy as a whole.

At the same time, women make up a greater proportion of older people because they tend to live longer. Because women generally live longer than men, and often have inconsistent employment patterns as a result of childrearing and part-time working, they are less likely to have the benefits of an occupational pension and are more likely to be dependent on welfare benefits in old age. This means that older people, especially women, make up a significant proportion of people suffering poverty, with associated ill health.

The impact of deprivation on children

Children also suffer from deprivation-related ill health or failure to thrive. An individual's health opportunities start from before birth and affect them throughout their life; this has remained constant. For children of mothers in the lower income groups, the mother's poor health is reflected in their children's health. For example, smoking in pregnancy is more common in lower socio-economic groups and increases the likelihood of still-birth, or premature or underweight babies. These babies are at high risk of respiratory disorders at birth and throughout infancy. There is less likelihood of disadvantaged mothers breastfeeding, which is partly cultural and partly because until recently, as part of the welfare food programme (a benefit in kind), milk tokens were provided which could be exchanged for artificial milk/infant formula. It is now known that breastfeeding gives babies many advantages: for example, they are less likely to be obese, they are less likely to suffer from heart disease and they are less likely to suffer from infections, including gastro-intestinal infections.

In households where there is someone with a disability, opportunities for maximising income through work are limited. For example, a child with a disability may need constant care, and an adult may not find suitable work locally that they are able to carry out or access. Such households are disproportionately dependent on welfare benefits, which provide subsistence levels of income.

Lone parents can be disadvantaged due to the lack of access to affordable childcare, which would enable them to work. Much childcare in the UK is provided privately, with little State subsidy, and it is highly regulated, making it expensive to deliver. For example, the national average cost of a place in a nursery for a 2-year-old is £110 per week, with regional differences of up to £70 or £80 per week; the cost of a childcare place in London can be approximately £200 a week. Lone parents without qualifications are likely to be particularly disadvantaged, since they are more likely to be in unskilled or in manual employment which attracts low pay. Because their income is unlikely to be able to cover the costs of childcare, these lone parents are more likely to be dependent on welfare benefits than other groups.

Problems associated with disadvantage

Wide gaps in income distribution make it difficult for individuals to manage the risks and challenges that life throws up unexpectedly. Financial insecurity is stressful and this makes it more difficult for people to adapt to changes in their lives – there is no 'safety net' – and 28 per cent of households have no savings, rising to 46 per cent for households with a weekly income of less than £200.

Problems associated with disadvantage are:

* it can cause depression, making someone less able to make decisions; they may make bad choices, or feel unable to choose at all
* financial insecurity may lead to a heightened sense of social isolation as people cannot afford to pay for leisure activities
* there is a lack of choices where income is only sufficient for the basic necessities; financial crises are frequent. For example, if the washing machine breaks down, there may be insufficient money to repair or replace it.

These stresses are reflected in health indicators that attempt to establish the level of social support that individuals have, such as the strength of social contacts, community ties and the availability of social support. These factors help to minimise the impact of challenge and change that people experience and help them to cope. Perceptions of social cohesion in society are not static; for example, when asked whether they felt that people 'looked out for one another', 40 per cent agreed in 1984, but only 31 per cent in 1992. This appears to indicate that social cohesion – a sense of 'society' – declined during this period. However, there has been something of a recovery and in the latest census (2001), 36 per cent felt that people looked after one another. This demonstrates the importance of friends, neighbours and local communities, which the government recognises.

SCENARIO A

Sonia

Sonia is 32 years old and has two children, aged 18 months and 7 years. Her husband has recently left the family home and Sonia is struggling to adjust to her changed circumstances, particularly a significant reduction in income.

Before she became a single parent, Sonia enjoyed her job working part-time at the local school helping with the lunches and playground supervision, even though she had no formal qualifications. Her young child was cared for during the short time she was at work by a neighbour who also had children at the school.

Since the break-up of her marriage Sonia has become depressed, as the money she has from her part-time job does not cover the bills. Although she has applied to the Child Support Agency for help in receiving maintenance from her husband, the process is taking a long time. Sonia also receives some welfare benefits, but is finding it difficult to cope and feels very stressed; she has taken up smoking, and often finds that she is not hungry. She has little energy to cook meals for the children, and tends to give them things that are easy to prepare or collects fish and chips on her way home from work. She is beginning to find the children irritating and has little patience when they misbehave. Her 7-year-old son has started to wet the bed at night, and her 18-month-old daughter has developed a nappy rash. Sonia has recently received a warning letter from the gas board, threatening to cut off the gas supply if she does not pay the bill.

SCENARIO B

Alison

Alison is also a single parent whose husband left 12 months ago. Prior to this, Alison stayed at home, bringing up her two children aged 3 and 8.

Like Sonia, Alison has no formal qualifications; she was a shop worker before her marriage; however, she has found a full-time job in the local nursing home as a care assistant. As part of her new role, Alison is required to undertake training and attends the local college for one day a week, paid for by her employer.

The college has a nursery and Alison has managed to secure a place for her 3-year-old, and has good support from her close friend Susan, who looks after her children one evening a week so that Alison can complete her college work. Although the money is not very good, she receives additional benefits and help with childcare costs, which enables her to pay her bills. Alison has set her sights on becoming a nurse and is working hard to achieve her qualification.

Consider this

Consider the two scenarios about Sonia and Alison.

1. Identify differences and similarities in the two women's circumstances.
2. Who is managing best?
3. Why do you think this is? Give examples to illustrate your reasons.
4. What health implications are there for the two women and their children?
5. What advice would you give to each woman?

Social change, lifestyle choices and public health issues

British society has changed significantly in the last 50 years in many areas:

* More women with dependent children now work, although the age of the children affects participation. For example, 55 per cent of women with children under 5 years old work, compared to 80 per cent of those with children aged 11–15
* There has been an increase in non-standard working such as self-employment and home-working, flexible hours and job sharing
* The white ethnic population is ageing
* Fertility rates among white ethnic females is decreasing
* Immigration patterns are changing, with an increase from Eastern European countries
* The population is diverse, with many ethnic groups, although those from Asian and Caribbean backgrounds predominate
* Women continue to earn less per hour than men – 82 per cent of men's full-time hourly earnings, although the differential is decreasing
* Women spend more time on child-related activities and housework than men, although men are participating more
* There has been an increase in home ownership
* There has been an increase in working hours.

Changes in society have been accompanied by changes in individual behaviour and changes in lifestyle and patterns of consumption, associated with changes in the pattern of health and disease. Individuals and groups will be affected to a greater or lesser degree, depending on the extent to which they take risks with their health, and whether they adopt healthy or unhealthy habits. The choices individuals make about how they live their lives are determined by a number of factors, in particular:

* their values – what is important
* their income
* culture – what is acceptable to family, friends and society
* physical and emotional health
* knowledge and information about available choices and their risks and benefits.

An example of the link between lifestyle choice and health issues is highlighted by issues surrounding food: in households with limited incomes, many people use loans or credit (such as credit cards) to manage household bills, and in such situations food becomes an item on which spending can be restricted in order to pay for other goods or services. Choices about food are determined by access, income, choice or preferences, knowledge and skills, time and advertising. See Figure 6.15.

As we saw in the Health Survey, people in lower socio-economic groups eat less fruit and vegetables and have diets that are higher in fat and salt. Young people, particularly young men, also have poor diets.

FACTORS THAT INFLUENCE FOOD CHOICES:	
Access	In recent years there has been a consolidation of food retailers, and the main supermarkets now supply the bulk of food for the majority of the population. There has been a tendency for such supermarkets or hypermarkets to be located on the outskirts of towns, which may be relatively inaccessible to families without a car. Local shops tend to offer convenience foods, which are high in fat, sugar and salt, and less fresh fruit and vegetables. This means that choice can be restricted for people without a car – for example, older people.
Income	Where individuals have a limited budget, food is an item of expenditure that can be restricted if necessary in order to pay for other things – for example, clothes and shoes, Christmas and birthday presents.
Choice	Food choices are closely linked to cultural values and norms. People tend to prefer the sort of food that they are used to, and if children are not introduced to a wide range of food at an early age, they may grow up with limited food preferences. A recent survey by the National Consumer Council compared different supermarkets according to a number of indicators, such as the amount of shelf space they gave to fresh foods, how much salt, sugar and fat is in the supermarket's own-brand processed food, whether they promote unhealthy foods more than healthy fresh foods in the store, and the quality of label information and advice. The stores with the highest rating for their contribution to a healthy diet were the supermarkets that had a clientele made up of higher socio-economic groups, and were also more expensive.
Knowledge and skills	Much of the knowledge that people have about food is obtained from the media, and there has been a decline in cooking skills among young people in particular. This is partly due to many schools removing cooking from the curriculum to make way for other subjects. If parents do not spend time cooking at home, it is more difficult for young people to acquire the skills and knowledge needed to prepare fresh foods.
Time	The increased number of women working outside the home, together with the long working hours of both men and women, restricts the time available for preparing meals using fresh ingredients and increases reliance on ready-prepared foods that are quick to cook. Eating habits have changed. For example, there has been a decline in families sitting down together to eat, and many children fail to eat breakfast; in a survey of teenage eating habits carried out by the Schools Health Education Unit, over 40 per cent of 14 and 15-year-olds said they missed breakfast. Many families eat in front of the TV or from take-away outlets. Such tendencies lead to a higher consumption of foods that are high in fat, salt and sugar – for example, some ready-prepared soups contain between one third and one half of the recommended daily intake of salt.
Advertising	There has been increased concern about the link between advertising unhealthy foods to children and the consumption of those foods. Supermarkets' promotional activities and discounts – for example, 2 for 1 offers – were found to be centred on unhealthy foods such as sugary drinks and sweets, often linked to popular films and sporting events.

FIGURE 6.16 *Some of the factors that influence choice of food*

Demographic and population changes

Other social changes that link to public health concerns centre around demographic and population changes. These are discussed below.

Change in population profile

The population profile is older, and older people suffer more ill health, especially degenerative diseases associated with ageing such as osteoarthritis, which affects mobility, and neurological diseases such as Alzheimer's, which affects memory and the ability to remain independent. The incidence of diseases such as cardiovascular disease and stroke increase, with age. Diabetes is also more common in older people.

People are marrying later and fewer babies are being born

The age at which people get married is rising, and there are fewer babies being born, although the rates are showing a slight rise – up from 2.3 to 2.5 per woman of childbearing age. However, more women are choosing to remain childless, perhaps to follow career pathways, and there has been an increase in infertility. The cause of this increase in infertility is uncertain, but it is likely to be the result of a combination of factors, including the increased incidence of chlamydia; this sexually transmitted infection causes inflammation of the fallopian tubes (pelvic inflammatory disease, PID) in women but has few symptoms in men, so the risk from unprotected sexual intercourse is not immediately evident. Chlamydia is now estimated to affect 1 in 10 women of childbearing age. Increased pollution, with exposure to toxic chemicals such as pesticides and hormone disrupters in the environment, is also thought to be a factor. At the same time, young single people are drinking more alcohol and having more sexual partners, factors that may also be linked to a decrease in fertility.

Ethnic minority groups

Ethnic minority groups, as we have seen, still suffer from a disproportionate degree of health disadvantage. This is likely to be the result of workplace discrimination, either covert or overt, together with health services that are not culturally sensitive and adapted to the needs of ethnic minority groups. In African and sub-Saharan countries, AIDS and HIV infection is endemic, and there is a higher prevalence among people from these groups in the United Kingdom.

Action is needed

In order to address the public health problems caused by social changes, action needs to be taken by a range of government agencies to address the multiple complex causes of health inequality.

Government targets

In *Saving lives: Our Healthier Nation* (White Paper, 1999), the government recognised the wider influences on health and the fact that there was a widening gap in health inequalities. They proposed a 'three-way deal for health' between individuals, communities and the government with the aims of:

* improving health
* reducing the health gap (tackling health inequalities).

The government put forward an action plan to address poor health by 2010. They identified four target areas for preventing illness, the aims of which are shown in Figure 6.17.

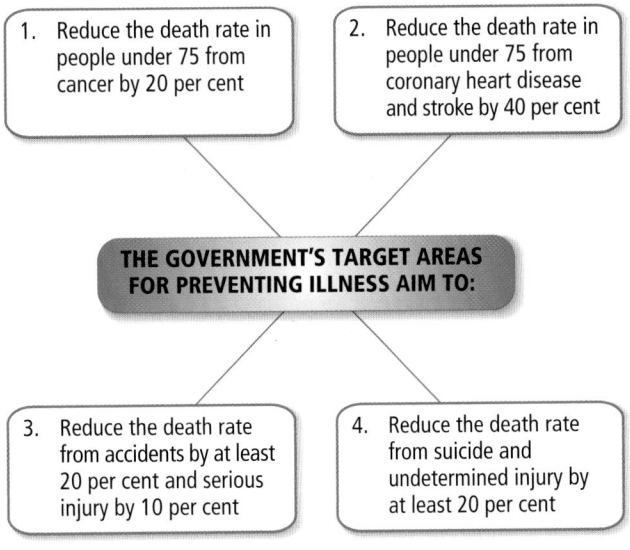

FIGURE 6.16 *The government's action plan to address poor health by 2010*

Source: White Paper (1999)

As part of reducing health inequalities, the government identified details of how the areas for action would be addressed in the document 'Tackling Health Inequalities: Programme for Action', launched in 2003. There are several main areas (outlined below) and the programme covers the years from 2003 to 2010.

Preventing illness and providing effective treatment and care

Details of targets concerned with smoking, cancer and coronary heart disease are shown in Figure 6.17.

Supporting families and children

Priority areas included improving infant mortality rates and life expectancy. Action was to be targeted in disadvantaged areas, and, as a result, the Sure Start Programme was introduced. The focus of this is set out in Figure 6.18.

Responsibilities were allocated to different government agencies such as Primary Care Trusts and the Sure Start Unit. The proposed development of children's centres was to be led by the Sure Start unit, together with improved access to high-quality nursery and childcare facilities, especially in disadvantaged areas. Other

TARGETS TO PREVENT ILLNESS AND PROVIDE TREATMENT AND CARE	
Reducing risks through effective prevention	Aims to reduce smoking rates within the adult population 800,000 smokers to quit and reduce the smoking prevalence in manual groups to 26 per cent by 2010 (from 32 per cent in 1998) Reduce to 18 per cent the number of women smoking during pregnancy National School Fruits scheme to reach all children aged 4 to 6 Reduce the number of adults killed in road traffic accidents by 40 per cent and the number of children by 50 per cent, with a corresponding reduction to 10 per cent in casualties
Early detection, intervention and treatment	Improve GP premises and add 250 extra one-stop centres Develop 500 primary care centres, 100 of which will be within rural communities Establish 20 Primary Care Trusts Update all practice registers to include all coronary heart disease patients
Improving access to effective treatment (aims to reduce cancer rates in the under-75 population and reduce coronary heart disease (CHD) death rates in the under 75 age group)	Increase breast cancer screening for women aged 65–70 by 100 per cent Maximum 2 month wait following urgent GP referral to treatment for all cancers and one month wait from diagnosis to treatment 1000 extra cancer specialists Reduce death from cancer in the under 75s by 20 per cent by 2009 Reduce the death rates from CHD in people under 75 by 25 per cent by 2005, and by 40 per cent by 2009 2 week wait for rapid access to chest pain clinics Achieve a 3 month wait for angiography and revascularisation

FIGURE 6.17 *Details of targets concerned with smoking, cancer and coronary heart disease*

proposals included improving educational standards among the disadvantaged, to be led by the Department for Education and Skills and providing children with at least two hours of PE and sport each week, led by DfES and the Department for Culture, Media and Sport. See Figure 6.19.

Addressing the underlying determinants of health

These targets cover Housing, Training and Skills, Jobs and Income, and Transport. They are consequently indirectly related to the health and comfort issues such as:

* reduce fuel poverty by improving energy efficiency in 800,000 homes
* improve the standard of housing, including 100 per cent of social housing to be a decent standard by 2010
* improving basic skills of 750,000 adults (Skills for Life)
* develop literacy, IT and numeracy for 20,000 health and social care staff and decrease the number of adults who lack NVQ level 2 or above by 40 per cent by 2010
* increase by 50 per cent the number of people aged 18 to 30 entering higher education
* incorporate accessibility planning in local transport plans.

Engaging communities and individuals

These targets are concerned with community support and reducing drug misuse. For example:

* increase the participation of drug users in treatment programmes by 55 per cent at the end of 2004 and by 100 per cent by 2008, with a 20 per cent reduction in drug-related deaths

FOCUS OF THE SURE START PROGRAMME	
Maternity and child health and child development (Aims to improve infant mortality and subsequent life expectancy)	Reduce by 25 per cent, the number of children in low-income homes, halve child poverty by 2010 and eradicate child poverty by 2020 Increase the take-up and duration of breastfeeding by 2 per cent per year, particularly among mothers in low-income groups Increase attendance of pregnant women at antenatal classes Set up 522 Sure Start Programme in disadvantaged areas by 2004 and visit all families within two months of birth by 2006 in each area Free nursery places for all 3-year-olds and 45,000 neighbourhood nursery places by 2004 Launch Healthy Start 2004 Reform the Welfare Foods Scheme by 2004, to include vouchers for fresh fruit and vegetables and encourage support of breastfeeding mothers Launch a development programme of preventive action to reduce inequalities in the dental health of young children, especially in areas without water fluoridation Develop multi-disciplinary family support teams, reflecting the needs of local children and families, and reduce by 10 per cent the number of children admitted to hospital with severe injury by 2010

FIGURE 6.18 *Focus of the Sure Start Programme*

OTHER GOVERNMENT PROPOSALS TO SUPPORT FAMILIES AND CHILDREN	
Improving life chances for children and young people (Aim is to improve the life chances and job opportunities of young people)	Narrow the gap in educational attainment for young people from disadvantaged backgrounds, including black and minority ethnic groups, and Looked After Children, e.g. through national literacy and numeracy strategies Focus the Healthy Schools Programme on disadvantaged areas and strengthen the teaching of personal, social and health education, including education on drugs, alcohol and tobacco, and sex and relationships education Develop a comprehensive mental health service for children and adolescents by 2006 Reduce truancy and improve basic skills and learning opportunities to improve job prospects and prevent crime (links to education targets, e.g. 85 per cent of 14-year-olds to achieve level 5 in English, maths and ICT) Develop sports facilities through the New Opportunities Programme Use culture and creativity to increase engagement and improve school attendance among pupils at risk of no educational attainment in disadvantaged areas, e.g. by increasing number of schools implementing school travel plans to 25 per cent by 2005
Reducing teenage pregnancy and supporting teenage mothers (Aim is to provide job opportunities for young mothers and better opportunities for their children)	Reduce the gap year-on-year in under-18 conceptions between the worst 20 per cent of electoral wards and the national average, e.g. reducing the under-18 conception rate by 15 per cent by 2005, increasing to 25 per cent by 2006 and 50 per cent by 2010 Provide early antenatal bookings and smoking cessation services in suitable settings, for teenage mothers and their partners Deliver specially tailored support and advice through the Sure Start Programme, and provide childcare places for 1.6 million children Help teenage parents to secure access to education, using personal advisers to liaise with other agencies and ensure parents have the best opportunities to engage in education training No lone parents aged 16 to 17 to be in unsupported tenancies by the end of 2004 Reduce by 12 per cent the number of under 3-year-olds in Sure Start areas living in households where no one is working

FIGURE 6.19 *Other government proposals to support families and children*

* increase to 30 per cent the number of supported older people able to live at home, including 50,000 more people to live independently and 50 per cent more people to benefit through community equipment, with 150,000 older people receiving intermediate care
* improve mental health care in prisons and develop early intervention teams and crisis resolution teams for mental health
* provide extra resources to Primary Care Trusts in Health Action Zone areas

* create 250 extended schools
* no homeless families with children in bed-and-breakfast accommodation, except for short-term and urgent cases, by 2004
* provide online resources for health issues in key languages by 2003.

Other financial initiatives for disadvantaged people

The focus of many of the above initiatives is to improve the chances of disadvantaged people and communities by increasing their job opportunities and subsequent income. Other financial initiatives are outlined below.

Minimum wage

A national minimum wage was introduced in 1998, with differential rates for different groups and younger people receiving less than adults.

New Opportunities scheme

This was introduced in 1998, with the aim of helping young people into work and off reliance on benefits, through advice, guidance and training.

Other strategies to improve the financial situation of those with low incomes

Examples of strategies to improve the financial situation of those with low incomes include adjusting taxes and benefits. Low-income households usually receive two kinds of benefits, illustrated in Figure 6.20.

These benefits are provided on a sliding scale: they are reduced as income increases. Tax contributions increase in line with earnings, so, for example, the top 20 per cent of households paid 24 per cent of gross income in direct tax in 2002 to 2003, whereas the bottom 20 per cent paid 9 per cent. Indirect taxes such as VAT have the opposite effect: because VAT is paid on purchases, some of which are necessities such as clothes, they take a high proportion of income from those on low incomes.

CASH BENEFITS	BENEFITS IN KIND
Income support, child benefit, incapacity benefit and working families tax credit. These benefits are most effective in reducing inequalities, contributing approximately 60 per cent of gross income for the poorest 20 per cent of households and 40 per cent for the next poorest group.	Free school meals, welfare foods, free dental treatment, free sight tests, free post-compulsory education, housing benefit

FIGURE 6.20 *Types of benefits*

The national public health strategy

A new public health White Paper was published in November 2004 ('Choosing Health: Making Healthy Choices Easier'), in which the population is recognised as consumers, and considering the impact that a consumer society has on individual health choices. Government intends to respond to the needs and wishes of the population by providing clear information about the health choices available to them through policies and practices that recognise the reality of people's daily lives. The White Paper has identified three core principles:

* **Informed choice** – providing clear, credible and trustworthy information to enable people to make their own decisions about health
* **Personalisation** – tailored, personal support for individuals in deprived groups and communities to enable them to choose healthy habits, especially where current services do not adequately meet their needs
* **Working together** – developing effective partnerships between communities, groups, business, advertisers, retailers and government agencies.

The existing health targets remain; however, there are new initiatives, including food labelling, providing information through a new agency – Health Direct – which will link to existing agencies such as the Food Standards Agency, plus regular briefings for the media from the Chief Medical Officer. The government intends to work with the food industry to introduce new standards, increasing the availability of healthier food by reducing the levels of sugar and salt in products, providing clear information on labels and developing guidance on portion sizes, reducing the trend towards bigger portions.

Other initiatives include restricting the advertising and promotion of foods that are high in fat, salt and sugar to children and the voluntary social responsibility code for alcohol producers and retailers. Tobacco advertising will be restricted.

In schools

There will be a drive towards integrating the planning and delivery of services, for example through Children's Trusts, and the School Health Service will be expanded and modernised. Children will be encouraged to take responsibility for their own health, through Personal Health Guides. Healthy Start is the name of a new reformed welfare foods scheme, which will provide fruit and vegetable vouchers as well as those for milk and vitamins. Plans are under-way to improve nutrition at school, to revise nutritional standards for school meals, and extend the standards to tuck shops and vending-machine services. School sports and physical education will be increased, and will include the development of specialist sports academies and partnership arrangements.

FIGURE 6.21 *Healthy Start is part of a plan to improve nutrition in schools*

In the community

Community initiatives include support for cookery clubs and food cooperatives to encourage an increased consumption of fruit and vegetables. The Public Health Observatories will be responsible for providing regular reports based on local health information. Partnership arrangements between Primary Care Trusts and local authorities will be expected to deliver health and well-being to local communities and a reduction in health inequalities.

Training and support is to be provided to help NHS staff to develop their understanding and skills in promoting health, and it is proposed that there will be 3,000 Community Matrons to take the lead in providing personalised health care and advice.

In the workplace

There are plans to improve health in the workplace and encourage more people to cycle to work.

Stronger links are to be made between academic institutions and practitioners to promote the evidence base for public health initiatives, and a new agency is to identify effective interventions – the National Institute for Public and Clinical Excellence.

Finally, there will be an obligation on government departments to undertake a Regulatory Impact Assessment on all future legislation; all proposals must carry out an assessment of the impact of their proposals on the health of the population so that health becomes integrated into all government policy.

It is clear that there are many factors other than biological ones implicated in ill health, such as personal views and attitudes to health risk, knowledge of health risks, access to preventive services and social and economic factors. The government has stated its commitment to improving the health of the population as a whole, and to reducing health inequalities using a range of strategies. They have set targets for achieving these aims, concentrating on reducing the incidence of major diseases such as cancer and heart disease and targeting vulnerable groups and individuals.

Summary of Section 6.2

The following key areas have been covered in this section:

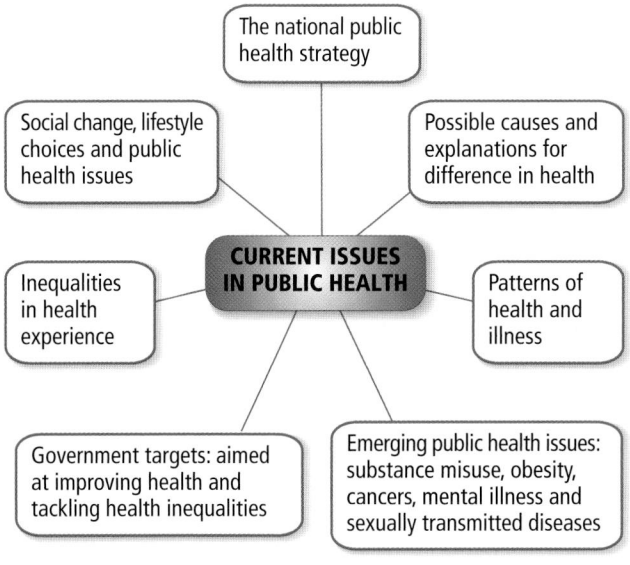

6.3 Promoting and protecting public health in the UK

Much of the responsibility for environmental health and well-being lies with local authorities. Local authorities may be based in an urban or built-up environment, a rural or green environment or an industrial environment; often, local authorities have a mixture of all of these areas within their boundaries.

Environmental measures

Environmental measures are intended to reduce the risk to human health posed by environmental hazards, which may relate to the external environment (outdoors) or the internal environment such as workplaces and homes. Examples of environmental hazards are shown in Figure 6.22.

HAZARD	EXAMPLES
Physical	Structures, buildings and materials, land, water or air
Chemical	Pesticides, fertilisers, plasticisers and chemicals used in manufacture
Biological	Vermin, poisonous plants, dangerous animals
Social	Noise pollution

FIGURE 6.22 *Examples of environmental hazards*

In modern society, there is no escape from environmental pollution; it is estimated that 80 per cent of cancers have an environmental link. As a result, the environment is regulated through the Environment Agency (see www.heinemann.co.uk/hotlinks (express code 370XP) for a link), part of the Department of Food and Rural Affairs (DEFRA), and enforced through local authority agents such as environmental health officers.

Reducing environmental harm

Local authorities are responsible for monitoring and regulating industrial, household and biological waste in their area. Sometimes these activities are carried out by other companies or agencies on behalf of the local authority, and there are specialist agencies who deal with hazardous wastes such as asbestos and other industrial waste.

The government is committed to providing sufficient housing while maintaining the countryside. As a result, there is increased pressure and financial incentives to build on 'brownfield sites'. These sites have been contaminated by previous manufacturing processes and industry, and often contain high levels of toxic waste, due to lack of regulation of such industries before the hazards were fully appreciated. Such land has to be dealt with, by making it clean and safe using specialist processes, to ensure that it doesn't harm future inhabitants.

Local authority planning and building regulations are responsible for monitoring all proposals for new housing and examining any plans to deal with toxic residues, for example heavy metals such as mercury, lead, arsenic and cadmium (from batteries), which might be found on brownfield sites. These heavy metals can cause breathing difficulties, skin complaints, lung cancer and damage to the kidneys and nervous system. They also disproportionately affect children, because of their small size and relatively immature body systems.

Monitoring of farming and agricultural methods

In rural areas, local authorities are responsible for monitoring farming and agricultural methods that may pose a threat to health – for example, ensuring that a farmer disposes of leftover chemicals in a risk-free manner that complies with regulations. Local authorities are also responsible for monitoring outbreaks of disease in animals that may be passed to humans; a recent example was the foot and mouth epidemic in which local authorities were responsible for the coordinated disposal of thousands of animal carcasses that had been infected with foot and mouth, in order to stop the epidemic. Slaughterhouses and associated food production methods are also regulated, monitored and inspected.

Air quality and atmospheric pollution

Air quality and atmospheric pollution are linked to the use of fossil fuels and traffic as well as industrial processes. Discharges of industrial fumes into the atmosphere are carefully regulated and monitored; however, the extent to which they are dispersed depends on the weather: the action of sunlight on some by-products of industry can change them into more dangerous pollutants. The UK has agreements with the European Union on atmospheric pollution and industrial discharges. The government has passed the responsibility for reducing these on to local authorities, with associated targets and payment incentives.

One of the major causes of atmospheric pollution is increasing traffic, particularly cars and lorries. Local authorities differ in their approach to traffic management, with some being 'car friendly' while others are perceived as penalising the motorist. This can be a divisive political issue locally. However, the government is encouraging integrated transport policies, with initiatives such as car-sharing and cycle lanes; increased, affordable public transport and traffic calming schemes – particularly in residential areas and new schools – to reduce the risk of accidents and contribute therefore to the government health targets in this area.

One of the health issues associated with traffic is the increased morning traffic, due to parents dropping their children off at school. Initiatives have not been successful in encouraging parents to let their children walk to school because of the perception that this is dangerous, and because time is at a premium first thing in the morning for working parents. Where subsidised school transport, for example a school bus, is available, this is seen as an acceptable alternative.

Think it over...

Take a walk round your local area and identify any traffic measures. These may include

* mini roundabouts
* restricted width
* bus lanes
* cycle lanes
* restricted access
* parking restrictions – for example, resident only parking .

Try to identify whether your local authority is 'pedestrian friendly', encourages cycle use and provides facilities for disabled pedestrians.

Give reasons for your answers. You may find the local paper provides a discussion of local traffic issues of concern to the population.

Water quality

Water quality in the UK has a high standard compared to other parts of the world. It is provided by different private companies and regulated by the government to ensure that the quality of the drinking water meets standards agreed by the European Union. Water standards are inspected and monitored by the Environment Agency, which oversees areas such as sewage treatment and river quality, and the Drinking Water Inspectorate (see www.heinemann.co.uk/hotlinks (express code 370XP) for a link to the DWI website).

Public health measures

Public health measures, as we have seen in this unit, are often directed at individuals – for example, screening and immunisation programmes.

Screening for babies and young children

There is a universal programme of screening for babies and young children, which specifies a minimum level of care and support the parents can expect wherever they may live in the UK. This programme starts at birth, and covers physical examinations, growth monitoring and nutrition, screening for hearing and vision defects, as well as immunisation and neonatal blood tests for metabolic disorders. Babies and young children are subjected to routine medical examinations at approximately 8 weeks, 8 months, and at school entry to detect any issues that may need intervention. Immunisation is carried out at 2, 3 and 4 months of age against diphtheria, tetanus, polio, pertussis (whooping cough), Hib (a dangerous type of influenza), and meningitis type C. At 13 months of age, immunisation against measles, mumps and rubella (MMR) is recommended, followed by a booster dose of diphtheria, tetanus, polio and pertussis, between 3 years and 4 months of age and 5 years. No further immunisations are given until between 10 and 14 years of age, when BCG is given to protect against tuberculosis. A further booster dose of diphtheria, tetanus and polio should be given between 13 and 18 years of age. This schedule protects against most of the major infectious diseases in the UK. However, additional vaccination may be needed before travelling, for example against hepatitis A.

Adult screening

Adult screening programmes are offered against breast cancer and cervical cancer for women, often in a special clinic devoted to women's health, where other issues may be discussed with the health professional. It is not uncommon for adults to undergo medical examination, which may include height and weight, blood pressure and blood tests, together with urine analysis. Increasingly, there are screening clinics for men, dealing with men's health issues such as prostate cancer, testicular cancer and cardiovascular disease.

Local and central government action

Central government develops policies and legislation relating to the environment and public health and safety; however, the responsibility for implementing these policies often lies with local government in the form of local authorities. For example, although food safety is monitored and controlled by the Food Standards Agency – a non-governmental organisation – the responsibility for monitoring food retail outlets, local manufacturers and producers lies with local authority personnel.

The local authority has responsibility for the disposal of household waste, including targets for recycling waste. Biological waste, such as clinical waste from hospitals, for example, has to be incinerated to reduce the risk of infection. Many authorities now provide receptacles for individual households to recycle their waste. Products recycled include:

* paper
* aluminium cans
* glass
* aluminium foil.

Some local authorities also provide facilities for recycling plastic. However, all local authorities vary in the extent to which they achieve their targets for recycling.

The Food Standards Agency monitors the quality of food produced by national and

Consider this

Local authorities must produce plans for Sustainable Development, which includes environmental targets (Local Agenda 21). Investigate your local authority's facilities for waste recycling, including:

* garden waste
* bottles
* plastic
* batteries
* electrical equipment
* paint
* furniture.

1. Compare these facilities with other authorities and assess how effective your council is at recycling. What additional facilities could be provided to encourage recycling?
2. How does recycling contribute to minimising the effects of climate change?
3. What are the other aspects of sustainable development?
4. Why is sustainable development important?

international manufacturers. Where a product is suspected of being unfit to eat, or may cause health problems, the agency issues a food alert on their website (see www.heinemann.co.uk/ hotlinks (express code 370XP) for a link). The number of food allergies appears to be increasing, particularly nut allergy and allergies to dairy produce, so products should be comprehensively labelled with their contents.

The roles and activities of public health workers

There is a wide range of people keen to protect the health of the public; these include public health clinicians, who will usually be doctors and are concerned with the monitoring and regulation of specific health threats such as epidemics. There are also public health practitioners, who have a degree in a particular area of public health and may be employed by the health service or local authorities or within the Environmental Protection Agency, for example. Some health service staff have a particular public health role, especially with regard to screening and prevention – for example, health visitors. Other public health workers are employed in specific roles with the local authorities; environmental health officers, for example, have responsibility for monitoring issues such as unfit housing, atmospheric pollution, pest control and food standards in a defined local area. The proposals within the White Paper *Choosing Health* (2004), suggest that more people will have public health as part of their role, and that some people will be specially trained to provide public health support – for example, health trainers. These individuals may be drawn from local communities and voluntary organisations for the health service, and will be specially trained to provide advice and guidance to individuals with health issues. In addition, general health workers are likely to have received training on the issues surrounding public health.

ENVIRONMENTAL CONCERNS	HEALTH IMPLICATIONS
Ozone layer The ozone layer, a natural protection against the harmful rays of the sun, is thinning and disappears in some parts of the world at certain times of the year	This is a known contributory factor in skin cancer, rates of which are increasing rapidly, especially in fair-skinned people from temperate climates such as the UK Frequent travel to hotter climates is also contributing to the increases in malignant melanoma (skin cancer)
Polluted seas and decreasing fish stocks Many fish, especially oily fish such as tuna and swordfish, are heavily contaminated with heavy metals as a result of polluted seas; other sea mammals such as dolphins are contaminated by dioxins, used in paper manufacturing	These pollutants are among those that accumulate in the body
Chemicals The widespread use of agricultural chemicals to produce 'perfect' fruit and vegetablesis of concern Often, these products are transported many miles by air from the growing regions to the shops , contributing to atmospheric pollution	This produce is grown in developing countries, where regulations are often less stringent than in the UK, the workers can be adversely affected by chemicals

FIGURE 6.23 *Environmental concerns and health implications*

The role of pressure groups

Climate change is causing grave concern globally, and the contribution of environmental pollution is a factor in climate change, which will have long-term implications for human health. The issues surrounding climate change are regularly discussed among world leaders, and agreements have been signed by many countries (though not all), to cut the emission of 'greenhouse gases' – gases that become trapped in the Earth's atmosphere and are in too great a concentration to be absorbed quickly enough by natural processes to prevent atmospheric warming.

Environmental concerns with health implications are outlined in Figure 6.23.

Many of these issues are the subject of campaigns by pressure groups such as Greenpeace, Friends of the Earth and Compassion in World Farming, which have succeeded in drawing attention to the problems. Their methods of attracting media attention are sometimes unorthodox, but they are taken seriously by responsible governments.

The World Health Organisation has responsibility for monitoring health trends worldwide, and has a major role in health issues across national and international boundaries, such as HIV and AIDS and infectious pandemics such as SARS. It also monitors international child health.

The United Nations deals with international peace and security, economic and social development and humanitarian issues, including human rights and international law. It was responsible for promoting the Human Rights Act, which has recently been adopted by this country.

Think it over...

Investigate the following organisations, using the Internet and identify their key priorities:

- World Health Organisation (Europe)
- Friends of the Earth
- Compassion in World Farming
- Greenpeace
- United Nations

How do the key priorities of these organisations contribute to global public health?

Give reasons why individual countries should be concerned about global public health.

The United Nations also provides aid to developing countries, particularly in the aftermath of war and environmental or international disasters.

The government takes the lead in deciding health priorities. However, many of the day-to-day responsibilities are devolved to other agencies, partly or wholly funded by government. In order to meet local health needs, many of the responsibilities are given to local authorities who can act at community level and contribute to meeting targets set by the government.

Good health involves quality of life as well as disease prevention, and this means acting to reduce adverse environmental influences on the health of communities. Public health operates across national and international boundaries, at national, regional and local level, and within communities, as well as being important to individuals. As such, it is everybody's responsibility.

Summary of Section 6.3

The following key areas have been covered in this section:

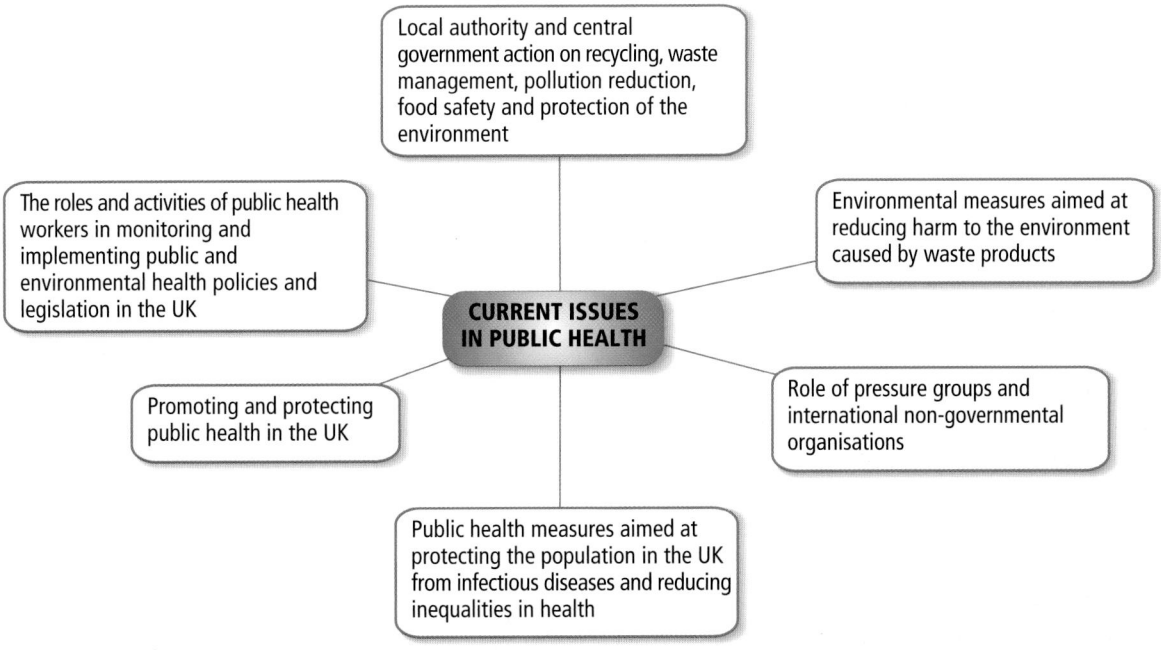

Consider this

You should by now have a view on the overall health of your local area.

Using concepts, can you identify?
The main environmental health issues in your locality and their likely effect on local communities.

Go further – can you analyse the issues using theory?
Assess the contribution to public health of two initiatives from each of these organisations:

* your local community health trust
* your local authority
* one or two local voluntary organisations.

Go further – can you evaluate using a range of theory?
Evaluate the extent to which these identified initiatives contribute to the government strategy for public health in your area.

FIGURE 6.24 *Worker wearing protective clothing*

UNIT 6 ASSESSMENT

How you will be assessed

The assessment of this unit will consist of a report of your investigation into a public health issue of your choice. You need to think carefully about your choice of subject and the availability of information about the health issue and its possible consequences. Your subject can be a disease or condition that is becoming more prevalent in particular groups. You will need to find information about the condition, causes, prevention and epidemiology, treatment and cost of treatment as well as the likely impact it will have if nothing is done to prevent the spread. You should consider the implications for individuals, families, communities and the economy.

Structure of your report

Your report should be structured with clear headings, for example:

* Content
* Background
* Introduction to the issue – you should include information about the disease or condition, for example signs and symptoms, prognosis (the short- and long-term effects), how it is transmitted or acquired, the incidence of the disease or condition and the scale of the current problem, the likely impact if untreated both on the particular service users affected and on the wider public health.
* Body of the report – it would be useful to organise the material into sections. You will need to make the links between social, environmental and lifestyle factors and analyse these. You should also make clear the public health issues and their impact, for example on services in the future. You should provide examples and case studies wherever possible to illustrate your points.
* Recommendations/suggested strategies – this section could include initiatives already underway as well as additional suggestions to protect the public, for example health education, health promotion, environmental initiatives.
* Evaluation – this section gives you an opportunity to state your views of the issue and the likely effectiveness of strategies to combat the health issue. You must back up your views with source material.

You will need to demonstrate your use of a wide range of sources, carefully referenced, and be aware of any ethical issues. Since health issues can be a very sensitive subject, particularly if lifestyle factors are a feature, it is not recommended that personal interviews are undertaken for this unit, except where stated in activities. Permission (preferably written) must be sought from all interviewees, who may request that they see the transcript of their interview. Confidentiality must be maintained at all times.

While there is no word limit on the report, it is useful to discuss it with your tutor before and during your work to ensure you are giving relevant information and are not repeating it in other sections. It is not the length of the report that is important but the quality of your research and findings.

Ideas for consideration

Some suggested areas for consideration include:

* **Hepatitis C:** this is an emerging public health issue, which will provide opportunities for you to discuss issues around compulsory and voluntary screening, how the health status of the population is monitored and the ethical issues involved. It will also provide opportunities to look at the impact on future health service provision and the associated social, economic, environmental and political issues.

* **Tuberculosis:** this disease was all but eradicated in Britain but is now re-emerging. You will have the opportunity to identify why this is the case, the global impact of TB, the associated issues such as access to services for affected groups, and current and emerging treatments. You will also have the opportunity to investigate the impact on services of containing and treating TB and the effectiveness of immunisation programmes.
* **Diabetes:** this disease is also on the increase and is linked to lifestyle factors; however, certain groups are more susceptible to diabetes than others, suggesting a genetic link. There are different forms of diabetes and this will provide an opportunity to consider a wide range of options for minimising the health risks from that disease.

Unit test

1. Public health has improved over the last 150 years. Give three examples illustrating how this has been achieved.
2. Identify three measures commonly used to assess health inequalities.
3. Suggest three reasons why health inequalities persist.
4. Why are governments interested in public health?
5. Identify three health issues that are of current concern to the government.
6. Explain lifestyle factors that can have a negative effect on health, giving two examples.
7. Explain what is meant by health screening and give two examples of screening programmes.
8. Explain the public health role of local authorities and their staff.
9. Explain two conditions that are more prevalent in some groups of people than in others.
10. Identify two types of regulations that are used to protect public health and well being.

References

Fraser, D. (1986) *The Evolution of the British Welfare State* (London, Macmillan)

Hall, D. and Elliman, D. (eds) (2003) *Health For All Children* (Oxford, Oxford University Press)
Note: This book gives a good overview of the principles of screening programmes, which are also relevant to adults.

Townsend, P. and Davidson, N. (ed) (1988) *Inequities in Health: The Black Report* (Pelican, London)

UNICEF (1993) *The Progress of Nations* (United Nations 45)

Whithead, M. (1988) *Inequalities in Health: The Health Divide* (Pelican, London)

Useful websites

Please see www.heinemann.co.uk/hotlinks (express code 370XP) for links to the following websites, which may provide more information:

Department of Food and Rural Affairs
Department of Health
Direct Government
Health Development Agency
Health Poverty Index
Health Protection Agency
Local Government Association
Joseph Rowntree Foundation
National Office of Statistics
Public Health Observatories

Answers to assessment questions

Unit 1

1a. (i) Later adulthood
(ii) 5
(iii) Middle adulthood
(iv) There is a lack of viable eggs in the ovary which causes reduced levels of hormones and declining menstrual cycles, eventually stopping completely. Sue cannot become pregnant again or bear any more children. This can be a relief or a sad time coinciding with the likelihood that grown-up children will start to move away. Sue may suffer from hot flushes, night sweats and changeable moods due to the menopause.

1b. (i) John may withdraw from many social activities as he feels ashamed and also cannot afford them due to a lower income. His self-esteem has lowered and his self-concept changed from positive to negative. This makes it harder to find a new job. He has lost status as the breadwinner and now depends on his wife's earnings. He often feels humiliated and depressed, as well as angry as losing of his job was not his fault. He gets so emotionally drained from discussing job prospects that he shuns company and is short-tempered with his family.
(ii) Husband being made redundant, shop is regularly vandalised, she is going through the menopause.
(iii) Stress causes release of adrenaline, which raises blood pressure. Constant stress results in hypertension producing heart disease and strokes. Lack of sleep affects daily performance and lowered immunity can result in more disease. Depression is more common and suicide rate increases.

2a. (i) Divorce, bereavement, moving house or business, and unemployment.
(ii) Danger of being attacked – especially at night. Surgeries, clinics get robbed and vandalised; poor facilities in the neighbourhood, no incentive to work in rundown area, little interest in healthy living and can get better paid job elsewhere in pleasant surroundings.
(iii) Stimulates and raises energy levels, outlet for feelings, gives her the 'feel-good' factor, makes new friends, puts worries in better perspective, improves resistance to disease, digestion, sleep, circulation and respiration. Provides a physical, emotional and social boost to life.
(iv) Advantages – Almost instantaneous treatment, no waiting for a doctor's appointment; often cheaper than prescription charge and easily available. Disadvantages – May have harmful side effects unknown to purchaser; may not be the most appropriate medicine for the illness; no control over purchase so abuse can occur readily.

2b. (i) More road accidents due to lack of adequate safe play facilities; poorer health and education; less likely to achieve physical, emotional, social and intellectual potential.
(ii) It is safer to belong to a gang than to be outside of the gang and risk harassment or bullying; individuals feel braver within gangs. Leaving a gang causes ridicule, taunting and bullying. Gang activities tend to be exciting and risky.
(iii) Self-esteem is the way in which you value or feel about yourself.
(iv) Self-esteem enables you to disagree with others; provides self-confidence and the ability to cope with difficulties. A person is liked by others and is therefore popular with peers. Generally speaking, an individual with high self-esteem is happier and more contented.

3a. (i) Adolescence

(ii) Infancy

(iii) Sarah will feel physically and emotionally drained at the end of the day. After some time, she may be fitter and healthier than before. She may feel younger having younger people living in her home, provided that Melanie gives Sarah some of her time. Sarah may feel as if she has no privacy and this may make her feel depressed.

(iv) During adolescence, friendships become the most important relationships even over family. It is important that Melanie still has those relationships for her emotional and psychological well-being. She will be able to trust her friends with secrets and confidences.

3b. (i) This is a disorder caused by a fault in the hereditary make-up of an individual.

(ii) Genes can be dominant or recessive; a dominant gene responsible for a fault will pass on the condition to any individual who receives the gene. The affected gene often miscodes a particular protein thus affecting every cell in the body. Where this is an important enzyme for metabolism, the condition can be severe. A recessive gene will only pass on the fault when it is present with another recessive gene for the same fault, but it miscodes the protein in exactly the same way, just tending to miss generations.

(iii) Smoking, occupation, air quality/pollution

(iv) Smoking is very harmful to health; raises blood pressure causing hypertension, heart disease and strokes; narrows the arteries and releases lipids into the bloodstream thereby causing reduced blood flow and poor oxygenation to vital organs; tars are carcinogenic, cancers of the mouth, tongue, lungs, stomach, bowel and bladder are common. Nicotine is addictive, so more and more cigarettes are smoked with increasingly poor health. Smokers are more likely to get respiratory infections that last longer. Pregnant mothers have smaller babies, increased risks of stillbirth or premature birth. Children from smoking families do less well at school.

(v) At various times, scientists have proclaimed that the qualities of the environment surrounding individuals were more important influences on human characteristics than inherited or genetic influences. At other times, scientists argued for the importance of genetic influences over environmental ones. This continuous argument is known as the nature versus nurture debate. Nowadays we believe that characteristics arise from both influences and are inextricably linked.

4a. (i) Local people will not buy more expensive fresh vegetables that they have to spend time preparing when tinned and frozen goods are available. Sue had a lot of wasted vegetables as a result and finally had to stop stocking them.

(ii) Generally, processed food contains more sugar, salt and hidden fat than fresh food. It has to have preservatives added, and because the food has been cooked at high temperatures, destroying natural vitamins, these must be added too. There is little fibre in processed food, so the 'feel full' factor is removed and hunger soon returns.

(iii) Recent research has shown that smoking as little as one cigarette each day has a serious effect on women's fertility. Foetuses carried by smoking mothers tend to be small and mothers suffer from more respiratory difficulties during pregnancy. There are more miscarriages and stillbirths in smokers than in non-smokers, and infants and children tend to be smaller than their peers, more prone to chest infections and to perform less well academically.

(iv) Children on the estate are likely to have orthodontal problems, decayed teeth and pain. This is likely because they have no regular dental check-ups, no dental treatment, no orthodontal service and do not consume the recommended daily allowance of fresh fruit and vegetables.

As self-esteem is low on the estate, it is possible that oral hygiene is carried out under poor supervision; this completes the loop for more dental problems in the future.

Unit 2

1. The eyes, face, posture, muscle tension, movement, gesture (with arms and hands), touch (hands), proximity (position of the body), orientation (use of face position).

2. Verbal: using a clear calm voice, speaking using normal tone and volume, using effective listening skills, using questions in order to negotiate.
   Non-verbal: relaxed or calm body language, varied eye contact, keeping arms at side, keeping hands open, avoiding tense muscles, avoiding postures or gestures that might suggest anger or fear.

3. Keeping head at the same height as the child's head, maintaining eye contact, increased use of smiling in order to create a safe friendly encounter, speaking in a soft voice, varying tone and pitch of voice to create interest and attention, using leading questions to try to influence the child.

4. Preparing a checklist of issues about care values in order to focus the interview; preparing a series of open questions; preparing appropriate probes and prompts that you can use to focus the interview; rehearsing your interview with another person before doing the real interview.

5. Using communication skills to learn about the beliefs, life and needs of service users; building a supportive relationship involving understanding, warmth and sincerity; respecting and valuing diversity; showing respect for others; maintaining the dignity of others when providing physical support or care; providing choice, supporting service user independence; maintaining confidentiality; praising children's achievement.

6. Use of open questions, probes and prompts; using active listening skills or using the communication cycle effectively; building a supportive relationship with the person; using appropriate non-verbal behaviour to show interest and involvement with the person; using appropriate language and body language in order to convey respect and value for the person.

7. Observing the behaviour of the service user, or possibly asking the service user how they feel. If a person is receiving respect and value they are likely to reflect respect and value back to the people working with them. If service users appear relaxed and confident when communicating with care workers this behaviour may indicate the meeting of emotional needs.

8. Emotional barriers, language barriers (including signed languages), cultural barriers, sensory barriers (hearing and vision), environmental barriers such as background noise, poor lighting, lack of privacy.

9. Understanding cultural differences is very important because misunderstandings, stereotyping or discrimination can result from making the assumption that everybody uses language or body language in exactly the same way. Learning to understand what an individual intends to communicate is critically important in order for active listening to work effectively and in order to build a supportive relationship. Understanding cultural differences is essential for the transmission of care values.

10a. Service users have legal rights that are established through Acts of Parliament such as the Disability Discrimination Act (1995). Acts of Parliament influence the design of national minimum standards, and the policies and procedures that employers design. In addition to legal rights, service users may be perceived to have more general moral rights associated with care values. Formal codes of practice such as the GSCC Code of Practice provide a basis for defining care values.

10b. Without identified rights it would be difficult to ensure that service users received a reasonable standard or quality of care service. Without identifiable rights service users would have no basis for challenging or complaining about poor quality services. Without rights and responsibilities it would be difficult to ensure that service users' emotional, social, and self-esteem needs were met. Without rights service users might be increasingly vulnerable to neglect, abuse or exploitation by others.

Unit 3

1. Values are beliefs that identify 'something that is valued' or 'valuable' in a situation. Values can influence what people do and the choices and decisions they make on a day-to-day basis within care. Care values may influence the way in which workers provide care. Care values are part of what is needed to provide quality and empowering care.

2. Empowering services aim to enable the service user to make choices and take control of his or her life; the opposite of empowerment is dependency where the staff have the power and the service user is dependent upon them. Empowering services for young people will stress the provision of learning opportunities so that children can develop self-confidence and self-esteem. Empowering services for older people will seek to enable older people to maintain personal decision-making and retain self-esteem. Direct payments may enable some older people to control the services that they receive.

3. Service users' security or safety could be put at risk if details of their property or behaviour are shared with inappropriate people. Service users could lose trust and confidence in care workers if personal information is made available without consent. A service user's self-esteem could be threatened by the sharing of personal information. A service user may feel disempowered if they cannot control the way personal information is used. Service users have legal rights to confidentiality defined in the Data Protection Act together with rights specified within National Minimum Standards by the CSCI.

4. Discrimination, communication barriers, organisational barriers, emotional barriers, geographical barriers.

5. Disempowerment, increased vulnerability, emotional stress and poorer physical or mental health, loss of confidence or failure to grow up as a confident person, loss of self-esteem, exclusion from social groups, failure to develop an effective identity.

6. Non-discrimination involves not damaging other people by providing some people with a better quality of service than others. Antidiscrimination involves actively identifying and challenging discriminatory behaviour – in yourself and others or in systems within a work setting.

7. The quality of communication skills; the accessibility and clarity of the organisation's policies and procedures; the training opportunities available to staff; the application of care values including the GSCC code of practice, the valuing of diversity and promotion of equality and the maintenance of confidentiality.

8. The Employment Equality Religion and Belief Regulations 2003 provide a legal right to protection from discrimination within the field of employment. Some limited rights are provided by the Race Relations Act.

9. Every service must have a complaints procedure; where a local authority has purchased the service the local authority's complaints procedure may also be accessed. A civil action for negligence can be taken; complaints that allege maladministration can be taken to the ombudsman. Commissions including the Commission for Social Care Inspection will hear complaints relevant to their role. Special courts called tribunals are involved in hearing certain kinds of complaint or appeal.

10. Legislation provides a framework that influences the design of policies and procedures that will be used at an organisational level to guide staff. Legislation also provides a framework for redress where service users can give evidence of a breach of their rights. Legislation cannot by itself control the moment by moment actions and decisions of care workers; care values guide the moment by moment decisions that workers make.

Legislation is therefore only part of what is needed in order to ensure that service users' rights are maintained and that high quality services are delivered.

Unit 4

Scenario 1

1. Physical consequences may include stress and tiredness. Intellectual consequences may include the need to learn new things (a wide range of concrete examples could be offered such as using new shops, learning new journeys). Social consequences may include losing contact or making new relationships with neighbours, friends and colleagues. Emotional consequences may involve coping with loss or transition, including the fear and joy of making new relationships.

2. Weight gain, heart disease and the range of additional threats associated with smoking.

3. Experiencing loss, uncertainty, fear in the new situation, the need for new learning, making new friends, understanding a new building, relationships with new teachers; emotional and physical reactions to these demands, such as stress and tiredness.

4. Practical help with tasks such as shopping, cooking and cleaning. Emotional buffering, or emotional support to cope with stress. The support of just having someone with you – company, someone to listen to you. Increased happiness and maintenance of self-concept. Improved physical health is associated with social support.

5. Phases associated with theories such as Hanson or Parkes. The need to protect a sense of self through denial and subsequent emotional work before being able to present a new sense of self that has accommodated the changes.

6. Discussion of the factors associated with low income and poverty including issues such as housing, neighbourhood, poor physical health, lower opportunities, increased exposure to crime and fear of crime.

7. Discussion of the degree to which people are constrained by social factors such as the response of family, friends and colleagues, past socialisation. The discussion could include reference to self-concept and self-efficacy.

Scenario 2

1. Primary means first and socialisation means learning the norms, beliefs and values of a social group as well as how to become social.

2. Jake often sees his father talking to friends about football as well as spending lots of time in football related activities.

3. Jake's father may have become interested in football through the friends he grew up with or may now mix with a group of people who reinforce his interest. Cultural influences might be expressed through newspapers and TV, influencing the circle of friends as well as directly influencing Jake's father.

4. Secondary socialisation may conflict with primary socialisation. It is not possible to know the outcome of any conflict but secondary socialisation would at least influence Jake and might result in a reduced expression of interest in football.

5. Broad social and media influences exert an influence on more local social groups. The community a person lives in will influence the family and friendship networks which in their turn will influence a person directly. Social influences interact and an individual selects their own behaviour in the context of a range of influences.

Scenario 3

1. 'In the past these people were put down as being too limited' suggests negative stereotyping of service users.

2. A stereotype is a fixed way of thinking involving generalisations and expectations about an issue or a group of people.

3. A selection of examples taken from the value base including freedom from discrimination,

the maintenance of confidentiality, celebration of diversity, the right to choice and independence, the importance of trust and appropriate relationships.

4. The value base issues of choice, promoting independence, respect for identity, needs and physical, perhaps appropriate communication, could be mentioned here.

5. Empowerment enables a service user to make choices and take control of their own life. Dependency is the opposite of empowerment. The approach focuses on enabling service users to make choices and take control of their own lives; the approach is centred on service users.

6. An empowering approach may result in helping service users to develop a higher level of self-esteem together with a self-concept as a person who can make decisions and choices.

7. A service user centred approach involves putting the service user at the centre of care. It involves focusing on the service user's own understanding of social, emotional and identity needs as well as supporting people to make choices and decisions that affect their own life. Examples include the expert patient initiative, person centred planning, a focus on personhood, and the focus on education in early years work.

Unit 5

1. Human needs can be broadly categorised into physical, intellectual, emotional and social requirements.

2. It's important to see a service user as a person with unique requirements, wishes and views. Activities should never be forced onto someone, and it's vital to work with a person, rather than to do something to him or her.

3. Theatre visit – This may satisfy intellectual needs (concentrating on the play, enjoying the plot and its outcomes). Emotional needs may be met if the person engages with the characters and feels that the play's outcome is satisfactory. Social needs may be met by the fact that this is a group outing. Walking to the coach, then into the theatre will satisfy some physical needs, especially if the person doesn't move around very much in a normal day.

   Line dancing – Physical needs will be met by this activity (gentle movement, deeper breathing, improved circulation). Social needs are met by the fact that this is a group activity. Intellectual needs are met by the requirement to memorise steps and movements. An enjoyment of the music can realise emotional needs.

   Group singalong – Physical needs are met by singing, which is good for respiration. Intellectual needs are met by the requirement to follow the words and hit the right notes. Social needs are met by joining in with this group activity. Emotional needs may be met by sharing in old memories, reinforcing a sense of identity (i.e. remembering times of having a role as a worker or a parent).

4. To *label* someone is to classify him or her in terms of one personal aspect (e.g. appearance or disability). If you refer to someone as a special needs person rather than as a person with special needs, then you are labelling that person. To stereotype someone is to assume that he or she will be the same as everyone else with the same characteristic. To assume that all people over a certain age suffer from incontinence and sit around all day doing nothing is a stereotypical view of older people.

5. Labelling or stereotyping someone can prevent you from seeing him or her as a unique individual, with very personal preferences, wishes, needs and abilities.

6. Any activity should be chosen in consultation with a service user and should be something that he or she wishes to do. Activities should never be detrimental to a person's self-confidence (e.g. because they are too difficult or physically demanding), neither should they be offensive (e.g. in terms of cultural or religious acceptability).

7. Make sure that you do not disclose the personal identity of a service user to anyone other than your tutor, or a relevant member of staff in a service setting (such as the person's

key or care worker). Make sure you anonymise your notes, and keep them in a safe place.

8. Check out what the establishment's policy is in the event of fire or other emergency. Find out what you are expected to do in the event of an emergency. Check that all furniture and equipment is safe with no sharp edges, loose fittings, wobbly legs etc. Check that there are no loose wires or loose connections on electrical equipment, and no faulty switches; all cabling should be taped down (if there is no proper cabling duct). Ensure that the room is not overcrowded with unnecessary furniture and/or equipment. Make sure there is adequate space for people to get in and out, and to move around within the room. Make sure that everyone knows how to get to the nearest emergency exit, in case of fire or other emergency.

9. Setting out anticipated benefits in advance of an activity gives something by which to measure its success.

10. An activity can be evaluated by:
    - observation
    - asking people for their views
    - reflection.

Unit 6

1. Three from the following: Provision of clean water and sewers to everyone; scientific advances such as germ theory leading to better understanding of the causes of diseases; advances in surgery; antibiotics and other drugs; access to a wider range of food (not better nutrition because having the food available does not mean it is eaten); improved housing conditions; immunisation and more money/better standard of living for most people.

2. Three from the following: home ownership, car ownership, life expectancy, infant mortality/mortality rate, single parenthood, socio-economic status, level of education or qualifications.

3. Three from the following: genetic factors, lack of knowledge, low income/poverty/unemployment/lack of access to work, lack of access to health services, unhealthy lifestyles.

4. We need a healthy workforce/to ensure Britain's international competitiveness and are concerned about the cost of ill health to the NHS.

5. Three from the following: obesity, mental health, heart disease and strokes, cancer, accidents, smoking/excessive drinking/substance abuse, teenage pregnancy, sexually transmitted diseases, infectious diseases/immunisation take-up/tuberculosis.

6. Two from the following, including their health effects:
    - Smoking – cancers, heart disease and stroke/high blood pressure
    - Lack of exercise/sedentary lifestyles – obesity, heart disease, diabetes
    - Poor diet/junk food – poor immunity, child behaviour, disease in later life
    - Low incomes – accidents, mental health problems, poor diet

7. Two from the following: child health screening, immunisation programmes, breast screening, cervical cancer screening, genetic screening for those at risk of certain diseases e.g. sickle cell anaemia.

8. Local authorities have responsibility for environmental health – recycling, pollution, traffic management to prevent accidents and food safety as well as safe communities (e.g. policing).

9. Sickle cell anaemia, thalassaemia, diabetes, high blood pressure are more common in South Asian communities and people of Afro-Caribbean descent.

10. Regulations protecting people at work (e.g. Health and Safety at Work Act), regulations concerned with protecting vulnerable people (e.g. The Children Act), regulations concerning drinking alcohol and substance abuse, traffic laws and the national minimum wage.

Glossary

absolute poverty not having sufficient resources to ensure survival.

accommodation developing new, internal knowledge by finding new ways of doing things.

Act of Parliament known as primary or statute law. Contains powers, duties and responsibilities.

active listening involves more than hearing, it also involves using the communication cycle and being able to demonstrate what you have understood when you listen to another person.

adolescence the life stage from 8–18 years and the total of the physical, emotional, social and intellectual changes taking place in this life stage.

advocacy arguing a case for another. In law, an advocate argues a legal case. In care work, an advocate tries to understand and argue from a service user's perspective.

anti-discriminatory practice professional practice that challenges both discrimination and the assumptions that may result in discrimination.

Asperger's syndrome a condition characterised by severe and sustained impairment in social interaction, and by restricted or repetitive behaviour patterns. This can lead to social and other problems.

assertiveness the skill of negotiating for your own needs whilst respecting the needs of others.

assimilation applying existing knowledge to a new situation.

autonomy having independence and control over local or personal issues. In the context of care work, autonomy implies control of decisions over daily living activities

axillary hair hair growing in the armpits.

babbling a pre-language stage of making meaningless sounds that may help in developing language at a later date.

bereavement and loss a process of transition, or coping with change, following a loss. This may be loss of a loved one, a skill or part of the body such as a limb. The process involves phases of shock, searching, using defences, denial, anger and guilt before final reconstruction is possible.

bill a statute law in draft form that goes through the House of Parliament, House of Lords and Royal Assent before it becomes an Act of Parliament.

Black Report a report first commissioned in 1980, chaired by Sir Douglas Black to gather information on differences in health status among social classes, identify likely causes, the implications for government policy and make recommendations. This was a major report on health inequalities.

bonding making an emotional attachment to a person.

buffering the way in which social relationships can absorb shock and protect us from stress.

care setting the place where health or social care is given. This could be a hospital, day unit, residential establishment, etc. But it could also be the service user's own home.

Care Standards Act 2000 an Act of Parliament that established the National Care Standards Commission.

care value base a series of principles that guide care practice. These principles were originally identified in National Vocational Qualifications but can also be identified in codes of practice.

census a regular population count, carried out on the same day nationally every 10 years, and which now also includes social and health information.

centile charts normal ranges of measurements of large numbers of infants or children at different ages.

cephalo-caudal development development that takes place from the head downwards towards the tail (or legs).

code of practice guidance document making recommendations for practice. This does not have the force of an Act of Parliament but still needs to be incorporated into health and social care practice.

cognition the process of thinking.

cognitive development the development of mental abilities such as problem solving, the increase in understanding and the acquisition of knowledge.

Commission for Social Care Inspection (CSCI) the inspection authority for care services that has taken over from the National Care Standards Commission and the Social Services Inspectorate.

communication barriers blocks which prevent communication. Examples might include blocks which prevent people from receiving a message, making sense of a message or understanding a message.

communication cycle the process of building an understanding of what another person is communicating.

concept a term used to classify, predict and explain physical and social reality. Concepts are probably dependent on experience of events and are useful to simplify experience and enable others to share.

concrete operations the third stage in Piaget's theory of intellectual development. In this stage, children are unable to cope with abstract things but can solve logical problems, providing that they can see or sense the objects they are working with.

culture the collection of values, norms, customs and behaviours that make a group distinct from others. Many cultures have values linked to religious beliefs. Our culture may be one of the biggest influences in our lives.

Data Protection Act 1998 provides people with legal rights with respect to the confidentiality of information.

dementia a range of illnesses involving the degeneration or wasting of the brain. It is not part of the normal ageing process.

depression loss of social and emotional functioning. Many people experience depression at some time in their lives.

deserving and undeserving poor poverty was seen as the fault of individuals, caused by moral weakness. The 1834 Poor Law Amendment Act distinguished between those 'deserving' or 'undeserving' of assistance; for example, widows and orphans deserved help, whereas the unemployed did not. In order to obtain relief, individuals had to be prepared to enter the workhouse.

determinants of health the factors that can positively or negatively affect health, either directly or indirectly; they may be environmental, biological, cultural, socio-economic, psychological or behavioural.

development increase in skills, abilities or capacities relevant to physical, social, emotional or intellectual development.

diversity the variation that exists between people's cultures and ways of living.

droplet infection infection that is spread by pathogens (bacteria and viruses) suspended in fluid, e.g. mucus. Most respiratory infections are spread this way – 'coughs and sneezes spread diseases'.

duties defined in law with the word 'shall'. Local authority and social workers must carry these out.

educational/behavioural approach or model of health promotion a model that emphasises information-giving to promote better knowledge and understanding of health matters so that individuals or groups can adopt healthier lifestyles.

electoral ward an official area containing people who vote in an election.

embryo the first 8 weeks of human infant development in the uterus.

emotional development a process of forming the feelings that individuals have in association with relationships.

empowerment enabling individuals to make their own choices (informed or personal) and direct their own lives and affairs.

endemic regularly found in a particular area.

environment the surroundings that people function in, such as air and water qualities, housing, landscape, crime, noise etc.

epidemic the widespread presence of disease or infection in the population, over and above that which would normally be expected.

epidemiology refers to how disease is spread and includes the incidence (rate of occurrence) and prevalence (numbers affected).

Equal Opportunities Commission a commission that has the duty of monitoring gender equality issues in the United Kingdom.

ethics the term used to describe moral principles in action and to refer to the behaviour of social workers and other professionals towards service users and carers.

European Union formed in 1993 of member states with common foreign and security policies and with a political and economic focus.

evaluation the process of assessing something, in particular its worth, value or importance.

fertilisation the union of a nucleus from the father's sperm with the nucleus of the mother's egg or ovum.

fine motor skills refers to the ability to coordinate the movement of the fingers in detailed activities such as writing, painting, etc.

foetus the technical term for a baby in the uterus from the 8th week until birth.

formal operations the final stage in Piaget's theory of intellectual development. People at this stage can think abstractly.

funnelling a system for organising questions so that closed questions are always 'led up to', using general open questions to prepare the respondent.

gender roles the different expectations associated with male and female behaviour.

gender the differences between males and females based on cultural or social expectations.

genetics the study of inheritance.

germ theory the theory of microbes (germs) causing disease.

gross motor skills refers to the ability to coordinate the larger muscles of **group maintenance** the social needs of group members when they are working. Maintenance activities create an appropriate social atmosphere to enable members to work effectively.

group a collection of individuals linked by common characteristics.

group task the work or activities that a group of people have come together to do.

group values help to explain and define group norms of behaviour. See **values**.

growth increase in physical size or complexity, getting taller or heavier.

GSCC code of practice a code that prescribes key principles to guide the professional conduct of care workers.

health the extent to which an individual or group is able, on the one hand, to realise aspirations and satisfy needs, and on the other hand, to change or cope with the environment. (WHO)

health education involves trying to influence or direct a change of attitude or behaviour in people as a result of giving information about health.

health inequality the extent to which people experience differences in their state of health and longevity, above that which would be considered normal for their biological, genetic or age profile.

health promotion the process of enabling people to increase control over and to improve their health.

herd immunity the levels of immunity within a population sufficient to prevent the spread of disease because there are too few people susceptible to it.

holistic health physical, social and mental well-being.

Holmes-Rahe scale a scale of life events that identifies stress levels associated with these events.

identity How an individual person identifies him or herself. Social identity might focus on social group membership personal identity might focus on an aspect of personality. ill health or disability.

immunisation the process of conferring immunity by introducing a foreign substance such as bacteria or virus into the body, usually in a weakened form that is sufficient to stimulate the body's natural defences.

immunity resistance to disease. It may be natural (inherited) or provided artificially through immunisation.

impairment damage to or loss of a physical function of the body.

income money that an individual or household gets from wages, benefits, investments, or other sources.

independence being able to function without being dependent on others.

infant mortality the number of deaths of children under one year of age, per 1,000 live births in any one year.

labelling classifying someone in a fixed way that refers only to one aspect of that person, e.g. physical appearance, nationality, disability, etc.

laissez-faire the principle of non-intervention, especially by governments. It is based on the assumption that there are natural laws in society, and in the economy, which will automatically achieve a balance without interference.

law set of rules made by Parliament that is enforceable by the courts and regulates the behaviour and responsibilities of individuals and public bodies.

less eligibility another principle of the 1834 Act was one of 'less eligibility'; in other words, conditions in the workhouse should never be better than those experienced by the lowest paid labourers outside, to deter individuals from making unnecessary claims. The Poor Law Commission was responsible for implementing and administering the 1834 Act, which was funded nationally through the Poor Law Unions, to which each parish contributed.

life course events a range of expected occurrences during a person's life within Western culture such as going to school, starting work and retiring.

lifestyle choice the way in which people choose to live their lives.

lifestyle how a person spends time and money to create a style of living.

low income an income worth 40 per cent less than the level of income enjoyed by the average person in the UK (60 per cent of median income). Low income provides a measure of relative poverty.

Maslow's hierarchy the psychologist Abraham Maslow's description of human needs as belonging to the following categories physical, safety, love and belonging, self-esteem and self-actualisation. Care should not only cover physical and safety needs.

medical approach to health promotion using medical science to prevent disease.

menarche the onset of menstruation.

menopause the gradual cessation of menstruation and fertility.

milestones of development significant events taking place at certain, average periods of time, used for monitoring progress.

monitoring the act of checking on the progress of something, or of someone's performance or behaviour, over a period of time.

morbidity the state of having ill health. It includes disability and chronic ill health, as well as episodes of illness. It is usually shown statistically, as the number of cases which occur each year per thousand of the population.

mortality rate this is the number of deaths across the whole population per year and includes cause of death. The data is 'standardised', that is account is taken of variables, such as age and sex to give an overall figure.

motor development the coordination of muscles to enable complicated movements to occur.

National Minimum Standards a set of requirements that forms the basis for inspection of care services. There are different sets of criteria for different services.

nature-nurture debate a long-standing debate on whether inheritance (nature) or environment (nurture) is most important in making people what they are. The modern view is that nature and nurture cannot be meaningfully separated.

neonatal mortality rate the number of infant deaths occurring in the first 4 weeks of life for every 1,000 live births in any one year.

neonate a newborn infant.

norm recognised standards of measurement.

norms patterns of behaviour that are followed by the members of a particular society, family or group.

object permanence the understanding that objects exist whether they can be seen or not. (Piaget).

pandemic an epidemic, which spreads over a wide area involving several countries and is sometimes worldwide.

PCS model a model developed by Neil Thompson (2001: Unit 2) to explain the different levels on which discrimination may operate and the levels on which anti-discriminatory practice needs to operate.

peer group a group of people who share common characteristics or circumstances and feel themselves to be like one another.

person-centred care care that places 'the person' at the centre of decision-making and activities, thereby valuing the individual 'personhood' of service users.

personhood recognition and respect for the self-concept and self-esteem needs of service users.

PIES categories the four broad areas of human needs, categorised as physical, intellectual, emotional and social.

Poor Law the first law was passed by Elizabeth I, making local parishes responsible for supporting the poor. This was done by a poor rate tax from local landowners and tenants to provide money for food to those living in their own homes who were unable to provide for themselves. By 1834, this had evolved into a national system for dealing with poverty.

Poor Law Amendment Act 1834 made the distinction between the 'able-bodied poor' and those who were infirm, elderly or children. It was intended that 'outdoor relief', i.e. assistance provided to people in their own homes, should be abolished and provided in workhouses instead.

poverty having insufficient resources to participate fully in society. Usually, but not always, measured in economic terms as a percentage of the mean or average of a benchmark, e.g. average wage. Being in poverty is currently considered to be where income is less than 60 per cent of average wage.

powers indicated by the word 'may' in an Act of Parliament. This means the local authority has a choice of whether to implement or not. Powers can change to become duties. An example is the Direct Payment Scheme, which started as a power or 'enabling piece of legislation' and it is now a compulsory duty for all local authorities to have one (and has been since 2003).

pre-operational the second stage of Piaget's theory of intellectual development. Infants in this stage cannot reason logically.

presbyopia long-sightedness developing in most people from the mid-forties onwards.

primary poverty the state where earnings are not eenough to live on.

primary socialisation the socialisation that takes place in early childhood, in which the language, norms and values of the society the child has been born into are acquired.

primitive reflexes temporary reflexes occurring in the newborn, replaced after a few months with learned responses.

puberty the physical changes taking place in adolescence.

pubic hair hair growing on the lower abdomen, between the legs.

public health refers to the health of whole populations, the factors that can affect this and how these risks can be minimised.

Race Relations Act 1976 (amended 2000) an Act of Parliament which makes discrimination on the basis of race illegal.

redress to remedy or put right something that is wrong. reflection the act of thinking about something critically and calmly.

Registrar-General's social classification a method of dividing the population along the lines of class or occupation.

relative poverty not having sufficient resources to live to the same standard as the majority of people do.

rights and responsibilities social values result in rights for people – but rights have boundaries. Rights are balanced with responsibilities.

role the behaviour adopted by individuals when they are interacting in social situations.

secondary poverty the state where earnings are above substistance but spent unwisely.

secondary socialisation the process by which we learn the norms, values and behaviour that makes us a member of a particular group. We learn the roles we are expected to play as a group member.

self-actualisation the highest level of development in Maslow's hierarchy. It means fulfilling your potential and everything you need to achieve.

self-concept the understanding that we have of ourselves. A learned idea of how we are distinct from other people.

self-confidence being assured of the ability to achieve something or cope with circumstances. Self-confidence may influence and be influenced by self-esteem.

self-efficacy the degree to which a person predicts that he or she will be successful in coping with tasks and challenges in life.

self-esteem the degree to which we value ourselves. Self-esteem is likely to influence how we relate to other people and how confident we are.

self-image how a person views him or herself.

sense of self the understanding of self. A set of concepts that we use to explain to ourselves what we are like.

sensori-motor the first stage of Piaget's theory of intellectual development. Infants learn to coordinate their muscle movements in relation to things that they sense.

service user centred relationships relationships that aim to empower the service user to be able to choose and make decisions about the services they receive.

Sex Discrimination Act 1975 (amended 1986) an Act of Parliament designed to make discrimination on the basis of a person's gender illegal.

social class the status given to different types of occupation or work. Socio-economic status is the current term used by the Registrar General; see Registrar General's classification of socio-economic groups.

social development a focus on the way groups may influence relationship patterns within a culture.

social exclusion being excluded from opportunity – people with fewer life chances become less economically prosperous than the majority of people.

social justice the concept of fairness within society; equal and non-discriminatory treatment.

social networks when people who are linked together provide help and support in times of need.

social support networks partners, friends, family, relatives and members of community groups who provide a source of support for own self-esteem.

socialisation the process by which we learn the norms, values and behaviour that makes us a member of a particular group – learning to become 'social' or a social member of a group.

societal approach or model of health promotion concentrates on changing society to improve the health of the population rather than the individual.

spatial awareness the ability to make sense of and respond appropriately to objects in space.

speech community people who share the same rules, behaviours and expectations about the way a language is used.

stereotyping a fixed way of thinking that involves generalisations and expectations about an issue or a group of people.

supportive relationship an encounter between people that conveys warmth, understanding and sincerity.

Tourette's syndrome a neurological condition characterised by repeated and involuntary body movements (also known as tics), together with uncontrollable vocal sounds.

transitions a life event that involves changing assumptions about life and moving from one way of life to a new way of living. Transitions include periods of change in life such as starting work, having children, or retiring.

values inherent beliefs, including moral beliefs such as perceptions of right and wrong, good and bad.

vulnerability being at risk of some kind of harm – not being protected from risk and harm.

Wanless Report 2004 securing good health for the whole population was concerned with identifying action that could be taken to improve the population's health in order to achieve similar levels as other developed countries. Forerunner to the 2004 White Paper *Choosing Health*.

wealth the value of the property and other investments and savings owned by a person. Wealth includes the value of houses, pensions, savings and other personal possessions.

Welfare State one in which government acts to reduce inequalities by providing resources, particularly to vulnerable members of society who have needs that they are unable to meet themselves, e.g. education, health care, housing support, income and disability support.

zygote an alternative technical name for a fertilised egg.

Index

A

absolute poverty 174, 175, 190, 261
accommodation development 213
Acheson, Donald 176
active listening 59, 98
activities
  benefits 204, 226
  choosing 232–4
  evaluating benefits 248
  evaluation 246–9
  implementation, explaining 238, 243
  intellectual needs 212–13
  physical needs 208
  planning, aims 237
  planning, checklists 237–42, 244
  planning, key principles 228
  timing 235–6
  types 204, 226
activities, cognitive development
  adults 216
  children 0–3 years 213
  children 3–7 years 213–14
  learning disabilities 214–15
  overview 212
  stimulation and interest 215–16
activities, emotional needs
  adults 216–19
  children 217, 221
  children 0–3 years 219–20
  children group activities 220
  dementia 218
  Kitwood's diagram 218–19
  overview 216
activities, physical needs
  children 0–3 years 209–10
  children 3–7 years 210–12
  older people 208–9
  overview 208
  public health 284
  special needs 209
activities, social needs
  adults 225
  children 225
  group membership 222
  overview 220–1
adolescence (9–18 years)
  effect of personal relationships 44
  emotional development 15
  intellectual skills 14
  physical changes 10
  physical skills 10
  puberty 5
  social skills development 18
Adult Protection Procedures 117
advocacy 72, 117, 136
age-appropriate behaviour 61
ageing 11–12
aggression 67–8
air pollutants 36–7, 301
air quality 36–7, 301
alcohol 28–9, 170–1, 283–4
Alzheimer's disease 191
anti-discriminatory practice 115
Argyle, Michael 166
Asperger's Syndrome 222
assertiveness
  non-verbal behaviour 68
  skills 66–8
  verbal behaviour 68
  winning and losing 67–8
assimilation development 213
autosomal disorders 21–2

B

Bazalgette, Joseph 261
beliefs 93, 131
benefits for disadvantaged people 297
bereavement 160, 162–3
Beveridge, William 261–2
Birth to Three Matters 213, 219
Black, Douglas 264
Blaxter, Mildred 166
body language 58, 61–2, 97
body mass index 282–3
body movement 63
Boer War 261
bonding 17
Booth, Charles 261
Braille 58
Breadline Britain Score 270
British Sign Language 71
buffering role 166–7

C

cancer 294
care group 75
care services
  Alzheimer's disease 191
  children's likes 229
  codes of practice 194
  dementia 191–2
  focus 190
  non-judgmental 229
  person-centred 191
  personhood 191
  stereotypes 192–5
  user-centred relationships 190–1
care setting
  definition 228
  facilities 234
care value base
  empowerment 129–30
  importance 128–9
  marginalisation 129
  principles 80–1
carers own needs 206
Carers' Charter 206
Caring for People [White Paper] 136
Census, The 265, 268
cephalo-caudal development 4
Chadwick, Edwin 260–1
change, coping with 166
chemicals 303
child offenders 147
children
  deprivation effects 289–90
  friendships 187
  physical activity reduced 276
  play 187
  poverty 288, 289
  public health 282–3
  stereotypes 193
  see also under activities
chromosome abnormalities 20–1
circles of influence 169
closed questions 65–6
codes of practice
  Adult Protection Procedures 117
  advocacy 117

Care Homes for Younger Adults 114
care organisations 117
care services 194
confidentiality 143
Early Years 84
employees 80–1
employers 90
General Social Care Council (GSCC) 194–5
Home Care agencies 117
mental health 148–9
nurses 83–4
service users 135
social care workers 80–1
cognitive development 12–13, 212
cohabiting 32
colour blindness [disorder] 23
'colour-blindness' [diversity ignorance] 185
Commission for Racial Equality (CRE) 82, 135
Commission for Social Care Inspection (CSCI) 84, 114, 117, 151
Commissioner for Local Administration 150
Commissions 151
communication
barriers 68–70, 119
cycle 59–60
difficulties 70
effective 96–7, 114–15, 132
emotional barriers 71
groups 72–3
interpreters 71–2
translators 71
types 58
community groups 34
community support factors 30
complaints procedures 149–50
confidentiality
boundaries 112
care organisations 136
codes of practice 143
giving information 113–14
inaccurate information 113
legislation 114, 143
management's need to know 112–13
need to know 112–13
overview 83, 111–14
conversation sandwich 65
conversation structure 65
cooperative play 17
Cri du chat syndrome 21
cultural beliefs 36
cultural variation
importance 60–1
respect 60–1
culture
differences 70
importance 131
'Curriculum Guidance for the Foundation Stage' 210–11
cycle of disadvantage 92–3

D

damages 150
dementia 14, 72, 191–2
demographic changes 293
deprivation in rural areas 271
deprivation indicators 268–70
Determinants of Health 272
development
cephalo-caudal 4
children 0–3 years 210
children 3–7 years 210–12
cognitive 12–13, 212
definition 2
environmental factors influencing 24
language 12
milestones 8
patterns 3–4, 4–7
predictable events 158–60
sensori-motor stage 12–13
tasks by life stages 3
thinking 12–13
diet 24–5, 169–70, 176, 284, 292–3
Direct Payments 130–1
disabilities
access 120–1, 138
assessment of needs 147–9
hearing 70
intellectual 70
visual 70
Disability Rights Commission 82, 135, 142–3
discipline 138
discrimination
anti- 115
anti-discriminatory practice 115
barriers to accessing services 121
challenging 133–4
consequences 125–6
cycle of oppression 123–4
direct 85–6, 121
disempowerment 126
effects 88, 122–3
equal opportunities 124
examples and challenges 134
exclusion 126
groups at risk 84–6
harassment 122
indirect 85–6, 121
labelling 87–8, 124–5
marginalisation 126
non- 115
permitted areas 142
practices 122
protection under legislation 122
recognising 122–3
redress 151
rights to protection 152
stereotypes 87–8, 115, 124–5
tribunals 151
types 87, 121–2
understanding 86–7
victimisation 122
diversity to be celebrated 84, 93–4
Down's syndrome 20–1
Down, Longdon 20
droplet infection 275
drugs misuse 27–8, 171
Duchenne's muscular dystrophy 23
Duchenne, Guillaume 23
Duck, Steve 165

E

early adulthood (18–45 years)
effect of personal relationships 44
emotional development 16
intellectual skills 14
physical skills 10–11
social skills development 18
early childhood (2–8 years)
effect of personal relationships 44
emotional development 15
intellectual skills 13–14
physical skills 9
social skills development 17–18
education 39
embryo 4
emotional barriers 120
emotional development 14–16
employment 159
employment, access to 37–9
empowerment 88–90, 115–16, 129–30, 195–8
empowerment – disempowerment 126
'empty nest' syndrome 16
environment factors 36–7
environment, positive 133–5

environmental concerns 303
environmental measures 300–1
epidemics 277
epidemiology 259–60
equal opportunities 124
Equal Opportunities Commission 82, 120
equal opportunity policies 135
ethics 108–9
ethnic groups
  categories 184
  crime victims 185
  importance 185
  poverty 183–5, 289
  unemployment 184
exclusion 126
exercise 25–6
Expert Patient Initiative 89
extended families 31

F

face-to-face positions 64
facial expressions 62–3
family relationships 42–3
family support
  insufficient 32–3
  types of families 30–2
farming methods 300–1
fine motor skills 8, 210
fish stocks 303
foetus 4
food choice factors 292–3
'food poverty' 176
formality, degree of 64–5
Framework for the Assessment of Children in Need and Their Families 228–9
friends 33, 187

G

gender roles 181, 183
gender-appropriate behaviour 61
General Household Survey 265
General Social Care Council (GSCC) 80, 194–5
genes 20
genetic inheritance 20
geographical barriers 120–1
gestures 63–4
glossary 315–19
grievances 138
gross motor skills 8, 210
groups
  activity 74–6, 78
  behaviour 76, 77
  care group 75
  communication 72–3
  concluding 76, 78
  formation 73
  use for challenging
discrimination 133
  values 74, 75–6
growth of body parts 6
growth pattern 3–4
growth profiles 6

H

haemophilia 23
harassment 122
health
  behaviour 169–71, 283–5
  defining 47
  diet 169–70
  education 47
  meaning 46–7
  promoting 46–7
Health Action Zones 271–2
Health Divide, The: Inequalities in Health in the 1980s 264
Health for All by the Year 2000 264
health inequality 256, 264, 288
health information 287
health promotion
  behavioural approach 49
  biomedical approach 48–9
  campaigns 47–50
  choice of approach 50
  educational approach 49
  environmental measures 300–1
  policies 274
  societal approach 50
health services 34 *and see also* public health
heart disease 294
height increases 5
herd immunity 274
hierarchy of needs 69, 96–7, 204–5
Holmes-Rahe scale 163–4
Home Care agencies 117
Hopson's seven-stage process 160–2
Hopson, Barrie 160
household tasks 183
human growth 2
human rights
  absolute rights 140
  legislation 140–1
  limited rights 140–1

I

identity 223
identity, importance 99–100, 131
income 173–4, 287
Index of Local Conditions 270
individual choice 116–17, 130–1
inequalities 91–3
infancy (0–2 years)
  effect of personal relationships 44
  emotional development 15
  intellectual skills 12–13
  physical skills 7–9
  social skills development 17
influenza 275, 277
informality 64
information
  exchange 58–9
  inaccurate 113
  see also confidentiality
'Inquiry into Inequalities in Health' 266
intellectual skills 12–14
interpreters 71–2

J

Jarman Score 266, 268–9
Jarman, Brian 266
Jenner, Edward 260
judicial review 150

K

key worker 137
Kitwood's diagram 218–19
Klinefelter's syndrome 21

L

labelling 87–8, 124–5, 229–30
language
  appropriate 64–5
  barriers 119
  basics 58
  correct and incorrect 231–2
  development 12–13
  differences 70
  speech communities 65
later adulthood (65+ years)
  characteristic traits 11
  effect of personal relationships 44
  emotional development 16
  intellectual skills 14
  physical skills 11–12
  social skills development 18–19
legislation
  Abortion Act 1967: 4
  Access to Health Records Act 1990: 83, 143
  Access to Personal Files Act 1987: 83, 143
  Care Standards Act 2000: 81, 83, 84, 117, 135, 137, 138, 151–2

Children Act 1989: 83, 117, 140, 144–7, 151–2
Data Protection Acts 1984 and 1998: 83, 114, 143–4
Disability Discrimination Act 1995: 82, 121, 124, 138, 142–3
Disability Rights Commission Act 1999: 82
Employment Directive Regulations Article 13: 124
Employment Equality (Culture and Belief) Regulations 2003: 124, 142
Employment Equality (Sexual Orientation) Regulations 2003: 124, 141
Equal Pay Acts 1970, 1975 and 1983: 82, 124
European Convention of Human Rights 140
Freedom of Information Act 2001: 144
Health and Safety at Work Act 1974: 137, 236
Human Rights Act 1998: 140–1
Local Authorities and Social Services Act 1970: 117, 150
Mental Health Act 1983: 148–9
NHS and Community Care Act 1990: 83, 117, 130, 147–8
Public Interest Disclosure Act 1998: 136, 150–1
Race Relations Act 1976 (amended 2000) 82, 121, 124, 141–2
Sex Discrimination Acts 1975 and 1986: 82, 124, 141
United Nations Convention on the Rights of the Child 146
legislation areas
anti-discriminatory 122, 124
child offenders 147
confidentiality 114
discrimination 141–3
equal opportunities 82–3
equity law 145
Home Care agencies 117
Northern Ireland 145
redress 117
service user's rights 140
service users 152–3
social care 144–7
social care workers 81–2
life events
Holmes-Rahe scale 163–4
Hopson's seven-stage process 160–2
impact within PIES categories 164–5
least stressful 163–4
predictable 158–60
stressful 163–4
unpredictable 160–2
life stages 2–3
lifestyle
air travel and health 275
changing patterns 275–7
choices 167–8
definition 167–8
factors 24–30
health behaviour 169–71
influences on 188
mental health 276–7
opportunities 168
poverty 180–1
public health 291–2
sedentary occupations 276
unemployment 276
work pattern changes 275–6
listening skills 59–60
local complaints procedures 149–50
lone-parent families 32
'Looking Glass' theory 199

M

marginalisation 126, 129
marriage 160
Marxism 130
Maslow's pyramid of needs 69, 96–7, 204–5
Maslow, Abraham 69, 96, 195, 204
memory session example 238–9, 242–4, 246–9
menarche 10
menopause 16
middle adulthood (46–65 years)
effect of personal relationships 44
emotional development 16
intellectual skills 14
physical skills 11
social skills development 18
'mirror of value' 199
mission statement 135
misunderstanding a message 69
mitigation 162
mnemonics
PIES categories 164–5, 205
monitoring 248
moral rights 81, 89–91
morbidity 256
Moro, Ernst 7
multifactorial disorders 23–4
muscle tension 63

N

named nurse 137
National Care Standards Commission (NCSC) 84
National Curriculum Key Stage 1: 210–11, 213
National Health Service (NHS) 263–4
National Minimum Standards (NMS) 117, 135
National Statistics socio-economic classification 35, 173
nature-nurture debate 43–5
needs
Maslow's pyramid 69, 96–7, 204–5
people first 206–7
PIES 205–6
needs assessment 228–9
negative self-concept 17
negligence 150
neonate 4
noise pollution 37
'normal' attitudes 185–6, 286
'norms' 128, 185–6, 286
nuclear families 31
Nursing and Midwifery Council (NMC) 83–4

O

obesity 284
object permanence 13, 213
Office for Standards in Education 151–2
Ofsted 151–2
Ombudsman 150
ONS Area Classification 270
open questions 65–6
opportunities 168
'Opportunity for All' 92, 178–9
organisational barriers 119–20
organisational culture 135
organisational factors 133–5
organisational policies and procedures 135–6
organisational positive practice 138
orientation 64
'over-the-counter' drugs 27
ozone layer 303

P

pandemics 277
parallel play 17
parents as 'buffers' 128

Parkes, Colin Murray 162
partner relationships 42–3
Pasteur, Louis 260
Patient's Charter 84
Person-Centred Planning process 136–7, 149, 234
personal space 64
personhood 191
physical barriers 121
physical skills development 7–12
Piaget, Jean 12–14
Plain Facts 231
play types 17
Poor Law Commission 260–1
positive care 110–11
positive practice 138
positive self-concept 15
posture 63
poverty
  absolute 174, 175, 190, 261
  children 288, 289
  crime 179
  diet 176
  disadvantages 175–6, 288–90
  education 179–80
  ethnic groups 289
  ethnicity 183–5
  food 176
  gender 181–3
  health 176
  housing 177–8
  impact 175–6
  lifestyle 180–1
  overview 174–5
  poor services 179
  primary 261
  relative 174, 175, 261
  research 261
  secondary 261
  smoking 177
  social class 176
  unemployment 178–9
  vicious circle 178
pregnancy, teenage 284, 296
prejudices 93
pressure groups 304
primary socialisation 18, 35, 186–7
primitive reflexes 7
probes 66
professional relationships 67–8
prompts 66
proximity 64
psychological factors 40
puberty 5
public health
  access to health care 285–6
  aims in UK now 271
  children 282–3
  chronology 262–3
  communicable disease 274
  cost 277
  current issues 280–99
  definition 256
  disease spread 275
  emerging issues 283–5
  environmental concerns 303
  epidemic prediction 277
  government action 302–3
  government involvement 257
  government targets 293–7
  group differences 282–3
  health behaviours 283–5
  identifying needs 273
  illness patterns 280–1
  infectious diseases 259
  lifestyle 291–2
  local differences 282
  local government action 302
  monitoring 272–3
  mortality historical 259
  national strategy 297–8
  new diseases 281
  origins 258
  overview 256–7
  pioneers and reformers 260–1
  planning healthcare 274–5
  promoting 300–1
  reforms 259–60
  regional differences 281–2
  risk reduction 273–4
  screening for adults 302
  screening for babies and children 301–2
  screening for early disease 273–4
  service use 283
  social change 291–2
  statistical data importance 265
  statistical data uses 266, 268
  timeline 262–3
  towns 258–9
  Welfare State 257–8
  workers' roles 303
Public Health Observatories 272

Q

questions 65–6

R

reconstituted families 32
redress 117
redress for service users 149–51
regional health authorities 266
  map
Registrars of Births, Marriages and Deaths 265
relationships
  active listening 98
  differences respected 100
  good and poor quality 165–7
  identity importance 99–100
  importance 187
  sincerity 99
  social 221–2
  supportive body language 97
  transmitting care values 101
  understanding 98
  warmth 97–8
relative poverty 174, 175, 261
respect for difference 84
responsibilities and rights 89–91
retirement 159–60
rights
  and the law, differences 152–3
  automatic 152–3
  individuals 89–91
  service users 152–3
  to consultation 153
  to information 153
Rowntree, Seebhom 261
Rubella 4
rural areas 120–1

S

safe base behaviour 187
safe neighbourhoods 39–40
SARS 278
Saving Lives: Our Healthier Nation 272, 280, 293
scenarios
  assessment needs 148
  autism 214
  bereavement 162, 205
  biomedical approach to health 48
  Bridge School 212
  care home arrival 132
  care home culture 134
  care home socialising 222
  care settings 192
  cerebral palsy 214
  companionship 219
  confidentiality 112, 113
  deprivation impact 181
  disabled child 233
  diversity celebrated 223
  early years centre 235
  early years setting 198
  educational approach to health 49
  family relationship 287

group activity 77
group membership 223–4
illness, serious 161
learning difficulty 196, 215
music 215
patient or person 207
progress slowly 207–8
retirement 160
school, starting 158
single parents 290, 291
state of health 46
'The Mansion' 108
Tourette's Syndrome 224
wheelchairs 231
work, starting 159
sea pollution 303
secondary socialisation 18, 33, 35–6, 187
Secretary of State powers 150
Securing Good Health for the Whole Population 256
self, sense of 162, 223
self-concept 14–15, 17, 40–3, 162, 171, 198–9
self-confidence 128
self-esteem 14, 40–3, 171, 198–9
self-image 14, 128
Seligman, M 167
sensori-motor stage of development 12–13, 213
service users
barriers to access 236–7
communicating with 229
labelling 229–30
learning difficulties 230–1
needs assessment 228–9
stereotypes 229–30
sex-linked genetic disorders 22–3
sexually transmitted infections 284
signed languages 58
silence 66
smoking 29–30, 170, 177, 257, 283, 294
Snow, John 260
social care workers code of practice 80–1
social class 34–5, 173
social justice 257
social reforms 261–3
social relationships 165–7, 221–2
social skills development 17–19
social support factors 30
socialisation 33, 35–6, 128, 185–7
socio-economic groups 266–7
spatial awareness 213
Special Education Needs Tribunal 142
speech communities 65
stereotypes 87–8, 115, 120, 124–5, 229–30
stress 26–7, 43
submission 67–8
supportive relationship 97
Sure Start programme 137, 295

T

thinking development 12–13
tolerance 84
touch 64
Townsend Score 268, 270
Townsend, Peter 174, 268
training requirements 137
translators 71
tribunals 151
trisomy 21: 21
turn-taking 74
Turner's syndrome 21

U

unemployment
ethnic groups 184
lifestyle 276
unifactorial disorders 21–3
uniqueness 188
Unit 1: human growth and development
assessment 51
assessment preparation 52–4
further reading 55
unit test 52–4, answers 308–10
websites 55
Unit 2: communication and values
assessment 102
assessment preparation 102–4
further reading 106
key resources 106
unit test 105, answers 310–11
websites 106
Unit 3: positive care environments
assessment 154
assessment preparation 154–5
further reading 156
unit test 155–6, answers 311–12
websites 156
Unit 4: social aspects and lifestyle choices
assessment 200
assessment preparation 200–2
further reading 202
unit test 200–2 answers 312–13
websites 202
Unit 5: activities for health and well-being
assessment 250–1
assessment guidance 251–2
references 253
unit test 252–3 answers 313–14
websites 253
Unit 6: public health
assessment 306
references 307
report structure 306–7
unit test 307 answers 314
websites 307
United Nations Convention on the Rights of the Child 146

V

values
overview 108–9
positive care 110–11
'Valuing People' [White Paper] 149
victimisation 122
voice tone 63
vulnerability 109–10

W

water quality 37, 301
wealth 173–4
Weil, Adolf 37
Welfare State 257–8, 263–4
West Nile Virus 277
whistle blowing 136, 150–1
women
inequality of opportunity 182–3
senior appointments 182
words to avoid 232
words to use 232

Z

zygote 4